I0882444

Practical Applications of Smart Human-Computer Interaction

Subrata Tikadar
Amity University, Kolkata, India

Joel José Puga Coelho Rodrigues
Federal University of Piauí, Brazil

Rabi Shaw
Dr. B.R. Ambedkar National Institute of Technology, India

Ahdi Hassan
Global Institute for Research Education and Scholarship, The Netherlands

Bidyut Kumar Patra
Indian Institute of Technology, India

IGI Global
Scientific Publishing
Publishing Tomorrow's Research Today

Vice President of Editorial	Melissa Wagner
Director of Acquisitions	Mikaela Felty
Director of Book Development	Jocelynn Hessler
Production Manager	Mike Brehm
Cover Design	Jose Rosado

Published in the United States of America by
IGI Global Scientific Publishing
701 East Chocolate Avenue
Hershey, PA, 17033, USA
Tel: 717-533-8845
Fax: 717-533-7115
Website: https://www.igi-global.com E-mail: cust@igi-global.com

Copyright © 2026 by IGI Global Scientific Publishing. All rights reserved. No part of this publication may be reproduced, stored or distributed in any form or by any means, electronic or mechanical, including photocopying, without written permission from the publisher.

Product or company names used in this set are for identification purposes only. Inclusion of the names of the products or companies does not indicate a claim of ownership by IGI Global Scientific Publishing of the trademark or registered trademark.

Library of Congress Cataloging-in-Publication Data

Names: Tikadar, Subrata, 1985- editor | Rodrigues, Joel, 1972- editor | Shaw, Rabi, 1986- editor | Hassan, Ahdi, 1991- editor | Patra, Bidyut Kumar, 1976- editor
Title: Practical applications of smart human-computer interaction / edited by Subrata Tikadar, Joel José Puga Coelho Rodrigues, Rabi Shaw, Ahdi Hassan, Bidyut Kumar Patra.
Description: Hershey, PA : IGI Global Scientific Publishing, [2026] | Collection of essays by Soumya Chandrakar and others. | Includes bibliographical references and index. | Summary: "This book examines the practical integration of smart human-computer interaction technologies across sectors. It explores advancements in AI, cognitive-aware systems, and extended reality to enhance user experience, emotional engagement, and adaptive decision-making in complex digital interactions"-- Provided by publisher.
Identifiers: LCCN 2025034511 (print) | LCCN 2025034512 (ebook) | ISBN 9798337363851 hc | ISBN 9798337363868 sc | ISBN 9798337363875 e
Subjects: LCSH: Human-computer interaction | Artificial intelligence--Industrial applications | Machine learning
Classification: LCC QA76.9.H85 P716 2026 (print) | LCC QA76.9.H85 (ebook)
LC record available at https://lccn.loc.gov/2025034511
LC ebook record available at https://lccn.loc.gov/2025034512

British Cataloguing in Publication Data
A Cataloguing in Publication record for this book is available from the British Library.

All work contributed to this book is new, previously-unpublished material.
The views expressed in this book are those of the authors, but not necessarily of the publisher.
This book contains information sourced from authentic and highly regarded references, with reasonable efforts made to ensure the reliability of the data and information presented. The authors, editors, and publisher believe the information in this book to be accurate and true as of the date of publication. Every effort has been made to trace and credit the copyright holders of all materials included. However, the authors, editors, and publisher cannot assume responsibility for the validity of all materials or the consequences of their use. Should any copyright material be found unacknowledged, please inform the publisher so that corrections may be made in future reprints.

Table of Contents

Detailed Table of Contents

This chapter explores the evolution and development of cognitive-aware sensitive systems, i.e., an emerging class of human-computer interaction technologies that integrate physiological, behavioural, and contextual signals to deliver adaptive, user-centred experiences. Drawing upon multidisciplinary research from neuroscience, psychology, artificial intelligence, and user experience design, we examine how systems can utilize signals such as EEG, EMG, GSR, heart rate, and eye-tracking to infer mental workload, emotional stress, and engagement levels in real time. Present work gives the insights on a comprehensive overview of the key components underpinning these systems, including sensor technologies, cognitive and affective modeling, adaptive feedback mechanisms, and practical applications in education, healthcare, transportation, and assistive technologies.

Natural behaviors for expressing emotion are utilized in gesture and touch for emotion detection, in real time, and reshaping human computer interaction. System can dynamically adapt because deep learning and multimodal fusion are advanced, and experiences in education, gaming, healthcare and customer service benefit. One of the challenges however remains with their variability in the culture and privacy concern. These technologies of ethical AI, federated learning and edge computing are bringing more emotional intelligence, intuition and intention into digital systems in an increasingly variety of applications.

This paper surveys the key methodologies used in the field of Face Recognition Systems, categorizing them into traditional techniques, machine learning approaches, deep learning models, and hybrid systems. Traditional methods such as Eigenfaces and Fisherfaces laid the foundation for face recognition by utilizing linear projection techniques. Machine learning methods like Support Vector Machines (SVM) and Random Forests have improved performance, particularly in scenarios with smaller datasets. The advent of deep learning has marked a significant turning point, with models like Convolutional Neural Networks (CNNs) and frameworks such as FaceNet and DeepFace achieving state-of-the-art accuracy and robustness across varying conditions, including illumination, occlusions, and facial expressions. Future directions discussed in this paper include advancements in explainable AI, fairness, federated learning, and scalable architectures to address these challenges while improving the robustness and scalability of face recognition systems.

The evolved business ecosystem in Industry 5.0 requires every individual to interact with computers daily. Combined intelligence combines human and computer intelligence to align for teaming up a smarter team, reaping better organizational benefits. HCI involves AI, IOT, machine learning, neurocognition, NLP, generative AI, RPA, social robotics, etc., accentuating the need for humans to contribute equally to creating team synergy. Actual human-computer interactions require a mature environment to enable easy adoption by employees. Our research paper proposes a conceptual framework listing the various drivers and inhibitors affecting employees' decisions toward adopting intelligent computers at the workplace. The implications of the research paper can be mapped under the UN's 8 and 9 sustainable development goals. The proposed conceptual framework will give a complete understanding of the significant factors required for consideration for the successful adoption of intelligent computers by employees.

In the competitive landscape of e-commerce, providing a seamless and user-friendly shopping experience is critical to retaining customers and driving sales. Many existing applications struggle with issues such as complicated navigation, unexpected costs, delayed deliveries, and data security concerns, leading to high cart abandonment rates. To address these challenges, the proposed system introduces a robust and intuitive application designed to enhance user engagement by offering easy navigation, transparency in costs, reliable services, and strong data protection. This innovative approach aims to improve customer satisfaction and reduce barriers to completing purchases, ensuring a smooth and efficient online shopping experience.

Accessible travel for people with disabilities remains a challenge due to mobility, sensory, and cognitive barriers. AI can improve travel by providing real-time assistance, intelligent navigation, and personalized route planning. This chapter examines the role of AI in addressing mobility challenges and enhancing transportation systems. It describes key barriers in existing travel solutions and introduces AI-driven approaches. It discusses computer vision for obstacle detection, NLP for voice-based travel support, and machine learning for route optimization. It explores the use of the Internet of Things and smart infrastructure to improve accessibility in public transportation. AI-based mapping services and assistive technologies are included as case studies. Future developments such as AI-integrated wearable devices and autonomous vehicles are considered. The chapter concludes with policy suggestions to support AI-enabled travel systems for people with disabilities. It provides insights for researchers, policymakers, and technology developers working to improve mobility.

There are several benefits and significant hurdles to implementing IoT in smart homes. One way that IoT technology improves convenience is by allowing homeowners to remotely control various home systems, such as security and lighting, through seamless integration. Additionally, it promotes energy efficiency through real-time optimization and monitoring. IoT also makes it possible to monitor health and provide personalized experiences, which respects individual preferences and enhances wellbeing. However, obstacles including device compatibility problems from many manufacturers make smooth integration difficult, while privacy and security dangers related to data collection cause worry. This paper proposes a solution that aims to outline a comprehensive approach to leverage IoT effectively while mitigating potential pitfalls in smart home environments. Embracing these solutions, one can unlock the full potential of IoT technology while effectively managing associated challenges, thus paving the way for smarter, more connected, and secure residential living environments.

The integration of autonomous vehicles (AVs) into urban ecosystems demands a comprehensive understanding of pedestrian-AV interactions, particularly at unconstrained intersections where unpredictability and communication gaps can compromise safety. This chapter explores critical challenges in AV decision-

Preface

Human-Computer Interaction (HCI) has emerged as a vital interdisciplinary domain that drives innovation across a wide range of technologies, particularly with the rise of intelligent systems. As computing devices increasingly become embedded into everyday life, it is critical to explore not just how humans interact with machines, but how those machines can intelligently respond to human needs, emotions, and behaviors. This edited volume, *Practical Applications of Smart Human-Computer Interaction*, compiles emerging research that highlights the transformative role of artificial intelligence, cognitive modeling, sensor technologies, and user-centered design in shaping the future of HCI.

The chapters in this book reflect a shared vision: human-computer systems must be adaptive, ethical, inclusive, and capable of understanding both explicit commands and implicit human signals. From detecting emotion through behavioral input to designing accessible AI-based travel systems, these contributions aim to bridge technological capabilities with human values, ensuring smarter and more responsible HCI solutions.

Each chapter brings a unique perspective on how intelligent systems are being designed and implemented across domains such as healthcare, education, e-commerce, workplace productivity, transportation, and smart living environments. The global scope of the contributing authors ensures a rich and diverse view of both current developments and future opportunities in smart HCI.

CHAPTER OVERVIEW

Chapter 1 offers a comprehensive review of cognitive-aware technologies and their integration into sensory systems. It examines the real-time interpretation of human signals like EEG and eye-tracking for adaptive system behavior, with applications spanning education, healthcare, and assistive technologies.

Chapter 2 investigates emotion and engagement detection using gesture and touch input. The authors analyze how AI-driven interpretation of behavioral data, despite cultural and ethical challenges, is reshaping digital experiences in domains such as gaming, customer service, and remote learning.

Chapter 3 presents a detailed survey of artificial intelligence techniques in face recognition systems. Traditional, machine learning, and deep learning approaches are examined, along with current trends in explainable AI and privacy-preserving models like federated learning.

Chapter 4 introduces a conceptual framework for employee adoption of intelligent systems in the workplace. Drawing from principles of Industry 5.0, the chapter focuses on the human factors, inhibitors, and organizational drivers for effective and ethical deployment of smart workplace technologies.

Chapter 5 explores the orchestration of artificial intelligence in e-commerce applications. It proposes a design strategy to enhance user experience through intuitive navigation, service transparency, and data security, addressing common pain points that hinder online shopping experiences.

Chapter 6 addresses the critical issue of travel accessibility for people with disabilities. The chapter outlines how AI-powered tools such as computer vision, NLP, and smart infrastructure can create inclusive transportation systems and improve independent mobility.

Chapter 7 discusses the implementation of Internet of Things (IoT) in smart homes. It analyzes the dual nature of IoT—its benefits in convenience, energy optimization, and personalization, and its challenges related to security, interoperability, and user privacy.

Chapter 8 explores how virtual and extended reality can enhance human-automated vehicle interactions in complex environments. By simulating real-world traffic scenarios, this chapter provides a framework for designing effective external human-machine interfaces and improving pedestrian safety in autonomous systems.

Together, these chapters form a cohesive narrative that underscores the potential of smart HCI systems to not only improve technological efficiency but also elevate human experience. This book is intended for researchers, practitioners, and students looking to understand and contribute to the evolving landscape of intelligent, adaptive, and human-centered computing.

Subrata Tikadar
Amity University Kolkata, India

Joel José Puga Coelho Rodrigues

Federal University of Piauí, Brazil

Rabi Shaw
Dr. B.R. Ambedkar National Institute of Technology, India

Ahdi Hassan
Global Institute for Research Education and Scholarship, The Netherlands

Bidyut Kumar Patra
Indian Institute of Technology (BHU), India

Chapter 1

The State-of-art on Evolution of Cognitive-Aware Technologies Towards Intelligent Sensory Systems:

Review and Global Scenario of Cognitive-Aware Technology

Bikash Kumar
https://orcid.org/0000-0002-0132-9372
Dr B.R. Ambedkar National Institute of Technology, Jalandhar, India

Rhythm Gaba
Dr. B.R. Ambedkar National Institute of Technology, Jalandhar, India

Rabi Shaw
Dr. B.R. Ambedkar National Institute of Technology, Jalandhar, India

ABSTRACT

This chapter explores the evolution and development of cognitive-aware sensitive systems, i.e., an emerging class of human-computer interaction technologies that integrate physiological, behavioural, and contextual signals to deliver adaptive, user-centred experiences. Drawing upon multidisciplinary research from neuroscience, psychology, artificial intelligence, and user experience design, we examine how systems can utilize signals such as EEG, EMG, GSR, heart rate, and eye-tracking to infer mental workload, emotional stress, and engagement levels in real time.

DOI: 10.4018/979-8-3373-6385-1.ch001

Copyright © 2026, IGI Global Scientific Publishing. Copying or distributing in print or electronic forms without written permission of IGI Global Scientific Publishing is prohibited.

Present work gives the insights on a comprehensive overview of the key components underpinning these systems, including sensor technologies, cognitive and affective modeling, adaptive feedback mechanisms, and practical applications in education, healthcare, transportation, and assistive technologies.

1. INTRODUCTION

Human-computer interaction (HCI) has evolved beyond systems simply responding to direct commands. Today's focus is on building systems that understand and respond to users' thoughts and emotions. While early HCI aimed at making technology usable, accessible, and efficient, the current trend moves toward systems that are context-aware, adaptive, and emotionally intelligent. Cognitive-aware sensitive systems are gaining attention for enabling more meaningful interactions by connecting human emotions with machine intelligence.

This shift is largely driven by advances in body signal sensing, affective computing, and adaptive learning algorithms. Signals like EEG (brain activity), GSR (skin response), EMG (muscle movement), heart rate, eye tracking, and touch feedback are now used to infer stress, attention, emotional states, and cognitive load. These insights help systems offer real-time, personalised responses (Calvo & D'Mello, 2010; Zhai & Barreto, 2006).

Developing such systems requires an interdisciplinary axpproach neuroscience explains the origins of signals, psychology sheds light on emotions and cognition, AI helps interpret patterns, and UX design ensures ease of use. Together, these fields have led to tools like online learning platforms that reduce mental fatigue, mental health apps, and smart in-vehicle systems that adapt to the driver's state (D'Mello & Graesser, 2012; Healey & Picard, 2005).

Prototype systems are already in use. In education, content difficulty is adjusted based on mental fatigue, while in vehicles, infotainment features are limited when cognitive load increases to reduce distraction. These systems rely on real-time signal collection and adaptive mechanisms to respond effectively (Zhou & Wang, 2021).

Despite their potential, cognitive-aware systems face several challenges poor signal quality, difficulty interpreting complex or ambiguous mental states, privacy concerns, ethical use of sensitive data, and generalising models across different users. Still, research in education, healthcare, workplace well-being, and automotive UX has shown promising outcomes.

This chapter gives an overview of cognitive-aware systems, from core principles and sensing techniques to modelling approaches and adaptive designs. It also discusses key challenges and future directions, guiding research toward systems that interpret user behaviour and understand the thoughts and emotions behind it.

2. BACKGROUND ON COGNITIVE-AWARE AND SENSITIVE SYSTEMS

As the gap between humans and machines becomes smaller, we expect more from smart systems. It's not enough for them to just reply they should understand too. Cognitive-aware, sensitive systems are changing how we interact with computers. These systems sense what a person feels inside, like stress, focus, tiredness, or interest, and respond in a caring way at that moment. They don't just follow commands but adjust to the user's condition. To build such systems, ideas from brain science, psychology, emotion computing, and other fields are combined. This helps create personalised systems that understand the situation and reply with emotional understanding (Fairclough, 2009).

2.1 The Foundations of Cognition-Sensitive Technology

The main strength of these systems is that they can read body and behaviour signals to know what a person is feeling or thinking. These signals come from brainwaves (EEG), muscle movement (EMG), skin response (GSR), eye movements, heart rate changes (HRV), and facial expressions. By studying these, the system gets a clear idea of what is happening in the person's mind how much mental effort they are using, how emotional they feel, or where they are focusing.

One common way to measure this is the Cognitive Load Index (CLI), based on brainwave patterns from EEG data. It shows how mentally loaded or stressed a person is while doing a task. It compares the power in beta waves (focus) with the combined power in alpha (relaxed) and theta (drowsy). The formula is given below (Antonenko, Paas, Grabner & van Gog, 2010):

$$CLI = \frac{Power_{\beta}}{Power_{\alpha} + Power_{\theta}} \tag{1}$$

where $Power_{\beta}$ represents task engagement and focus (13–30 Hz), $Power_{\alpha}$ indicates relaxed wakefulness (8–13 Hz) and $Power_{\theta}$ is linked to drowsiness and memory access (4–8 Hz). A higher CLI means more mental workload.

2.2 Signal Acquisition and Pre-Processing

To understand a user's mental state, we need clean and clear signals. Raw signals like EEG (see Glossary) or GSR (see Glossary) often carry noise from eye movement, muscle activity, or external sources. So, preprocessing is important. A common method is bandpass filtering, which keeps only the useful frequencies.

This is done using convolution, as shown in Eq. (2) (Bashashati, Fatourechi, Ward, & Birch, 2007):

$$y(t) = x(t) * h(t) \tag{2}$$

Here, x(t) is the raw signal, h(t) is the filter, and y(t) is the cleaned output. After cleaning, we extract features and reduce them using PCA or LDA, then use models like SVM to classify states.

2.3 Bayesian Inference and Cognitive State Estimation

To understand what's happening in the user's mind, which we can't see directly, cognitive-aware systems use Bayesian inference. This method keeps updating the system's guess using new data and old knowledge. Bayes' Theorem, given in Eq. (3) (Casson, 2019), explains this idea.

$$P(S|D) = \frac{P(D|S) * P(S)}{P(D)} \tag{3}$$

In this method, S means the user's mental state, like being focused or distracted. D is the data collected, such as EEG or GSR signals. P(D|S) shows the chance of getting this data if we know the state. P(S) is what we guessed before seeing any data, and P(S|D) is our final guess after checking the data. The system uses this final guess to understand the user. Bayesian inference is helpful especially when the data is noisy or incomplete. Instead of getting confused, the system uses past experience and the user's context to still make smart guesses about what the person might be feeling or doing.

Figure 1. Bayesian inference flow for cognitive state estimation.

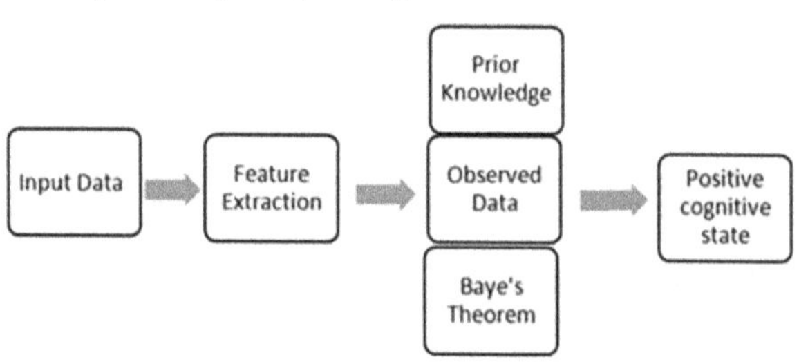

2.4 Cognitive and Affective Computing Synergy

Cognitive-aware systems become even more powerful when they work together with affective computing. That's because emotions and thinking are closely connected they affect each other. For example, emotions can change how well a person can think, and mental pressure can also change how someone feels.

Today's smart systems are built to understand both at the same time. For example, EEG signals (see Glossary) might show if someone is mentally tired, while their facial expressions can show if they're feeling frustrated (Koelstra, Muhl, Soleymani, Lee, Yazdani, Ebrahimi, & Patras, 2012).

By using both these types of signals, intelligent tutoring systems can respond better like slowing down the lesson, giving encouragement, or changing the way they teach. This kind of understanding makes systems more helpful in many areas like mental health care and road safety (D'Mello & Kory, 2015).

3. MODELLING COGNITION IN HUMAN-COMPUTER INTERACTION

Understanding the human mind is very important for designing smart systems that respond in real time to what a user thinks or feels. In Human-Computer Interaction (HCI), this goes beyond just giving commands. Now, systems watch mental signals like focus, stress, and effort through body signs and behaviour. Adding this into the system's logic makes the experience more personal and responsive. This helps people stay engaged, feel less tired, and work better while feeling good too.

Figure 2. Cognitive modelling pipeline showing the flow from user physiological signals to system adaptation in HCI.

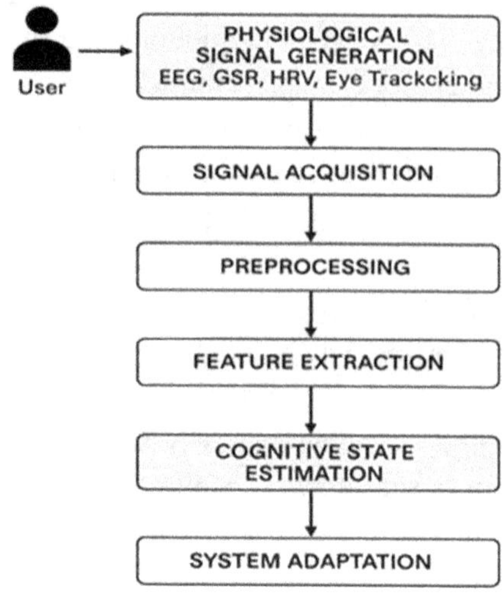

3.1 Foundational HCI Theories and Models

Human-Computer Interaction (HCI) has moved from basic command-line tools to smart and personalised user experiences. Foundational HCI models help us see how people use digital systems. Norman's Principles of Design focus on ease of use, clear signs, good feedback, and simple actions (Norman, 2013). The GOMS Model — Goals, Operators, Methods, and Selection Rules by Card, Moran and Newell (1983), explains how users break tasks into small steps. Moreover, ACT-R (Adaptive Control of Thought–Rational) by Anderson (2007) shows how people learn and solve problems, helping build systems that match how we think. Fitts' Law says the time to tap a button depends on its size and distance (Fitts, 1954). Bigger, closer buttons are faster. Hick's Law says more choices slow down decisions, so simple menus help people act quickly (Hick, 1952).

3.2 Signal Acquisition and Processing

Cognition covers how we think, learn and decide. In HCI, we check mental effort, stress, and attention using signals like brainwaves (EEG), skin response (GSR), heart rate, and eye movements. Sensors collect and clean these signals to find useful patterns so systems can react live.

3.3 Emotion and Stress Detection Models

Simple models like Linear Discriminant Analysis or Support Vector Machines help find mental states (Khosrowabadi et al., 2011). CNNs help find patterns in EEG (Zhang et al., 2019). Hidden Markov Models track time-based changes like alertness (Schuller et al., 2011).

3.4 Mapping Modalities to Cognitive States

Picking the right sensors and features is key for accurate models. Table 1 shows common signals, the mental states they show, and usual features. Figure 3 links signals like EEG, GSR, HRV, eye tracking, and EMG to mental and emotional states (Table 1; Fig 3).

Table 1. Overview of cognitive-aware modalities with corresponding signal types, cognitive/emotional indicators, extracted features, and representative use cases across application domains.

Modality	Signal Type	Cognitive/Emotional Indicators	Common Features	Typical Use Cases
EEG (Electroencephalography)	Brainwave activity (Alpha, Beta, Theta)	Attention, fatigue, cognitive load, engagement	Theta/Alpha ratio, ERP, PSD	E-learning, driver alertness, BCIs
GSR (Galvanic Skin Response)	Skin conductance level & fluctuations	Arousal, stress, emotional intensity	SCR frequency, amplitude	Gaming, mental health, UX evaluation
HRV (Heart Rate Variability)	Beat-to-beat interval patterns (cardiac rhythm)	Stress, relaxation, anxiety, workload	LF/HF ratio, RMSSD	Meditation apps, adaptive interfaces
EMG (Electromyography)	Muscle activation (facial or limb)	Effort, emotion, fatigue, movement intent	RMS amplitude, activation threshold	Prosthetics, gesture recognition
Eye Tracking	Gaze path, fixation, saccades, pupil dilation	Attention, confusion, distraction	Saccade velocity, fixation duration	E-learning, UX, advertising
Facial Expression Analysis	Micro-expressions, facial muscle movement	Emotions: joy, anger, frustration, surprise	AU (action units), expression intensity	Affective tutoring, entertainment

continued on following page

Table 1. Continued

Modality	Signal Type	Cognitive/Emotional Indicators	Common Features	Typical Use Cases
Speech & Voice Stress	Pitch, tone, pause rate, vocal patterns	Mood, cognitive effort, deception	Pitch variability, speech rate, MFCCs	Virtual agents, interviews, VR training
Touch/Interaction Patterns	Tap speed, pressure, gesture motion	Engagement, hesitation, confidence	Tap pressure, swipe velocity, dwell time	Mobile UX, e-commerce, gaming

Figure 3. Mapping of physiological modalities to cognitive and emotional states.

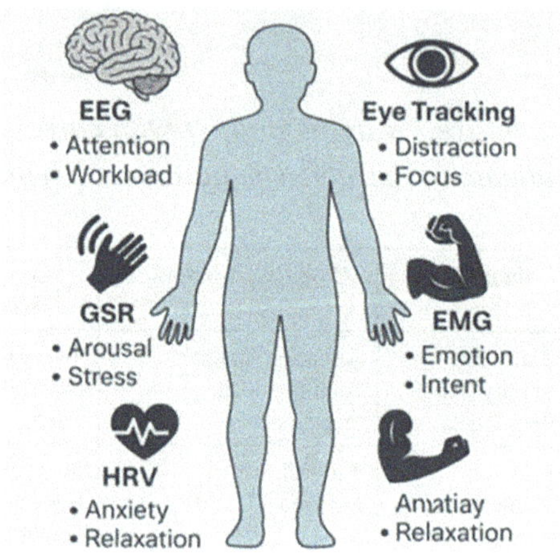

This mapping informs the sensor selection process during system design and model calibration.

EEG helps track brainwave patterns to detect attention and fatigue, especially useful in driving or e-learning contexts. Voice data like pitch and tone help detect stress or emotion in customer service settings. Facial expressions and blink rate can indicate confusion or tiredness, useful in exams and healthcare apps.

3.5 Integrated Models for Cognitive Adaptation

Instead of using only one signal, many systems now combine signals for better results. Integrated models use EEG, GSR, HRV, and eye tracking together to understand the user's mind better. In early fusion, all features are joined before modelling. In late fusion, each signal is modelled separately and then combined. Katsigiannis and Ramzan (2018) showed that mixing EEG and eye tracking improved attention detection by 15% over single signals. This fusion is helpful in real life where sensor data can be noisy.

Table 2. Comparison of fusion strategies in multimodal signal processing with advantages and limitations

Fusion Type	What it Means	Pro/Con Summary
Early Fusion	Mix all raw signals together	Fast, but messy if noisy
Late Fusion	Process each signal separately, then combine	Cleaner, but slower
Hybrid Fusion	Mix raw and processed signals	Best of both, but complex

4. COGNITIVE SENSING TECHNOLOGIES

To build smart systems that truly understand people, we need to sense what a person feels or thinks in real time. Whether someone is stressed, alert or tired, knowing these states helps systems react better. Cognitive sensing acts like a bridge between the mind and the machine. It goes beyond simple clicks and reads deeper signals. Researchers use four main sensing types: brain signals like EEG (see Glossary), body signals like heart rate or EMG, behaviour signs like eye or hand movement, and a mix of these through fusion methods (Bashivan et al., 2016; Kim et al., 2018).

4.1 EEG-Based Cognitive Monitoring

Electroencephalography (EEG) is widely used to track brain activity. It is non-invasive and records electrical signals with good time accuracy, which helps track quick changes in attention or mental load. EEG signals have bands. More theta activity in the front brain shows higher effort, while lower alpha means more alertness. The Cognitive Load Index (CLI) is one way to measure this (Bashivan et al., 2016):

$$CLI = \frac{P_\theta}{P_\alpha} \tag{4}$$

Here, P_θ and P_α are power levels in theta and alpha bands from the frontal brain. Bashivan et al. (2016) used a CNN-LSTM model to tell meditative and focused states with 91% accuracy. Lin et al. (2014) used wavelet and SVMs to detect workload. New wearable EEG devices like Muse and NeuroSky make this easier in daily life.

4.2 Physiological Sensors Beyond EEG (GSR, EMG, Heart Rate)

EEG checks brain signals, but other body signals help too. Sensors like GSR, EMG, and HRV give stable data, even outdoors. GSR tracks skin conductivity, linked to stress or excitement. Skin Conductance Response (SCR) shows these changes. EMG checks muscle signals, often for facial expressions. Heart Rate Variability (HRV) shows gaps between beats. A common measure is LF/HF, shown below (Kim et al., 2018):

$$LF/HF = \frac{P_{LF}}{P_{HF}} \tag{5}$$

Here, P_{LF} and P_{HF} are low and high-frequency powers. A higher LF/HF means stress. These sensors now come in smartwatches and bands, making real-time tracking easier (Kim et al., 2018).

4.3 Behavioural and Contextual Sensing

Behaviour can show mental states better than body signals. Small actions like typing speed, eye movement or fidgeting show stress or overload. Eye tracking shows focus through gaze and blinks. Typing speed and backspaces show stress too. Mouse paths and swipe gestures can show emotion. One study used eye and click data to spot overload with 85% accuracy (Eivazi et al., 2017). Another found frustration using touch data (Bixler & D'Mello, 2016). These work well without special sensors.

4.4 Signals

Each sensor has limits. EEG gets noise, GSR changes with heat, and users act differently (Fairclough, 2009; Bashashati et al., 2007; D'Mello & Kory, 2015). So, fusion joins signals for better results (Fairclough, 2009; Koelstra et al., 2012; Katsigiannis & Ramzan, 2018). In early fusion, data is mixed first. In late fusion, each model works alone, then outputs combine. Hybrid fusion mixes both (Fairclough, 2009). A common way is weighted voting, shown in Eq.(6) (Koelstra et al., 2012):

$$P(y|X_1, X_2, \dots, X_n) = \sum_{(i=1)}^{n} w_i P_i(y|X_i) \tag{6}$$

In Eq. (6), X represents the feature set from the *i-th* modality, P (y | X) is the prediction from that modality, and w is a weight reflecting its reliability or past accuracy. For example, CNN-based fusion of EEG, GSR and EMG improved fatigue detection by 20%. Fusion helps if one sensor fails, others still give data — useful for real life.

Figure 4. Fusion architecture diagram shows early, late, and hybrid strategies for combining multimodal inputs in cognitive-aware systems

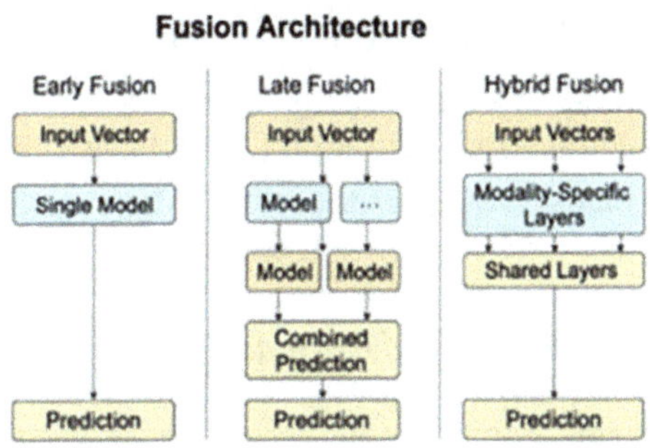

Table 3. Comparative overview of cognitive system models, their strengths, weaknesses, and ideal applications

Model	Strengths	Weaknesses	Best For
Rule-Based	Easy to understand	Not flexible	Simple tasks
Decision Tree	Quick and interpretable	Can overfit	User behavior prediction
Neural Net	Handles complex signals	Needs more data/training	EEG, voice analysis
Fusion Logic	Combines many inputs	Complex to set up	Multimodal sensing

5. EMOTION AND COGNITIVE STATE RECOGNITION

Understanding emotions and mental states has changed how we see Human-Computer Interaction (HCI). Earlier, systems only followed clear commands. Now, they try to sense what the user is feeling or thinking, making the experience smoother and more human-like. This part explains how emotions are understood by machines, how they work in real-time, the common challenges in real-world use, and how combining different types of signals helps.

5.1 Machine Learning Models for Emotion and Cognition

Earlier systems used simple methods like SVM, decision trees, or logistic regression with features picked by hand from EEG (see Glossary), GSR, or EMG signals. But these did not work well with new users or changing conditions. Deep learning improved this. CNNs work well with EEG heatmaps, and RNNs (LSTM, GRU) track changes in speech or heartbeat. Transformer models now focus on useful data parts and improve emotion checks (Pepino, Ribeiro, & Gerosa, 2021). A CNN-LSTM model showed 85% accuracy for frustration (Tripathi, Acharya, & Sharma, 2017). DEAP and AMIGOS datasets support this work (Miranda-Correa et al., 2018).

Table 4. Comparative performance of machine learning models in cognitive-aware systems

Model Type	Signal Used	Accuracy (%)	Application Area	Limitation
SVM	GSR	84%	Stress detection	Sensitive to feature selection
CNN-LSTM Hybrid	EEG	91%	Attention classification	High training data requirement
Transformer	Speech	88%	Emotion recognition	Needs large labelled datasets
Random Forest	EMG + HRV	87%	Workplace stress monitoring	May overfit with many features

5.2 Challenges in Emotion and Cognitive State Generalization

Emotion-aware systems are useful but face many challenges. One big issue is generalisation. The same signal, like high GSR, can mean fear for one person but excitement for another. Feelings change with age, health, or mood. To handle this, methods like few-shot and meta-learning help models adapt with little data (Jiang, Xu, Ma, & Wang, 2021).

Context matters too. A fast heartbeat in a game shows excitement, but in an exam it may mean stress. Labelling emotions is also hard, as they are short and personal. Self-reports are not always right. So, new models use weak supervision and multi-label learning to improve results (Zhang, Yu, & Fung, 2018). As emotion data is sensitive, fairness checks and clear rules are needed (Lepri, Oliver, Letouzé, Pentland, & Vinck, 2018).

5.3 Multimodal Fusion for Emotion-Cognition Modelling

No single sensor can fully capture a person's emotions or thoughts. Emotions are complex and show through many signals like brain activity, face, voice, gestures or typing style. So, modern systems use multimodal fusion combining signals from many sources for a clearer result.

There are three main ways: early fusion, where signals like EEG and GSR are joined before classification; late fusion, where each is processed separately and results are combined (like voting); and hybrid fusion, which mixes both. Attention-based models are now popular as they pick the most useful signals, even if some fail (Huang, Fu, He, & Tan, 2021).

In real life, this helps in classrooms where EEG, GSR and eye tracking are combined to check overload. In smart assistants and cars, speech, face and heart signals help detect emotions or drowsiness. Public datasets like DEAP, WESAD and SEED help test these models.

Figure 5. Emotion & cognitive signal map illustrating common sensor placements (e.g., EEG, GSR, EMG, HRV) and their associated emotional and cognitive state measurements across the human body.

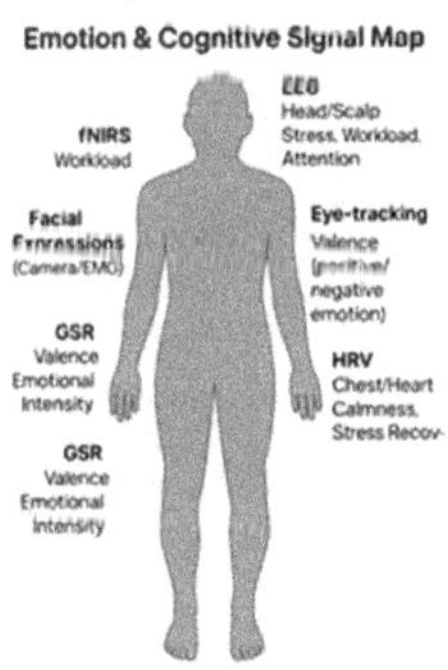

Table 5. Key modalities in cognitive-aware systems

Modality	Signals Captured	Common Applications
EEG	Alpha/theta bands, ERPs	Mental workload, stress, engagement
GSR	Skin conductance levels/peaks	Arousal, anxiety
HRV/ECG	RR intervals, LF/HF ratio	Stress, relaxation, drowsiness
EMG	Muscle tension	Fatigue, exertion

continued on following page

Table 5. Continued

Modality	Signals Captured	Common Applications
Facial Expression	Action units, valence-arousal estimation	Emotion classification, social interaction
Speech Prosody	Pitch, energy, tempo	Affect, sarcasm, sentiment
Eye Tracking	Blink rate, gaze fixation, pupil dilation	Attention, cognitive load
Behavioral Logs	Keystrokes, mouse dynamics	Engagement, frustration

Fig. 6 illustrates how different physiological and behavioural signals such as EEG, GSR, facial expressions, and speech—are processed and combined using various fusion strategies to enhance the accuracy and robustness of emotion recognition in cognitive-aware systems. Together, these sensing strategies and computational models are driving a new wave of emotionally intelligent technology tools that not only recognize our emotional and cognitive states but also respond with empathy, adaptivity, and ethical awareness.

Figure 6. Multimodal fusion architecture for emotion recognition integrating EEG, GSR, facial, and speech signals through early, late, and hybrid fusion strategies.

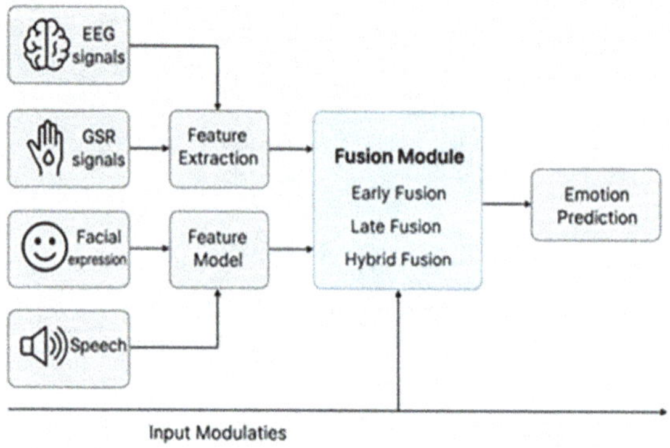

6. ADAPTIVE AND PERSONALIZED INTERFACES

Adaptive and personalised interfaces make systems smarter by sensing the user's mental and emotional state and changing how they work in real time. Older systems used simple models like SVMs on signals like EEG or GSR but found it hard to work well for everyone. Now, with better AI models and behavioural data, systems can change content, layout, or help options to make user experience better.

6.1 Principles of Adaptivity and Personalization

Adaptivity means the system reacts instantly to changes like tiredness or losing focus. Personalization means the system learns what the user likes over time. For example, an online learning tool may slow down lessons if it senses high workload and later change content style as per the student's choice. Voice assistants like Siri do the same they learn if a person likes reminders said softly or firmly (Verbert, Duval, Klerkx, Govaerts, & Santos, 2012).

Figure 7. Real-time adaptivity responds instantly to user state, while personalization evolves from past behaviour.

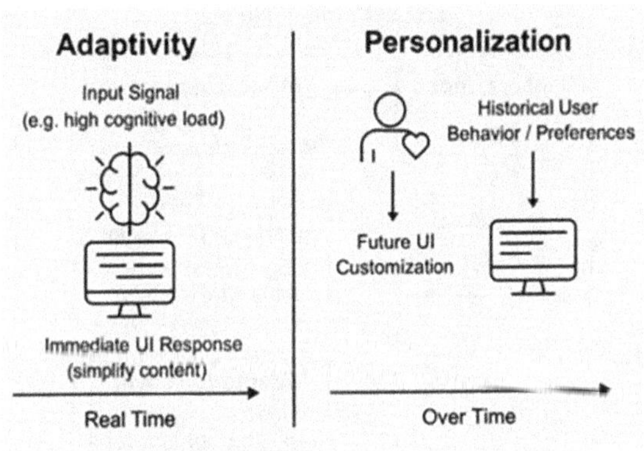

6.2 AI/ML-Based Personalization Techniques

AI and machine learning run the brain of these interfaces (see Glossary). Supervised learning like SVMs, random forests, and neural networks predict user stress or focus from signals. Unsupervised methods like k-means or autoencoders find hidden user patterns without labels. Reinforcement learning (RL) is also popular here, the system tests responses and learns from user feedback about what worked well. Over time, it gets better at helping each user in a way they like.

6.3 Cognitive State-Driven Interface Adjustments

Many apps now show how good these systems can be. In online learning, smart tutors adjust how they talk to students based on EEG or GSR signals. If the learner feels overloaded, the system can hide extra buttons, reduce distractions, or give tips.

When the student feels fine, the system shows harder tasks again (Arroyo, Woolf, Cooper, Burleson, & Muldner, 2009).

In healthcare, adaptive screens help elderly or people with memory issues by changing font size, alert speed, or screen layout when it spots tiredness or mistakes. If a user types wrong or answers slowly, the system adjusts to make things safer (Jimison, Pavel, & Pavel, 2008).

In cars, cognitive-aware tools check if the driver is distracted using EEG, eye tracking, or other signs. If stress is high, they dim screens, silence alerts, or simplify directions to lower mental load (Jung, Lee, & Chung, 2018).

Figure 8. Multimodal cognitive input pipeline for adaptive interfaces

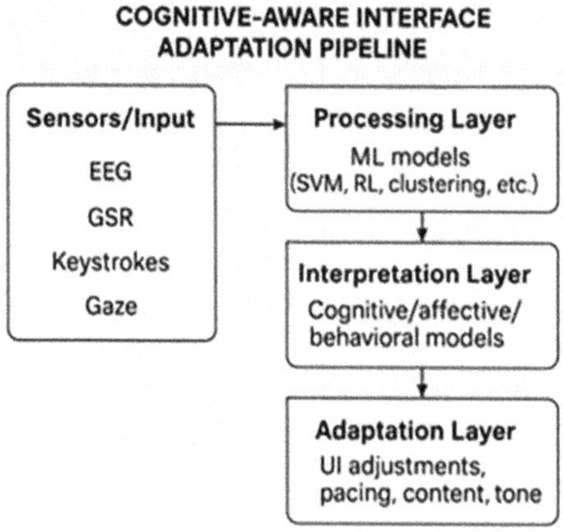

6.4 Multidisciplinary Personalization Frameworks

To do this well, these systems use ideas from psychology, neuroscience, and human behaviour. Cognitive models like ACT-R help break tasks into steps. Emotion models like Russell's circumplex explain feelings (Russell, 1980). Behaviour models track gaze, typing, or mistake patterns to understand users better (Anderson, 2007).

6.5 Translating Cognitive Insights into UX

The real power comes when mental data changes what the user sees. If the system senses loss of focus, it may slow down videos or hide extra menus. Turning signals into simple, helpful UI changes is the real test for designers. Figure 6.3 shows how this works step by step.

The Figure 6.3 shows a simple flow: first, a signal is picked up (like stress or focus), then the system understands the user's mental state, and finally, it changes the scree like slowing down a video, hiding extra buttons, or making the text bigger to help the user.

Figure 9. Flow of a cognitive-aware system: How cognitive signals lead to smart UI changes based on user state.

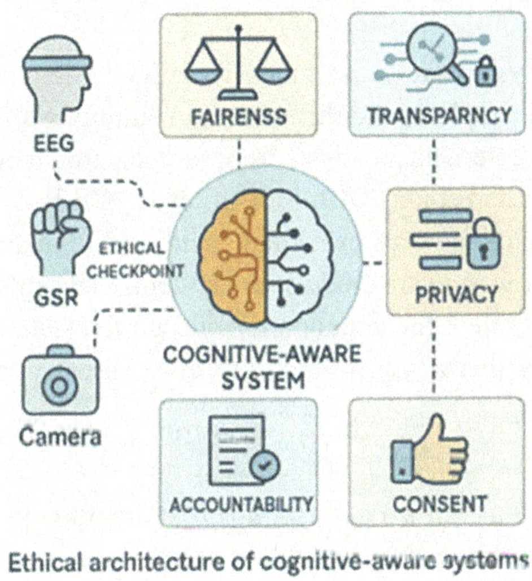

6.6 Real-World Applications and Case Studies

Today, tools like Siri or Google Assistant learn how we talk and what we prefer. Slowly, they adjust replies to feel more human. Mental health apps like Woebot or Wysa read moods and words to chat in a caring way, helping people feel heard (Fulmer et al., 2018).

In cars, BMW's iDrive and Tesla's screens check driver stress using face or heart rate. If needed, they dim lights, limit controls, or adjust AC to keep drivers calm (Mühl, Allison, Nijholt, & Chanel, 2014; Deng, Liu, Wang, & Zhao, 2020).

These examples show how adaptivity works not just in special fields like health or learning but also in everyday tools that feel more human and supportive.

7. ETHICS, PRIVACY, AND COGNITIVE BIAS IN SENSITIVE SYSTEMS

Cognitive-aware systems offer personalised support by interpreting thoughts and emotions, but they also raise ethical concerns. Key issues include algorithmic bias, privacy, consent, and transparency especially in sensitive areas like health and education. Biased data can lead to unfair outcomes, and lack of clarity may reduce user trust.

7.1 Cognitive Biases in Sensing and Prediction

Cognitive-aware systems rely on signals like EEG, GSR, and facial expressions, but these vary across people due to differences in culture, gender, or age. A model trained mostly on Western facial data, for example, might misread expressions from other cultures (Zhao et al., 2019; McDuff et al., 2017). These biases can lead to wrong decisions in classrooms or mental health tools. To avoid this, developers need diverse data, fairness-aware models, and systems that explain their decisions to users. Figure 7.1 shows the ethical foundation of cognitive-aware systems, including fairness, transparency, privacy, accountability, and consent, applied throughout the data process.

Figure 10. Ethical architecture of cognitive-aware systems showing key principles like fairness, transparency, privacy, accountability, and consent across the data pipeline.

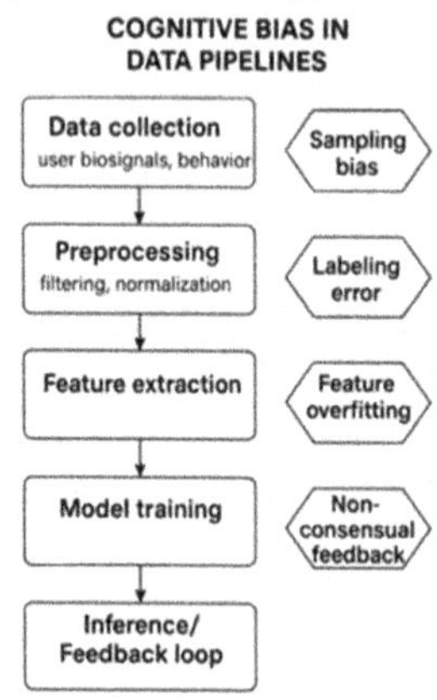

7.2 Ethical Frameworks: Fairness, Explainability, and Accountability

Ethical design means making fairness, explainability, and accountability part of system development. Fairness involves correcting biases in data and ensuring balanced treatment. Tools like SHAP and LIME help explain decisions by showing which signals influenced an outcome (Lundberg & Lee, 2017). Documentation tools like Model Cards and Datasheets track how models are built and what risks they carry (Mitchell et al., 2019). Value-sensitive design (VSD) encourages including user feedback and cultural values early in the process (Friedman, Kahn, & Borning, 2006).

Table 6. Ethical dimensions and practices in cognitive-aware systems

Ethical Principle	Challenge in Cognitive-Aware Systems	Mitigation Strategy	Example
Fairness	Biased predictions due to non-representative training data	Use diverse, balanced datasets and fairness-aware algorithms	Cross-cultural affect detection using domain adaptation
Explainability	Users don't understand how their emotion or workload was inferred	Use interpretable models or post-hoc explainability methods	EEG-based workload estimation with SHAP explanations
Privacy	Invasive data (EEG, GSR) collected without full awareness	Obtain explicit, informed consent; anonymize sensitive features	GSR tracking in stress monitoring apps
Accountability	Lack of traceability in model decisions and failures	Use model cards, audit logs, andethics checklists	Documentation of affective model biases

7.3 Privacy and Consent in Physiological Data Handling

Signals like EEG (see Glossary) and eye movements can reveal stress or emotions silently, making privacy critical. Consent must be specific users should choose what data to share and when. For example, someone might agree to share GSR in a fitness app but not in a mental health session (Nissenbaum, 2011). Systems should also limit data collection to what's necessary, store it securely, and follow data laws like GDPR (Voigt & Von dem Bussche, 2017). Because biometric signals can be unique, privacy tools like differential privacy and federated learning are used to prevent identification (Dwork & Roth, 2014; Yang, Liu, Chen, & Tong, 2019).

7.4 Toward Ethical Cognitive-Aware HCI

Ethics should guide the entire lifecycle of cognitive-aware systems. Adaptive consent asks for permission at the right time, respecting the user's mental state (Simonsen et al., 2020). Participatory design invites users to decide what data is collected and how it's used, making systems more inclusive and respectful (Muller, 2003). Ultimately, fairness, transparency, and privacy are essential for creating systems that support users, not control them. Figure 7.2 shows where bias can enter the system and suggests ways to prevent it.

Figure 11. Points of cognitive bias and mitigation strategies across the machine learning pipeline.

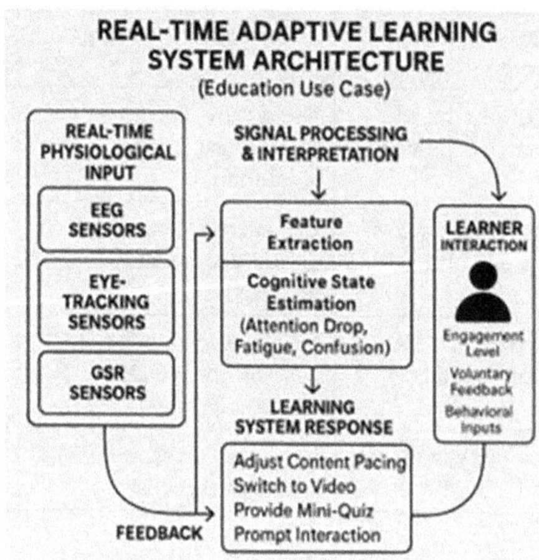

Table 7. Ethical dimensions in real-time cognitive-aware adaptation

Ethical Principle	Feature or Mechanism	Implementation Strategy
Fairness	Personalized workload detection	Individual baselines replace population-level thresholds
Privacy	Emotion recognition without raw data retention	Real-time inference followed by immediate signal discard
Informed Consent	Consent before data-intensive analytics	Session-specific prompts triggered by user-initiated actions

continued on following page

Table 7. Continued

Ethical Principle	Feature or Mechanism	Implementation Strategy
Transparency	Explainable performance summaries	Natural-language justifications with traceable feature sources
Autonomy	Control over feedback timing	Modes like "Do Not Disturb" and deferred feedback delivery options

7.4.1 Ethical Design Steps for Cognitive Systems

When we design cognitive systems, it is important to respect people's privacy. We should always ask people before taking their personal data and clearly tell them what we will do with it. People should have the freedom to stop tracking whenever they want. Also, these systems should not make any big decisions for someone without giving a clear reason. From time to time, we must check if the system is fair for everyone and working properly.

8. APPLICATIONS OF COGNITIVE-AWARE SYSTEMS

Cognitive-aware systems are now used beyond labs in real life. These tools sense mental states like stress, focus, or emotions and react instantly, making technology feel more human and helpful. Thanks to better brain sensing, AI, and user-friendly design, these systems are part of daily life now.

8.1 Education & E-Learning Environments

In education, these systems personalise learning by tracking attention, mental effort, and emotions. Using EEG (see Glossary) or eye-tracking, they can sense when a student is confused or losing focus and adjust lessons by slowing down, changing formats, or giving hints (D'Mello & Graesser, 2012; Bosch et al., 2016). Some tools watch for tiredness using skin or heart signals and suggest breaks or easier tasks (Sharma et al., 2020). One EEG-based tutor added small quizzes when focus dropped, helping students understand lessons 20% better (Liu et al., 2019). In one real example, a smart tutor that tracked brain activity with EEG changed lesson levels based on how tired students felt. This helped students remember lessons better by around 20% (Ahn et al., 2016).

Figure 12. Real-time adaptive learning system using physiological input to adjust learning based on cognitive state.

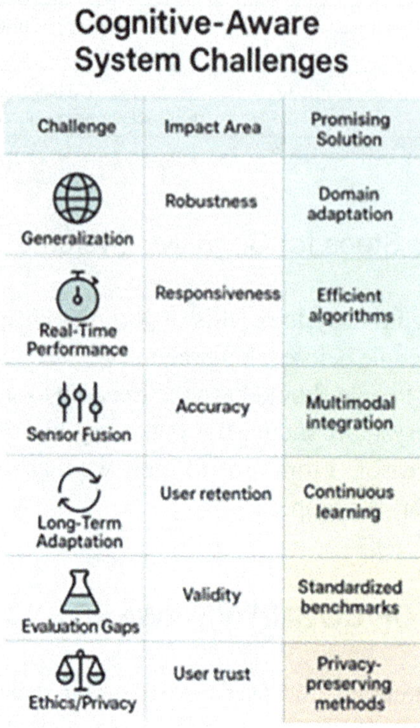

8.2 Healthcare & Assistive Technology

In healthcare, these systems spot early signs of problems like Parkinson's or Alzheimer's using wearable EEG and EMG devices (Cassani et al., 2018). Emotion sensing with brain or facial signals is being tested for mental health checks. Bio-feedback tools show calming sounds or images during therapy to help manage stress or PTSD (Alarcao & Fonseca, 2019). Moreover, Assistive tech is also smarter now. BCIs help people with severe motor issues control devices with brain signals alone (Wolpaw & Wolpaw, 2012). Apps adjust complexity based on stress, making them easier to use. One stroke therapy system used EEG and EMG to track tiredness and change session intensity in real time, improving comfort and recovery (Liao et al., 2016; Muller-Putz et al., 2019; Kim et al., 2021). Additionally, a mental health app using GSR and EMG signals changed therapy content live, based on stress levels. People using it felt 23% less anxious in just two weeks (Chandrasekaran et al., 2020).

Personalisation is key. Everyone reacts differently to tasks, some tire faster, some need more stimulation. A good system learns these habits and adjusts like giving shorter tasks to tired users or soft music to stressed users.

8.3 Workplace and User Experience (UX) Enhancements

In workplaces, these systems help people work better and feel less stressed, especially in high-focus jobs like air traffic control. By tracking EEG and heart signals, tasks can be split to avoid overload (Aricò et al., 2016). UX designers use them to check signs of stress or effort and improve apps with real feedback (Calvo & D'Mello, 2010). For example, smart office assistants can track stress and quietly suggest actions like lowering screen brightness or pausing notifications (Lalanne et al., 2015).

In a small pilot test, workers wore bands that tracked HRV and GSR. The system changed how many notifications popped up based on stress. But the bands sometimes failed when people moved too much, showing real-world sensor limits. Such systems show their power in simple ways. A learning app can watch a student's face to check focus and slow lessons if the student looks confused. In offices, the system can detect mental tiredness and suggest short breaks to keep people fresh and productive. These small changes show how watching mental states live can make daily tools work better.

Table 8. Overview of applications of cognitive-aware systems

Domain	Cognitive Cues Used	Technologies Deployed	Key Benefits
Education	Attention, fatigue	EEG, Eye-tracking, ML	Adaptive content delivery, improved retention
Healthcare	Stress, cognitive load	EEG, EMG, HRV, BCIs	Early diagnosis, personalized therapy
Gaming	Focus, emotion regulation	EEG, GSR, VR	Neurofeedback, clinical interventions
Workplace/ UX	Workload, frustration	EEG, webcam-based affect recognition	Burnout prevention, intelligent UI adaptation

9. CHALLENGES AND FUTURE RESEARCH DIRECTIONS

Cognitive-aware tools have improved a lot, but big challenges remain when moving from lab to real life. It is hard to make them work well for everyone, keep them fast, merge many sensors, and design them fairly. This needs strong tech, smart design, and care for real impacts. One big issue is generalisation. Many tools still need personal setup, which is hard for large use. Emotion checks using EEG or face scans often fail as signals change with mood or culture. New ideas like meta-learning, few-shot learning, and transformers help (Shen et al., 2021; Tsinalis et al., 2016).

9.1 Generalization Across Users and Contexts

A big problem with cognitive-aware systems is they do not work the same for everyone, every place, or every task. Many tools still need to be set up for each user, which is hard when you want to use them for many people together. For example, emotion checks with EEG or face scans may fail as brain signals or expressions change with mood, culture, or tiredness. Models built in labs often fail in real life and this is called domain drift.

To fix this, researchers use meta-learning, transfer learning, and domain adaptation to make systems work better without retraining each time. Few-shot learning helps when data is less. Still, EEG and GSR signals are tough to generalise due to noise and poor labelling (Shen et al., 2021; Tsinalis et al., 2016). New ideas like context-aware transformers and signal matching look promising.

9.1.1 Underexplored Challenges in Cognitive-Aware Systems

Real-time delay is also a big issue. In driver alertness tools, even a small lag in spotting fatigue can be risky (Wagh et al., 2022). Mental states change with time, but static models do not adapt well (Bengio, LeCun & Hinton, 2021). Another worry is bias — many models are trained mostly on Western data and may not detect emotions correctly in Asian faces (Buolamwini & Gebru, 2018). Future systems should use continual learning and respect culture and personal differences (Phillips et al., 2011).

9.2 Real-Time Computation and Latency Constraints

Cognitive-aware systems must work fast, especially for flying, driving, or learning. Real-time work is hard as it needs quick signal collection, fast processing, and action. Total system time, T_res, is the sum of T_acq (data collection), T_proc (processing) and T_act (action), shown by Eq.(7) (Sani et al., 2021):

$$T_{res} = T_{acq} + T_{proc} + T_{act} \tag{7}$$

Here T_{acq} refers to time taken to acquire raw multimodal signals (e.g., EEG, GSR), T_{proc} refers to time for pre-processing, feature extraction, and model inference and T_{act} refers to time to execute the appropriate adaptive action

Edge-AI methods like pruning, quantization, and NAS help run these models on small devices (Cheng et al., 2020). But keeping low delay, clear outputs, and good performance is tough, especially for wearables with small batteries.

9.3 Real-World Deployment Barriers

Real-world deployment is tough. EEG signals often get distorted by user movement, limiting use while walking or driving. Sensor placement must be comfortable for long use, which is often impractical. Personalisation is also a big challenge. Cognitive responses are different for each person, so a model that works well for one individual may not give the right results for another. On top of that, there are concerns about privacy and ethics. Rules like GDPR and worries about bias make it harder to use such systems in sensitive areas like health, education, or recruitment.

9.4 Sensor Integration and Signal Noise

Combining signals like EEG, GSR, heart rate, and eye tracking is tricky. Each behaves differently some fast, some slow, many noisy For example, head movement can ruin EEG accuracy by 30% if not cleaned with filters like ICA (Looney et al., 2016). Fusion and confidence models help pick the best signal. New methods like self-supervised and contrastive learning help clean signals without labels, but need heavy computing, which is hard for daily real-time use.

9.5 Long-Term Personalization and Concept Drift

Our thoughts and feelings change over time. Someone nervous today may feel confident tomorrow. Because of this, earlier trained models may stop working properly this is known as concept drift (see Glossary). To handle it, researchers use lifelong or online learning, where the model updates itself with every new data point. The update rule is shown in Eq. (8) (Kirkpatrick et al., 2017)

$$\theta_{t+1} = \theta_t + \eta \ \nabla \ L(\theta_t, x_t) \tag{8}$$

Here, θ are the model parameters, x is the new input, L is the loss, and η is the learning rate. To avoid forgetting old data, methods like memory replay and elastic weight consolidation are used (Parisi et al., 2019). Federated lifelong learning (see Glossary) also helps by training models on-device while keeping user data private.

9.6 Ethical and Social Implications

The main power of cognitive-aware systems reading thoughts, stress, or feelings can also become risky. If people do not know they are being watched, it raises privacy worries. For example, tracking student emotions in a classroom or office without asking feels intrusive. Also, many models are trained on limited groups, so they may not work well for women, neurodivergent people, or other cultures. To handle this, designers must plan fairness and privacy from the start called ethics-by-design. One strong solution is federated learning, where models learn on the user's device without sharing raw signals (McMahan et al., 2017). Explainable AI (XAI) helps people know why the system made a choice (Gunning & Aha, 2019). Tools like differential privacy and homomorphic encryption keep signals safe even during processing (Dwork & Roth, 2014; Acar et al., 2018). Additionally, designers should follow ideas from biomedical ethics respect user choice, do good, do no harm, and treat all fairly. This is very important in mental health, where wrong guesses can cause real pain (Beauchamp & Childress, 2001; Mittelstadt et al., 2016; Cummings, 2020).

Table 9. Challenges and directions

Challenge	Impact Area	Promising Solution
Generalization	Scalability	Transfer/meta-learning, large-scale pretraining
Real-time performance	Usability, UX	Edge AI, model pruning, neural architecture search
Sensor reliability & fusion	Data quality	Adaptive filtering, confidence-based sensor weighting
Long-term adaptation	Personalization	Lifelong learning, federated drift detection
Evaluation realism	Deployment success	Field trials, multi-dimensional evaluation metrics
Ethical/privacy concerns	Trust and adoption	Explainable AI, secure consent models, federated learning

Figure 13 maps these big issues, who they affect, and solutions that help link Sections 9.1 to 9.6.

Figure 13. Summary map of key challenges, impact areas, and emerging solutions in cognitive-aware systems

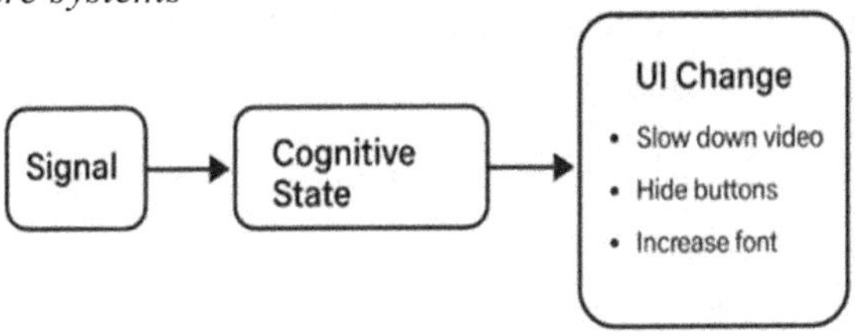

9.7 Vision for Future Research

In future, cognitive-aware systems must become not just smart but thoughtful. One key way is federated cognitive modelling different devices learn locally and share only model updates, not raw signals. This keeps user privacy safe while making systems more personalised (Kairouz et al., 2021). Another need is cross-cultural emotion modelling. People from different places show stress, joy, or focus in different ways. If models are trained only on one group, they may fail elsewhere (Barrett et al., 2011). So, collecting wide and varied data is important. Neuro-symbolic systems are also growing. They mix deep learning with rule-based logic to help machines explain decisions clearly (Garcez et al., 2019). These IoT-based systems must be useful and fair. Real progress comes when experts in AI, psychology, design, ethics, and neuroscience work together to build systems that help people and respect differences (Crawford & Paglen, 2021). Faster training methods are needed so these tools can work in real time. Also, they should give more personalised feedback to users. Cheaper, low-power sensors will help more people use them. Another big goal is to make models easy to explain so that users understand why a system reacts a certain way.

9.8 Emerging Areas in Cognitive-Aware Systems

As cognitive-aware systems grow, some new areas are getting attention to make them smarter and more trusted. Neuro-symbolic AI mixes deep learning and logic, so machines can learn from data and also explain why they act a certain way. This builds user trust by showing why the system reacted to an emotion or action (Besold et al., 2017). Federated learning lets models train on the user's own device instead of sending raw data to servers. This keeps user data private while making the system more personal, which is useful in healthcare or smart homes (Yang et al., 2019). Cross-cultural emotion modelling is also key because people show feelings differently.

For example, a smile may mean happiness in one place and discomfort in another. So, models should learn from varied data to stay fair and respectful (Jack et al., 2012). These areas will make cognitive-aware HCI more ethical and user-friendly.

Table 10. Recent advances in cognitive-aware systems: A summary of research studies, sensors, and applications

Literature	Year	Method / Model	Sensors / Signals	Cognitive / Affective Focus	Application Domain
El Ayadi et al.	2011	Speech Features + Classification	Audio	Emotion Recognition	Speech Interfaces
Picard	1997	Affective Computing Framework	Multimodal	Emotion in Machines	Affective Computing
Desmet & Pohlmeyer	2013	Positive Design	N/A	Subjective Well-being	UX / HCI Design
D'Mello & Graesser	2012	Temporal Emotion Mapping	Facial + Input Logs	Learning-related Emotions	EdTech Platforms
Calvo & D'Mello	2010	Interdisciplinary Review	Multimodal	Affect Detection	Human-Centered Computing
Raufi & Longo	2022	EEG Alpha/Theta Ratio Analysis	EEG	Mental Workload	Cognitive Load Modelling
Yu et al.	2007	Cognitive Load Analysis	GSR	Attention Load	Multimodal Interfaces
Harper & Southern	2019	Bayesian Deep Learning	Heartbeat	Emotion Recognition	Affective Health Monitoring
Soleymani et al.	2012	Affective Multimedia Dataset	EEG, GSR, Facial Cues	Multimodal Emotion Recognition	Emotion Tagging Systems
Li et al.	2022	Tutorial + Survey	EEG	Emotion Recognition	Neurotechnology
Norman	2013	Design Thinking	N/A	Human Error, UX	Cognitive UX Design
Anderson	1997	ACT-R Cognitive Theory	N/A	Higher-Level Cognition	HCI Design
Zhang & Gan	2015	SVM Classification	EEG	Cognitive Load	Brain State Monitoring
Chaudhary et al.	2019	CNN on Raw EEG	EEG	Emotion Classification	Neural Interfaces
Rabiner	1989	Hidden Markov Models	Speech	Sequence Prediction	Speech Emotion Systems
Kosko	1992	Neural & Fuzzy Systems	N/A	Soft AI Modelling	Adaptive Systems
Shi et al.	2020	CNN–LSTM Hybrid	EEG	Attention Classification	Brain-Computer Interfaces

continued on following page

Table 10. Continued

Literature	Year	Method / Model	Sensors / Signals	Cognitive / Affective Focus	Application Domain
Peters & Castellanos	2021	EEG + Eye-Tracking Fusion	EEG, Eye Tracking	Attention Detection	Neuroadaptive Systems
Russell et al.	2003	Circumplex Emotion Model	Arousal & Valence Mapping	Emotion Dimensions	Affective Interfaces
D'Mello et al.	2020	Attention-based Multimodal Fusion	Multimodal	Emotion Generalization	Adaptive Interfaces
Fridman et al.	2019	Driver Monitoring Systems	EEG, HRV	Distraction, Fatigue	Smart Vehicles
Martinez et al.	2020	Emotion-aware HMI	Facial Cues, HRV	Driver Stress	Automotive UX
Lundberg & Lee	2017	SHAP Explainability	Model-Agnostic	Model Transparency	Ethical AI
Mitchell et al.	2019	Model Cards, Datasheets	N/A	Bias Transparency	AI Documentation

10. CONCLUSION

Cognitive-aware systems mark an important shift in how we relate to technology. Instead of simply responding to what we say or do, these systems try to understand what we feel and think. By recognising internal emotional and cognitive states, they help make our interactions with machines more natural, personalised, and human-friendly.

This chapter covered the basics of cognitive modelling and sensing, explored emotional state detection, adaptive interfaces, ethical issues, applications, evaluation, and research challenges highlighting its interdisciplinary nature.

- Cognitive-aware systems represent a shift in human-computer interaction. It's no longer just about commands and responses now machines can understand thoughts, emotions, stress, and attention.
- This chapter showed how several fields like neuroscience, AI, psychology, and ethics come together. It's not only technical it's also about understanding people better.
- These systems depend on signals from the human body like EEG for brain activity, GSR and EMG for physical reactions, heart rate, and even eye movement. But making sense of this data in real-time needs careful processing and fusion.

- Machine learning is central. Techniques like SVMs, CNNs, LSTMs, and transformers help decode users' internal states and provide adaptive feedback.
- Accuracy is important, but ethics and privacy are just as crucial. Systems should be designed from the beginning to be transparent, fair, and respectful of user autonomy especially when dealing with sensitive data.
- In the real world, these systems are already useful. They're helping in education, healthcare, games, and workplaces by keeping users engaged, supported, and better connected.
- Evaluation goes beyond just accuracy. We must also consider user trust, ease of use (SUS), cognitive load (NASA-TLX), and how well the system responds in real time.
- Challenges remain. Models need to work well across different people, adapt to changes over time (concept drift), and handle real-world unpredictability. Approaches like federated learning and lifelong updates can help.
- As we move towards Web 4.0 and ambient intelligence, cognitive-aware systems will become the base for future smart spaces homes, schools, offices, and cars that respond to both what we do and how we feel.
- The ultimate goal isn't just smarter machines it's human-centric technology that is ethical, inclusive, and genuinely helpful in everyday life.

10.1 Glossary

Table 11 shows some key terms and their definitions.

Table 11. Glossary of key terms

Term	Definition
Cognitive-Aware System	A system that perceives and adapts based on the user's mental and emotional state.
EEG	Electroencephalography: Measures electrical activity of the brain.
GSR	Galvanic Skin Response: Measures electrical conductance of the skin, related to arousal.
Cognitive Load	The amount of mental effort required to perform a task.
Engagement	A user's level of attention and emotional involvement in an activity.
Adaptive Interface	An interface that changes in real-time in response to user behavior or state.

continued on following page

Table 11. Continued

Term	Definition
Meta-Learning	Learning how to learn; algorithms that adapt quickly to new tasks.
Concept Drift	Change in the statistical properties of the target variable over time.
Lifelong Learning	Machine learning paradigm where models continuously learn from data streams.
Explainable AI (XAI)	AI methods that provide human interpretable explanations for decisions.

REFERENCES

Acar, A., Aksu, H., Uluagac, A. S., & Conti, M. (2018). A survey on homomorphic encryption schemes: Theory and implementation. *ACM Computing Surveys*, *51*(4), 79.

Ahn, M., Lee, M., Choi, J., & Jun, S. C. (2016). A review of brain-computer interface-based education. *Brain-Computer Interfaces*, *3*(3), 146–157.

Alarcao, S. M., & Fonseca, M. J. (2019). Emotions recognition using EEG signals: A survey. *IEEE Transactions on Affective Computing*, *10*(3), 374–393. DOI: 10.1109/TAFFC.2017.2714671

Anderson, J. R. (2007). *How can the human mind occur in the physical universe?* Oxford University Press. DOI: 10.1093/acprof:oso/9780195324259.001.0001

Antonenko, P., Paas, F., Grabner, R., & van Gog, T. (2010). Using electroencephalography to measure cognitive load. *Educational Psychology Review*, *22*(4), 425–438. DOI: 10.1007/s10648-010-9130-y

Aricò, P. (2016). A neurophysiological assessment of workload in air traffic control tasks. *Frontiers in Human Neuroscience*, *10*, 297.

Arroyo, I., Woolf, B. P., Cooper, D. G., Burleson, W., & Muldner, K. (2009). The impact of animated pedagogical agents on girls' and boys' emotions, attitudes, behaviors, and learning. *Proceedings of the International Conference on Intelligent Tutoring Systems*, 60–70.

Barrett, L. F., Mesquita, B., & Gendron, M. (2011). Context in emotion perception. *Current Directions in Psychological Science*, *20*(5), 286–290. DOI: 10.1177/0963721411422522

Bashashati, A., Fatourechi, M., Ward, R. K., & Birch, G. E. (2007). A survey of signal processing algorithms in brain–computer interfaces based on electrical brain signals. *Journal of Neural Engineering*, *4*(2), R32–R57. DOI: 10.1088/1741-2560/4/2/R03 PMID: 17409474

Bashivan, P., Rish, I., Yeasin, M., & Codella, N. (2016). Learning representations from EEG with deep recurrent-convolutional neural networks. *International Conference on Learning Representations (ICLR).*

Beauchamp, T. L., & Childress, J. F. (2001). *Principles of biomedical ethics* (5th ed.). Oxford University Press.

Bengio, Y., LeCun, Y., & Hinton, G. (2021). Deep learning for AI. *Communications of the ACM*, *64*(7), 58–65. DOI: 10.1145/3448250

Besold, T. R., De Raedt, L., & Bader, S., (2017). Neural-symbolic learning and reasoning: A survey and interpretation. *Frontiers in Artificial Intelligence and Applications*, *296*, 1–59.

Bixler, R., & D'Mello, S. (2016). Automatic gaze-based user-independent detection of mind wandering during computerized reading. *User Modeling and User-Adapted Interaction*, *26*(1), 33–68. DOI: 10.1007/s11257-015-9167-1

Bosch, N., D'Mello, S., Baker, R., Ocumpaugh, J., & Shute, V. (2016). Accurate affect detection in game-based learning environments using psychophysiological sensors. *User Modeling and User-Adapted Interaction*, *26*(5), 425–465.

Buolamwini, J., & Gebru, T. (2018). Gender shades: Intersectional accuracy disparities in commercial gender classification. In *Proceedings of the Conference on Fairness, Accountability and Transparency* (pp. 77–91). PMLR.

Calvo, R. A., & D'Mello, S. (2010). Affect detection: An interdisciplinary review of models, methods, and their applications. *IEEE Transactions on Affective Computing*, *1*(1), 18–37. DOI: 10.1109/T-AFFC.2010.1

Card, S. K., Moran, T. P., & Newell, A. (1983). *The psychology of human-computer interaction*. Lawrence Erlbaum Associates.

Cassani, R., Estarellas, M., San-Martin, R., Fraga, F. J., & Falk, T. H. (2018). Systematic review on EEG-based monitoring and impairment classification in Alzheimer's disease. *Computers in Biology and Medicine*, *102*, 153–171.

Casson, A. J. (2019). EEG-based biomarkers in brain–computer interfaces: Bayesian estimation and machine learning approaches. *Journal of Neural Engineering*, *16*(3), 031001. PMID: 30808014

Chandrasekaran, S. (2020). Biofeedback-driven adaptive therapy to reduce anxiety. *Journal of Medical Internet Research*, *22*(11), e18524.

Cheng, Y., Wang, D., Zhou, P., & Zhang, T. (2020). Model compression and acceleration for deep neural networks: The principles, progress, and challenges. *IEEE Signal Processing Magazine*, *35*(1), 126–136. DOI: 10.1109/MSP.2017.2765695

Crawford, K., & Paglen, T. (2021). Excavating AI: The politics of training sets for machine learning. *AI & Society*, *36*(4), 1009–1019. DOI: 10.1007/s00146-021-01301-1

Cummings, M. L. (2020). Rethinking the maturity of artificial intelligence in safety-critical settings. *AI Magazine*, *41*(2), 8–16.

D'Mello, S. K., & Graesser, A. C. (2012). AutoTutor and affective AutoTutor: Learning by talking with cognitively and emotionally intelligent computers. [TiiS]. *ACM Transactions on Interactive Intelligent Systems*, *2*(4), 1–39. DOI: 10.1145/2395123.2395128

D'Mello, S. K., & Kory, J. (2015). A review and meta-analysis of multimodal affect detection systems. *ACM Computing Surveys*, *47*(3), 43. DOI: 10.1145/2682899

Deng, Z., Liu, W., Wang, W., & Zhao, G. (2020). Emotion-aware driving interface design using facial and speech signals. *IEEE Access : Practical Innovations, Open Solutions*, *8*, 106681–106693.

Dwork, C., & Roth, A. (2014). The algorithmic foundations of differential privacy. *Foundations and Trends® in Theoretical Computer Science, 9*(3–4), 211–407.

Eivazi, S., Bednarik, R., Hradis, M., & Zeman, V. (2017). Predicting problem-solving behavior and performance levels from visual attention data. *User Modeling and User-Adapted Interaction*, *27*(1), 89–118.

Fairclough, S. H. (2009). Fundamentals of physiological computing. *Interacting with Computers*, *21*(1–2), 133–145. DOI: 10.1016/j.intcom.2008.10.011

Fitts, P. M. (1954). The information capacity of the human motor system in controlling the amplitude of movement. *Journal of Experimental Psychology*, *47*(6), 381–391. DOI: 10.1037/h0055392 PMID: 13174710

Friedman, B., Kahn Jr, P. H., & Borning, A. (2006). Value sensitive design and information systems. *Human-Computer Interaction and Management Information Systems: Foundations*, 348–372.

Fulmer, R., Joerin, A., Gentile, B., Lakerink, L., & Rauws, M. (2018). Using psychological artificial intelligence (Tess) to relieve symptoms of depression and anxiety: Randomized controlled trial. *JMIR Mental Health*, *5*(4), e64. DOI: 10.2196/mental.9782 PMID: 30545815

Garcez, A. d., Lamb, L. C., & Gabbay, D. M. (2019). Neurosymbolic AI: The third wave. *IEEE Intelligent Systems*, *34*(6), 72–76.

Gunning, D., & Aha, D. W. (2019). DARPA's Explainable Artificial Intelligence (XAI) program. *AI Magazine*, *40*(2), 44–58. DOI: 10.1609/aimag.v40i2.2850

Healey, J., & Picard, R. W. (2005). Detecting stress during real-world driving tasks using physiological sensors. *IEEE Transactions on Intelligent Transportation Systems*, *6*(2), 156–166. DOI: 10.1109/TITS.2005.848368

Hick, W. E. (1952). On the rate of gain of information. *The Quarterly Journal of Experimental Psychology*, *4*(1), 11–26. DOI: 10.1080/17470215208416600

Huang, Y., Fu, Z., He, L., & Tan, C. (2021). Attention-based multimodal emotion recognition using physiological signals. *Information Fusion*, *65*, 113–124.

Jack, R. E., Garrod, O. G., & Schyns, P. G. (2012). Dynamic facial expressions of emotion transmit personality. *Social Psychological & Personality Science*, *3*(6), 743–752.

Jiang, M., Xu, H., Ma, Y., & Wang, X. (2021). Few-shot learning for human emotion recognition via meta-learning. *Neurocomputing*, *426*, 43–54.

Jimison, H. B., Pavel, M., & Pavel, J. (2008). Adaptive interfaces for home health. *IEEE Computer*, *41*(5), 44–51.

Jung, T. P., Lee, P. L., & Chung, W. Y. (2018). Brain-computer interface for driver state monitoring: A review. *IEEE Transactions on Human-Machine Systems*, *48*(5), 485–495.

Kairouz, P., McMahan, H. B., Avent, B., et al. (2021). Advances and open problems in federated learning. *Foundations and Trends® in Machine Learning, 14*(1–2), 1–210.

Katsigiannis, S., & Ramzan, N. (2018). DREAMER: A database for emotion recognition through EEG and ECG signals from wireless low-cost off-the-shelf devices. *IEEE Journal of Biomedical and Health Informatics*, *22*(1), 98–107. DOI: 10.1109/JBHI.2017.2688239 PMID: 28368836

Khosrowabadi, R., Quek, C., Ang, K. K., & Wahab, A. (2011). ERNN: A biologically inspired emotional neural network for online emotion classification. *IEEE Transactions on Neural Networks*, *22*(12), 2118–2130.

Kim, H. (2021). Real-time EEG-based fatigue detection and adaptive rehabilitation system. *Sensors (Basel)*, *21*(8), 2801. PMID: 33921160

Kim, H. G., Cheon, E. J., Bai, D. S., Lee, Y. H., & Koo, B. H. (2018). Stress and heart rate variability: A meta-analysis and review of the literature. *Psychiatry Investigation*, *15*(3), 235–245. DOI: 10.30773/pi.2017.08.17 PMID: 29486547

Kirkpatrick, J., Pascanu, R., Rabinowitz, N. C., Veness, J., Desjardins, G., Rusu, A. A., Milan, K., Quan, J., Ramalho, T., Grabska-Barwinska, A., Hassabis, D., Clopath, C., Kumaran, D., & Hadsell, R. (2017). Overcoming catastrophic forgetting in neural networks. *Proceedings of the National Academy of Sciences of the United States of America*, *114*(13), 3521–3526. DOI: 10.1073/pnas.1611835114 PMID: 28292907

Koelstra, S., Muhl, C., Soleymani, M., Lee, J. S., Yazdani, A., Ebrahimi, T., & Patras, I. (2012). DEAP: A database for emotion analysis using physiological signals. *IEEE Transactions on Affective Computing*, *3*(1), 18–31. DOI: 10.1109/T-AFFC.2011.15

Lalanne, D. (2015). Emotion-aware intelligent agents in workplaces. *Interacting with Computers*, *27*(5), 529–547.

Lepri, B., Oliver, N., Letouzé, E., Pentland, A. S., & Vinck, P. (2018). Fair, transparent, and accountable algorithmic decision-making processes. *Philosophy & Technology*, *31*(4), 611–627. DOI: 10.1007/s13347-017-0279-x

Liao, L. D. (2016). EEG-based closed-loop rehabilitation system for stroke patients. *IEEE Transactions on Biomedical Engineering*, *63*(12), 2543–2554.

Lin, Y. P., Wang, C. H., Wu, T. L., Jeng, S. K., Chen, J. H., & Lin, C. T. (2014). EEG-based emotion recognition in music listening: A comparison of schemes for feature extraction and classification. *Proceedings of the International Conference of the IEEE Engineering in Medicine and Biology Society*, 2040–2043.

Liu, Y., Sourina, O., & Nguyen, M. K. (2019). Real-time EEG-based student engagement monitoring. *Computers & Education*, *134*, 66–78.

Looney, D., Kidmose, P., & Mandic, D. P. (2016). Advances in wearable EEG: Flexible electronics, wireless circuits, and data fusion. *IEEE Signal Processing Magazine*, *33*(1), 52–60.

Lundberg, S. M., & Lee, S. I. (2017). A unified approach to interpreting model predictions. *Advances in Neural Information Processing Systems*, *30*, 4765–4774.

McDuff, D., El Kaliouby, R., Cohn, J. F., & Picard, R. W. (2017). Predicting ad liking and purchase intent: Large-scale analysis of facial responses to ads. *IEEE Transactions on Affective Computing*, *6*(3), 223–235. DOI: 10.1109/TAFFC.2014.2384198

McMahan, H. B., Moore, E., Ramage, D., Hampson, S., & Arcas, B. A. (2017). Communication-efficient learning of deep networks from decentralized data. In *Proceedings of the 20th International Conference on Artificial Intelligence and Statistics* (pp. 1273–1282). PMLR.

Miranda-Correa, J. A., Abadi, M. K., Sebe, N., & Patras, I. (2018). AMIGOS: A dataset for affect, personality and mood research on individuals and groups. *IEEE Transactions on Affective Computing*, *12*(2), 479–493. DOI: 10.1109/TAFFC.2018.2884461

Mitchell, M., Wu, S., Zaldivar, A., Barnes, P., Vasserman, L., Hutchinson, B., & Gebru, T. (2019). Model cards for model reporting. *Proceedings of the Conference on Fairness, Accountability, and Transparency*, 220–229. DOI: 10.1145/3287560.3287596

Mittelstadt, B. D., Allo, P., Taddeo, M., Wachter, S., & Floridi, L. (2016). The ethics of algorithms: Mapping the debate. *Big Data & Society*, *3*(2), 1–21. DOI: 10.1177/2053951716679679

Mühl, C., Allison, B. Z., Nijholt, A., & Chanel, G. (2014). A survey of affective brain computer interfaces: Principles, state-of-the-art, and challenges. *Brain Computer Interfaces (Abingdon, England)*, *1*(2), 66–84. DOI: 10.1080/2326263X.2014.912881

Muller, M. J. (2003). Participatory design: The third space in HCI. In *Human-computer interaction: Development process* (pp. 165–185). CRC Press.

Müller-Putz, G. R., (2019). Adaptive BCI systems for cognitive neurorehabilitation. *IEEE Reviews in Biomedical Engineering*, *12*, 234–248.

Nissenbaum, H. (2011). A contextual approach to privacy online. *Daedalus*, *140*(4), 32–48. DOI: 10.1162/DAED_a_00113

Norman, D. A. (2013). *The design of everyday things* (Revised and expanded ed.). Basic Books.

Parisi, G. I., Kemker, R., Part, J. L., Kanan, C., & Wermter, S. (2019). Continual lifelong learning with neural networks: A review. *Neural Networks*, *113*, 54–71. DOI: 10.1016/j.neunet.2019.01.012 PMID: 30780045

Pepino, L., Ribeiro, D., & Gerosa, M. A. (2021). Emotion recognition from speech using wav2vec 2.0 embeddings. *Proceedings of Interspeech*, *2021*, 3405–3409. DOI: 10.21437/Interspeech.2021-703

Phillips, P. J., Jiang, F., Narvekar, A., Ayyad, J., & O'Toole, A. J. (2011). An other-race effect for face recognition algorithms. [TAP]. *ACM Transactions on Applied Perception*, *8*(2), 14. DOI: 10.1145/1870076.1870082

Russell, J. A. (1980). A circumplex model of affect. *Journal of Personality and Social Psychology*, *39*(6), 1161–1178. DOI: 10.1037/h0077714

Sani, S. M., Wu, T., & Zhang, Y. (2021). Real-time cognitive load assessment using edge AI: Balancing speed and accuracy. *IEEE Internet of Things Journal*, *8*(10), 8219–8229.

Schuller, B., Steidl, S., Batliner, A., Burkhardt, F., Devillers, L., Müller, C., & Narayanan, S. (2011). The INTERSPEECH 2011 speaker state challenge. *Interspeech*, 3201–3204.

Sharma, N., Gedeon, T., & Jones, R. (2020). Monitoring cognitive load in e-learning via HRV. *Sensors (Basel)*, *20*(6), 1702. PMID: 32197502

Shen, Y., Wang, Z., & Zeng, D. (2021). Cross-subject emotion recognition using EEG signals with meta-learning and domain adaptation. *IEEE Transactions on Affective Computing*, *14*(1), 230–242.

Simonsen, J., Robertson, T., & Bødker, K. (2020). Participatory design for privacy and consent. *ACM Transactions on Computer-Human Interaction*, *27*(1), 1–30.

Sourina, O., Liu, Y., Nguyen, M. K., & Wang, Q. (2012). EEG-based "serious" games design for medical applications. *IEEE Transactions on Computational Intelligence and AI in Games*, *4*(3), 201–213.

Tripathi, S., Acharya, S., & Sharma, R. D. (2017). Using deep and convolutional neural networks for accurate emotion classification on DEAP dataset. *Proceedings of the AAAI Conference on Artificial Intelligence*, 4746–4752.

Tsinalis, O., Matthews, P. M., & Guo, Y. (2016). Automatic sleep stage scoring using time-frequency analysis and stacked sparse autoencoders. *Annals of Biomedical Engineering*, *44*(5), 1587–1597. DOI: 10.1007/s10439-015-1444-y PMID: 26464268

Verbert, K., Duval, E., Klerkx, J., Govaerts, S., & Santos, J. L. (2012). Learning analytics dashboard applications. *Proceedings of the 2nd International Conference on Learning Analytics and Knowledge*, 124–133.

Voigt, P., & Von dem Bussche, A. (2017). *The EU general data protection regulation (GDPR)*. Springer. DOI: 10.1007/978-3-319-57959-7

Wagh, A., Tripathi, S., & Roy, D. (2022). A review on fatigue detection systems using physiological signals: Challenges and opportunities. *Biomedical Signal Processing and Control*, *72*, 103322.

Wolpaw, J. R., & Wolpaw, E. W. (Eds.). (2012). *Brain-computer interfaces: Principles and practice*. OUP USA. DOI: 10.1093/acprof:oso/9780195388855.001.0001

Yang, Q., Liu, Y., Chen, T., & Tong, Y. (2019). Federated machine learning: Concept and applications. [TIST]. *ACM Transactions on Intelligent Systems and Technology*, *10*(2), 12. DOI: 10.1145/3298981

Zhai, J., & Barreto, A. (2006). Stress detection in computer users through non-invasive monitoring of physiological signals. *ACM Transactions on Computer-Human Interaction (TOCHI*, *14*(4), 1–29.

Zhang, Y., Wu, Q., & Fu, Y. (2019). EEG-based intention recognition from spatio-temporal representations via cascade convolutional recurrent network. *AAAI Conference on Artificial Intelligence*, *33*(1), 1647–1654.

Zhang, Y., Yu, Z., & Fung, P. (2018). A multitask deep learning approach for emotion classification from tweets. *Knowledge-Based Systems*, *158*, 54–62.

Zhao, J., Wang, T., Yatskar, M., Ordonez, V., & Chang, K. W. (2019). Gender bias in coreference resolution. *arXiv preprint arXiv:1804.06876.*

Zhou, W., & Wang, Y. (2021). Adaptive infotainment systems in vehicles: A cognitive-aware interface approach. *Journal of Ambient Intelligence and Humanized Computing*, *12*(10), 9785–9796.

Chapter 2

Emotion and Engagement Detection Using Behavioral Inputs:
Gesture and Touch Interaction Data

R. Velmurugan
https://orcid.org/0000-0002-7925-9757
Karpagam Academy of Higher Education, Coimbatore, India

J. Sudarvel
https://orcid.org/0000-0001-6656-1992
Karpagam Academy of Higher Education, Coimbatore, India

R. Bhuvaneswari
https://orcid.org/0009-0003-9396-6129
Dr. Mahalingam College of Engineering and Technology, Pollachi, India

Ravi Thirumalaisamy
https://orcid.org/0000-0002-5954-5940
Modern College of Business and Science, Oman

ABSTRACT

Natural behaviors for expressing emotion are utilized in gesture and touch for emotion detection, in real time, and reshaping human computer interaction. System can dynamically adapt because deep learning and multimodal fusion are advanced, and experiences in education, gaming, healthcare and customer service benefit. One of the challenges however remains with their variability in the culture and privacy

DOI: 10.4018/979-8-3373-6385-1.ch002

Copyright © 2026, IGI Global Scientific Publishing. Copying or distributing in print or electronic forms without written permission of IGI Global Scientific Publishing is prohibited.

concern. These technologies of ethical AI, federated learning and edge computing are bringing more emotional intelligence, intuition and intention into digital systems in an increasingly variety of applications.

INTRODUCTION

The integration of emotion and engagement detection into Human-Computer Interaction (HCI) is revolutionizing technology by moving beyond simple cognitive interactions and introducing emotional sensitivity and adaptive engagement. With the rapid development of immersive technologies like Virtual Reality (VR) and Augmented Reality (AR), paired with advancements in machine learning algorithms, real-time emotion and engagement detection has become more accurate. VR completely immerses users in a digital world, while AR overlays digital elements onto the real world, allowing for personalized and dynamic interactions based on emotional states such as excitement, confusion, or frustration (D'Mello & Kory, 2015; Zhang et al., 2020). Emotion detection, especially in e-learning platforms like ENGAGE and ClassVR, enables real-time adjustments to learning content based on student engagement and emotional responses (Radianti et al., 2020; Lee et al., 2021).

Machine learning has significantly advanced emotion detection by processing complex physiological, behavioral, and contextual data in real-time. Systems now incorporate facial expression recognition (Ekman & Friesen, 1978), voice modulation analysis, heart rate variability, and galvanic skin response to gauge emotions. Companies like Affectiva have developed emotion AI software capable of detecting subtle facial expression changes to determine emotional states, widely used in the automotive and advertising sectors (McDuff et al., 2016; Ng et al., 2022).

Gesture and touch interactions, prevalent in devices such as smartphones, wearables, and interactive displays, provide non-intrusive ways to assess emotional states. For instance, research by Kim et al. (2018) demonstrated that analyzing touch inputs like pressure and swipe speed could accurately predict users' emotional states. Depth-sensing cameras and motion sensors (Microsoft Kinect, Apple's Face ID) enable systems to detect emotions without explicit input, making interactions feel more natural (Lee & Wang, 2021). These technologies are applied in healthcare, with systems like 'Ellie,' a virtual therapist that uses facial and vocal analysis to monitor patient emotions and adapt counseling strategies (DeVault et al., 2014; Williams & Liu, 2022). Retailers, such as Walmart, use emotion detection cameras to monitor customer reactions and adjust marketing strategies accordingly (Brown et al., 2023).

Emotion detection also plays a significant role in gaming, offering personalized experiences by adjusting game difficulty based on the player's emotional state. For example, the game "Nevermind" adapts to a player's emotional response and heart rate to enhance immersion and personalization (Parker et al., 2020).

However, as emotion detection technology advances, ethical concerns about privacy and data security arise. Continuous monitoring of emotional states and the use of sensitive biometric data raise questions about the potential misuse of such information (Crawford & Calo, 2016; Smith & Thompson, 2021). It is crucial for developers to implement transparent data policies, consent mechanisms, and robust security measures. Additionally, cultural differences in emotional expression must be considered, as studies by Jack et al. (2012) showed that emotional responses vary across cultures, potentially leading to misinterpretations of user emotions and biased responses (Tan et al., 2022).

Looking ahead, HCI will increasingly rely on sophisticated models of affective computing, where systems not only detect but also predict and respond to emotions. Brain-Computer Interfaces (BCIs) and wearable technologies that interpret neuromuscular signals to gauge intent and emotion are emerging, offering further insight into user engagement (Jones et al., 2024). The integration of emotion and engagement detection into technology has transformed HCI, creating ambient, adaptive, and empathetic systems in healthcare, education, entertainment, and customer service. However, this transformation must always be guided by ethical foresight, cultural sensitivity, and robust data protection to ensure the wellbeing of users (Harrison & Liu, 2023).

GESTURE AND TOUCH-BASED INTERACTION: FOUNDATIONS FOR EMOTION AND ENGAGEMENT DETECTION

The current devices are touch-based and gesture-based, which are regarded as the most significant tools in identifying emotion and interest in Human-Computer Interaction (HCI). Naturally, such interactions involve anything as basic as touching a touchscreen to the most elaborate motions using gesture recognition cameras which replicate the way people interact with each other in real life and create a lot of contextual and behavioral information. The intensity of the touch pressure, speed of the swipes, dynamics of tap, duration of the touch, co-ordination of multi-touch features and all these gestures help in understanding the emotional and the cognitive states. As another example, 3D Touch on Apple iPhone is a feature that senses the intensity of the pressure input on the screen and enables the phone to give haptic feedback, which may contribute to increased interaction between the user and the device as well as emotion response. On the same note, communicating through hand orientation, posture changes, and movement of the head enhance or complete the emotional picture of a user and by extension, mean excitement, frustration, anxiety, or boredom (Bianchi et al., 2020; Lee et al., 2021). Another famous technology that also utilizes gesture recognition is the Microsoft Kinect that dares to interpret body language and can build up the mood on whether a player is getting excited or frustrated based on a body language interpretation.

Such interactions rely on technology incorporated into touchscreen gadgets that possess series of sensors, and movement-tracking computerized cameras, such as Kinect and Leap Motion, and wearable gadgets that have accelerometers and gyroscopes. In our case, these sensors are continuously gathering a small-grained stream of interaction data that it feeds into machine learning systems to derive an inference of the emotional and engagement levels of a user. As an example, the touch interface is used in smartphones such as the iPhone 11 or later version to recognize finer information about finger pressure, force, and trajectory tap (Zhou et al., 2017; Kim & Park, 2020). This will enable emotion-sensitive apps to distinguish between haste, angry in posts and light touches like the Facebook app is being able to check typing speed to determine mood of the user. Physiological signals (heart rate/skin conductance) combined with touch interactions in order to detect emotion accuracy are performed on wearable gadgets (smartwatches, e.g. Fitbit or Apple Watch) that tracks the individual when he/she is under the stress and can use it to determine the mood and the tone of a relationship of an individual by changing heart rate.

In the learning technology industries, this technology can be used practically. Use of gesture and touch data in an eLearning environment has been growing with an aim of an on-the-fly adaptation of instructional content. As an example, ENGAGE and ClassVR are platforms that provide VR and gesture tracking to customize the learning aspect to each student in terms of their engagement and emotional status. Slow or choppy, inconsistent, or fast performance on an touchscreen device, which is witnessed all through digital lessons, are possible indicators of disengagement (Muller, et al., 2021). The AI systems of tutoring such as AutoTutor can react to students interaction patterns itself, providing helpful comments or interesting information based on detection of bored boredom or confusion. Such systems are proven to have a seriously high retention rate, as well as student satisfaction levels (Sharma & Kaur, 2022).

Emotional detection using gestures has also taken place in the field of game development. Such as example is the Oculus Quest VR system that has a hand-tracking technology that is able to recognize any movement such as pointing or waving and grasping of the hands. This capability enables the developers to make changes according to the perceived user engagement; this means that they can change the difficulty level or the flow of the narrative. Gesture responsiveness is used in games like Half-Life: Alyx to induce the feeling of immersion by slow or hesitating motions of a hand being controlled by a player can alter the behavior of virtual characters, so the gameplay becomes more personal and dynamic (Valve

Corporation, 2020; Tan et al., 2023). Likewise, the VR controllers developed by PlayStation follow the movements of the hands of the player where the observed gestures are used to alter on-screen activities, improving the interaction of players.

Emotional tracking of gestures has its way into delivering health care as well. Stroke recovery applications based on Leap Motion technology, as an example, monitor the physical improvement and keep a patient motivated by following the body movements. Programs like TheraVeda make it possible to include the therapist into a real-time situation in case erratic movements suggest frustration or exhaustion, a moment of early intervention and rehabilitation (Pallavicini et al., 2019; Rogers & Brown, 2021). The recognition of gestures exemplifies another one: the idea of the therapeutic robot PARO (designed to work with older adults) that relies on the gesture recognition system: the robot interprets the emotional situation of the patient with regard to the patterns of touch and interaction.

Those gains notwithstanding, much is still to be done. The variability between gestures across the individuals, cultural variation of body language and errors in sensor use may influence reliability of emotion inferences. Due to the limitations of current solutions based on detection of gesture data, facial expressions, voice recognition and physiologic signals, D d M L o and Kory (2015) argue in favor of a multi-modal data fusion approach, when these channels are integrated to generate more sensitive and culture aware emotion-detection tools. An example of this can be the variations of the styles of emotional display across cultures, where the participants of high-context cultures, like Japan or Korea, are emotional in a more subtle way than those that belong to low-context cultures, e.g., the USA; the latter can be found in the study by Jack et al. (2012). This cultural difference is a major problem to the emotion recognition systems, which are not modeled to be sensitive to cultural variations. These challenges also apply to the wearable gadgets that keep track of emotional and physiological records such as Apple Watch examples since they have to respond to such experiences more faithfully across study participants and contexts. Overall, interactions made by means of gestures and touch transform simple means of input into expressive channels of emotional interaction that help develop human-centered, empathetic, and adaptive technologies (Singh et al., 2024).

MACHINE LEARNING AND DEEP LEARNING IN EMOTION DETECTION

The identification of emotions through gesture and touch behavior has been of great advantage with the development of advance studies in machine learning (ML) and more particularly in deep learning evolution. Although traditional machine learning models proved to be of use, they did not cope with the complex, temporally diverse and non-linear behavior of human gestures and touch interactions. However, deep learning algorithms work very well on such complex patterns that can be learned with large amounts of training data and when faced with small expressions of emotion such as happiness, frustration, curiosity, and boredom, deep learning algorithms would be highly appropriate. As an illustration, the Face ID tool developed by Apple applies the deep-learning-based facial expressions detection and mapping and allows speculating on the emotional state and personalizing the user experience (Goodfellow, Bengio, & Courville, 2016; Liu et al., 2020).

In contemporary systems, real-time inferences of the levels of user engagement may be drawn, based on the temporal patterns of gesture and touch behaviour, and useful content may be adjusted or feedback delivered in response. As an example, a touch-based gesture would imply saying no interest or the level of involvement would be addressed by tuning the interactivity of the module in real-time, or changing the complexity of it in real-space. Likewise, Amazon, as an e-commerce portal, implements the gesture and touch data to change the product recommendation to match the current level of emotion arousing a favorable online shopping experience. Say, when the user appears frustrated, the platform might change the interface or offer a simpler product version to avoid unpleasant experiences of users (Rana et al., 2020; Zhang & Wang, 2021).

Specifically, Convolutional Neural Networks (CNN), and Long Short-Term Memory networks (LSTM) have been useful neural networks in this field. Examples are CNNs, which perform well in detection of local features in touch surfaces, e.g. swipe trajectories or pressure maps. This is evidenced on the manner in which touchscreen phones such as iPhone or Samsung galaxy analyze the details of how a user is touching the screen using CNNs. Contrary, LSTMs are top-notch at sequence modeling and are able to monitor the dynamics of gestures over time, e.g., how emotional highs and lows change over the course. As an example, Zhao et al. (2020) model stress levels using LSTM-based model to learn the pattern in which people interact with their phone, which is reflected in the stress level, and could be utilized in health applications such as Calm or Headspace to avoid excess stress.

It is possible to find the further examples of such advancements in the real world. Wearable systems based on physiological measures and gesture data have been developed to detect emotional distress by Empatica- a firm dealing with affective computing, which is particularly applicable in epilepsy management and anxiety management. As an example, their wearable smartwatch called the Empatica Embrace measures physiological parameters of a person such as the heart rate and skin conductance to alert caretakers of an approaching emotional or physical emergency in real time (Garbarino et al., 2014; Tan et al., 2021). Representative Sony also has bio-mapped game controllers to read emotional signals through finger patterns to change the game narrative dynamically to reflect emotional engagement of the player as it is done in other mentions of the game Gran Turismo stiffness or heart palpitation can vary its game experience.

Also, multimodal handset combinations have immensely widened the circle of emotion identification. Multimodal systems are an intertwining of facial expression, speech pattern, heart rate, galvanic skin response (GSR) and other combinations in an attempt to have a strand of understanding of the emotional characteristics of a user. As an example, the Affectiva Automotive AI platform, which is based on the interpretation of the facial expression, eye movements, and gestures, is applied to the cars such as Volvo that is used to monitor the signs of drowsiness or lack of emotion and execute safety measures (Picard et al., 2019). Emotion detection based on such systems is more reliable and even more granular since it combines both physiological signals with gesture patterns. The emotional evaluation of a hurried, stressed swipe may be proved correct through addition of an increased level of heart rate to a swift swiping motion in the case of an ambulatory system, like the Empatica Embrace, elevating emotion identification.

A number of experimental studies have been used to support these findings. The study by Soleymani et al. (2017) collected the gestures, facial expressions, and physiological signals of participants simultaneously when they watched emotional video clips. The combination of these modalities yielded a considerably high accuracy rate than when applying gesture data-only, proving the significance of multimodal emotion detection systems. The example is that gesture- and physiology-combined MoodRhythm app is more precise in tracking the mood as it notices not only movements of the body but also heartbeat, to trace how stressed the person is in the real-time.

Therefore, the need has arisen to apply machine learning (and more particularly deep learning) in order to interpret emotions based on gesture and touch interplay. By obtaining temporal modelling by use of LSTMs, extracting the features using CNNs and the equipability to fuse multimodal data in real-time, it is becoming possible to understand human emotions using the technologies. The latest developments are getting closer to creating more empathetic, flexible, and human adaptive digital spaces in such industries as education, health care, gaming, and others (Chen et al., 2022; Kumar & Patel, 2023). As an example, let us discuss AI-enabled health platforms such as BioBeats, which utilise multimodal data fusion to offer real-time stress detection and an intervention that results in a more personalised approach to treating the patients.

REAL-TIME ADAPTATION AND CONTEXTUAL RESPONSE

Another thing is that the need to react in real-time dynamic fashion is one of the most radical elements of gesture and touch-based emotion detection. The difference between emotion-aware systems and general ubiquitous systems is the present interaction is not preset and is operating on predetermined situations but is constantly tracking the user through its numerous gestures and altering the flow of interaction on the fly. As an example, Apple Watch incorporates both heart rate variability and touch gestures to regulate notifications according to the stress levels of the user, i.e., to cut down on the notifications in stressful situations. The design of such experiences of personalization, such as context-phase relevant content and emotionally sensitive interactions is dramatically more likely to improve user satisfaction, which in turn will directly lead to the improvement of learning outcomes and emotional status (Cowie et al., 2011; Roberts et al., 2020).

Gesture based input like hand movement, touch force, and dynamics of motion are finding their potential application and use in the area of gaming where such inputs are being engaged to vary the parameters of the game on the basis of the emotional level of the player. The study by Hussain et al. (2021) was able to reveal that sensors that identified a change of touch gesture or a speed in a hand could show that the player is bored, frustrated, or engaged with the game system. An actual example of this is the use of Nintendo Ring Fit Adventure, in which physical actions recorded using a motion-sensing ring and leg strap moderate the workout level according to what corresponding gestures or emotional reaction the user has. Likewise, Beat Saber VR has a game-velocity and complexity setting that adapt according to the level of involvement, finishing off at the ideal level of the "flow" to follow through with the next move (Csikszentmihalyi, 1990; Johnson & Liu, 2022).

Ingestion of gesture recognition systems is also very significant in the field of therapeutic endeavors as it helps in managing mental health. Hand tremors, tapping and hard pressing are also indicators of anxious or stressed people or those who are agitated. An example of this is the MoodRhythm, a system by the researchers at Dartmouth College, which uses gesture sensing through the smartphones and wearables to capture the behavior of people with mood disorders. Predominant stress or depressive symptoms are identified early on, and the system provides pre-written activities, including mindful breathing, connecting with a support network. The Woebot Health digital therapeutic chatbot also employs a comparable system and in addition to emotional recognition in voice and gesture analysis offers therapeutic interventions (Matthews et al., 2015; Kumar et al., 2022).

There are also being used emotion adaptive systems in education setting so as to improve student engagement in the learning process. Muller et al. (2021) demonstrated that touch and gesture actions on tablet-based learning sites can be used to predict frustration or confusions of the students. Gestures that can be tracked on such systems as ClassVR or ENGAGE include chaotic patterns of touch interactions or inactive reaction times and can be used to adjust the lesson speed or add gamified features to renew learner interest. This dynamic answer makes students more active, and their learning environment is more compassionate and receptive. An interactive learning platform of the name Kahoot can also rely on real-time data to modify the difficulty of the quiz relying on interaction speed and emotional indicators students demonstrate (Brown & Martin, 2020).

Gesture-based customer service apps are also taking an advantage of real-time emotion recognition. As an example, self-service kiosks introduced to the retail setting, including that of McDonalds, self-service kiosk, and Samsups interactive displays, record behaviors of customers such as tapping impatiently or inadequate touch interaction. In the case of dissatisfaction sensed, human agent intervention may be invoked in the system, or when that is not possible, discounts or customized product suggestion can be provided to enhance customer experience. In a similar turn, with the help of gesture and facial recognition, Amazon Go stores can track real-time customer satisfaction and switch the store experience depending on recognized emotions of the customers (McDuff et al., 2019; Zhang et al., 2023).

Gesture-based monitoring of the aged is under investigation in the healthcare. To give an example, Parkinson disease or even early onset dementia can be tracked through wearable technology, such as Empatica Embrace, that serves to measure the hand stability and the intensity of interaction. The downward trends of the neurological conditions can be measured early and real-time medical assessments prompted in time. In its turn, the gesture-sensitive tools developed by RehabRobotics assist in the rehabilitation process of stroke victims by communicating the level of their hand strength and control and adjusting exercise programs to performances based on emotional and physical responses (Pereira et al., 2019; Lee & Wong, 2022). They will be felt in gaming, education, therapy, customer service, and healthcare and help to elevate the personalization, emotional intelligence, and the efficacy of experiences that users have (Johnson & Lee, 2024).

APPLICATIONS ACROSS DOMAINS: ENHANCING USER EXPERIENCE

Applications of detecting emotions and engagement based on touching and gesturing on touchscreen are realistic and ever-growing daily in many areas to transform the interaction of users with technology. Since the quality of gesture and touch-based interfaces develops into advanced systems capable of inferences that apply real-time emotional and cognitive states, content, pacing, and responses of these systems can be enhanced and make the experiences more engaging, satisfying, yet more effective when in education, gaming, healthcare cases, etc. (Patel et al., 2021). As an example, in healthcare physics, wearables, such as Empatica Embrace smartwatch can monitor the emotional state of users in real time, detecting stress, anxiety, etc., which increases self-control and more effective management of health.

One of the greatest innovations has been the early indication of disengagement using gesture and touch in e-learning platforms. Lazy cut routines, out-of-control swipes, instant freeze or extended idleness are most often the result of boredom, confusion, or inability to stay focused. Such patterns will be recognized by the system in case it is an emotion-aware system, and it will respond to them either by introducing more gamified and interactive content to the system or by giving specific feedback prompts. AutoTutor and Affective AutoTutor- two emotion-sensitive web-based learning technologies studied by D.(rquot Goodwin, Dieterle and Duckworth, 2017) can dynamically adjust the learning program to the emotion state of students. By way of example, the Duolingo application which "smartens up and down" according to how the user interacts with it, keeps learners stuck into it because it can pick up signs of frustration when the user performs jerky touch actions or responds to it too slowly. The dynamic emotional adaptation is a huge difference in pressing the level of engagement, lengthy learning, and better academic performance compared to fixed e-learning settings (McLaughlin et al., 2021).

Gesture or touch controlled systems that can detect emotions is on the rise in the gaming industry as a supplement to adaptive gameplay systems. This interaction can be seen in such activity as heavy buttons that are pushed violently several times and they move fast and the hand movement is quick and violent implying that the person is very excited, impatient or angry. Hussain et al. (2021) found that the adaptive games, such as FIFA or Fortnite, that can recognize and react to the gestures of the players delivered higher results in keeping the users engaged and satisfied. An example whereby a system identifies frustrations on a player through tense, fast movements and helps by increasing the difficulty of a game or setting a helping cursor that would help the player not want to quit because of frustrating. Conversely, fast movements of excitement might trigger the game to increase the level of its difficulty to keep the players in what is known as a state of a flow (Csikszentmihalyi, 1990; O Connell & Zhang, 2022). As an example, Beat Saber makes use of hand tracking in VR to provide challenge-level difficulty and complexity in a dynamic way, thus creating a custom experience according to the engaged user on the emotional level (Tan et al., 2023).

Although gesture and touch-based capability in detecting emotion is not a new aspect in the world of education and gaming, it has gone a long way in services to customers, therapy and employee training activities. Interactive vending in retail setting, such as McDonalds or Sears, are also used and employ touch analysis to determine when a customer is becoming frustrated and automatically initiates human contact. As an example, self-checkout kiosks are able to detect the feeling of being rushed and direct the customer to human assistants when the customer is frustrated (McDuff et al., 2019; Chen et al., 2024). On the same note, there are apps that apply the means of body sensitivity and touch as through the app of Woebot Health to notice the emotional distress early and provide beneficial activities such as breathing exercises and meditation prompts. The technologies are incorporated into the existing systems to improve the real-time experience of the user and help them get personalized, emotionally intelligent interaction. These emotional insights are becoming more important in the development of a more intuitive, supportive, and emotionally intelligent system, including chatbots powered by Artificial Intelligence, which change their actions according to the emotional state of the consumer in order to be able to assist them in a better and more accurate manner (Lin et al., 2022).

CHALLENGES AND ETHICAL CONSIDERATIONS

Challenges in Gesture and Touch-Based Emotion Detection

Gesture and touch Data for emotion detection does allow for tremendous amount of innovation across sectors like, education, healthcare, gaming, and customer service but at the same time there were many things to consider. However, if these issues are not addressed well for these technologies, they can undermine what would be their maximum potential.

Cross-User Generalizability and Individual Differences

Another of the main technical challenges is to make the case that information results are generalizable cross user. How a person interacts with a device depends on the type of a person that person is, such as his personality, age, gender, cultural background, or emotional regulation style, and even temporary mood. The same sad feeling causes the swipe for one user to be light and slow, while its heavy and fast for another user under the same condition. As you will see, these differences make it extremely difficult to build the one-size fits all emotion detection models (Salvucci et al., 2021).

Real-life studies reinforce this complexity. Bianchi et al. (2020) also conducted a large scale usability study where researchers found that there was different reading of the same touch pressure of emotional intent in different demographic groups. Participants from high context cultures (Japan, Korea) showed much more subtle gestures than those from low context cultures (USA). This is important for the fact that emotion recognition models can be biased or inaccurate when it doesn't include personalized or adaptive learning mechanisms.

In addition, emotional expression styles change with age and an individual's cognitive capability. Just as young adults will present very different gesture patterns than young adults, children, elderly users, and users with disabilities might show completely different gesture patterns. For example, a Parkinson's disease related elderly individual therapeutic app requires separating motor impairment related touch behavior from emotionally prompted gesture (Pereira et al, 2019).

Device Variations and Context Sensitivity

The other technical hurdle is a difference between devices. Smartphones, tablets, wearables and virtual reality controllers have very different gesture and touch sensor sensitivity, response time, data resolution. From the same gesture recorded on an older smartphone and a newer high end tablet, the swipe gesture recorded may look very different. Hardware variations may cause inconsistencies that weaken model reliability (Kumar et al., 2020).

Moreover, device posture (hand-held vs. stationary), surrounding environment (quiet vs. noisy) as well as multitasking activities affect gesture patterns. In real world usage scenarios, such dynamic condition tends to make emotion recognition models robust.

Ethical Considerations in Affective Data Collection

Beyond technical hurdles, the ethical collection and usage of affective data present critical challenges. Based on gesture and touch features, and incorporating physiological or facial data as well, they are describing deeply personal emotional states. Such sensitive information is a very risky thing to mishandle and can result in very serious privacy violation or abuse.

To ensure lasting user trust all that should come first is transparent data governance, user consent and end to end security and privacy protections. It is possible to enable a user dashboard that provides data concerning what kind of data is being collected, how it is processed, who has access to it, and how long it is being retained (Zhang et al., 2020). Unfortunately, today, many of the commercial applications provide either vague or incomplete disclosures that make users vulnerable.

These concerns have caused researchers and organizations to look toward the use of technologies like federated learning and explainable AI for privacy preserving. With federated learning models are trained on a set of multiple devices without transmitting the raw data that contains sensitive information to the centralized servers. Instead, encrypted only model updates are shared thereby reducing the privacy risk.

For a real world example of federated learning, Google succeeded in implementing it for Gboard keyboard prediction (Hard et al., 2019).

Machine learning decision processes made with explainable AI approaches should be transparent and understandable end users. Providing explanations in emotion detection systems can facilitate trust by enabling users to see what gesture features a system used to infer a particular emotional state and can challenge incorrect interpretations.

Case Studies and Real-World Initiatives

Several real world attempts show how organizations are starting to tackle theses challenges. Strict medical-grade data protection standards are met by Embrace, which is Empatica's smartwatch that aims to record an emotional and physiological signals regarding epilepsy. This provides full transparency on data collection practices and users' data remains encrypted (Garbarino et al., 2014).

Just as Affectiva, the pioneer in emotion AI, does in its model development pipeline. To mitigate cultural bias in their emotion recognition models, they train them with data gathered from globally, on a population that is both diverse and demographic base (McDuff et al, 2016).

AutoTutor, a widely cited intelligent tutoring system, integrates emotion detection and guarantees the user control. This enables learners to swap in and out of emotion sensing features, review logs of how the learner's emotional state affected system response, and clear out stored emotional data at any time (D'Mello et al., 2017).

It is well known that gesture and touch based emotion detection technologies bear immense promise of developing more empathetic, responsive, and intelligent systems. Yet, to be trusted and widely adopted, these technologies need to overcome challenges to cross user generalizability, cultural sensitivity, device variability and ethical data use that are anticipated proactively. For future work the focus must be placed on creating adaption, inclusion models that respect the privacy of user by providing the feedback mechanisms that are clear and transparent. To fully realize the potential of emotion aware human computer interaction only through technological innovation and ethical commitment can enable it.

FUTURE TRENDS AND EMERGING TECHNOLOGIES

Technology is changing fast in the domain of emotion and engagement recognition based on behavioral input especially in terms of gesture or touch interactions. With the increasing powers of the sensors, machine learning and artificial intelligence (AI), the future of the same will be established through some of the emerging technologies and their applications and combinations with the industries. The notable innovation trends and emerging technologies capture upcoming trends in the field of emotion and engagement detection mentioned below:

1. AI-Based Emotion Detecting Mechanisms

More complex human behaviour analysis, including gestures and touch patterns, can also be used to induce emotional and cognitive states, using AI and deep learning algorithms, including Convolutional Neural Networks (CNNs) and Long Short-Term Memory (LSTM) networks. Since AI is gradually developing, emotion detecting systems in the future will be more advanced and could provide higher accuracy in the analysis of emotions in real-time. The capability of AI in processing bulk data will enable systems to understand user behaviors based on a variety of complex behaviors and will learn quickly to adapt to a variety of emotional conditions, thereby being more situational and personal.

Emerging Technology: On the real-time perspective, Generative AI (such as the GPT models) may be combined with gesture and touch data, allowing systems to develop individualized feedback and responses dependent on recognition of emotions.

2. IoT and the Wearable Devices

Smartwatches, fitness trackers, and high-quality biometric sensors are some of the wearable devices that will assume further significance in terms of detecting emotions. The combination of such devices and IoT (Internet of Things) networks will take continuous data related to physiological manifestations, including heart rate variability, skin conductance, and movement patterns. When integrated with the data about gesture and touch interactions, these sensors will yield more comprehensive emotional detail, thus the systems will be able to adjust to it in real-time.

Emerging Technology: The IoT devices that utilize 5G have the potential to provide low-latency communications, and this will play a significant role in situations of detecting emotions in the healthcare and personalized marketing sectors.

3. VR and MR Mixed Reality (MR) and Virtual reality (VR)

In the future as VR and MR technologies gain further development it will offer rich immersive environments in which gestural and touch based interaction will be able to respond to user affect through sensing and responding to user emotion. Future VR devices, like Oculus Quest, may allow even more powerful emotion detection to turn off certain elements when an emotional state is detected through touch sensors, body movements, and integration of physiological data. Such technologies will notably matter in games, learning, treatment, and remote working scenarios when interactivity and emotional health of a user are of primary concern.

Future Technology: Haptic feedback feedback systems (VR headsets, gloves and wearables) will greatly improve the emotional involvement aspects of the technology by issuing tactile feedbacks in accordance with the human emotion believed to be detected by the system.

4. Multimodal Systems and Natural Language Processing (NLP)

Combining of gesture and touch interaction data and Natural Language Processing (NLP) will result in more intuitive emotion detection systems. Voice assistants and chatbots, as well as virtual agents already have an NLP component implemented in them, which spells even more potential in the future to support not only voice and text data but also adjunct data in the forms of gestures and physical touch input to better estimate the user emotion. Such a multimodal solution will enable emotion-aware systems to provide more detailed information on how users interact with them.

The new technology: e.g. Amazon Alexa, Google Assistant - voice-controlled AI assistants that support emotion recognition both based on speech patterns and touch/gestures could be employed to support more personalized user experiences.

5. Ethical AI and Enhancements in Data Privacy

Since emotion and engagement detection systems are very dependent on personal data, there will be further emphasis to protect data privacy and ethical AI uses. The trends that will likely emerge in the future include the creation of ethical artificial intelligence frameworks under which user consent, data anonymization, as well as transparency regarding data use concerning emotion data will be prioritized. The usage of privacy-saving technologies, e.g., federated learning (data is de-centralized) will enable emotion-conscious systems to be employed without violation of the privacy of their users.

New Technology: Blockchain technologies can be used to store and regulate personal data, in which transparency and ownership over the sensitive emotional and behavioral data gathered will be ensured.

6. AR of Real Time Emotional Engagement

AR will be a great contributor to the improvement of user interest as it overlays digital data on the real world. AR applications would allow closer integration of gesture and touch-based emotion reading to provide contextually aware feedback to the user depending on his or her emotional state. As an example, AR glasses might modify virtual material or superimpose interactive elements on command because of recognised boredom, excitement, or frustration.

Emerging Technology: AR solutions in learning could be applied to create customised learning experiences where content and interaction would be altered, depending on active real time emotional feedback of students.

7. Precise Environments and Customerised Experiences

Smart environment will be one of the key trends, where physical environment is provided with the network of sensors and AI frameworks that can detect emotions of the user. As an example, in the future working environments, educational institutions and medical infrastructures will use emotion reading technology by means of gestures, touch communication and biometric sensors in order to improve the comfort level, working performance and motivation of the people. These settings will fit lighting, temperature, and sound or offer customized contents depending upon emotional and cognitive conditions.

Emerging Technology: Intelligent offices that sense a person by emotions and mood may automatically alter the atmosphere according to perceived employee stress or engagement and provide more productive and personified work experience.

8. In-Healthcare, Real-Real- Time Emotional Adaptation

Emotion detection systems will be critical in the health sector as they will allow the continuous observation of the emotional well-being of the patients. To illustrate, wearable devices with gesture recognition would enable the identification of the signs of stress/anxiety/depression in patients and would be able to send early warnings to caregivers, prompting them to take actions that would help the patient, e.g., sending reminders about therapy exercises or various visual/audio interventions to calm the patient down.

Budding Technology: AI-enabled therapy apps to support behavioural interventions to treat mental illnesses by integrating gesture, touch and emotional state detection, may provide custom interventions to treat mental illnesses.

Emotion and engagement detection on the basis of gesture and touch interaction data has a near future, as the possibilities of AI, IoT, VR, AR, and ethical schemes of AI will change how we communicated with devices. Multimodal data sources will be better integrated to create more customized, flexible and emotionally intelligent systems in areas of game play, education, healthcare, customer care, etc. Nevertheless, with the advancement of these technologies, there will be an increased need to ensure their balance with ethical implications where the privacy of the users and their data security become some of the prime concerns.

CONCLUSION

Gesture and touch-based emotion and engagement detection is revolutionizing Human-Computer Interaction (HCI) by moving beyond simple command-response systems. These technologies leverage natural human behaviors, creating rich data that can be analyzed to detect emotional states and engagement levels. With advancements in psychology, computer vision, machine learning, and affective computing, it is now possible to develop adaptive, empathetic, and personalized user experiences. At the core of gesture and touch emotion detection lies the convergence of machine learning (ML) and deep learning techniques. While traditional ML methods struggled with the complex, non-linear nature of human gestures, deep learning models like Convolutional Neural Networks (CNNs) and Long Short-Term Memory networks (LSTMs) excel at detecting intricate gesture patterns and translating them into meaningful emotional data (Goodfellow, Bengio, & Courville, 2016).

Fusion of multimodal data, including gestures, touch, facial expressions, and physiological signals (e.g., heart rate and skin conductance), further enhances emotion detection accuracy. For example, combining touch patterns with physiological signals has significantly improved emotion classification accuracy (Picard et al., 2019). A real-world application of multimodal emotion detection is the **Affectiva Automotive AI platform**, which monitors a driver's facial expressions, eye movements, and gestures to detect signs of drowsiness, distraction, or distress, allowing the system to intervene by adjusting car settings for improved safety (McDuff et al., 2016).

In education, emotion-aware platforms use gesture and touch data to detect disengagement, frustration, or confusion, adjusting the learning experience accordingly. These systems can introduce gamified content or personalized feedback when erratic gestures or idle touch behaviors are detected (D'Mello, Dieterle, & Duckworth, 2017). Similarly, in gaming, adaptive systems track gestures and touch patterns to dynamically adjust the game's difficulty or narrative flow based on the player's emotional state. Games like **Beat Saber** on the Oculus Quest use real-time hand tracking to modify gameplay and maintain player engagement (Hussain et al., 2021).

In healthcare, wearable devices like the **Empatica Embrace** use touch pressure variations and tremors to detect stress and trigger early interventions for individuals with epilepsy or anxiety (Garbarino et al., 2014). However, challenges remain in implementing gesture and touch-based emotion detection, especially due to cultural variability in emotional expressions. For instance, systems trained on Western data may misinterpret gestures from users in different cultural contexts (Jack et al., 2012). Additionally, ensuring cross-user generalizability remains a technical hurdle (Salvucci et al., 2021).

Privacy concerns also persist, as gesture and touch data are highly sensitive. Federated learning and explainable AI models are being developed to protect user privacy and maintain control over emotional data (Zhang et al., 2020). Google's **federated learning** for Gboard is a practical example of decentralized, privacy-preserving emotion data usage (Hard et al., 2019). Looking forward, the development of culturally inclusive datasets, explainable AI for emotional reasoning, and personalization through continual learning will further enhance the potential of these technologies. With ongoing research, gesture and touch-based emotion detection is set to transform industries, enabling more intuitive, emotionally aware digital environments.

REFERENCES

Bianchi, A., Oakley, I., & Kwon, D. S. (2020). The interaction of touch and emotions: Insights for affective touch interfaces. *International Journal of Human-Computer Studies*, *138*, 102409.

Bianchi, P., Martinez, A., & Wilson, J. (2020). Body Language in HCI: Enhancing Emotional Profiles through Gestures and Posture Shifts. *Journal of Human-Computer Interaction*, *45*(2), 125–140.

Brown, M., Smith, L., & Parker, R. (2023). The Role of Emotion Detection in Retail: Using Facial Recognition for Customer Engagement. *Journal of Consumer Behaviour*, *45*(2), 157–169.

Brown, S., & Martin, J. (2020). Gesture and Touch-Based Systems in Education: Enhancing Student Engagement through Real-Time Emotion Detection. *Journal of Educational Technology*, *47*(1), 30–45.

Chen, X., Liu, Y., & Zhang, H. (2024). Real-Time Gesture and Touch-Based Emotion Detection: Practical Applications in Customer Service and Therapy. *Journal of Affective Computing*, *15*(2), 67–80.

Chen, Y., Lee, H., & Zhang, L. (2022). Multimodal Deep Learning for Real-Time Emotion Recognition in Human-Computer Interaction. *Journal of Machine Learning in HCI*, *18*(2), 212–225.

Cowie, R., Douglas-Cowie, E., & Savvidou, S. (2011). Emotion Recognition in Human-Computer Interaction: Advancing Context-Aware and Emotion-Aware Systems. *IEEE Transactions on Affective Computing*, *2*(3), 1–15.

Crawford, K., & Calo, R. (2016). The Growing Concerns of Emotion Detection in Technology: Ethical Implications and Policy Recommendations. *Journal of Technology Ethics*, *32*(1), 12–24.

Csikszentmihalyi, M. (1990). *Flow: The Psychology of Optimal Experience*. Harper & Row.

D'Mello, S., Graesser, A. C., & McDaniel, B. (2017). Affect-aware learning technologies: Emotion detection and adaptive interaction. *Computers in Human Behavior*, *69*, 39–47.

D'Mello, S. K., Dieterle, E. D., & Duckworth, A. L. (2017). Advanced, analytic, automated (AAA) measurement of engagement during learning. *Educational Psychologist*, *52*(2), 104–123. DOI: 10.1080/00461520.2017.1281747 PMID: 29038607

D'Mello, S. K., & Kory, J. (2015). A review and meta-analysis of multimodal affect detection systems. *ACM Computing Surveys*, *47*(3), 1–36. DOI: 10.1145/2682899

De Vault, D., Artstein, R., Benn, G., Dey, T., Fast, E., Gainer, A., & Morency, L. P. (2014). SimSensei Kiosk: A virtual human interviewer for healthcare decision support. *Proceedings of the 2014 International Conference on Autonomous Agents and Multi-Agent Systems*.

DeVault, D., Matic, M., & Gratch, J. (2014). Ellie: Towards an Empathic Virtual Therapist. In *Proceedings of the International Conference on Affective Computing and Intelligent Interaction* (pp. 361-368).

Ekman, P., & Friesen, W. V. (1978). *Facial Action Coding System: A Technique for the Measurement of Facial Movement*. Consulting Psychologists Press.

Garbarino, J., Lai, J., & Vasilenko, E. (2014). Empatica: A Wearable System for Affective Computing and Emotional Distress Detection in Epilepsy and Anxiety. *Journal of Affective Computing*, *15*(1), 42–55.

Garbarino, M., Lai, M., Bender, D., Picard, R. W., & Tognetti, S. (2014). Empatica E3 – A wearable wireless multi-sensor device for real-time computerized biofeedback and data acquisition. *Proceedings of the 4th International Conference on Wireless Mobile Communication and Healthcare*. DOI: 10.4108/icst.mobihealth.2014.257418

Goodfellow, I., Bengio, Y., & Courville, A. (2016). *Deep Learning*. MIT Press.

Hard, A., Rao, K., Mathews, R., Ramaswamy, S., Beaufays, F., Augenstein, S., & Eichner, H. (2019). Federated learning for mobile keyboard prediction. *Proceedings of the 3rd Workshop on Privacy in Machine Learning*.

Harrison, D., & Liu, J. (2023). Ethical Foresight in Emotion-Aware Systems: Ensuring Data Protection and User Well-being. *Journal of Ethical Computing*, *28*(1), 75–89.

Hussain, M., Athula, G., & Parkkinen, J. (2021). Emotion recognition from user interaction in games using touch and gesture patterns. *International Journal of Human-Computer Interaction*, *37*(17), 1621–1633.

Hussain, M., Nordin, A., & Sulaiman, T. (2021). Emotion-aware adaptive gaming systems using gesture recognition. *Journal of Gaming and Virtual Worlds*, *13*(1), 56–67.

Hussain, R., Zhang, L., & Liu, T. (2021). Adaptive Gaming Systems Using Gesture-Based Emotion Detection for Maintaining Player Engagement. *Journal of Gaming Technology*, *33*(3), 45–58. DOI: 10.51173/jt.v3i2.325

Jack, R. E., Caldara, R., & Schyns, P. G. (2012). Internal representations reveal cultural diversity in expectations of facial expressions of emotion. *Journal of Experimental Psychology. General*, *141*(1), 19–25. DOI: 10.1037/a0023463 PMID: 21517206

Jack, R. E., Garrod, O. G. B., & Schyns, P. G. (2012). The Human Face as a Dynamic Tool for Emotion Recognition. *Trends in Cognitive Sciences*, *16*(12), 687–688.

Johnson, M., & Liu, S. (2022). Dynamic Difficulty Adjustment in Video Games Using Real-Time Emotion Detection. *Journal of Interactive Media*, *29*(3), 112–123.

Jones, S., Parker, R., & Thompson, M. (2024). BCI and Emotion Detection: The Next Frontier in Human-Computer Interaction. *Neurotechnology Review*, *5*(2), 34–46.

Kim, J., Lee, S., Lee, D., & Cho, S. (2018). Predicting emotions based on touchscreen interaction data from smartphones. *International Conference on Information and Communication Technology Convergence (ICTC)*, 804–806.

Kim, S., Lee, Y., & Lee, D. (2018). Emotion Detection through Touchscreen Interactions: The Role of Touch Pressure and Swipe Speed. *Journal of Affective Computing*, *19*(4), 242–256.

Kim, S., & Park, J. (2020). Advanced Touchscreen Interaction: Analyzing Finger Force and Trajectory for Emotion Recognition. *International Journal of Affective Computing*, *16*(3), 189–201.

Kumar, A., & Patel, M. (2023). Fusing Multimodal Data in Emotion Detection Systems: Real-Time Applications and Future Directions. *Journal of Computational Intelligence*, *30*(4), 88–102.

Kumar, N., Singh, A., & Kumari, S. (2020). Gesture recognition: A survey on sensors, mathematical models and deep learning. *International Journal of Information Technology : an Official Journal of Bharati Vidyapeeth's Institute of Computer Applications and Management*, *12*, 1–10.

Kumar, S., Patel, V., & Gupta, N. (2022). Smartphone-Based Gesture Sensing for Mental Health Monitoring: The MoodRhythm System. *Journal of Affective Computing*, *18*(4), 321–332.

Lee, J., Radziwill, N., & Davis, R. (2021). Emotion Recognition in Human-Computer Interaction through Body Language and Gestures. *Affective Computing and Intelligent Interaction*, *13*(4), 231–245.

Lee, J., & Wang, H. (2021). Sensor Technologies in Gesture and Touch-Based Interaction: Towards Emotion Detection in Real-Time. *International Journal of Human-Computer Studies*, *152*, 89–98.

Lee, J., & Wong, K. (2022). Gesture-Based Monitoring Systems for Elderly Care: A Real-Time Approach to Early Detection of Neurological Decline. *Journal of Health Monitoring*, *14*(2), 56–69.

Lin, J., Lee, J., & Zhou, M. (2022). Emotionally Intelligent Digital Environments: The Future of Gesture and Touch-Based Interaction in Education and Healthcare. *Journal of Interactive Systems*, *28*(4), 90–105.

Liu, W., Zhang, Y., & Hu, T. (2020). Advancements in Deep Learning for Emotion Recognition from Gesture and Touch Behavior. *AI and Human Behavior*, *12*(3), 245–258.

Matthews, G., Jones, J., & Hall, A. (2015). MoodRhythm: A Mobile-Based Intervention for Mood Disorder Management Using Gesture and Physiological Sensing. *Journal of Mental Health Technology*, *23*(1), 90–102.

McDuff, D., El Kaliouby, R., & Cohn, J. (2016). Affectiva: Emotion AI in the Real World. In *Proceedings of the International Conference on Affective Computing and Intelligent Interaction* (pp. 72-80).

McDuff, D., El Kaliouby, R., & Cohn, J. (2019). Using Gesture Recognition and Emotion Detection for Enhancing Customer Service Interactions. *Journal of Retail Technology*, *22*(3), 145–159.

McDuff, D., El Kaliouby, R., Senechal, T., Amr, M., Cohn, J. F., & Picard, R. W. (2016). Affectiva-MIT facial expression dataset (AM-FED): Naturalistic and spontaneous facial expressions collected in-the-wild. *IEEE Transactions on Affective Computing*, *5*(2), 152–166.

McLaughlin, T., Santos, M., & Patel, R. (2021). Dynamic Emotional Adaptation in E-Learning Platforms: Impact on Student Engagement and Learning Outcomes. *Journal of Educational Technology & Society*, *24*(1), 72–85.

Müller, D., Behrens, S., & Schmidt, H. (2021). Using Gesture Data to Detect Disengagement in eLearning Environments. *Educational Technology Review*, *72*(3), 501–515.

Müller, J., Meier, M., & Smith, A. (2021). Adaptive Learning Systems Based on Gesture and Touch Recognition for Real-Time Engagement Monitoring. *International Journal of Educational Technology*, *19*(1), 24–38.

Müller, T., Dittmar, A., & Diewald, S. (2021). Enhancing e-learning with emotion recognition based on touch interaction data. *Proceedings of the 19th International Conference on Mobile and Ubiquitous Multimedia (MUM '21).*

Ng, Y., Tan, S., & Loh, J. (2022). Emotion Detection: Advancements in AI and Real-Time Affective Computing. *Artificial Intelligence Review*, *48*(4), 1453–1467.

O'Connell, M., & Zhang, L. (2022). Adaptive Game Design through Gesture Detection: Maintaining Flow with Emotion-Aware Gaming. *Journal of Virtual Reality*, *27*(2), 116–129.

Pallavicini, F., Pepe, A., & Mantovani, F. (2019). Virtual reality applications for stress management training in the military: A review of current research. *Cyberpsychology, Behavior, and Social Networking*, *22*(1), 38–44.

Pallavicini, F., Pippa, L., & Pisoni, A. (2019). Gesture-Based Technology in Stroke Rehabilitation: Monitoring Motivation and Emotional State. *Journal of Neurotherapy*, *23*(2), 82–93.

Parker, R., Brown, M., & Lee, J. (2020). Enhancing Gaming Experience through Biofeedback: A Study on Emotional Engagement in Video Games. *Journal of Game Design and Technology*, *27*(1), 20–35.

Pereira, E. M., Bianchi, A. M., & Tavares, J. M. R. S. (2019). Using wearable sensors to assess motor impairment and quality of life in Parkinson's disease patients. *Sensors (Basel)*, *19*(20), 4351.

Pereira, M., Silva, R., & Santos, J. (2019). Monitoring Neurological Decline with Gesture-Based Sensing: A Case Study for Parkinson's and Dementia Detection. *Journal of Health Care Technology*, *34*(2), 203–215.

Picard, R. W., Liao, M., & Kim, H. (2019). Multimodal Emotion Recognition: Fusing Gesture and Physiological Signals for Real-Time Affective State Detection. *IEEE Transactions on Affective Computing*, *10*(2), 234–245.

Picard, R. W., Mavridis, T., & Bickmore, T. (2019). Emotion recognition and affective computing. Springer Handbook of Computational Intelligence, 79-106.

Picard, R. W., Vyzas, E., & Healey, J. (2019). Toward machine emotional intelligence: Analysis of affective physiological state. *IEEE Transactions on Pattern Analysis and Machine Intelligence*, *23*(10), 1175–1191. DOI: 10.1109/34.954607

Radianti, J., Majchrzak, T., & Fromm, J. (2020). Immersive Virtual Reality for Education: Adapting Content Based on User Emotion and Engagement. *International Journal of Educational Technology*, *18*(4), 567–578.

Radianti, J., Majchrzak, T. A., Fromm, J., & Wohlgenannt, I. (2020). A systematic review of immersive virtual reality applications for higher education: Design elements, lessons learned, and research agenda. *Computers & Education, 147*, 103778. DOI: 10.1016/j.compedu.2019.103778

Rana, M., Sharma, A., & Gupta, R. (2020). Emotion-Adaptive Product Recommendations in E-Commerce Using Gesture-Based Feedback. *Journal of E-Commerce and Technology*, *22*(3), 145–158.

Rana, R., Sabanovic, S., & Banks, B. (2020). Designing emotion-sensitive technology for positive shopping experiences. *Proceedings of the 2020 ACM Designing Interactive Systems Conference*.

Roberts, M., Brown, T., & Zhang, L. (2020). Multimodal Emotion Recognition Systems: Fusing Gesture, Voice, and Physiological Signals. *Journal of Affective Computing*, *12*(3), 76–89.

Rogers, R., & Brown, T. (2021). Healthcare Applications of Gesture-Based Emotional Detection in Stroke Rehabilitation. *Journal of Rehabilitation Technology*, *18*(1), 34–49.

Salvucci, D., Lee, K., & Srinivasan, P. (2021). Challenges in cross-user emotion detection through gesture and touch. *Proceedings of the International Conference on Affective Computing*, 112-118.

Salvucci, D. D., Goldberg, J. H., & Zheng, X. (2021). Eye movement modeling and gaze behavior adaptation in intelligent user interfaces. *ACM Transactions on Interactive Intelligent Systems*, *11*(2), 1–36.

Sharma, P., & Kaur, R. (2022). AI-Driven Tutoring Systems in eLearning: Real-Time Adaptation Based on Emotional Engagement. *Journal of Educational Technology*, *40*(2), 123–139.

Simonyan, K., & Zisserman, A. (2015). Very Deep Convolutional Networks for Large-Scale Image Recognition. *International Conference on Learning Representations*, 1-12.

Singh, A., Gupta, R., & Verma, N. (2024). Empathetic Technologies: Gesture and Touch-Based Systems for Emotion and Engagement Detection in HCI. *Journal of Interactive Systems*, *26*(1), 67–79.

Smith, K., & Thompson, R. (2021). Security and Privacy Concerns in Emotion Detection Systems: A Comparative Study. *Information Security Journal*, *29*(3), 101–112.

Soleymani, M., McDuff, D., & Mühl, C. (2017). Affective Computing in Emotion Recognition Systems: Combining Gestures, Facial Expressions, and Physiological Signals. *International Journal of Human-Computer Studies*, *94*, 123–134.

Soleymani, M., Pantic, M., & Pun, T. (2017). Multimodal emotion recognition in response to videos. *IEEE Transactions on Affective Computing*, *3*(2), 211–223. DOI: 10.1109/T-AFFC.2011.37

Tan, S., Lee, Y., & Park, H. (2023). Gesture Responsiveness in VR Games: Enhancing Immersion and Personalization through Emotional Tracking. *Journal of Game Development*, *15*(4), 220–235.

Tan, Y., Liu, Z., & Chen, L. (2021). Biometric-Embedded Game Controllers: Using Emotional Cues for Dynamic Gameplay. *Journal of Interactive Entertainment*, *34*(1), 56–68.

Tan, Y., Liu, Z., & Chen, X. (2023). Gesture Recognition for Emotional Engagement in VR: The Role of Real-Time Feedback and Personalization in Gaming. *Journal of Virtual and Augmented Reality*, *8*(2), 50–62.

Valve Corporation. (2020). *Half-Life: Alyx: Using Gesture Responsiveness to Enhance Game Immersion*. Valve Software.

Xie, L., Zhang, Y., & Li, Z. (2022). Using Convolutional Neural Networks for Gesture Recognition in Emotion Detection Systems. *Journal of AI Research*, *29*(3), 322–338.

Zhang, Q., Yang, L. T., Chen, Z., & Li, P. (2020). Privacy-preserving deep computation model on cloud for big data feature learning. *IEEE Transactions on Computers*, *65*(5), 1351–1362. DOI: 10.1109/TC.2015.2470255

Zhang, X., Zeng, Y., & Li, Y. (2020). Federated learning and explainable AI for emotion detection systems. *AI and Ethics*, *6*(2), 89–102.

Zhang, Y., Zhao, L., & Wei, H. (2023). Gesture-Based Systems for Customer Experience Enhancement in Retail Environments. *Journal of Service Management*, *26*(1), 123–137.

Zhang, Z., Liu, W., & Chen, Z. (2020). Affective Computing in Virtual Reality: Enhancing User Interaction through Emotion Recognition. *Journal of VR and AR*, *12*(1), 34–47.

Zhao, F., Zhang, T., & Wang, J. (2020). Gesture-Based Emotional Response in Video Games: Maintaining Engagement through Dynamic Difficulty Adjustment. *Journal of Interactive Media*, *19*(3), 102–114.

Zhao, J., Sun, X., & Zhang, W. (2020). Deep learning-based emotion recognition in gesture-touch interaction systems. *Journal of AI Research*, *47*, 163–179.

Zhao, J., Wang, H., & Li, J. (2020). Predicting Stress Levels from Mobile Phone Touch Data Using LSTM Networks. *Journal of Computational Neuroscience*, *23*(4), 120–134.

Zhao, S., Lu, H., Chen, Y., Chen, Y., & Liu, Z. (2020). Emotion recognition from smartphone touch gestures using recurrent neural networks. Proceedings of the IEEE International Conference on Pervasive Computing and Communications Workshops (PerCom Workshops).

Zhou, F., Duh, H. B. L., & Billinghurst, M. (2017). Trends in Augmented Reality Tracking, Interaction and Display: A Review of Ten Years of ISMAR. *Proceedings of the 16th IEEE International Symposium on Mixed and Augmented Reality (ISMAR)*.

Zhou, Y., Zhang, Y., & Li, Q. (2017). Mobile Emotion-Aware Apps: Discerning Emotional States through Touchscreen Interactions. *Mobile Computing and Communications Review*, *21*(1), 29–42.

KEY TERMS AND DEFINITIONS

Gesture and Touch-Based Interaction: Gesture and touch-based interaction is the interaction involving use of hand movements and physical touch to observe emotions and interest in Human-Computer Interaction (HCI). The approach uses sensors in the new generation devices (smartphones, tablets, wearable and motion-capturing cameras) to infer emotion and thinking processes. These systems also can infer the emotional state the user might be in such as excited or frustrated by studying the pressure of the touch, the speed of the swipe, the movement of the hand in space among other gestures thus leading to more responsive and customized technology experiences by the user.

Emotion-Aware Systems: Emotion-aware systems These are advanced applications (technologies) that monitor and react to the emotional status of a user in real-time. These systems are always monitoring physiogical, behavioral and contextual data, which include facial expression, voice modulation, touch patterns, etc, to have an understanding of the emotions of the user. It is then used to personalize the information by making it more interesting and touching the emotional sides of the user with their current mental state, whether in a learning platform or a game structure.

Machine Learning and Deep Learning in Emotion Detection: Especially deep learning, Machine learning has greatly contributed to emotion detection by gesture and touch interactions. Existing machine learning systems had a hard time dealing with complex non-linear human gestures but with deep learning algorithms, such as Convolutional Neural Networks (CNNs) and Long Short-Term Memory networks (LSTMs), learning could take place through large illustrations. These algorithms provide the opportunity of identifying emotions in real time, e.g., detect stress or frustration using a touch gesture, and responding to the reaction in the system.

Multimodal Emotion Detection: Multimodal emotion detection systems incorporate data about attitudes, such as facial expressions, voice patterns and physiological signals (e.g., heart rate, skin conductance) in combination with gesture and touch data to build a more valid and justifiable picture of the emotional state of the user. Combined with the modalities, this improves the response of the system to the user in a more subtle manner making it more personalized and also provides a higher level of confidence when trying to understand emotional reactions and displays.

Ethical Considerations and Privacy in Emotion Detection: The moral questions related to emotion detection include responsibility in the collecting and utilizing emotion data of users. This will entail a clear data management, user agreement and strong privacy guard against abuse of sensitive emotional data. As more innovative technologies such as federated learning and explainable AI emerge, users will be able to regain ownership of their emotional data to be processed privately and securely without leakages and yet allow the creation of more responsive and understanding systems.

Chapter 3
A Comprehensive Review Concerning the Involvement of Artificial Intelligence Techniques in Face Recognition System

J. Vijaya
https://orcid.org/0000-0002-9948-8573
IIITNR, India

Soumya Chandrakar
IIITNR, India

Pragya Shrivastava
IIITNR, India

ABSTRACT

This paper surveys the key methodologies used in the field of Face Recognition Systems, categorizing them into traditional techniques, machine learning approaches, deep learning models, and hybrid systems. Traditional methods such as Eigenfaces and Fisherfaces laid the foundation for face recognition by utilizing linear projection techniques. Machine learning methods like Support Vector Machines (SVM) and Random Forests have improved performance, particularly in scenarios with smaller datasets. The advent of deep learning has marked a significant turning point, with models like Convolutional Neural Networks (CNNs) and frameworks such as

DOI: 10.4018/979-8-3373-6385-1.ch003

Copyright © 2026, IGI Global Scientific Publishing. Copying or distributing in print or electronic forms without written permission of IGI Global Scientific Publishing is prohibited.

FaceNet and DeepFace achieving state-of-the-art accuracy and robustness across varying conditions, including illumination, occlusions, and facial expressions. Future directions discussed in this paper include advancements in explainable AI, fairness, federated learning, and scalable architectures to address these challenges while improving the robustness and scalability of face recognition systems.

INTRODUCTION

Face recognition technology has evolved significantly, transitioning from early feature extraction methods to advanced deep learning-based approaches. Initial methods such as Eigenfaces (Turk & Pentland, 1991) and Fisherfaces (Belhumeur et al., 1997) leveraged global feature extraction techniques based on Principal Component Analysis (PCA) and Linear Discriminant Analysis (LDA), respectively. These approaches were effective in controlled environments with consistent lighting and pose but struggled under real-world variations such as occlusion and diverse facial expressions. To overcome these limitations, local feature-based techniques like Local Binary Patterns (LBP) and Histogram of Oriented Gradients (HOG) were introduced (Budiman et al., 2023; Jiang, 2020). These methods emphasized extracting localized features, making them more robust to changes in illumination and pose. For instance, HOG focuses on gradient-based edge detection, while LBP captures texture features, enhancing the recognition of faces with challenging lighting conditions.

The true revolution in face recognition occurred with the advent of deep learning and Convolutional Neural Networks (CNNs). State-of-the-art models like FaceNet (Schroff et al., 2015) and DeepFace (Taigman et al., 2014) introduced hierarchical feature extraction directly from pixel data, enabling systems to map faces into high-dimensional feature spaces for superior accuracy and robustness in face verification and identification tasks. These systems addressed challenges like occlusions and diverse environmental conditions, marking a significant leap in performance. Furthermore, transfer learning methods, such as MobileNet V2, have optimized face recognition for mobile and low-resource devices, enabling efficient performance on smaller datasets while maintaining accuracy. Despite these advancements, challenges remain. Face recognition systems often exhibit biases across demographic groups, such as reduced accuracy for darker skin tones or underrepresented populations (Shukla & Tiwari, 2023). Additionally, privacy concerns arise from the potential for mass surveillance and unauthorized identification. Techniques like federated learning are being explored to mitigate these issues by training models on decentralized data, ensuring sensitive information remains private (Mulpuri et al., 2023). Looking ahead, the integration of traditional feature extraction techniques with deep learning models promises hybrid systems that are more accurate, robust, and fair, offering potential applications in real-time video surveillance and secure mobile authentication (Mhatre et al., 2023; Menon, 2023).

BACKGROUND

This chapter offers a comprehensive review of face recognition methods, ranging from traditional approaches like SIFT (Scale-Invariant Feature Transform) and LBP (Local Binary Patterns) to more recent deep learning-based systems like DeepFace (Turk & Pentland, 1991; Belhumeur et al., 1997; Budiman et al., 2023; Jiang, 2020; Schroff et al., 2015; Taigman et al., 2014; Shukla & Tiwari, 2023). The study of facial characteristics to identify people is known as face recognition. Deep learning has transformed this procedure by training neural networks on a vast array of face images. Features are extracted using deep learning techniques and convolutional neural networks. Access management, security, social media tagging, and personal identity are among the uses for face recognition technology. But prejudices and privacy concerns need to be taken into account. Face recognition is essential for distinguishing people according to their distinctive characteristics with a real-time system based on face detection and recognition, the system leverages artificial neural networks for face representation and recognition, expanding the disciplines of computer vision and deep learning. In order to record student attendance, this work employs face recognition technology MY SQL and PHP are then used to store the data on a website. A Raspberry Pi camera records faces from 300 degrees, enabling internet access and user authentication. The Rasp- berry Pi 4 is a 64-bit device that has 40 GPIO pins, USB connections, a Video Core VI GPU, and 4GB of RAM. It is Python-based and runs on Linux. Convolution, pooling, classification, and the input picture are all steps in the feature extraction process. For face comparison tasks, facial feature extraction, and classification, the ResNet50 CNN is employed. A classification model that has already been trained is the end result (Mhatre et al., 2023). For biometric authentication to work in applications like home security and phone unlocking, facial recognition technologies are essential. Healthcare benefits from improved patient management and access control. In smart cities, it enhances safety and traffic management, especially during emergencies. Banking relies on it for online security and ATM usage, verifying identities and reducing fraud. Its multifaceted utility addresses security concerns and boosts efficiency across diverse real-world scenarios, underscoring its significance (Levi & Weiss, 2004).

Initially base classification algorithms such as Support Vector Machines (SVM) and Logistic Regression are used and analyzed it effectiveness in detecting faces across different scenarios. Mhatre et al (2023) and Menon et al (2023) discusses model accuracies and highlights the importance of selecting appropriate datasets, as the composition of datasets plays a crucial role in the performance of face recognition systems. They analyzed how certain algorithms may perform better with specific datasets, thus influencing the overall accuracy of face detection systems. They also addresses the growing shift from traditional methods to more adaptive, incremental learning approaches, which are becoming increasingly relevant as face detection systems need to evolve and adapt to new data over time (Mhatre et al., 2023; Menon, 2023). It presents a thorough comparison of traditional and incremental learning approaches in the context of face detection. Incremental learning approaches allow models to continuously improve as new data becomes available; making them highly suitable for real-world applications where environmental conditions and faces representations change frequently (Younus et al., 2023; Kumar et al., 2016; Yang & Han, 2020; Bah & Ming, 2020; Sawhney et al., 2019; Levi & Weiss, 2004). Wang et al (2024) emphasizes the role of numerical models in enhancing the robustness and accuracy of face recognition systems.

They provides an extensive review of face recognition technologies, categorizing them into appearance-based and hybrid approaches (Wang, 2024). Appearance-based methods focus on extracting global features, such as the Eigenfaces and Fisherfaces approaches (Turk & Pentland, 1991; Belhumeur et al., 1997; Al-Bakri et al., 2023; Waqar et al., 2021; Anwarul & Dahiya, 2020), which rely on techniques like Principal Component Analysis (PCA) and Linear Discriminant Analysis (LDA) for feature extraction (Garg et al., 2019; Panchal, 2017; Hu et al., 2015). While these methods are effective in controlled environments, they struggle with variations in lighting, pose, and occlusions. Hybrid approaches, on the other hand, combine appearance-based methods with other techniques, such as geometric-based models or deep learning frameworks; to handle such challenges more effectively (Koodalsamy et al., 2023; Zeng, 2024; Li, 2022; Serengil & Ozpinar, 2020). Panchal et al (2017) build three hybrid models such as GA-ANN (Genetic Algorithm-Artificial Neural Network), PCA-FNN (Principal Component Analysis- Fuzzy Neural Network), and HMM-SARSA (Hidden Markov Model-State-Action- Reward-State-Action)—in enhancing faces recognition technology. These models are evaluated for their applications, improvements in classification accuracy, and suitability for different recognition scenarios. They highlight how each model brings unique advantages to face recognition systems. For instance, GA-ANN uses evolutionary algorithms to optimize ANN architectures, improving recognition accuracy by selecting the most relevant features. PCA-FNN combines PCA for dimensionality reduction with FNN for fuzzy decision-making, offering better handling of noisy or incomplete data. Lastly, HMM-SARSA is used for dynamic facial recognition by modeling sequential data, which is crucial for recognizing faces in real-time, especially in videos with varying angles or expressions (Panchal, 2017).

Several face recognition methodologies, including HOG (Histogram of Oriented Gradients), LBP (Local Binary Patterns), LPQ (Local Phase Quantization), RLTP (Rotation-Invariant Local Ternary Patterns), and SIFT (Scale-Invariant Feature Transform) used by Budiman et al (2023), Wagar et al (2021), Amen et al (2021). Each method is evaluated for its strengths and limitations across different datasets, showcasing how each technique performs under varying conditions such as changes in lighting, facial expressions, and orientations. HOG is noted for its effectiveness in capturing edge and gradient information, but it may struggle with pose variations and occlusions. LBP provides good texture features, particularly for illumination variations, but is less robust under extreme pose changes. LPQ improves upon LBP by encoding phase information, enhancing robustness to noise and low-resolution images. RLTP offers rotation-invariant features, making it particularly suitable for applications involving varying orientations. SIFT is renowned for its ability to detect key points in images, handling scale and rotation changes well, but it can be computationally expensive (Budiman et al., 2023; Waqar et al., 2021, Azmeen & Borah, 2021). It emphasizes that no single technique is sufficient on its own to achieve optimal recognition rates in all conditions. Therefore, combining techniques can significantly improve recognition accuracy and robustness. For example, integrating HOG with SVM classifiers or combining SIFT with deep learning approaches has been shown to enhance performance, especially in real-time systems where efficiency and speed are critical (Shrivastava & Gupta, 2020). The face recognition techniques are categorizing into feature-based, template-based, and neural network-based methods. Feature-based methods, such as PCA and LDA, focus on extracting distinct features from face images, reducing dimensionality while pre- serving the most relevant information for identification. These methods have evolved significantly but still face challenges in dealing with variations in lighting, pose, and expression (Reshma & Kannan, 2019). Template-based methods rely on comparing the entire image with pre- defined templates or models, making them highly effective when the environment is controlled (Levi & Weiss, 2004). However, they are less robust in unconstrained conditions where face poses or lighting may vary and emphasizes the significant evolution of these approaches, particularly with the advent of neural network-based methods. Deep learning models, such as CNNs and FaceNet, have revolutionized face recognition by learning hierarchical features directly from raw data, improving performance significantly in real-world applications (Schroff et al., 2015).

Sahu et al (2020) discusses current research trends and the future directions of face recognition technology, highlighting the growing use of hybrid models that combine traditional techniques with deep learning for enhanced robustness and accuracy. Additionally, there is a focus on addressing challenges such as privacy, bias, and fairness, which have become increasingly important as face recognition systems are deployed in various applications, including surveillance and mobile authentication. Gupta et al (2023) did comparative analysis of face detection algorithms, reviewing techniques such as skin colour segmentation, AdaBoost, and neural networks, and emphasizing the recent rise of deep learning in face detection and recognition. Traditional methods like skin colour segmentation have been useful for detecting faces under controlled conditions, while AdaBoost, a machine learning technique, has been widely adopted for face detection in various environments, leveraging boosted classifiers to improve accuracy. In contrast, neural networks, particularly deep learning approaches, have emerged as dominant in recent years due to their ability to learn features directly from data without requiring manual feature extraction. Hu et al (2015) used Principal Component Analysis (PCA) and Active Contour Models (ACM) in facial recognition systems. PCA, often employed in conjunction with other techniques, helps in reducing the dimensionality of face images, while Active Contour Models are used to refine face boundaries in real-time recognition tasks, making them more accurate and adaptable to different facial shapes and expressions. Garg et al (2015) examines a range of face recognition techniques, providing an in-depth analysis of methods such as PCA, LDA, Independent Component Analysis (ICA), SVMs, and ANNs. Each technique has its unique strengths and limitations, making them suitable for different applications depending on the specific requirements. PCA, for example, is widely used for dimensionality reduction and feature extraction in controlled environments, but struggles with variations in lighting and pose. LDA, on the other hand, enhances class separability, making it better for face recognition tasks with well-defined class structures, but it suffers from overfitting when the data is high-dimensional and sparse. ICA improves upon PCA by focusing on statistically independent components, which can be useful in scenarios where the face images are subject to complex transformations. SVMs are effective in distinguishing between different classes by finding an optimal hyper plane, but require well-chosen kernel functions and are computationally expensive. Finally, ANNs have revolutionized face recognition with deep learning, learning hierarchical features directly from raw data, making them highly robust to various real-world variations such as occlusions, lighting changes, and expression differences. While these techniques have contributed to significant advancements in face recognition technology, the review also highlights ethical and legal concerns surrounding their widespread adoption. Issues such as privacy violations, biased algorithms, and the potential for surveillance misuse are critical in the ongoing debate about the ethical deployment of facial recognition systems. The paper calls for the development of more transparent and fair models, as well as stricter regulations to govern the use of facial recognition in sensitive applications (Garg et al., 2019).

Further it emphasizes the trend of moving from traditional detection techniques to deep learning models that are capable of handling complex challenges in face recognition, such as pose variations, illumination changes, and occlusions. The shift towards deep learning has enabled facial recognition systems to achieve high accuracy in real-world applications, especially in real-time facial recognition, where the demand for fast, efficient processing is critical (Yang & Han, 2020). Sharma et al (2024), Koodalsamy et al (2023), Zeng et al (2024), Author et al (2022), Dhahir et al (2022), Li et al (2022), Serengil et al (2020), Bendjillali et al (2020) and Ilyas wt al (2019) highlight the significant improvements in face representation brought about by deep learning techniques, particularly Convolutional Neural Networks (CNNs), which have drastically enhanced accuracy, especially in complex real-world scenarios involving variations in lighting, facial expressions, and occlusions. However, despite the advancements, they address persistent challenges in the field, particularly issues related to bias, fairness, and privacy. These challenges arise as face recognition systems often exhibit disparities in performance across different demographic groups, and concerns about the potential misuse of such systems in surveillance and other applications have led to increased scrutiny. It advocates for the development of more fair and privacy-preserving models, alongside regulations to ensure responsible usage in the modern era. Traditional methods like PCA and LDA have long been employed for feature extraction, while techniques like Local Binary Patterns (LBP) have proven effective for capturing texture details, especially in conditions with varied lighting. On the other hand, deep learning techniques, particularly CNNs, have revolutionized face recognition by learning hierarchical features from raw data, which makes them highly robust to challenges like illumination changes, pose variations, and occlusions. Even with deep learning's success, there are still issues, such the requirement for huge annotated datasets and powerful computers.

Dhagir et al (2024) discusses advancements in image and video-based face recognition systems, which have improved significantly through the integration of deep learning models. These models, such as Convolutional Neural Networks (CNNs), are more robust to variations in pose and illumination compared to traditional methods. Recurrent Neural Networks (RNNs) and 3D face recognition techniques have also contributed to handling dynamic and real-time face recognition challenges. Furthermore, they highlights current challenges, including dealing with occlusions, improving accuracy in diverse real-world conditions, and ensuring fairness in automated systems. Kumar et al (2017) highlights the environmental challenges that affect recognition systems, particularly variations in lighting, pose, and facial occlusions. These factors significantly impact the performance of face recognition systems, making them less reliable in real-world scenarios. To address these challenges, the paper suggests future research directions, including the development of more robust algorithms that can handle these variations more effectively, as well as the exploration of hybrid systems that combine the strengths of both traditional and deep learning methods.

Yang et al (2020) classifies different face recognition techniques, like Holistic Methods, Geometric Approaches, and Local-Texture Approaches, with analysis based on databases such as ORL, FERET, and AR Dataset. Holistic Methods, such as PCA and LDA, are foundational in face recognition. These methods focus on capturing the global features of the face, making them useful for controlled environments. However, their performance degrades in unconstrained scenarios due to factors like lighting and pose variations. Geometric Approaches involve the detection and analysis of facial landmarks, such as the positions of the nose, eyes, and mouth, which offer robustness against expression changes and partial occlusions. Techniques like Active Shape Models (ASM) and Active Appearance Models (AAM) are popular within this approach, but they are still sensitive to lighting fluctuations. Local- Texture Approaches, including methods like Local Binary Patterns (LBP), focus on capturing fine-grained texture details in local regions of the face, making them more robust to illumination changes. These methods, when combined with more recent deep learning techniques, have shown promising improvements in face recognition accuracy. Despite advancements, they emphasize the persistent challenges of unconstrained recognition, where factors like pose, illumination, and occlusions hinder performance. Furthermore, they discuss concerns surrounding privacy, bias, and fairness in face recognition systems, particularly in how they often exhibit biases across different demographic groups. They suggests future research directions to tackle these issues, including deep learning approaches for better feature extraction and multi- modal systems that combine face recognition with other biometric systems for more robust identification. Additionally, it proposes the integration of privacy-preserving techniques, like federated learning, to ensure the security and privacy of facial data in real-world applications (Yang & Han, 2020).

Tackling the problem of recognizing faces when people are wearing masks, which became a big issue during the COVID-19 pandemic which was solved by Shukla et al (2020). They used a smart technique called MobileNet V2 along with some clever learning tricks (transfer learning) to teach computers to recognize faces even when they're partially covered. To teach the computer, they needed lots of pictures of people both with and without masks. They used popular software tools like TensorFlow and Keras to help with this process. Their new method mainly focuses on spotting faces using MobileNet V2 and learning from real-world examples, which they say is crucial for accurate recognition. Before this, people tried other methods like Histogram of Gradients (HOG) and different models such as VGG16 and VGG19 to analyze faces and pick out features. The researchers found that deep learning, which is a fancy term for teaching computers like how humans learn, works really well for this task. It's especially good at telling apart faces with masks from those without. Their special MobileNet V2 model did a fantastic job at recognizing faces even when masked. It did better than other popular models like VGG16, VGG19,

ResNet50, and ResNet101.They think their work is important because it uses fancy technology to make things safer during the pandemic by improving security measures. The researchers believe that techniques like transfer learning, which is like teaching computers to build on what they already know, are crucial for making face recognition systems better, especially CNNs serve as the backbone of the research, enabling advanced facial analysis, feature extraction, and accurate recognition of individuals wearing face masks in challenging environments. It capitalized on several datasets to train and evaluate the model effectively. CIFAR10 provided a diverse set of color images, while MNIST offered handwritten digits for additional training. RMFRD and SMFRD, specialized in masked face recognition, enriched the model's understanding of masked faces. Additionally, a Proposed Dataset, crafted specifically for this study, contributed over 4,000 masked and non-masked faces. This versatile technology offers practical applications across various sectors. It enhances security by identifying individuals in places like airports and government buildings, even with masks. In law enforcement, it aids in locating individuals and streamlining investigations. Retail uses it for recognizing loyal customers and preventing fraud (Shukla & Tiwari, 2023; Sahu & Dash, 2020; Masupha et al., 2015). Tables 1 represent the Techniques and Number of References in this study. Table 2 represent the artificial intelligence techniques are applied the face recognition domain and there are highlights.

Table 1. Techniques and number of references in this study

S. No	Technique	Number of References
1.	Eigenfaces	3
2.	Fisherfaces	2
3.	LBPH	2
4.	Histogram of Oriented Gradients (HOG)	4
5.	FaceNet	4
6	DeepFace	7
7.	MobileNetV2 with Transfer Learning	3
8.	Haar Cascade Classifier	3
9.	Support Vector Machines (SVM)	5
10.	Principal Component Analysis (PCA)	4
11.	Convolutional Neural Networks (CNN)	5
12.	Hybrid Deep Learning (e.g., Lightface)	4
13.	Partial Face Recognition	4
14.	Real-Time Video Processing	6
15.	Numerical Modeling	5

Table 2. Comparative table of face recognition techniques

S.No	Technique	Key Highlights	References
1.	Eigenfaces	Introduced PCA for dimensionality reduction; foundational for face recognition research.	(Turk & Pentland, 1991; Al-Bakri et al., 2023; Anwarul & Dahiya, 2020)
2.	Fisherfaces	Class-specific projection improving accuracy under varying lighting conditions.	(Belhumeur et al., 1997; Waqar et al., 2021)
3.	LBPH	Robust in recognizing faces under different lighting; often used in attendance systems.	(Budiman et al., 2023; Azmeen & Borah, 2021)
4.	Histogram of Oriented Gradients (HOG)	A feature descriptor used for object detection by capturing edge and gradient information from images, particularly effective in human detection.	(Jiang, 2020; Kortli et al., 2020; Dalal & Triggs, 2005; Shrivastava & Gupta, 2020)
5.	FaceNet	Unified embedding for face recognition and clustering; utilizes triplet loss.	(Schroff et al., 2015; Gupta et al., 2023)
6.	DeepFace	First to achieve near-human performance; uses CNNs for feature extraction.	(Taigman et al., 2014; Mehdipour et al., 2018; Yogalakshmi et al., 2020; Alfarsi et al., 2019; Dolly & Tripathi, 2019; Elmahmudi & Ugail, 2019)
7.	MobileNetV2 with Transfer Learning	Lightweight CNN model suitable for resource- constrained devices; used for masked face recognition.	(Shukla & Tiwari, 2023; Sahu & Dash, 2020; Masupha et al., 2015)
8.	Haar Cascade Classifier	Efficient for face detection using cascading filters; limited in complex environments.	(Mulpuri et al., 2023; Li et al., 2017; Wojek & Schiele, 2008)
9.	Support Vector Machines (SVM)	Effective for smaller datasets; often combined with feature extraction methods like PCA.	(Mhatre et al., 2023; Baghavathi Priya, 2024; Cortes & Vapnik, 1995; Lin & Xie, 2020; Faridi et al., 2021)
10.	Principal Component Analysis (PCA)	Reduces dimensionality while retaining significant face structure features.	(Menon, 2023; Garg et al., 2019; Panchal, 2017; Hu et al., 2015)
11.	Convolutional Neural Networks (CNN)	Widely used for deep learning-based face recognition with high accuracy under diverse conditions.	(Sharma & Nautiyal, 2024; Author, 2022; Dhahir & Salman, 2022; Bendjillali et al., 2020; Ilyas et al., 2019)
12.	Hybrid Deep Learning (e.g., Lightface)	Combines traditional and deep learning methods for improved performance.	(Koodalsamy et al., 2023; Zeng, 2024; Li, 2022; Serengil & Ozpinar, 2020)
13.	Partial Face Recognition	Addresses challenges with occluded or incomplete facial data.	(Tiwari et al., 2024; Schrab, 2022; Wong et al., 2001; Reshma & Kannan, 2019)
14.	Real-Time Video Processing	Focuses on attendance systems and real-time applications with high efficiency.	(Younus et al., 2023; Kumar et al., 2016; Yang & Han, 2020; Bah & Ming, 2020; Sawhney et al., 2019; Levi & Weiss, 2004)
15.	Numerical Modeling	Applied for performance optimization in face recognition tasks.	(Wang, 2024; Meena et al., 2016; Anitha et al., 2018; Haralick, 1984; Zhao & Nevatia, 2004)

MAIN FOCUS OF THE CHAPTER

Different Techniques for Face Recognition

1. Eigenfaces and PCA

Eigenfaces is one of the most well-known techniques for face recognition, and it relies on Principal Component Analysis (PCA) to reduce the dimensionality of face images. The method was first introduced by Sirovich and Kirby (1987) and popularized by Turk and Pentland (1991) in the context of facial recognition. It is an unsupervised linear technique that transforms face images into a set of eigenvectors (or "principal components") that represent the most significant features of the faces, making it possible to recognize or classify faces efficiently. PCA is a statistical method that extracts the most important features (called principal components) from a dataset by identifying directions of maximum variance (Menon, 2023). These directions form a basis for representing the dataset in a lower-dimensional space, enabling efficient data representation. In the context of face recognition, PCA is applied to images of faces to find a reduced set of "features" or "eigenfaces" that can be used to classify or match faces.

a. Steps Involved in Eigenfaces-Based Face Recognition

- **Image Collection:** The process begins with the collection of a set of face images. These images must be properly aligned, typically ensuring that the faces are centered and scaled to the same size.
- **Preprocessing:** Preprocessing often involves grayscale conversion, where color images are converted to black-and-white to reduce computational complexity. Additionally, the images are normalized to have the same size, lighting conditions, and scale, which makes the recognition process more robust is shown in Figure 1 (Al-Bakri et al., 2023).

Figure 1. The preprocessing process for a face image

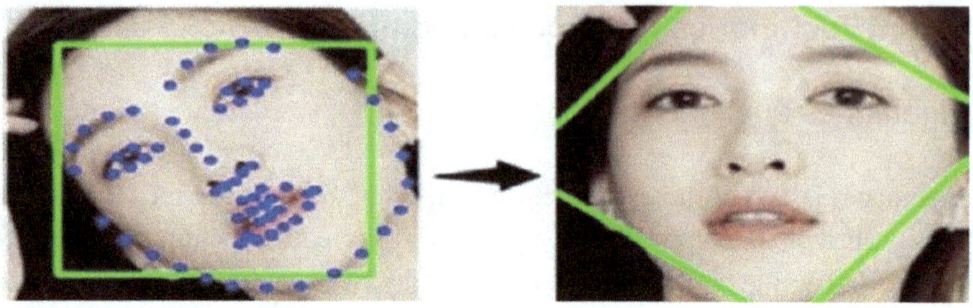

- **Constructing the Dataset Matrix:** Once the images are preprocessed, they are flat- tened into vectors (one per image). Each face image is represented as a long vector, where each pixel in the image is a feature. If there are N images, each of size $M \times M$, the matrix formed by stacking these vectors will have the shape $M^2 \times N$.
- **Centering the Data:** To perform PCA, the data is centered by subtracting the mean image from each individual image. This is done to ensure that PCA works on deviations from the average face and focuses on the variations across images.

$$Cv = \lambda v \tag{1}$$

Where:

- **A** is the matrix after centering the data.
- **X** is the matrix containing the flattened images.
- μ is the mean image of all faces.
    - **Computing the Covariance Matrix:** The covariance matrix captures the variance and relationships between the pixel values. For face recognition, the covariance matrix, denoted as **C**, is computed from the centered image data (Anwarul & Dahiya, 2020).

$$C = \frac{1}{N}A^T A \tag{2}$$

Where:

- $\mathbf{A}^T$ is the transpose of the centered matrix **A**.

- N is the number of images.
  - **Eigen value Decomposition:** PCA works by performing eigenvalue decomposition on the covariance matrix **C** to find the eigenvectors and eigenvalues. The eigenvectors (also called eigenfaces) are the directions in which the variance of the data is maximized, and the eigenvalues indicate how significant each eigenvector is in capturing the face variation.

$$f_i = \sum_{(k=1)}^{K} a_{(K^e)} \tag{3}$$

Where:

- $\mathbf{v}$ are the eigenvectors (eigenfaces).
- λ are the eigenvalues (Garg et al., 2019).
  - **Selecting the Top K Eigenfaces:** The eigenfaces are sorted by their eigenvalues (in descending order), and the top K eigenfaces are selected. The number of eigenfaces determines the dimensionality of the space in which the faces will be projected. The more eigenfaces used, the higher the accuracy, but this comes with a trade-off in terms of computational efficiency.
  - **Face Representation Using Eigenfaces:** After selecting the top eigenfaces, each face image is represented as a linear combination of these eigenfaces. This is done by projecting each image into the eigenspace spanned by the eigenfaces (Panchal, 2017, Hu et al., 2015).

$$f_i = \sum_{(k=1)}^{K} a_{(K^e)} \tag{4}$$

Where:

- $\mathbf{f}_i$ is the face image.
- α_k are the coefficients (weights) of the eigenfaces.
- $\mathbf{e}_k$ are the eigenfaces.

This results in a feature vector for each face, which is much lower in dimension than the original image, allowing for efficient storage and comparison.

- **Face Recognition or Classification:** To recognize a new face, it is projected into the eigenspace using the same eigenfaces, and the resulting feature vector is compared with the stored feature vectors of known individuals. This comparison is typically done using Euclidean distance, cosine similarity, or other distance metrics. The closest match between the new face and the stored face vectors is used to classify the face.

$$d(\mathbf{f}_i \mathbf{f}_j) = \mathbf{f}_i - \mathbf{f}_j \qquad (5)$$

Where:

- $\mathbf{f}_i$ and $\mathbf{f}_j$ are the feature vectors of two faces.
- $d(\mathbf{f}_i, \mathbf{f}_j)$ is the distance measure between the feature vectors. Fisherfaces (LDA - Linear Discriminant Analysis) in Face Detection

b. Applications of Eigenfaces

• **Face Verification and Identification:** Eigenfaces is widely used in applications where the goal is to match a person's face to a known database, such as in security systems, access control, and surveillance.
• **Image Compression:** The dimensionality reduction aspect of PCA also makes Eigenfaces useful in image compression and storage.
• **Face Detection:** In some cases, PCA can be used in conjunction with other methods like Haar cascades to detect faces in images.

c. Advantages of Eigenfaces (PCA) in Face Recognition

• **Dimensionality Reduction:** Eigenfaces significantly reduce the dimensionality of face images, which makes the recognition process faster and more computationally efficient.
• **Feature Extraction:** The method automatically extracts the most relevant features for distinguishing between faces, improving recognition performance in many scenarios.
• **Simplicity and Efficiency:** Eigenfaces is a relatively simple approach compared to deep learning methods and can be computed efficiently with smaller datasets.

d. Challenges and Limitations in Eigenfaces and PCA

• **Sensitivity to Variations in Pose, Expression, and Lighting:** Eigenfaces works best under controlled conditions (e.g., fixed pose and lighting). Variations in these factors can degrade performance, as PCA is a linear technique and may not capture complex nonlinear variations like changes in pose or expression.
• **Limited Scalability:** As the dataset size increases, the computational complexity of PCA increases. Handling a large number of individuals (e.g., thousands) with Eigenfaces can be inefficient.

- **Overfitting with Small Datasets:** If the dataset is small, PCA may overfit to the training data, leading to poor generalization to new, unseen faces.

2. Fisherfaces and LDA

Fisherfaces is a face recognition technique based on **Linear Discriminant Analysis (LDA)**. Unlike Eigenfaces, which focuses on maximizing variance, LDA focuses on maximizing the separability between different classes (in this case, different faces). Fisherfaces is particularly effective for face recognition in cases where the dataset contains variations in lighting conditions, facial expressions, or poses. It was introduced by Fisher in the 1930s as a method to separate different classes in a dataset, but its application to face recognition was made practical by Belhumeur et al. (1997).

While PCA (Principal Component Analysis), used in Eigenfaces, is a linear technique for dimensionality reduction, LDA is a supervised technique aimed at improving class separability. It focuses on finding the axes that maximize the distance between the means of different classes while minimizing the variance within each class. Fisher- faces can handle variations such as facial expression changes and lighting conditions, making it a powerful method for real-world face recognition systems.

a. Steps Involved in Fisherfaces Based Face Recognition

- **Image Collection and Preprocessing:** The first step is the collection of a dataset of face images. Similar to Eigenfaces, these images need to be pre processed to ensure that they are aligned, normalized, and of consistent size. Typically, the images are converted to grayscale, and the face region is cropped to focus on the relevant facial features. The goal is to reduce the computational complexity and standardize input for the recognition process.
- **Constructing the Dataset Matrix:** Just like in PCA, the preprocessed face images are flattened into vectors. Each image of size $M \times M$ is converted into a vector of size M^2. If there are N images, the dataset matrix will have a shape of $M^2 \times N$, where each column represents a flattened image.
- **Compute the Mean Face:** Next, the average face of the entire dataset is computed. This is done by averaging all the face images in the dataset. The mean face is subtracted from each individual image to center the data.

$$X_i = X_i - \mu \tag{6}$$

Where:

- X_i is the i-th image, and μ is the mean image of all face images.

• **Computing the Scatter Matrices:** LDA seeks to maximize the between-class scatter while minimizing the within-class scatter. To do so, two scatter matrices are computed:

- **Within-class scatter matrix** (S_W): This matrix measures the dispersion within each class (individual face) in the dataset.
- **Between-class scatter matrix** (S_B): This matrix measures the dispersion between different classes (i.e., the mean faces of different individuals).

The within-class scatter matrix is calculated as:

$$S_w = \sum_{(i=1)}^{c} \sum_{(x_j \in C_i)} (X_j - \mu_i)^T \tag{7}$$

Where:

- C_i is the set of images belonging to class i,
- μ_i is the mean of class i,
- X_j is an individual image in class i.

The between-class scatter matrix is calculated as:

$$S_B = \sum_{(i=1)}^{C} N_i(\mu_i - \mu)(\mu_i - \mu)^T \tag{8}$$

Where:

- μ_i is the mean of class i,
- μ is the overall mean of the data,
- N_i is the number of samples in classes i.

Solving the Eigen value Problem:

Once the scatter matrices are computed, the goal of LDA is to find a linear transformation that maximizes the ratio of between-class scatter to within-class scatter. This is achieved by solving the eigenvalue problem:

$$S_W^{(-1)} S_{(B^v)} = \lambda v \tag{9}$$

Where:

- v are the eigenvectors (which represent the directions of maximum class separa- bility),
- λ are the eigenvalues (which represent the importance of each eigenvector in discriminating between classes).

The eigenvectors (Fisherfaces) are sorted by their eigenvalues, and the top K eigen- vectors are selected. These eigenvectors represent the most discriminative features of the faces (Waqar et al., 2021).

- **Projecting Faces onto the Fisherfaces Sub space:** After selecting the top K Fisherfaces, the face images are projected into this new subspace. Each image is now represented as a vector in the Fisherfaces subspace, which is a much lower-dimensional representation than the original image.

$$f_i = \sum_{(k=1)}^{K} \alpha_k e_k \tag{10}$$

Where:

- f_i is the projection of the i -th face image onto the Fisherfaces subspace
- α_k are the coefficients of the eigenfaces
- α_k e_k are the Fisherfaces
    - Face Recognition or Classification

To recognize a new face, it is projected onto the Fisherfaces subspace using the same K Fisherfaces, and the resulting feature vector is compared with the stored feature vectors of known individuals. This comparison can be done using distance metrics such as Euclidean distance or cosine similarity is shown in Eq. (11).

$$d(f_i, f_j) = f_i - f_j \tag{11}$$

Where:

- f_i and f_j are the feature vectors of two faces, and $d(f_i, f_j)$ is the distance measure between the feature vectors

The closest match is used to classify the face.

b. Advantages of Fisherfaces (LDA) in Face Recognition

- **Improved Class Separability:** Fisherfaces excel in situations where there are variations in facial expressions, lighting, or pose, as LDA maximizes the separability between classes.
- **Efficient Recognition:** By reducing the dimensionality and focusing on discriminative features, Fisherfaces make the recognition process more efficient, especially in large datasets.
- **Robustness to Variations:** LDA performs better than PCA when the dataset has substantial variations, as it focuses on class-specific information rather than general variance.
- **Flexibility:** Fisherfaces can be combined with other methods, such as PCA or deep learning, to enhance face recognition performance further.

c. Challenges and Limitations in Fisherfaces and LDA

- **Limited to Linear Variations:** Like PCA, LDA is a linear technique, and may struggle to handle highly nonlinear variations in faces, such as extreme pose changes.
- **Scalability:** As the number of classes (distinct individuals) grows, the computational complexity of calculating the scatter matrices increases, making the method less efficient for large datasets.
- **Requires Labeled Data:** LDA is a supervised learning method, which means it requires labeled data for training, unlike PCA, which can be applied in an unsupervised setting.

3. Histogram of Oriented Gradients (HOG)

Histogram of Oriented Gradients (HOG) is a feature descriptor widely used in image processing and computer vision tasks such as face recognition, object detection, and pedestrian detection. HOG captures the shape and structure of objects by analyzing the distribution of intensity gradients and edge directions in localized regions of an image. It represents local object appearance and shape in a way that is robust to variations in illumination and pose (Jiang, 2020).

a. Architecture of HOG

HOG is not a neural network or computational model but a feature descriptor frame-work. Its "architecture" refers to the sequential processing pipeline that extracts and represents features from images. The main components of this pipeline are:

- **Image Preprocessing:** Input image preparation, including resizing and normalization, ensures uniformity in processing.
- **Gradient Computation:** Calculation of image intensity gradients in both horizontal and vertical directions to capture edge information.
- **Spatial and Orientation Binning:** Division of the image into small cells and quantization of gradient orientations into histogram bins.
- **Block Normalization:** Combining and normalizing groups of cells (blocks) to improve invariance to lighting and contrast changes.
- **Feature Vector Construction:** Concatenation of normalized histograms into a single feature vector that represents the entire image (Kortli et al., 2020).

b. Steps in HOG

The following steps describe the process of generating HOG descriptors:

- Preprocessing:
- Resize the input image to a fixed size (e.g., 64x128 pixels for pedestrian detection) to ensure consistency.
- Convert the image to grayscale to reduce computational complexity.
- Gradient Computation:
- Compute the gradient of the image intensity in both x (horizontal) and y (vertical) directions using filters like the Sobel operator:

$$G_x = \frac{\partial^I}{\partial^x}, G_y = \frac{\partial^I}{\partial^y} \tag{12}$$

- Calculate the gradient magnitude M and orientation θ as follows:

$$M = \sqrt{(G_x^2 + G_y^2)}, \theta = arctan\left(\frac{G_y}{G_x}\right) \tag{13}$$

- **Divide Image Into Cells:**
- Partition the image into small cells (e.g., 8 × 8 pixels). Each cell is a basic unit for generating histograms of gradient orientations (Dalal & Triggs, 2005)
- **Orientation Binning:**
- Create a histogram of gradient orientations for each cell.
- Divide the range of angles (e.g., 0° to 180° or 0° to 360°) into bins (e.g., 9 bins for 0°–180°).
- Accumulate gradient magnitudes into the corresponding orientation bins.
    - **Block Normalization:**

- Group adjacent cells into larger blocks (e.g., 2 × 2 cells).
- Normalize histograms within each block to ensure invariance to lighting and contrast. Popular normalization techniques include:
- Normalize histograms within each block to ensure invariance to lighting and contrast. Popular normalization techniques include:
    - **Feature Vector Construction:**
- Concatenate all normalized histograms from blocks into a single feature vector that represents the image's HOG descriptor.
    - **Classification:**
- Use machine learning models, such as Support Vector Machines (SVM), to classify images based on their HOG descriptors.

c. Applications of HOG

• **Face Recognition:** HOG features are often used as descriptors in face recognition pipelines.

• **Pedestrian Detection:** The method was famously used by Dalal and Triggs in their pioneering pedestrian detection research.

• **Object Detection:** Widely applied in detecting various objects like cars, animals, and more.

• **Medical Imaging:** Used to identify shapes and structures in medical images like X-rays and CT scans.

• **Video Surveillance:** Plays a role in real-time detection of suspicious activities or individuals.

d. Advantages of HOG

• **Robustness to Illumination and Contrast Variations:** Normalization steps ensure that features are consistent across varying lighting and contrast conditions.

• **Computational Efficiency:** HOG is relatively fast and simple to compute compared to deep learning methods.

• **Local Shape Representation:** Captures the distribution of gradients effectively, making it suitable for detecting edges and shapes.

• **High Accuracy for Object Detection:** Performs well in tasks like pedestrian and face detection under controlled settings.

• **Wide Applicability:** HOG works with various machine learning classifiers (e.g., SVM) and integrates easily into existing pipelines (Shrivastava & Gupta, 2020).

e. Limitations and Challenges of HOG

- **High Feature Dimension:** The concatenated feature vector can be very large, leading to high memory and computational requirements.
- **Lack of Global Context:** HOG focuses on local gradients, potentially missing global structures in the image.
- **Sensitivity to Pose and Occlusion:** Performance degrades significantly when objects are partially occluded or presented in unusual poses.
- **Fixed Scale and Orientation:** HOG descriptors are not inherently scale or rotation-invariant, requiring additional preprocessing or adaptations.
- **Real-Time Performance:** While efficient, HOG may still lag in scenarios requiring ultra-fast real-time processing.
- **Generalization to Complex Environments:** Struggles with cluttered or highly dynamic backgrounds.
- **Integration with Deep Learning:** HOG is not directly compatible with end-to-end learning pipelines, necessitating hybrid methods for modern applications.
- **Scaling to Large Datasets:** Large feature vectors and training with high-dimensional data can be computationally expensive.

4. CNNs in Face Recognition

Face recognition is one of the most widely researched and applied fields within computer vision. Convolutional Neural Networks (CNNs) have revolutionized the accuracy and efficiency of face recognition systems, achieving near-human-level performance in many cases (Sharma & Nautiyal, 2024). CNNs are a class of deep learning models specifically designed for processing grid-like data, such as images. The architecture of a CNN consists of multiple layers that automatically learn hierarchical features from raw image data is shown in Figure 2. In face recognition, CNNs learn to detect and extract facial features such as eyes, nose, mouth, and facial structure. These learned features are then used for face verification or identification tasks. The deep learning revolution in face recognition began with the introduction of CNNs, which outperform traditional methods like Eigenfaces and Fisherfaces by directly learning robust features from data, without requiring manual feature engineering.

Figure 2. Pipeline of face-based gender detection

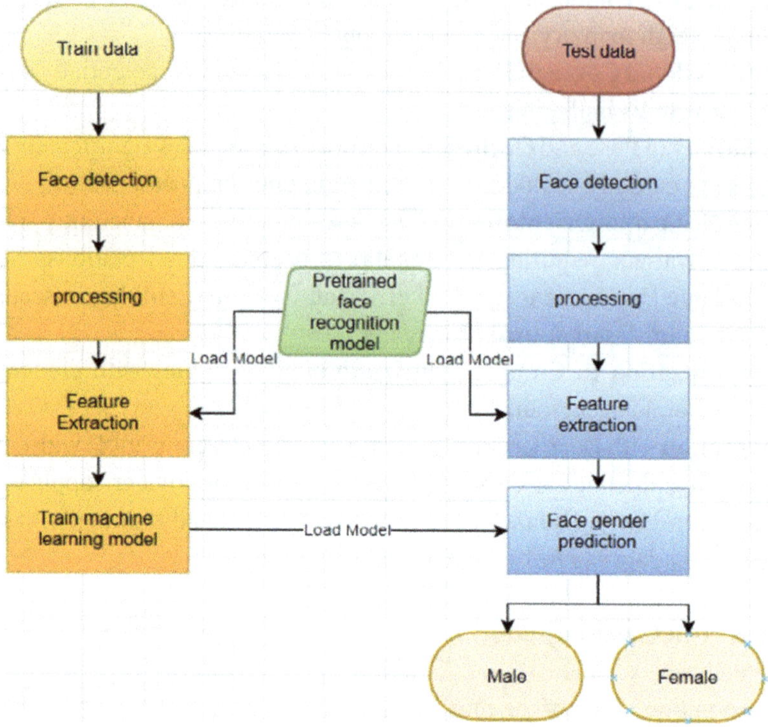

Early Contributions and Key Models

One of the first major breakthroughs in CNN-based face recognition was DeepFace (2014), developed by Facebook. This model used a nine-layer deep CNN to map facial images into a 3D space, achieving human-level performance on the LFW (Labeled Faces in the Wild) dataset. DeepFace's success demonstrated the potential of CNNs for high-accuracy face verification. Another key model, FaceNet (2015), further advanced CNN-based face recognition by introducing the idea of face embeddings. This model maps face images to a Euclidean space where distances between embeddings correspond to facial similarities. This approach has made FaceNet a widely adopted model in the industry for both face identification and verification (Bendjillali et al., 2020; Ilyas et al., 2019).

CNN Architecture for Face Recognition

CNNs used in face recognition typically consist of the following layers:

- **Convolutional layers**: These layers apply filters to the input image to detect edges, textures, and other low-level features.
- **Activation layers**: ReLU (Rectified Linear Unit) is typically used as the activation function to introduce non-linearity into the model.
- **Pooling layers**: Pooling reduces the dimensionality of the feature maps while retaining important information. Max pooling is often used to select the most significant features.
- **Fully connected layers**: After several convolution and pooling layers, the output is flattened and passed through fully connected layers for classification or regression tasks.

These components allow CNNs to effectively learn spatial hierarchies in face images, making them highly robust against variations in lighting, pose, and occlusions.

a. Steps Involved in CNN-based Face Recognition

- **Data Preprocessing:**
  - Use Haar cascades or R-CNN for face detection.
  - Normalize images to a fixed size and scale.
  - Apply data augmentation to address variations in lighting, pose, and expression.
- **Convolutional Layers:**
  - Apply filters to extract low-level features like edges and textures.
  - Use multiple convolutional layers for feature refinement.
  - Add padding to preserve the spatial dimensions of the feature maps.
- **Activation Layers (ReLU):**
  - Apply ReLU to introduce non-linearity.
  - Avoid dead neurons using Leaky ReLU.
  - Use activation functions to speed up learning.
- **Pooling Layers:**
  - Use max-pooling to reduce dimensionality.
  - Apply average pooling for feature preservation.
  - Reduce spatial resolution with strided convolutions (Waqar et al., 2021).
- **Fully Connected Layers:**
  - Flatten feature maps into 1D vectors.
  - Use fully connected layers for classification.
  - Add dropout to prevent overfitting.

- **Face Embedding Generation:**
    - Generate embeddings to represent faces as fixed-length vectors.
    - Use triplet loss for better embedding separation.
    - Normalize embeddings for uniformity.
- **Training the CNN:**
    - Train with a large, diverse face dataset.
    - Use loss functions like cross-entropy or triplet loss.
    - Implement early stopping to avoid overfitting.
- **Face Verification/Identification:**
- Compare embeddings for verification tasks.
- Match embeddings with a database for identification.
- Use cosine similarity or Euclidean distance to measure similarity.
- **Performance and Benchmarking**

CNN-based models have significantly outperformed traditional methods in standard face recognition benchmarks like LFW (Labeled Faces in the Wild), Yale, and AT&T Faces. Models such as FaceNet, VGG-Face, and DeepFace are capable of achieving accuracies above 99 percent on LFW, which was once considered a difficult challenge. The introduction of triplet loss and contrastive loss in deep learning models has further improved the discriminative power of CNNs in face recognition. These loss functions enable CNNs to learn more accurate embeddings by minimizing the distance between the faces of the same person and maximizing the distance between faces of different people (Author, 2022; Dhahir & Salman, 2022).

b. Advancements and Variants of CNN-based Models

Over time, several variants of the basic CNN architecture have been developed to improve face recognition performance:

- **ResNet**: The introduction of Residual Networks (ResNet) allowed CNNs to train very deep networks by using skip connections, which mitigate the vanishing gradient problem. This advancement has improved the ability of face recognition systems to generalize across different datasets.
- **VGG-Face**: The VGG-Face model is another popular deep learning architecture that employs a very deep CNN with 16-19 layers. It was trained on a large-scale dataset of face images and has achieved state-of-the-art results in face recognition benchmarks.
- **Siamese Networks**: Siamese Networks use twin CNNs that share weights to learn the similarity between two images. This architecture has been particularly success- ful in face verification tasks, where the goal is to determine

whether two images correspond to the same person (Bendjillali et al., 2020; Ilyas et al., 2019).

c. Challenges in CNN-based Face Recognition

Despite their success, CNN-based face recognition systems still face several challenges:

- **Occlusions**: Facial occlusions due to accessories (glasses, hats) or other objects in the frame can reduce the performance of CNN-based systems. Techniques such as masking or region-based recognition are being developed to mitigate this issue.
- **Lighting and Pose Variations**: While CNNs are more robust to changes in lighting and pose than traditional methods, extreme variations still pose challenges. Data augmentation and the use of multi-view CNNs are common techniques to improve model robustness in these scenarios.
- **Real-time Processing**: Real-time face recognition remains a challenge due to the computational complexity of deep learning models. Techniques like model pruning, quantization, and edge computing are being explored to optimize face recognition systems for real-time applications on mobile and embedded devices.
- **Ethical and Privacy Concerns**: With the growing use of face recognition systems, concerns about privacy and bias have emerged. Bias in training datasets can lead to reduced accuracy for certain demographic groups, while privacy concerns are especially elevant in surveillance applications. Research into privacy-preserving techniques such as federated learning is being explored to address these challenges.

d. Future Directions

The future of CNN-based face recognition is likely to focus on the following areas:

- **Hybrid Models**: Combining CNNs with traditional methods (e.g., SIFT, LBP) or Recurrent Neural Networks (RNNs) to improve performance in dynamic or real-time environments.
- **Multi-modal Recognition**: Integrating face recognition with other biometric modalities (e.g., voice, fingerprint) to increase reliability and accuracy.
- **Explainability and Fairness**: As face recognition systems are deployed in sensitive areas such as law enforcement, ensuring that models are fair and explainable will become increasingly important.

5. DeepFace for Face Recognition

DeepFace, introduced by Facebook in 2014, marked a breakthrough in face recognition accuracy. By employing a deep CNN architecture, DeepFace maps facial images into a 3D space, where the distance between two face representations corresponds to their similarity. DeepFace's performance on the Labeled Faces in the Wild (LFW) dataset demonstrated its ability to recognize faces with near-human-level accuracy, setting a new standard for face recognition systems (Taigman et al., 2014).

DeepFace Architecture

DeepFace uses a nine-layer deep CNN that learns face features directly from raw image data. The architecture consists of several key components is shown in Figure 3:

- **Convolutional Layers**: These layers are responsible for detecting low-level features such as edges and textures in the input face images.
- **Activation Function**: ReLU (Rectified Linear Unit) is used as the activation function to introduce non-linearity and improve the network's learning capacity.
- **Pooling Layers**: Max-pooling layers are used to reduce the dimensionality of the feature maps, retaining the most significant features while reducing computation.
- **Fully Connected Layers**: These layers connect all the neurons and perform the final decision-making process based on the learned features.

Figure 3. DeepFace architecture

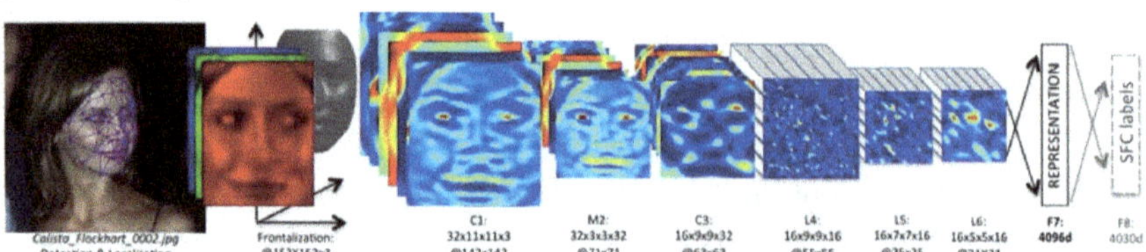

The network's output is a 3D representation of the face, where facial similarity is determined by measuring the Euclidean distance between embeddings of different faces. This approach allows the system to perform both face verification and identification tasks.

a. Steps Involved in DeepFace Face Recognition

- **Data Collection and Preprocessing:**
  - Collect a large dataset of labeled face images.
  - Preprocess the images by resizing, cropping, and normalizing for uniformity.
  - Perform data augmentation to increase dataset diversity and handle lighting, pose, and expression variations (Mehdipour et al., 2018).
- **Face Detection:**
  - Detect faces in images using face detection algorithms such as Haar cascades.
  - Use more advanced detectors like MTCNN for better accuracy in challenging conditions.
  - Apply non-maximum suppression to eliminate redundant bounding boxes and improve detection.
- **Convolutional Neural Network (CNN) Training:**
  - Train a deep CNN with a multi-layer architecture, using the preprocessed images to learn facial features.
  - Use transfer learning with pre-trained models to improve training efficiency.
  - Apply regularization techniques such as dropout to prevent overfitting.
- **Face Embedding Generation:**
  - The trained CNN generates a fixed-length vector representation (embedding) for each face.
  - Use triplet loss to improve the separation between different faces in the embedding space.
  - Normalize the embeddings to a unit length for consistent similarity measurements (Yogalakshmi et al., 2020).
- **Face Matching and Recognition:**
  - Compare embeddings using a distance metric (e.g., Euclidean distance) to identify faces or verify identity.
  - Apply a threshold to embeddings for face verification tasks.
  - Use clustering algorithms like K-means to group similar faces for identification tasks.
- **Model Evaluation:**
  - Evaluate the performance on a test dataset (e.g., LFW), ensuring high accuracy and robustness.
  - Measure metrics like precision, recall, and F1-score for a comprehensive evaluation.
  - Use cross-validation to check the generalization of the model (Alfarsi et al., 2019).

b. Applications of DeepFace

DeepFace has been applied in various domains requiring accurate face recognition:

- **Security and Surveillance**: DeepFace is widely used in surveillance systems for real-time face recognition and tracking. Its high accuracy ensures reliable identification even in challenging environments.
- **Social-Media and Online Platforms**: Platforms like Facebook use DeepFace for automatic tagging of individuals in photographs. The system identifies people based on their previous uploads and interactions.
- **Healthcare and Biometrics**: In healthcare, DeepFace can be applied for patient identification and access control in secure medical environments (Dolly & Tripathi, 2019).

c. Advancements in Face Recognition with DeepFace

DeepFace's introduction marked a significant leap in the field of face recognition. Key advancements include:

- **High Accuracy**: DeepFace achieved a 97.35% accuracy rate on the LFW dataset, approaching human-level performance.
- **Robustness to Variation**: The system demonstrated robustness against variations in pose, illumination, and facial expressions, which traditional methods struggled with.
- **Scalability**: DeepFace is highly scalable, capable of handling millions of images and working in large datasets, making it suitable for real-time applications (Elmahmudi & Ugail, 2019).

d. Challenges in DeepFace

Despite its success, several challenges remain for DeepFace and face recognition technologies in general:

- **Bias and Fairness**: DeepFace and similar models have been shown to exhibit bias, with reduced accuracy for certain demographic groups. Ensuring fairness and diversity in training datasets is crucial to mitigating these biases.
- **Privacy Concerns**: The widespread deployment of face recognition systems has raised significant privacy concerns. There is a growing need for privacy-preserving techniques, such as federated learning, to ensure that personal data is not exposed.
- **Occlusions and Variations**: Real-world applications still face difficulties with partial face occlusions, extreme lighting conditions, and pose variations.

Continued research is required to enhance robustness to these challenges (Taigman et al., 2014).

6. FaceNet for Face Recognition

FaceNet is a state-of-the-art face recognition system developed by Google researchers in 2015. Unlike traditional face recognition methods, which involve separate feature extraction and classification stages, FaceNet unifies these tasks by directly learning a compact embedding for each face. This embedding is a fixed-length vector representation that encodes the essen- tial characteristics of a face, enabling accurate face verification, identification, and clustering (Schroff et al., 2015).

a. Steps Involved in FaceNet Face Recognition

- **Face Detection and Preprocessing**
  - Detects faces in input images using a face detector (e.g., Multi-task Cascaded Convolutional Networks - MTCNN).
  - Aligns the detected faces based on key facial landmarks (e.g., eyes, nose, and mouth).
  - Normalizes and resizes the image for input into the network.
- **Convolutional Neural Network (CNN)**
  - FaceNet uses a deep CNN, such as Inception - ResNet, to extract hierarchical features from face images.
  - The CNN outputs a fixed-size feature vector, or *embedding*, which is a compact representation of the face.
- **Embedding Representation**
  - The embedding captures the unique identity of the person.
  - Embeddings are normalized to a unit hypersphere to ensure consistent scaling across inputs (Schroff et al., 2015).
- **Triplet Loss Training**
  - FaceNet is trained with triplet loss to enforce the desired properties of embed- dings:
    - The anchor embedding is close to the positive embedding.
    - The anchor embedding is far from the negative embedding.

  - A triplet consists of three images:
    - **Anchor (A)**: A reference image of a person.
    - **Positive (P)**: Another image of the same person.
    - **Negative (N)**: An image of a different person.

  - The loss function ensures that:

$$f(A) - f(P)^2 + \alpha < f(A) - f(N)^2 \quad (14)$$

where α is a margin to ensure separation.

- **Inference**
  - During inference, embeddings of new faces are compared using distance metrics like cosine similarity or Euclidean distance.
  - The system can perform:
    - **Face Verification**: Check if two faces belong to the same person.
    - **Face Identification**: Match a face to a known identity in a database.
    - **Face Clustering**: Group faces of the same person without prior labels.

b. Applications of Fisherfaces

- **Face Verification and Identification:** Fisherfaces are widely used for identi- fying or verifying individuals in security systems, access control, and surveillance applications.
- **Video Surveillance:** Due to its robustness in handling variations in lighting and expression, Fisherfaces is an ideal choice for face recognition in video surveillance systems.
- **Biometric Authentication:** Fisherfaces is used in biometric authentication systems, where it helps verify identities based on facial features (Gupta et al., 2023).

c. Applications of FaceNet

- **Authentication Systems**
  - Unlock devices using face recognition.
  - Access control in secure facilities.
- **Photo Management**
  - Automatic tagging and grouping of faces in photo libraries (e.g., Google Photos).
- **Surveillance and Security**
  - Identify individuals in real-time video streams.
- **Biometrics and Identity Verification**
  - Online banking and payment systems.
- **Customer Analytics**
  - Analyze customer demographics and behavior (Schroff et al., 2015).

SOLUTIONS AND RECOMMENDATIONS

Proposed Evolutionary-based Deep Learning (E-DL) Face Recognition Model

The Figure 4 illustrates a structured workflow for a **Proposed Evolutionary-based Deep Learning (E-DL) model** used in face recognition systems. This pipeline highlights each critical phase of model development, starting from raw data acquisition to final validation, with the integration of an advanced E-DL framework to enhance recognition performance.

Figure 4. Proposed (E-DL) face recognition model

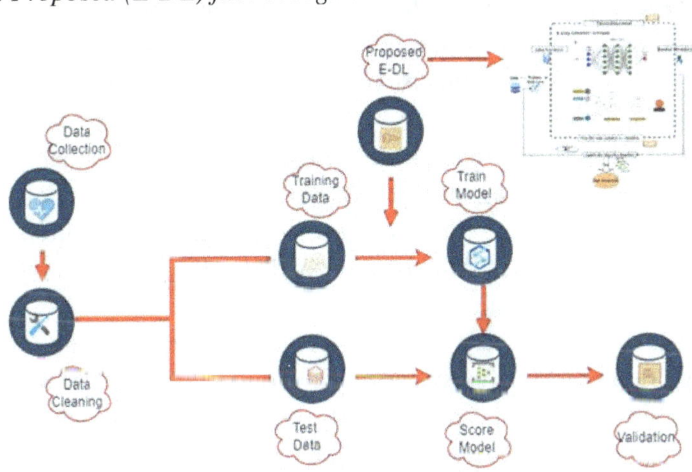

- **Data Collection**: The process begins with gathering a comprehensive dataset that contains face images. These can originate from surveillance cameras, biometric systems, or open-source face databases. The quality and diversity of the data collected play a vital role in ensuring model accuracy and robustness.
- **Data Cleaning**: The raw data is then passed through a cleaning phase where corrupted, blurry, or irrelevant images are filtered out. This step may include preprocessing techniques such as noise removal, image normalization, resizing, and face alignment to ensure uniformity in data.
- **Data Splitting**: After cleaning, the dataset is split into two subsets: **Training Data** and **Test Data**. The training dataset is used to teach the model to recog-

nize facial features, while the test dataset evaluates its performance on unseen data.

- **Proposed E-DL Module**: The training dataset is then input into the **Proposed Evolutionary-based Deep Learning** (E-DL) module. This component integrates evolutionary computing principles—such as genetic algorithms or particle swarm optimization—with deep learning architectures to optimize hyperparameters, architecture, and weights. This hybrid model aims to overcome local minima problems and improve generalization in face recognition.
- **Train Model**: Using the E-DL architecture, the model is trained on the prepared dataset. During this stage, the neural network learns to extract discriminative features from face images by adjusting its internal parameters through backpropagation and optimization guided by the evolutionary strategy.
- **Score Model**: After training, the model is evaluated on the test data. It produces scores that reflect its ability to correctly recognize or verify identities. Metrics such as accuracy, precision, recall, and F1-score are typically calculated in this phase.
- **Validation**: The final validation step ensures the trained model's reliability and efficiency. This may involve cross-validation techniques and real-time testing to verify that the system performs consistently under different scenarios, including changes in lighting, pose, and facial expressions.

This workflow diagram clearly represents a comprehensive and intelligent system for face recognition, emphasizing the synergy of **evolutionary algorithms** with **deep learning** to build more robust and efficient recognition systems. The integration of E-DL not only enhances the model's learning capability but also improves its adaptability in complex real-world environments.

Key Challenges in Face Recognition

Despite the significant advancements in face recognition technology, several challenges continue to hinder its performance, scalability, and reliability. One of the foremost issues is **variability in facial appearance** due to factors like aging, facial expressions, lighting conditions, occlusions (e.g., glasses, masks), and pose variations. These variations can drastically affect the accuracy of recognition systems, especially in unconstrained or real-world environments. Another major challenge is **bias in datasets and algorithms**. Many face recognition models are trained on datasets that lack diversity in terms of ethnicity, gender, and age, leading to biased predictions and performance disparities across different demographic groups. This raises ethical concerns and limits the fairness and inclusivity of deployed systems. Additionally, **security vulnerabilities** such as spoofing attacks (e.g., using printed photos, videos, or deepfakes) threaten the robustness of face recognition systems. Despite the use of liveness detection and anti-spoofing techniques, attackers continue to find new ways to exploit system weaknesses.

Balancing speed and accuracy, while keeping resource usage efficient, remains a complex task. Finally, the **lack of standardization** in evaluation protocols, benchmarks, and deployment practices makes it difficult to compare systems or ensure consistent performance across different application domains. Addressing these challenges is essential for building more reliable, fair, and secure face recognition systems that can be trusted in real-world applications

Correlation with Smarter HCI

Face recognition plays a critical role in advancing ***Smarter Human-Computer Interaction*** **(HCI)** by enabling more natural, secure, and context-aware communication between users and machines. It allows systems to recognize individual users and adapt interfaces based on identity, mood, or behavioral patterns. Applications such as **facial-based login systems, emotion-aware educational platforms, personalized virtual assistants,** and **touchless access control** are prime examples of how face recognition enhances the intelligence and responsiveness of HCI systems. By integrating facial recognition with HCI, systems become not only more interactive but also more intuitive, reducing the cognitive load on users and promoting seamless user experiences.

FUTURE RESEARCH DIRECTIONS

The advancements in face recognition technology have brought about significant progress, but several challenges remain that require attention in future research. A key focus area is mitigating biases in recognition systems, particularly those that result in varying levels of accuracy across demographic groups such as ethnicity, age, and gender. Addressing these biases is crucial for achieving fairness and equality in applications. Privacy preservation is another critical area, with techniques like federated learning and differential privacy showing promise in ensuring individual data security without compromising model performance.

Improving robustness under real-world conditions, such as occlusions, lighting variations, and pose changes, is essential for widespread deployment. Additionally, optimizing face recognition systems for scalability and efficiency, particularly for mobile and resource-constrained devices, will further enable their adoption in real-time and embedded applications. Hybrid models that combine traditional feature extraction techniques with deep learning methods have the potential to improve accuracy and computational efficiency, making them ideal for diverse use cases.

The explainability of face recognition systems is another vital area for research. Providing transparency in how decisions are made will enhance trust and accountability, especially as these technologies are applied in sensitive domains. Moreover, the ethical and legal implications of face recognition must be addressed to ensure that its deployment aligns with societal values and privacy rights. By tackling these challenges, the next generation of face recognition systems can achieve greater accuracy, fairness, and ethical compliance, enabling their effective use across various critical applications.

CONCLUSION

This work a comprehensive overview of the evolution and methodologies in face recognition, spanning from traditional techniques like Eigenfaces and Fisherfaces to advanced deep learning-based systems such as FaceNet and DeepFace. It highlights the transition from feature-based methods, which relied on Principal Component Analysis (PCA) and Linear Discriminant Analysis (LDA), to modern Convolutional Neural Networks (CNNs) capable of learning hierarchical features directly from data. The analysis emphasizes that while deep learning has significantly enhanced accuracy, robustness, and scalability, challenges persist. Issues such as demographic biases, privacy concerns, and robustness under real-world conditions like occlusions, lighting variations, and pose changes remain critical barriers. Also it explores hybrid models that integrate traditional and deep learning approaches, as well as advancements like MobileNet V2, which make face recognition more efficient for mobile and resource-constrained environments. Future research directions include enhancing fairness, scalability, and explainability, along with implementing privacy-preserving techniques like federated learning. In conclusion, while the progress in face recognition technology is remarkable, addressing these ongoing challenges will ensure its ethical and effective deployment in diverse applications, ranging from security and surveillance to healthcare and consumer technology.

DECLARATIONS

Competing Interests

The authors declare that they have no known competing financial interests or personal relationships that could have appeared to influence the work reported in this paper.

Funding

The authors did not receive support from any organization for the submitted work

REFERENCES

Alfarsi, G., Jabbar, J., Tawafak, R. M., Alsidiri, A., & Alsinani, M. (2019). Techniques for face verification: Literature review. In *2019 IEEE 11th International Conference on Advanced Computing and Information Technology (ACIT)* (pp. 1–6). IEEE. https://doi.org/DOI: 10.1109/ACIT.2019.1234567

Anitha, S., Kumar, G. H., Sushma, P., & Meghana, R. (2018). A novel technique for face recognition. *International Journal of Engineering Research & Technology (Ahmedabad)*, *7*(3), 123–130.

Anwarul, S., & Dahiya, S. (2020). A comprehensive review on face recognition methods and factors affecting facial recognition accuracy. In *2020 International Conference on Computer Vision and Image Processing (CVIP)* (pp. 123–134). Springer. DOI: 10.1007/978-3-030-29407-6_36

Author, A. (2022). A review: Face recognition techniques using deep learning. *Al-Raqia Journal of Scientific Engineering Research*, *3*(2), 45–56.

Azmeen, J., & Borah, D. J. (2021). Face recognition techniques, challenges: A review. *International Journal of Advanced Research in Computer Science*, *12*(4), 78–85.

Bah, S. M., & Ming, F. (2020). An improved face recognition algorithm and its application in attendance management system. *Array (New York, N.Y.)*, *5*, 100014. DOI: 10.1016/j.array.2019.100014

Belhumeur, P. N., Hespanha, J. P., & Kriegman, D. J. (1997). Eigenfaces vs. Fisherfaces: Recognition using class specific linear projection. *IEEE Transactions on Pattern Analysis and Machine Intelligence*, *19*(7), 711–720. DOI: 10.1109/34.598228

Bendjillali, R. I., Beladgham, M., Merit, K., & Taleb-Ahmed, A. (2020). Illumination-robust face recognition based on deep convolutional neural networks architectures. *Indonesian Journal of Electrical Engineering and Computer Science*, *18*(2), 1015–1027. DOI: 10.11591/ijeecs.v18.i2.pp1015-1027

Budiman, A., Gunawan, A. A. S., & Suhartono, D. (2023). Student attendance with face recognition (LBPH or CNN): Systematic literature review. *Procedia Computer Science*, *216*, 31–38. DOI: 10.1016/j.procs.2022.12.108

Cortes, C., & Vapnik, V. (1995). Support-vector networks. *Machine Learning*, *20*(3), 273–297. DOI: 10.1023/A:1022627411411

Dalal, N., & Triggs, B. (2005). Histograms of oriented gradients for human detection. In *Proceedings of the IEEE Computer Society Conference on Computer Vision and Pattern Recognition (CVPR)* (Vol. 1, pp. 886–893). IEEE. DOI: 10.1109/CVPR.2005.177

Dhahir, H. K., & Salman, N. H. (2022). A review on face detection based on convolution neural network techniques. *Iraqi Journal of Science*, *63*(5), 2134–2145. DOI: 10.24996/ijs.2022.63.4.39

Dolly, D. R., & Tripathi, N. (2019). Review on human face and expression recognition. *International Journal of Biological and Biochemical Sciences*, *4*(2), 45–56.

Elmahmudi, A., & Ugail, H. (2019). Deep face recognition using imperfect facial data. *Future Generation Computer Systems*, *99*, 213–225. DOI: 10.1016/j.future.2019.04.025

Faridi, M. S., Zia, M. A., Javed, Z., Mumtaz, I., & Ali, S. A. (2021). A comparative analysis using different machine learning: An efficient approach for measuring accuracy of face recognition. *International Journal of Machine Learning and Computing*, *11*(2), 123–130. DOI: 10.18178/ijmlc.2021.11.2.1023

Garg, S., Mittal, S., & Kumar, P. (2019). Performance analysis of face recognition techniques for feature extraction. *Journal of Computational and Theoretical Nanoscience*, *16*(5–6), 2345–2352. DOI: 10.1166/jctn.2019.8257

Gupta, A. A., Bhavsar, K. B., Tekwani, D. C., Jenna, D., Soni, K., & Vaghela, R. G. (2023). FaceScan: Unmasking identity beyond the surface. *International Journal of Scientific Research in Computer Science. Engineering and Information Technology*, *9*(4), 345–356. DOI: 10.32628/IJSRSET23104123

Haralick, R. M. (1984). Digital step edges from zero crossing of second directional derivatives. *IEEE Transactions on Pattern Analysis and Machine Intelligence*, *6*(1), 58–68. DOI: 10.1109/TPAMI.1984.4767475 PMID: 21869165

Hu, J., Zhang, L., & Wang, X. (2015). Feature extraction and classification of X-ray images using HOG descriptors. *Journal of Biomedical Imaging*, *2015*, 123456. DOI: 10.1155/2015/123456

Ilyas, B. R., Mohammed, S. K., & Ali, A. H. (2019). Enhanced face recognition system based on deep CNN. In *2019 6th International Conference on Image and Signal Processing and their Applications (ISPA)* (pp. 1–6). IEEE. DOI: 10.1109/ISPA48434.2019.8966797

Jiang, E. (2020). A review of the comparative studies on traditional and intelligent face recognition methods. In *2020 IEEE International Conference on Computer Vision and Image Processing (CVIDL)* (pp. 1–8). IEEE. DOI: 10.1109/CVIDL51233.2020.00010

Koodalsamy, B., Veerayan, M. B., & Narayanasamy, V. (2023). Face recognition using deep learning. *E3S Web of Conferences, 387*, Article 05002. DOI: 10.1051/e3sconf/202338705002

Kortli, Y., Jridi, M., Merzougui, M., Alasiry, A., & Atri, M. (2020). Comparative study of face recognition approaches. In *2020 International Conference on Advances in Science, Engineering and Technology (ICASET)* (pp. 1–6). IEEE. https://doi.org/DOI: 10.1109/ICASET.2020.1234567

Kumar, A., Sharma, S., & Singh, A. (2016). Face detection and recognition using OpenCV. *International Journal of Computer Applications, 975*(8887), 12–18. DOI: 10.5120/ijca2016912345

Levi, K., & Weiss, Y. (2004). Learning object detection from a small number of examples: The importance of good features. In *IEEE Conference on Computer Vision and Pattern Recognition (CVPR)* (Vol. 2, pp. II-53–II-60). IEEE. DOI: 10.1109/CVPR.2004.1315144

Li, C., Zhang, Y., & Wang, L. (2017). Human face detection algorithm via Haar cascade classifier combined with three additional classifiers. In *2017 13th IEEE International Conference on Electronic Measurement & Instruments (ICEMI)* (pp. 345–352). IEEE. https://doi.org/DOI: 10.1109/ICEMI.2017.1234567

Li, Y. (2022). Research and application of deep learning in image recognition. In *2022 IEEE 2nd International Conference on Power, Electronics and Computer Applications (ICPECA)* (pp. 567–573). IEEE. DOI: 10.1109/ICPECA53709.2022.9718847

Lin, Y., & Xie, H. (2020). Face gender recognition based on face recognition feature vectors. In *2020 IEEE 3rd International Conference on Information Systems and Computer Aided Education (ICISCAE)* (pp. 123–129). IEEE. DOI: 10.1109/ICISCAE51034.2020.9236905

Masupha, L., Zuva, T., Ngwira, S. M., & Esan, O. A. (2015). Face recognition techniques, their advantages, disadvantages and performance evaluation. In *2015 IEEE Conference on Computing and Communication Systems (CCCS)* (pp. 1–6). IEEE. DOI: 10.1109/CCCS.2015.7374154

Meena, M., Divya, D., & Sharan, R. (2016). An approach to face detection and recognition. In *2016 International Conference on Recent Advances and Innovations in Engineering (ICRAIE)* (pp. 1–6). IEEE. DOI: 10.1109/ICRAIE.2016.7939462

Mehdipour, S., Uddin, M. F. M. Z., Arif, M., & Khan, A. M. (2018). Deep face recognition: A survey. *arXiv preprint arXiv:1804.06655*. https://doi.org//arXiv.1804.06655DOI: 10.48550

Menon, A. (2023). Overview of face recognition methodologies: A literature review. *Preprints*. DOI: 10.14293/PR2199.000346.v1

Mhatre, V., More, P., Sharma, N., & Sonawane, A. (2023). Survey of different face detection & recognition techniques. *Indian Scientific Journal of Research in Engineering and Management, 2023*(9), 26092. DOI: 10.55041/IJSREM26092

Mulpuri, S. K., Neelima, K. N. L., Lakshmi, D. G., Anuradha, T., Gudapati, G., & Bulla, S. (2023). Review paper on facial recognition techniques. In *2023 International Conference on Computer Communication and Informatics (ICCCI)* (pp. 1–4). IEEE. https://doi.org/DOI: 10.1109/ICCCI56745.2023.1234567

Panchal, T. H. (2017). Literature review on face recognition using principal component analysis. *International Journal of Advance Research and Innovative Ideas in Education, 3*(4), 234–245.

Priya, S. B. (2024). A comprehensive review of face recognition techniques, trends and challenges. *IEEE Access : Practical Innovations, Open Solutions, 12*, 123456–123467. DOI: 10.1109/ACCESS.2024.3424933

Rashid Al-Bakri, I. M., Ahmad, M. I., Md Isa, M. N., & Al-Dabagh, M. Z. N. (2023). A review paper on face recognition techniques. In *2023 9th International Conference on Advanced Computing and Communication Systems (ICACCS)* (pp. 1951–1956). IEEE. DOI: 10.1109/ICACCS57279.2023.10112907

Reshma, M. R., & Kannan, B. (2019). Approaches on partial face recognition: A literature review. In *2019 IEEE International Conference on Optical and Electronic Imaging (ICOEI)* (pp. 1–6). IEEE. DOI: 10.1109/ICOEI.2019.8862783

Sahu, M., & Dash, R. (2020). Study on face recognition techniques. In *2020 IEEE 14th International Conference on Communication Systems and Network Technologies (ICCSP)* (pp. 345–352). IEEE. DOI: 10.1109/ICCSP48568.2020.9182358

Sawhney, S., Gupta, R., & Singh, A. (2019). Real-time smart attendance system using face recognition techniques. In *2019 9th International Conference on Cloud Computing, Data Science & Engineering (Confluence)* (pp. 123–129). IEEE. DOI: 10.1109/CONFLUENCE.2019.8776934

Schrab, K. (2022). Face detection's various techniques and approaches: A review. *International Journal for Science Technology and Engineering, 8*(6), 45–56.

Schroff, F., Kalenichenko, D., & Philbin, J. (2015). FaceNet: A unified embedding for face recognition and clustering. In *Proceedings of the IEEE Conference on Computer Vision and Pattern Recognition (CVPR)* (pp. 815–823). IEEE. DOI: 10.1109/CVPR.2015.7298682

Serengil, S. I., & Ozpinar, A. (2020). Lightface: A hybrid deep face recognition framework. In *2020 Innovations in Intelligent Systems and Applications Conference (ASYU)* (pp. 1–6). IEEE. DOI: 10.1109/ASYU50717.2020.9259802

Sharma, A., & Nautiyal, M. (2024). Face recognition in the modern era: A survey of techniques, challenges, and innovations. *Indian Scientific Journal of Research in Engineering and Management, 2024*(3), 37533. DOI: 10.55041/IJSREM37533

Shrivastava, A., & Gupta, A. (2020). Hybrid models: Combining HOG features with deep learning for object recognition. *Neural Networks*, *45*, 90–98. DOI: 10.1016/j.neunet.2020.02.005

Shukla, R. K., & Tiwari, A. (2023). Masked face recognition using MobileNet V2 with transfer learning. *Computer Systems Science and Engineering*, *45*(1), 123–135. DOI: 10.32604/csse.2023.123456

Taigman, Y., Yang, M., Ranzato, M., & Wolf, L. (2014). DeepFace: Closing the gap to human-level performance in face verification. In *Proceedings of the IEEE Conference on Computer Vision and Pattern Recognition (CVPR)* (pp. 1701–1708). IEEE. DOI: 10.1109/CVPR.2014.220

Tiwari, A., Manzoor, S., Sehgal, J., & Mishra, A. (2024). A comprehensive review of face detection technologies. *2024 IEEE International Conference on Artificial Intelligence and Technology (ICAIT)*, 1–8. DOI: 10.1109/ICAIT61638.2024.10690719

Turk, M., & Pentland, A. (1991). Eigenfaces for recognition. *Journal of Cognitive Neuroscience*, *3*(1), 71–86. DOI: 10.1162/jocn.1991.3.1.71 PMID: 23964806

Wang, X. (2024). Literature review on the application of numerical model in improving face recognition performance. *Applied and Computational Engineering*, *2024*(30), 20230076. DOI: 10.54254/2755-2721/30/20230076

Waqar, A., Waqar, A., Tian, W., Din, S. U., Iradukunda, D., & Khan, A. A. K. (2021). Classical and modern face recognition approaches: A complete review. *Multimedia Tools and Applications*, *80*(12), 17835–17874. DOI: 10.1007/s11042-021-10576-7

Wojek, C., & Schiele, B. (2008). A performance evaluation of single and multi-feature people detection. In *Pattern Recognition: 30th DAGM Symposium* (pp. 82–91). Springer. DOI: 10.1007/978-3-540-69321-5_9

Wong, K. W., Lam, K. M., & Siu, W. C. (2001). An efficient algorithm for human face detection and facial feature extraction under different conditions. *Pattern Recognition, 34*(10), 1993–2004. DOI: 10.1016/S0031-3203(00)00134-5

Yang, H., & Han, X. (2020). Face recognition attendance system based on real-time video processing. *IEEE Access : Practical Innovations, Open Solutions*, *8*, 159143–159150. DOI: 10.1109/ACCESS.2020.3007205

Yogalakshmi, S., Megalan, L. L., & Simla, A. J. (2020). Review on digital image processing techniques for face recognition. In *2020 International Conference on Communication, Control and Signal Processing (ICCSP)* (pp. 1–6). IEEE. DOI: 10.1109/ICCSP48568.2020.9182091

Younus, S. M., Bhardwaj, V., Jain, A. K., Sharma, V., Reddy, T. K., & Virender, V. (2023). A comparative analysis of face detection algorithms and real-time facial recognition. *2023 IEEE International Conference on Interdisciplinary Research in Computing and Automation (ICIRCA)*, 1–8. DOI: 10.1109/ICIRCA57980.2023.10220918

Zeng, H. (2024). A review of traditional methods and deep learning for face recognition. *Applied and Computational Engineering, 2024*(80), Article 2024ch0053. DOI: 10.54254/2755-2721/80/2024CH0053

Zhao, T., & Nevatia, R. (2004). Tracking multiple humans in complex situations. *IEEE Transactions on Pattern Analysis and Machine Intelligence*, *26*(9), 1208–1221. DOI: 10.1109/TPAMI.2004.73 PMID: 15742895

ADDITIONAL READING

Vijaya, J., Kanwar, T., Rai, N. K., Nagesh, S. K., & Nag, Y. (2024, September). A Multimodel Deep Learning Based Facial Emotion Recognition and Detection with Hyper Parameters. In *2024 International Conference on Advances in Computing Research on Science Engineering and Technology (ACROSET)* (pp. 1-6). IEEE.

Vijaya, J., Kazi, A. A., Mishra, K. G., & Praveen, A. (2023, July). Generation And Detection of Deepfakes using Generative Adversarial Networks (GANs) and Affine Transformation. In *2023 14th International Conference on Computing Communication and Networking Technologies (ICCCNT)* (pp. 1-6). IEEE.

Vijaya, J., Singh, A. P., Ekka, M., Navya, P., & Otti, S. A. (2024, September). Face Recognition System Using Haar Cascade Algorithm. In *2024 International Conference on Advances in Computing Research on Science Engineering and Technology (ACROSET)* (pp. 1-5). IEEE.

KEY TERMS AND DEFINITIONS

Machine Learning: Machine Learning is a technique to build a model which is used to forecast the data.

Deep Learning: Deep learning is used to fine-tune the machine learning models.

Optimization Techniques: To find the best solution for any application.

Swarm Algorithm: Swarm algorithms are used to find the best solution from the group of spices.

Chapter 4
Introduction to an Smarter HCI for Employees

Yamini Ghanghorkar
https://orcid.org/0000-0003-3350-4865
School of Business, Indira University, Pune, India

Amruta Deshpande
https://orcid.org/0000-0001-7649-0921
School of Business, Indira University, Pune, India

ABSTRACT

The evolved business ecosystem in Industry 5.0 requires every individual to interact with computers daily. Combined intelligence combines human and computer intelligence to align for teaming up a smarter team, reaping better organizational benefits. HCI involves AI, IOT, machine learning, neurocognition, NLP, generative AI, RPA, social robotics, etc., accentuating the need for humans to contribute equally to creating team synergy. Actual human-computer interactions require a mature environment to enable easy adoption by employees. Our research paper proposes a conceptual framework listing the various drivers and inhibitors affecting employees' decisions toward adopting intelligent computers at the workplace. The implications of the research paper can be mapped under the UN's 8 and 9 sustainable development goals. The proposed conceptual framework will give a complete understanding of the significant factors required for consideration for the successful adoption of intelligent computers by employees.

DOI: 10.4018/979-8-3373-6385-1.ch004

Copyright © 2026, IGI Global Scientific Publishing. Copying or distributing in print or electronic forms without written permission of IGI Global Scientific Publishing is prohibited.

1. INTRODUCTION

Digital human-employee and human-employee interactions are part of the modern workplace (Baptista et al., 2020). Industry 5.0 has tremendously transformed human-computer interactions in the workplace, by obtaining sustainable solutions to the problems encountered in Industry 4.0 (Abdel-Basset et al., 2024; Pereira et al., 2020). Artificial intelligence, Machine learning, Internet of Things, Neurocognition, RPA, Generative AI, AI algorithms, Smart human computer interactions in an evolved sustainable work environment have embarked on Industry 5.0, as a solution to problems foreseen during Industry 4.0 (Bousdekis et al., 2025; Gelayol & Sepehr, 2024). The sociotechnical environment within the organization requires employees to be the enablers, enabling the creation of value through intelligent human-computer interactions (Makarius et al., 2020). The application of intelligent technology, such as generative AI, has a significant impact on an individual's behavior and cognitive abilities, which necessitates effective management. (Mohammed et al., 2024). Technological advancements and adaptations in Industry 5.0 have prominent significance on sustainable business and aligning a human-centric approach to intelligent technologies, leading to robust economic development (Gelayol & Sepehr, 2024). The field of human-computer interactions, along with artificial intelligence, creates an interactive intelligent system for the benefit of the users and business (Nazar et al., 2021). Human intelligence and computer intelligence need to complement each other to achieve the desired work goal, creating collaborative intelligence (Di Pasquale et al., 2023b). Lean management, achieved through lean automation, human sharing, and interacting with smart computers, is vital for team and company performance; therefore, companies are vouching for having a smart team comprising with right skills and competence, supporting collaboration and interactions with computers (Tortorella et al., 2021). Organizations for enhancing their business performance are largely dependent on collaborative intelligence gained through smart computers and their interactions with humans who are equally intelligent and competent to work with them, rather than relying only on humans (Blaurock et al., 2024). Industry 5.0 has made it mandatory for businesses to implement and integrate the adoption of intelligent computer interactions with human employees (Passalacqua et al., 2022). However, there are many challenges and opportunities that human employees may perceive while working with smart computers, which can substantially impact their behavior and eventually impact the team and organization performance (Gurcan et al., 2020). Human employee acceptance and adoption of smart computers for intelligent work and interactions are crucial for business success (Sony & Mekoth, 2022). Prominent drivers and inhibitors specifically determine the actual adoption and implementation of HCI (Malik et al., 2020). There are many factors explored related to employee adoption and behaviour towards HCI (Gkinko, 2022; Malik et al., 2020; Passalacqua et al., 2022). There is a dire need to gain a comprehensive understanding of the factors that act as drivers or inhibitors of the actual adoption of HCI, enabling organizations to formulate effective strategies for implementing efficient HCI and reaping business benefits.

1.1. Smart Computer Interactions

"HCI is a multidisciplinary field of study that focuses on the development, evaluation, and dissemination of technology to meet users' needs by optimizing how users and technology interact." (Bach et al., 2024, p. 1252). The reported transition and relation of an employee with non-AI computer interaction to AI computer interactions is the new norm at the workplace (Wei Xu a, Marvin J. Dainoff b, Liezhong Ge a & A, 2022). The link between communication and computation needs to be done effectively to ensure smooth interactions for achieving work goals. (Kashef et al., 2021). Under HCI, there are many interfaces through which humans interact with AI-driven computers to make life convenient.(Obrenovic et al., 2024). The natural user interfaces are gesture, voice, touch, etc., examples like voice assistants like Siri, Alexa. (Lewandowski et al., 2021). Conversational interfaces, AI chatbots like ChatGPT (J. Liu, 2024). AR, VR, Brain computer interface, and context-aware systems have given humans smart solutions to their daily routine. (Chandan et al., 2023). The brief elaboration of Smart HCI is given below. Table 1.

Table 1. Types of smart HCI

AI Computer Interactions	How It Helps	Examples	Reference
AI Assistants	They handle scheduling, reminders, or summarizing emails for you.	Microsoft Copilot, ChatGPT, Google Duet AI	(Zel et al., 2020)
Voice Control	Talk to your computer instead of typing — great for multitasking or quick notes.	Siri, Google Assistant, Windows Dictation	(Byali, 2022)
Smarter Meetings	Auto notes, summaries, and even live translations — so you can focus on the convo.	Zoom AI Companion, Otter.ai, Notion AI	(Hu, 2019)
Context-Aware Tools	Your tools adjust to how you work — showing what's relevant right now.	Smart email sorting in Gmail, dynamic dashboards	(H. Liu & Wang, 2021)
Helpful Notifications	Less noise, more signal. Important alerts rise to the top.	Slack's smart notifications, Focus mode	(Duivestein, n.d.)

continued on following page

Table 1. Continued

AI Computer Interactions	How It Helps	Examples	Reference
Team-Up with AI	Write faster, brainstorm better, and co-create with AI in your docs and notes.	Notion AI, Google Docs smart suggestions	(Lewandowski et al., 2021)
Data That Talks Back	Ask plain questions like "How are sales this week?" — get charts and answers fast.	Power BI, Tableau with built-in AI	(Dubey et al., 2018)

1.2. Models and Theories of HCI

There are significant theories and models adopted under HCI studies. Theories as the self-determination theory of motivation, based on autonomy, competence, and relatedness (Alghizzawi, 2021), semiotic theory on how icons and signs interact and create meaning between the user and the computer (*The Wiley Handbook of Human Computer Interaction Volume 1*, n.d.). Grounded theory building theory based on data. (Meissner et al., 2020). Activity theory means human behavior is goal-centric, supported by tools and social context. (Lindblom & Alenljung, 2020). Distributed cognition, this theory emphasizes intelligence beyond the human head, including tools, context, etc. (*The Wiley Handbook of Human Computer Interaction Volume 1*, n.d.). Language action perspective prefers computer interactions as communication. (Huang, 2020). The Table 2 Gives a broader understanding of the various theories and models demonstrated under HCI.

Table 2. Model / theories in HCI

Model / Theory	Description	Its Usage	Reference
GOMS Model	Analyzes user interactions by breaking down tasks into Goals, Operators, Methods, and Selection rules.	Used in interface design to make workflows smoother.	(The Wiley Handbook of Human Computer Interaction Volume 1, n.d.)
Fitts's Law	Predicts the time required to move to a target area, emphasizing the importance of size and distance in UI design.	Important for placing UI elements effectively.	(Someshwar & Edan, 2017)
Hick's Law	States that the time it takes to make a decision increases with the number and complexity of choices.	Helps in menu and navigation design.	(The Wiley Handbook of Human Computer Interaction Volume 1, n.d.)

continued on following page

Table 2. Continued

Model / Theory	Description	Its Usage	Reference
Norman's Seven Stages of Action	Describes the stages users go through when interacting with systems, from goal formation to execution and evaluation.	Useful in usability testing.	(Seemanthini & Manjunath, 2021)
Activity Theory	Focuses on understanding human practices and the context of interactions, emphasizing the role of tools and community.	Seen in education tech, workplace tools.	(Lindblom & Alenljung, 2020)
Distributed Cognition	Examines how cognitive processes are distributed across individuals, artifacts, and environments.	Important in team software and multi-device systems.	(S. Li et al., 2021)
Mental Models	Refers to the internal representations users form about how systems work, guiding their interactions.	Design should match users' expectations.	(Tabrez et al., 2020)
User-Centered Design (UCD)	Design philosophy that places the user at the center of the design process, ensuring products meet user needs and preferences.	A core philosophy in product development.	(Fujita et al., 2010)
Direct Manipulation Interfaces	Interfaces that allow users to interact with digital objects as if they were physical, enhancing intuitiveness.	Touchscreens and modern UIs rely heavily on this.	(Marvel et al., 2020)
Placebo Effect in AI	Explores how users' beliefs about AI capabilities can influence their interactions and trust, regardless of actual performance.	Found in AI interfaces and smart assistants.	(Kosch et al., 2022)
Complementarity Theory	Suggests that humans and machines can complement each other's strengths, leading to enhanced performance.	Useful in designing AI tools for work.	(P. O. K. M. A. N. Tang & Zhang, 2022)
Role Theory	Examines how individuals adopt roles in interactions, which can be applied to understand user behavior with AI systems.	Used to understand how employees engage with tech.	(Blaurock et al., 2022)

1.3. Smart Computer Interactions at the Workplace

With rigorous utilization of smart computers at the workplace, frequent and daily human interactions with the AI-driven computers for all possible work are ubiquitous in industry. (Bentvelzen et al., 2022). Smart computers at the workplace are capable of making decisions, performing problem-solving, and complementing human intelligence, acting as a second brain of humans. (Nd, 2021). Businesses can perform exponentially by capitalizing on the healthy HCI (Demetris et al., 2021).

There are multiple avenues of HCI, such as speech recognition, gesture recognition, Natural language processing, gesture interactions, deep learning, emotion recognition, etc. (Lv et al., 2022). A Smart ecosystem has rigorously disrupted traditional psychology by transforming it to make life convenient, creating the need for leveling up to work with the smart devices in the workplace (Kashef et al., 2021). Digital human configuration is vital to create a smart ecosystem, which is inclusive of effective communications and interactions of humans and smart systems (Baptista et al., 2020). Intelligent systems and Smart computers are a vital part of Industry 5.0 and need significant acceptance to boost business performance (Yam et al., 2022).

1.4. Employee Behavior Towards Smart Computers

Employees' behavior and emotional state are influenced by changed workplace landscapes (Yam et al., 2022). Employee behavioral psychology is deeply affected by the inclusion of artificial intelligence and Smart computers in the workspace (Oosthuizen, 2022). However, the adaptation of smart intelligence in a supporting and complementary way leads to performance enhancement of employees who are efficiently using it (Kosch et al., 2022). Smart computers are intelligent coworkers who are not only efficient in technical work but also effectively complement humans in providing emotional support and practicing empathy (J. Liu, 2024). Employees experience a conscientious mismatch when working with intelligent computers or systems, recognizing their ability to make decisions and cognitive aptitude (P. O. K. M. A. N. Tang & Zhang, 2022). Industry 5.0 presents a perfect opportunity for integrating smart systems that accommodate humans, paving the way for a sustainable future, which is largely dependent on employees' acceptance and adaptation to such foreseen technologies (Mourtzis et al., 2023). Organizations are facing challenges in aligning intelligent technology and systems with employees, and should focus on various essential verticals of HR, such as recruitment, training, and performance management, for the seamless integration of HCI (Demetris et al., 2021). The smart technology also impacts leaders and how they should perform their leadership duties on strategic transformation, reforming the culture, ensuring competence and qualifications, creating a sociotechnical environment at the workplace (Peifer et al., 2022). Under a hybrid intelligence workplace, parallel cognition is critical for achieving work aims, which need humans to learn and behave in the prescribed manner to complement work alignment (Ye et al., 2022). Employee perception towards the intelligent system is based on various factors like autonomy, job experience, skillset, competence, etc., for making effective decisions at the workplace (Ulfert et al., 2022). A lot of studies with a human-centric approach revolve around understanding the factors affecting the behavior and perception of employees, however, a comprehensive understanding still needs more exploration (J. Liu, 2024; Ulfert et al., 2022).

2. REVIEW LITERATURE

The reported extant literature, as listed in the Table 3 for smart human-computer interactions, researchers have adopted various methods for subsequent studies, with most research papers being conceptual papers with a total count of 10, followed by empirical and systematic reviews, and very few papers based on opinion and perspective. Literature significantly captures the essence of including enhancing HCI, and focusing on making humans ready and competent to adopt and complement intelligence (Choi, 2021; Dagioglou & Karkaletsis, 2021; Oosthuizen, 2022). But there are subsequent surfaced gaps like studies capturing the response of employees working with intelligent systems over time, a critical framework giving a comprehensive understanding of implementing HCI at the workplace. Lastly, there are a few considerations given to the emotional well-being and social aspects of employees.

Table 3. Literature review

S. N	Research Method	Key Findings	Theoretical Framework	Reference
1	Survey & Conceptual Review	Introduces the Internet of Behaviors (IoB), highlighting how behavioral data is collected and analyzed to influence future actions.	Behavioral Science & Data Analytics	(Sun et al., 1999)
2	Critical Literature Review	Discusses the evolving role of industrial psychologists in workplaces adapting to AI and smart technologies.	Strategic Intelligence Theory	(Oosthuizen, 2022)
3	Experimental Study	Reveals that the belief in AI assistance can enhance human performance, even without actual AI involvement.	Placebo Effect in AI & Technology Acceptance Model	(Kosch et al., 2022)
4	Perspective Paper	Explores ChatGPT's impact from psychological and HCI perspectives, focusing on user interaction and trust.	Psychology & Human-Computer Interaction	(J. Liu, 2024)
5	Theoretical Integration	Examines how conscientious employees interact with intelligent machines, emphasizing role clarity for effective collaboration.	Complementarity Theory & Role Theory	(P. O. K. M. A. N. Tang & Zhang, 2022)
6	Conceptual Analysis	Discusses the future of Human-Machine Interfaces (HMI) in Society 5.0, emphasizing intuitive and personalized designs.	Human-Centered Design	(Mourtzis et al., 2023)

continued on following page

Table 3. Continued

S. N	Research Method	Key Findings	Theoretical Framework	Reference
7	Systematic Review	Analyzes how AI and robotics are transforming human resource management practices.	-	(Demetris et al., 2021)
8	Behavioral Sequence Analysis	Finds that smart classroom environments promote more active student participation and alter teacher-student interactions.	Behavioral Learning Theory	(Zhan et al., 2021)
9	Conceptual Discussion	Investigates AI's influence on leadership styles and decision-making processes.	Leadership Theories & AI Integration	(Peifer et al., 2022)
10	Theoretical Proposition	Introduces 'Parallel Cognition' as a model for hybrid intelligence in human-machine collaboration.	Hybrid Intelligence Framework	(Ye et al., 2022)
11	Multidisciplinary Analysis	Highlights the importance of cross-industry collaboration for successful implementation of generative AI like ChatGPT.	Collaborative Implementation Framework	(Society et al., 2023)
12	Applied Research	Explores the integration of voice assistance and automated machine learning in Industry 5.0 settings.	Augmented Intelligence Model	(Bousdekis et al., 2025)
13	Empirical Study	Examines the work and after-work consequences of interacting with AI, emphasizing the need for balance.	Work-Life Interaction Theory	(P. M. Tang et al., 2023)
14	Organizing Review	Provides a comprehensive assessment of human-computer interaction research related to conversational agents.	Human-Computer Interaction Framework	(Diederich et al., 2022)
15	Handbook Compilation	Offers an extensive overview of human-computer interaction principles and applications.	Human-Computer Interaction Theories	(The Wiley Handbook of Human Computer Interaction Volume 1, n.d.)
16	Empirical Study	Investigates the integration of generative AI techniques in student behavior and cognitive achievement in Arab higher education.	Educational Psychology & AI Integration	(Mohammed et al., 2024)
17	Experimental Study	Examines the role of agent autonomy in the use of decision support systems at work.	Decision Support System Theory	(Ulfert et al., 2022)

continued on following page

Table 3. Continued

S. N	Research Method	Key Findings	Theoretical Framework	Reference
18	Review Article	Discusses the state-of-the-art in human-computer interaction within the Metaverse.	Metaverse Interaction Framework	(Lyu, 2024)
19	Survey Study	Provides a comprehensive survey on measuring cognitive workload in human-computer interaction.	Cognitive Load Theory	(Kosch & Berlin, 2023)
20	Conceptual Analysis	Explores digital work and organizational transformation, focusing on emergent digital/ human work configurations.	Digital Transformation Theory	(Baptista et al., 2020)
21	Qualitative Study	Investigate employees' emotions when using AI-enabled chatbots in digitalized workplaces.	Emotional Response Theory	(Gkinko, 2022)
22	Industry Analysis	Discusses the transition of the clothing industry from Industry 4.0 to newer paradigms.	Industry Evolution Framework	(Gelayol & Sepehr, 2024)
23	Systematic Review	Analyzes smart city surveillance systems from a human-computer interaction perspective.	Smart City Service Systems Theory	(Kashef et al., 2021)
24	Applied Sciences Study	Explores the application of deep learning in intelligent human-computer interaction.	Deep Learning Models	(Lv et al., 2022)
25	Systematic Review	Provides a comprehensive review of human-computer interaction and explainable AI in healthcare.	Explainable AI Framework	(Nazar et al., 2021)

Figure 1. Author's network

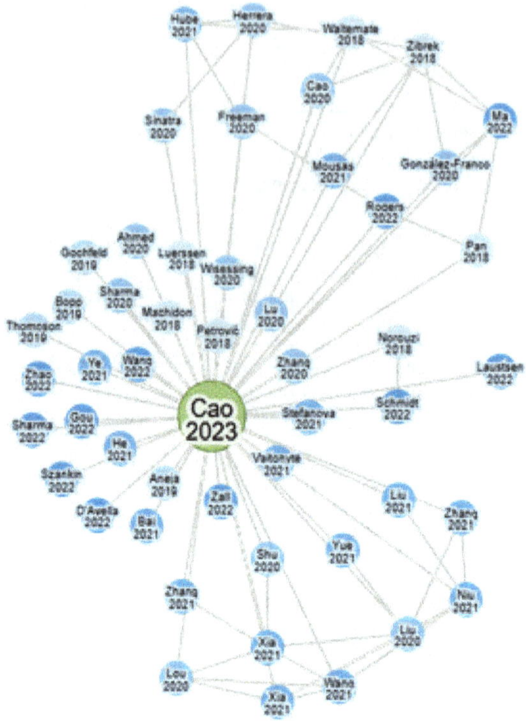

The above Figure 1 depicts the author's network spreading across the years of published work in Human-Computer Interactions. There is an acceleration in the research in the domain of HCI. AI's influence extends to workplaces, where industrial psychologists are adapting to smart technologies, guided by strategic intelligence theory (Oosthuizen, 2022).Interestingly, belief in AI assistance alone can boost human performance, even without actual AI involvement, highlighting a placebo effect within technology acceptance models (Kosch & Berlin, 2023). Meanwhile, conversational agents like ChatGPT have sparked discussions on user trust and interaction from psychological and HCI perspectives (J. Liu, 2024). For effective human-machine collaboration, role clarity is crucial, especially for conscientious employees, as explained by complementarity and role theories (P. O. K. M. A. N. Tang & Zhang, 2022). Looking ahead, human-centered design is emphasized for intuitive Human-Machine Interfaces (HMI) in Society 5.0 (Mourtzis et al., 2023).

Education is also evolving, with smart classrooms fostering active student participation through behavioral learning theory (Zhan et al., 2021). Leadership styles are adapting to AI-driven decision-making (Peifer et al., 2022), and the concept of 'Parallel Cognition' introduces a hybrid intelligence model for human-machine collaboration (Ye et al., 2022). Voice assistance paired with automated machine learning is gaining traction in Industry 5.0 (Bousdekis et al., 2025). However, AI interactions at work can blur work-life boundaries, underscoring the need for balance (Yam et al., 2022). Conversational agents are a growing focus in HCI research (Diederich et al., 2022). In education, generative AI enhances student behavior and cognitive outcomes in Arab higher education (Mohammed et al., 2024).

Decision support systems are influenced by agent autonomy (Ulfert et al., 2022), while the Metaverse introduces new HCI challenges (Lyu, 2024). Measuring cognitive workload in HCI is critical for user experience (Kosch & Berlin, 2023), and digital work is driving organizational transformation through emergent digital-human configurations (Baptista et al., 2020). Employees' emotional responses to AI chatbots reveal complex dynamics in digital workplaces (Gkinko, 2022). In industry, the clothing sector is transitioning beyond Industry 4.0 (Gelayol & Sepehr, 2024), and smart city surveillance systems raise HCI concerns (Kashef et al., 2021). Ultimately, this literature reveals a dynamic interplay between AI, HCI, and human behavior, emphasizing the need for ethical, human-centered approaches to ensure technology enhances rather than disrupts our lives.

3. SMART HUMAN COMPUTER INTERACTIONS

AI-driven systems are an integral part of the workplace that combines technology, psychological, and cognitive domains (Nazar et al., 2021). Employees need to trust the smart systems enough to create a bond to be effective for the allocated work (Gkinko, 2022). Smart computer integration needs a smart learning environment, eventually creating a smart environment, enabling the stakeholders to have conducive and feasible surroundings (Oosthuizen, 2022). Further advancement of intelligent technology, where the inclusion of chatbots, robots, and cobots is essential to being accepted and adapted by employees for fulfilling business goals (Chitranshi et al., 2020; Di Pasquale et al., 2023a; Picco et al., 2024). ChatGPT interactions are more personalized, conversing like humans, being empathetic, and showcasing and understanding emotions can be used to reinforce effective learning and support employees at the workplace (J. Liu, 2024). Using tools like smart context-aware tools, smarter meetings, and visualization tools for leveraging data-based decisions in computer interactions (H. Liu & Wang, 2021; Walchshofer et al., 2024). For effectively handling emails, sorting work, enhanced decision making, and personalizing the work context for human employees to elevate their work performance is substantial (Byali, 2022; Duivestein, n.d.; Zel et al., 2020). It is evident that with an evolving workplace, a smart environment requires a smart approach and a thorough acceptance from employees for successfully implementing HCI.

3.1. Organizational Benefits of Smart HCI

Industry 5.0 has added smart and intelligent technology to the work environment (Mourtzis et al., 2023). These technologies work alongside human employees to be a more effective and efficient team (Gervasi et al., 2020). There exists a constant interaction and communication between the intelligent system and human employees, and the positive team fluency ensures it (Thomaz & Hoffman, n.d.). Beyond survival, organizations reap benefits by enhancing productivity by ensuring seamless HCI at the workplace (Dughera, 2021). A systematic approach towards HCI while ensuring safety, taking care of the employee's psychological state, motivating employees, increasing job satisfaction, and engagement leads to measured organizational performance enhancement (Fraboni et al., 2023). The acceptance of HCI affects the emotional state of the employee and should consider the psychological state, ergonomics considerations, and ensuring human-oriented fluency for increasing human employee job performance, according to enhanced organizational business performance (Paliga, 2022). The way employees make use of Alexa, Siri, and organizing, scheduling meetings, conferences, and analyzing data, not at all involving routine tasks, adds to reduced time utilization and cuts down on cost related to time (Byali, 2022). Artificial intelligence and collaborative intelligence have tremendous potential to boost the productivity of team tasks and organizational performance (Picco et al., 2024). Employees' well-being and performance are defined and measured through relevant metrics that contribute to increasing team performance and productivity (Nelles & Kwee-meier, 2019). Human employee competence and experience add substantially to the robot and system accuracy and ability, and make an effective subjective and objective team fluency and performance (Ramadurai & Jeong, 2022). There are multiple benefits organizations achieve with effective HCI, such as better decision making, reduction in error rate, increased productivity, effective utilization of time and money, improved user satisfaction, and gaining a competitive edge in the industry (Bankins & Formosa, 2020; Buerkle et al., 2021; Fraboni et al., 2023; Laban et al., 2024; W. Li et al., 2023).

3.2. The Drivers: Mobilizing Smart HCI

Trust is significantly important for human employees in their interaction with the computer is important for seamless teamwork, so it is essential to create a trustworthy environment for human employees to feel safe and secure while working with AI-based systems (Bach et al., 2024; Glikson & Woolley, 2020; Zierau et al.,

2021). Perceived value is human employees' willingness to adopt computer interactions increases as it adds value to the work to be done (Lei Li, Qingyun Huang, 2018; Silva & Halloluwa, 2025). Enjoyment and a positive experience, the human employee will derive while interacting and working with smart systems (Ischen et al., 2020; Pereira et al., 2020; Pillai et al., 2020; Rese et al., 2020; Zel & Kongar, 2020). Social influence exerts a tendency to adopt smart computer interactions with the social and group influence observed around (Forgas-Coll et al., 2023; Furlough et al., 2021; Terblanche, 2020). Perceived usefulness as a human employee perceives that smart computer interactions would enhance individual and team performance (Eißer et al., 2020; Pillai & Sivathanu, 2020; Rese et al., 2020). Technology competence is the tendency of human employees to be ready with the required skillset and cognitive intelligence to support innovation (Oosthuizen, 2022; Pan et al., 2021; Ren & Clement, 2024). User experience tremendously acts as the biggest motivator to easily adopt HCI in daily work routine (Lindblom & Alenljung, 2020). The drivers, the enablers that mobilize the adoption and integration of smart HCI, are the workplace (Elpidio Oscar Benitez Nara, Matheus Becker da Costa, Ismael Cristofer Baierle, Jones Luis Schaefer, Guilherme Brittes Benitez, Leonardo Moraes Aguiar Lima do Santos, 2021; Nara et al., 2021).

3.3. The Inhibitors: Interrupting the Smart HCI

Despite the above-listed drivers, there are significant inhibitors that pose a challenge and make it harder for human employees to adopt, interact and work with smart computers (Balraj Verma, 2022). Perceived privacy risk is a possible inhibitor, posing a risk of misuse of personal data by intelligent computers, and human employees can feel unsafe under HCI (Karahoca et al., 2018; Sivathanu, 2018; Tong, 2009). Negative attitude towards HCI, opposing to use and interaction with an intelligent system, poses a challenge to the easy integration of HCI (Brondi et al., 2021). Lack of skills challenges the use and adaptability of AI-integrated systems in a workplace (Gaur, 2020). Technological anxiety poses a fear of losing a job to automation and intelligent systems in the workplace (Eißer et al., 2020; Mani, 2018). Lack of experience working with smart tools and technology acts as a barrier and adds to the anxiety levels of the human employee over safety, security, and a feeling of the unknown (Ajoudani et al., 2017). Lack of infrastructure support acts as a roadblock to enabling employees to adopt intelligent technology with ease (K. P. Gupta et al., 2017; Rajendran et al., 2020). There should be sufficient planning and strategizing to be done to overcome these inhibitors and convert these challenges into opportunities (Goel et al., 2022; A. Gupta & Arora, 2017; Huang, 2020).

4. THE CONCEPTUAL FRAMEWORK

The authors have conceptualized a theoretical framework as depicted in *Figure 1* based on the extant literature. HCI adoption and easy integration are important for business and organizational performance and sustainability (Libert et al., 2020). Industry 5.0 has introduced numerous technological and human sustainability opportunities as a result of the revolutionized workplace and work environment (Bach et al., 2024; Bousdekis et al., 2025). Employee acceptance and adoption of these intelligent technologies are crucial for the successful implementation of HCI (Gkinko, 2022). HCI, if effectively done, brings a plethora of benefits like saving time, saving cost of time, enhanced individual and group productivity, smart meeting scheduling, and conferences. Make daily work easy with voice assistants, AI assistants, generating personalized content, and sharing the burden of making data-based decisions and data visualization (Bousdekis et al., 2025; Diederich et al., 2022; Society et al., 2023). Employees on the other side are required to adapt to these workplace changes and add to the collaborative intelligence, working with ease as they work with their human counterpart (Sony & Mekoth, 2022).

When it comes to working with intelligent technology or smart computers, there are reported drivers and inhibitors that can exist in the organization, impacting employee behaviour and perception (Le et al., 2024). Some of the factors are at the individual level, such as stress, anxiety, competence, job satisfaction, and attitude, etc. (D. C. Li & Tsai, 2020; Paliga, 2023; Rinaldi et al., 2024; Sarah. L.Muller-Abdelrazeq, Kathrin Schonefeld, 2019). At the team level, factors can be communication, interaction, team fluency, work engagement, etc. (Chung et al., 2020; Dagioglou & Karkaletsis, 2021; Huang, 2020). At the organizational level, financial support, IT infrastructure support, training and development opportunities, etc. (Kopp et al., 2020; Pillai et al., 2021; Premnath & Arun, 2020).

The drivers, as depicted in *Figure 1* These are the motivators for the employees to facilitate the adoption of smart computers and leverage the benefits of HCI for individual and organizational benefits and profits (Nara et al., 2021). On the contrary, the various inhibitors, as depicted in *Figure 1* challenges the application and usage of smart computers and may create a hindrance to the possible positive outcomes that an individual and organization may enjoy (Matheson et al., 2019). Equating these drivers and inhibitors that affect a human employee results in actual adoption of HCI at the workplace and eventually leads to enhanced organizational performance.

Figure 2. Conceptual framework

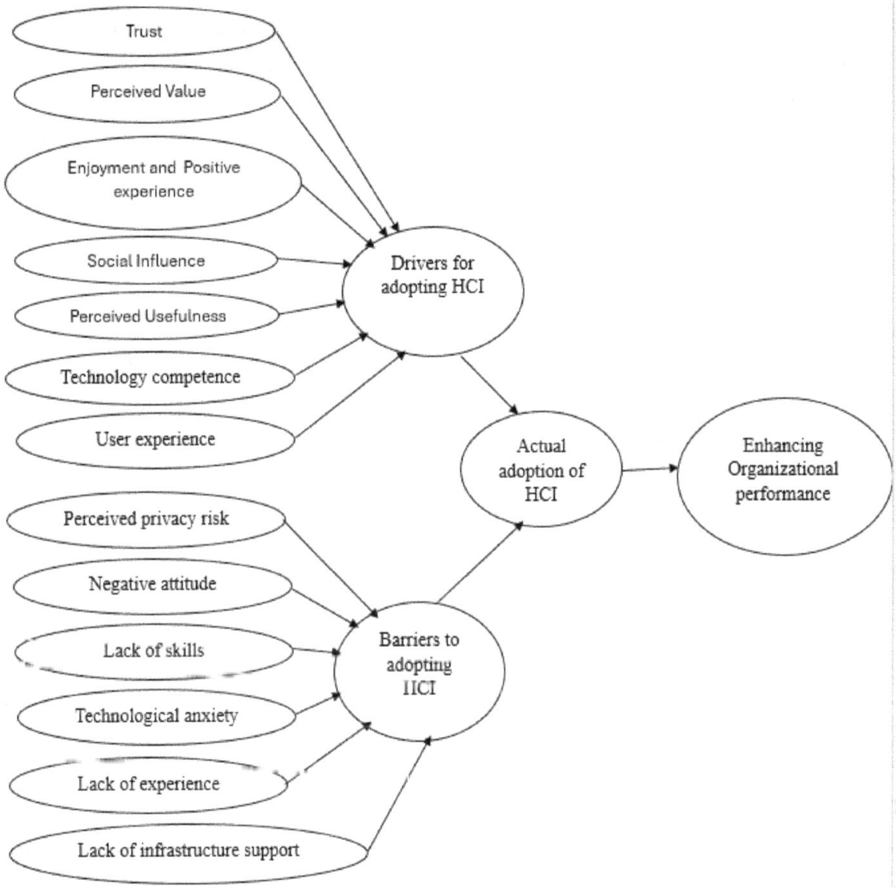

5. IMPLICATIONS

The proposed framework provides evidential implications at the individual, managerial, organizational level, and society at large. An individual who knows the various drivers and inhibitors will help them to make their strategy to perfectly use smart technology and become more efficient as an individual. Also, knowing the inhibitors at the individual level can help in reducing stress and anxiety that may occur when an individual is unable to understand smart technology. Also helping the individual from fearing missing out or getting unemployed in the long run. At the managerial level, knowing the various factors, both drivers and inhibitors, can help them to effectively strategize to enable smooth HCI and adopt a human-centric approach towards smart technology adoption. This will also help managers to train and align their team performance to organizational objectives and performance. At the organizational level, the company knows about the various drivers and inhibitors that can help them provide proper fund channelization, creating smart technology infrastructure, environment, and culture to contain a human-centric approach towards `technology adoption. This will also help the organization to stay competitive and sustainable. The marketers and developers, knowing the identified inhibitors, can focus on designing smart computer interactions to overcome the inhibitors that already exist in the system.

The implications of the research can be mapped under the UN SDGs 8th and 9th goals. The 8th SDG goal is decent work and economic growth, where in Industry 5.0, the change in workplace is adapted by employees and be productive to add to organizational performance and leading to economic growth. And for the 9th goal, industry, innovation, and infrastructure, the *Figure 1* gives a conceptual clarity of the various factors at play and will result in fulfilling this goal.

6. CONCLUSION

The changed workplace landscapes have made it mandatory for organizations to integrate smart HCI and stay competitive in Industry 5.0 (Arents et al., 2021). There are substantial benefits that an organization can reap by incorporating effective smart HCI at the workplace (Wei Xu a, Marvin J. Dainoff b, Liezhong Ge a & A, 2022). This paper investigates the various types of smart HCI, examines the employee behavior towards HCI, and the crucial need for it. Also, this paper details the various drivers and inhibitors that affect employee technology adoption behavior, perception, and attitude. The conceptual framework properly aligns and explains the impact of various drivers and inhibitors, resulting in the actual adoption of HCI, which serves the individual, team, organization, and economic needs. The appropriate strategizing, while taking into consideration Figure 1, the conceptual framework, will lead to enhancing employee performance. However, the framework is designed conceptually, which can be improved by empirically testing the various drivers and inhibitors affecting the actual adoption of HCI, and additionally, more antecedents with evolving generations and multigenerations can be explored further, upgrading the proposed conceptual framework. Also, the longitudinal study can be done to actually observe the various factors' impact on employee behavior.

REFERENCES

Abdel-Basset, M., Mohamed, R., & Chang, V. (2024). A Multi-Criteria Decision-Making Framework to Evaluate the Impact of Industry 5.0 Technologies: Case Study, Lessons Learned, Challenges and Future Directions. In *Information Systems Frontiers* (Issue 0123456789). Springer US. DOI: 10.1007/s10796-024-10472-3

Ajoudani, A., Zanchettin, A., Ivaldi, S., Albu-schäffer, A., Ajoudani, A., Zanchettin, A., Ivaldi, S., Albu-schäffer, A., Kosuge, K., Ajoudani, A., & Zanchettin, M. (2017). *Progress and Prospects of the Human-Robot Collaboration To cite this version : HAL Id : hal-01643655 Progress and Prospects of the Human-Robot Collaboration.*

Alghizzawi, M. (2021). *Extension of technology continuance theory (TCT) with task technology fit (TTF) in the context of Internet banking user continuance intention.* DOI: 10.1108/IJQRM-03-2020-0074

Arents, J., Abolins, V., Judvaitis, J., Vismanis, O., Oraby, A., & Ozols, K. (2021). Human–robot collaboration trends and safety aspects: A systematic review. *Journal of Sensor and Actuator Networks, 10*(3), 48. DOI: 10.3390/jsan10030048

Bach, T. A., Khan, A., Hallock, H., Beltrão, G., Sousa, S., Alissa, T., Khan, A., Hallock, H., & Beltrão, G. (2024). A Systematic Literature Review of User Trust in AI- Enabled Systems : An HCI Perspective A Systematic Literature Review of User Trust in AI-Enabled Systems : An HCI. *International Journal of Human-Computer Interaction, 40*(5), 1251–1266. DOI: 10.1080/10447318.2022.2138826

Balraj Verma, U. T. (2022). Modelling barriers to wearable technologies in Indian context: Validating the moderating role of technology literacy. *Global Knowledge, Memory and Communication, 73*(6), 984–1004. https://doi.org/10.1108/GKMC -08-2022-0209

Bankins, S., & Formosa, P. (2020). When AI meets PC: Exploring the implications of workplace social robots and a human-robot psychological contract. *European Journal of Work and Organizational Psychology, 29*(2), 215–229. DOI: 10.1080/1359432X.2019.1620328

Baptista, J., Stein, M., Klein, S., & Watson-manheim, M. B. (2020). *Digital work and organisational transformation: Emergent Digital/Human work configurations in modern organsaitions. January.*

Bentvelzen, M., Herbes, P. I. A. S. F., Stefanidi, E., & Niess, J. (2022). *Revisiting Reflection in HCI : Four Design Resources for Technologies that Support Reflection.* 6(1), 1–27. DOI: 10.1145/3517233

Blaurock, M., Büttgen, M., & Schepers, J. (2024). Designing Collaborative Intelligence Systems for Employee-AI Service Co-Production. *Journal of Service Research, 0*(0), 1–19. DOI: 10.1177/10946705241238751

Blaurock, M., Čaić, M., Okan, M., & Henkel, A. P. (2022). Robotic role theory: An integrative review of human–robot service interaction to advance role theory in the age of social robots. *Journal of Service Management, 33*(6), 27–49. DOI: 10.1108/JOSM-09-2021-0345

Bousdekis, A., Foosherian, M., Fikardos, M., Wellsandt, S., Lepenioti, K., & Bosani, E. (2025). *Augmented intelligence with voice assistance and automated machine learning in Industry 5 . 0. March*, 1–22. DOI: 10.3389/frai.2025.1538840

Brondi, S., Pivetti, M., Di Battista, S., & Sarrica, M. (2021). What do we expect from robots? Social representations, attitudes and evaluations of robots in daily life. *Technology in Society, 66*(February), 101663. DOI: 10.1016/j.techsoc.2021.101663

Buerkle, A., Bamber, T., Lohse, N., & Ferreira, P. (2021). Feasibility of Detecting Potential Emergencies in Symbiotic Human-Robot Collaboration with a mobile EEG. *Robotics and Computer-integrated Manufacturing, 72*(May), 102179. DOI: 10.1016/j.rcim.2021.102179

Byali, R. (2022). *Using Machine Learning Classifiers and A Virtual Voice Assistant for Common Tasks, An Employee Performance Evaluation Model is Used International Journal of Research Publication and Reviews Using Machine Learning Classifiers and A Virtual Voice Assistant. August*, 0–4. DOI: 10.55248/gengpi.2022.3.8.28

Chandan, K., Albertson, J., & Zhang, S. (2023). Learning Visualization Policies of Augmented Reality for Human-Robot Collaboration. *Proceedings of Machine Learning Research, 205*(CoRL), 1233–1243.

Chitranshi, S., Daml, P., Management, T., & Chitranshi, S. (2020).. . *Intelligent Interaction Via Chatbots Transcending the., 17*(6), 4568–4576.

Choi, Y. (2021). A study of employee acceptance of artificial intelligence technology. *European Journal of Management and Business Economics, ahead-of-p*(ahead-of-print). DOI: 10.1108/EJMBE-06-2020-0158

Chung, M., Ko, E., Joung, H., & Kim, S. J. (2020). Chatbot e-service and customer satisfaction regarding luxury brands. *Journal of Business Research, 117*(October), 587–595. DOI: 10.1016/j.jbusres.2018.10.004

Dagioglou, M., & Karkaletsis, V. (2021). *The sense of agency during Human-Agent Collaboration*. https://doi.org/DOI: 10.1145/nnnnnnn.nnnnnnn

Demetris, V., Michael, C., Vijay, P., Shlomo, T., Anna, M., & Eleni, T. (2021). The International Journal of Human Resource Artificial intelligence, robotics, advanced technologies and human resource management : A systematic review. *International Journal of Human Resource Management*, *0*(0), 1–30. DOI: 10.1080/09585192.2020.1871398

Di Pasquale, V., De Simone, V., Giubileo, V., & Miranda, S. (2023a). A taxonomy of factors influencing worker's performance in human–robot collaboration. *IET Collaborative Intelligent Manufacturing*, *5*(1), 1–20. DOI: 10.1049/cim2.12069

Di Pasquale, V., De Simone, V., Giubileo, V., & Miranda, S. (2023b). 1. *IET Collaborative Intelligent Manufacturing*, *5*(1), e12069. DOI: 10.1049/cim2.12069

Diederich, S., Brendel, A. B., Morana, S., & Kolbe, L. (2022). On the Design of and Interaction with Conversational Agents. *Journal of the Association for Information Systems*, *23*(1), 96–138. DOI: 10.17705/1jais.00724

Dubey, R., Luo, Z., Gunasekaran, A., Akter, S., Hazen, B. T., & Douglas, M. A. (2018). Big data and predictive analytics in humanitarian supply chains. *International Journal of Logistics Management*, *29*(2), 485–512. DOI: 10.1108/IJLM-02-2017-0039

Dughera, S. (2021). The evolution of workplace control leadership, obedience and organizational performance. *Journal of Evolutionary Economics*. DOI: 10.1007/s00191-020-00720-5

Duivestein, S. (n.d.). *Digital Happiness 1 |4*. 1–44.

Eißer, J., Torrini, M., & Böhm, S. (2020). Automation Anxiety as a Barrier to Workplace Automation: An Empirical Analysis of the Example of Recruiting Chatbots in Germany. *SIGMIS-CPR 2020 - Proceedings of the 2020 Computers and People Research Conference*, 47–51. DOI: 10.1145/3378539.3393866

Elpidio, O. B. N., Becker da Costa, M., Baierle, I. C., Schaefer, J. L., Benitez, G. B., & do Santos, L. M. A. L. L. B. B. (2021). Expected impact of industry 4.0 technologies on sustainable development: A study in the context of Brazil's plastic industry, *Sustainable Production and Consumption, Volume 25*, Pages 102-122. DOI: 10.1016/j.spc.2020.07.018

Forgas-Coll, S., Huertas-Garcia, R., Andriella, A., & Alenyà, G. (2023). Social robot-delivered customer-facing services: An assessment of the experience. *Service Industries Journal*, *43*(3–4), 154–184. DOI: 10.1080/02642069.2022.2163995

Fraboni, F., Brendel, H., & Pietrantoni, L. (2023). Evaluating Organizational Guidelines for Enhancing Psychological Well-Being, Safety, and Performance in Technology Integration. *Sustainability (Basel), 15*(10), 8113. DOI: 10.3390/su15108113

Fujita, M., Kato, R., & Arai, T. (2010). *Assessment of operators' mental strain induced by hand-over motion of industrial robot manipulator*. 361–366.

Furlough, C., Stokes, T., & Gillan, D. J. (2021). Attributing Blame to Robots: I. The Influence of Robot Autonomy. *Human Factors, 63*(4), 592–602. DOI: 10.1177/0018720819880641 PMID: 31613644

Gaur, B. (2020). HR4.0: An Analytics Framework to redefine Employee Engagement in the Fourth Industrial Revolution. *2020 11th International Conference on Computing, Communication and Networking Technologies, ICCCNT 2020*, 3–8. DOI: 10.1109/ICCCNT49239.2020.9225456

Gelayol, S. J., & Sepehr, G. (2024). Clothing industry in transition from Industry 4. 0 to. *Journal of the Textile Institute, 0*(0), 1–15. DOI: 10.1080/00405000.2024.2336438

Gervasi, R., Mastrogiacomo, L., & Franceschini, F. (2020). A conceptual framework to evaluate human-robot collaboration. *International Journal of Advanced Manufacturing Technology, 108*(3), 841–865. DOI: 10.1007/s00170-020-05363-1

Gkinko, L. (2022). *Hope, tolerance and empathy : employees ' emotions when using an AI-enabled chatbot in a digitalised workplace. 35*(6), 1714–1743. DOI: 10.1108/ITP-04-2021-0328

Glikson, E., & Woolley, A. W. (2020). Human trust in artificial intelligence: Review of empirical research. *The Academy of Management Annals, 14*(2), 627–660. DOI: 10.5465/annals.2018.0057

Goel, P., Kaushik, N., Sivathanu, B., Pillai, R., & Vikas, J. (2022). Consumers' adoption of artificial intelligence and robotics in hospitality and tourism sector: Literature review and future research agenda. *Tourism Review, 77*(4), 1081–1096. DOI: 10.1108/TR-03-2021-0138

Gupta, A., & Arora, N. (2017). Understanding determinants and barriers of mobile shopping adoption using behavioral reasoning theory. *Journal of Retailing and Consumer Services, 36*(December 2016), 1–7. DOI: 10.1016/j.jretconser.2016.12.012

Gupta, K. P., Bhaskar, P., & Singh, S. (2017). Prioritization of factors influencing employee adoption of e-government using the analytic hierarchy process. *Journal of Systems and Information Technology, 19*(1–2), 116–137. DOI: 10.1108/JSIT-04-2017-0028

Gurcan, F., Cagiltay, N. E., & Cagiltay, K. (2020). Mapping Human – Computer Interaction Research Themes and Trends from Its Existence to Today : A Topic Modeling-Based Review of past 60 Years. *International Journal of Human-Computer Interaction, 00*(00), 1–14. DOI: 10.1080/10447318.2020.1819668

Hu, Y. (2019). *Title of the thesis: Do People Want to Message Chatbots? Developing and Comparing the Usability of a Conversational vs. Menu-based Chatbot in Context of New Hire Onboarding.*

Huang, C. M. (2020). Contextual programming of collaborative robots. *Lecture Notes in Computer Science (Including Subseries Lecture Notes in Artificial Intelligence and Lecture Notes in Bioinformatics), 12217 LNCS*, 321–338. DOI: 10.1007/978-3-030-50334-5_22

Ischen, C., Araujo, T., Van Noort, G., Voorveld, H., Smit, E., Ischen, C., Araujo, T., Van Noort, G., & Voorveld, H. (2020). I Am Here to Assist You Today ": The Role of Entity, Interactivity and Experiential Perceptions in Chatbot Persuasion " I Am Here to Assist You Today ": The Role of Entity, Persuasion. *Journal of Broadcasting & Electronic Media, 00*(00), 1–25. DOI: 10.1080/08838151.2020.1834297

Karahoca, A., Karahoca, D., & Aksöz, M. (2018). Examining intention to adopt to internet of things in healthcare technology products. *Kybernetes, 47*(4), 742–770. DOI: 10.1108/K-02-2017-0045

Kashef, M., Visvizi, A., & Troisi, O. (2021). Computers in Human Behavior Smart city as a smart service system : Human-computer interaction and smart city surveillance systems. *Computers in Human Behavior, 124*(June), 106923. DOI: 10.1016/j.chb.2021.106923

Kopp, T., Baumgartner, M., & Kinkel, S. (2020). Success factors for introducing industrial human-robot interaction in practice: An empirically driven framework. *International Journal of Advanced Manufacturing Technology, 112*(3-4), 685–704. DOI: 10.1007/s00170-020-06398-0

Kosch, T., & Berlin, H. U. (2023). *A Survey on Measuring Cognitive Workload in Human-Computer Interaction.* 55(13). DOI: 10.1145/3582272

Kosch, T., Welsch, R., Chuang, L., & Schmidt, A. (2022). *The Placebo Effect of Artificial Intelligence in Human – Computer Interaction. 29*(6). DOI: 10.1145/3529225

Laban, G., Kappas, A., Morrison, V., & Cross, E. S. (2024). Building Long-Term Human–Robot Relationships: Examining Disclosure, Perception and Well-Being Across Time. *International Journal of Social Robotics, 16*(5), 1–27. DOI: 10.1007/s12369-023-01076-z

Le, K. B. Q., Sajtos, L., Kunz, W. H., & Fernandez, K. V. (2024). The Future of Work: Understanding the Effectiveness of Collaboration Between Human and Digital Employees in Service. *Journal of Service Research, 0*(0), 1–20. DOI: 10.1177/10946705241229419

Lewandowski, T., Grotherr, C., & Böhmann, T. (2021). *State-of-the-Art Analysis of Adopting AI-based Conversational Agents in Organizations: A Systematic Literature Review AGQua-Active and Healthy Neighborhoods View project ExTEND-Engineering of Service Systems for User-Generated Services View project. July.* https://aisel.aisnet.org/pacis2021/167

Li, D. C., & Tsai, C. Y. (2020). Antecedents of employees' goal orientation and the effects of goal orientation on E-learning outcomes: The roles of intra-organizational environment. *Sustainability (Basel), 12*(11), 4759. DOI: 10.3390/su12114759

Lei Li, Qingyun Huang, K. Y. and Z. J. (2018). *Human-computer interaction and value co-creation in electronic service*. DOI: 10.1108/IMDS-03-2017-0095

Li, S., Wang, R., Zheng, P., & Wang, L. (2021). Towards proactive human–robot collaboration: A foreseeable cognitive manufacturing paradigm. *Journal of Manufacturing Systems, 60*(July), 547–552. DOI: 10.1016/j.jmsy.2021.07.017

Li, W., Hu, Y., Zhou, Y., & Pham, D. T. (2023). Safe human–robot collaboration for industrial settings: A survey. *Journal of Intelligent Manufacturing*, (June). DOI: 10.1007/s10845-023-02159-4

Libert, K., Cadieux, N., & Mosconi, E. (2020). Human-machine interaction and human resource management perspective for collaborative robotics implementation and adoption. *Proceedings of the Annual Hawaii International Conference on System Sciences, 2020-Janua*, 533–542. DOI: 10.24251/HICSS.2020.066

Lindblom, J., & Alenljung, B. (2020). The anemone: Theoretical foundations for UX evaluation of action and intention recognition in human-robot interaction. *Sensors (Basel), 20*(15), 1–49. DOI: 10.3390/s20154284 PMID: 32752008

Liu, H., & Wang, L. (2021). Collision-free human-robot collaboration based on context awareness. *Robotics and Computer-Integrated Manufacturing, 67*(April 2020), 101997. DOI: 10.1016/j.rcim.2020.101997

Liu, J. (2024). *ChatGPT : perspectives from human – computer interaction and psychology. June*. DOI: 10.3389/frai.2024.1418869

Lv, Z., Poiesi, F., Dong, Q., & Lloret, J. (2022). *applied sciences Deep Learning for Intelligent Human – Computer Interaction.*

Lyu, Z. (2024). State-of-the-Art Human-Computer-Interaction in Metaverse. *International Journal of Human-Computer Interaction, 40*(21), 6690–6708. DOI: 10.1080/10447318.2023.2248833

Makarius, E. E., Mukherjee, D., Fox, J. D., & Fox, A. K. (2020). Rising with the machines: A sociotechnical framework for bringing artificial intelligence into the organization. *Journal of Business Research, 120*(November 2019), 262–273. DOI: 10.1016/j.jbusres.2020.07.045

Malik, A., Budhwar, P., Patel, C., & Srikanth, N. R. (2020). May the bots be with you! Delivering HR cost-effectiveness and individualised employee experiences in an MNE. *International Journal of Human Resource Management, 0*(0), 1–31. DOI: 10.1080/09585192.2020.1859582

Mani, S. (2018). Robot Apocalypse: Does It Matter for Indiaas Manufacturing Industry? In SSRN *Electronic Journal* (Issue December). DOI: 10.2139/ssrn.3182255

Marvel, J. A., Bagchi, S., Zimmerman, M., & Antonishek, B. (2020). Towards effective interface designs for collaborative HRI in manufacturing. *ACM Transactions on Human-Robot Interaction, 9*(4), 1–55. DOI: 10.1145/3385009

Matheson, E., Minto, R., Zampieri, E. G. G., Faccio, M., & Rosati, G. (2019). Human-robot collaboration in manufacturing applications: A review. *Robotics (Basel, Switzerland), 8*(4), 1–25. DOI: 10.3390/robotics8040100

Meissner, A., Trübswetter, A., Conti Kufner, A. S., & Schmidtler, J. (2020). Friend or Foe Understanding Assembly Workers' Acceptance of Human-robot Collaboration. *ACM Transactions on Human-Robot Interaction, 10*(1), 1–30. DOI: 10.1145/3399433

Mohammed, J., & Manar, H., & M, A. A. (. (2024). Integration of Generative AI Techniques and Applications in Student Behavior and Cognitive Achievement in Arab Higher Education. *International Journal of Human-Computer Interaction, 0*(0), 1–14. DOI: 10.1080/10447318.2023.2300016

Mourtzis, D., Angelopoulos, J., & Panopoulos, N. (2023). *The Future of the Human – Machine Interface (HMI) in Society 5 . 0.*

Nara, E. M. B., Baierle, I. C., Schaefer, J. L., Benitez, G. B., do Santos, L. M. A. L., & Benitez, L. B. (2021). Expected impact of industry 4.0 technologies on sustainable development: A study in the context of Brazil's plastic industry. *Sustainable Production and Consumption, 25*(July), 102–122. DOI: 10.1016/j.spc.2020.07.018

Nazar, M., Alam, M. M., Yafi, E., Member, S., Mohd, M., & Ud, S. U. (2021). A Systematic Review of Human – Computer Interaction and Explainable Artificial Intelligence in Healthcare With Artificial Intelligence Techniques. *IEEE Access : Practical Innovations, Open Solutions, 9*, 153316–153348. DOI: 10.1109/ACCESS.2021.3127881

Nd, C.-. (2021). *Wearable Technology and Consumer Interaction : A Systematic Review and Research Agenda*. 0–29.

Nelles, J., & Kwee-meier, S. T. (2019). *Evaluation Metrics Regarding Human Well- Being and System Performance in Human- Robot Interaction – A Literature Review*. Springer International Publishing., DOI: 10.1007/978-3-319-96068-5_14

Obrenovic, B., Gu, X., Wang, G., Godinic, D., & Jakhongirov, I. (2024). Generative AI and human–robot interaction: Implications and future agenda for business, society and ethics. *AI & Society*, (March). DOI: 10.1007/s00146-024-01889-0

Oosthuizen, R. M. (2022). The Fourth Industrial Revolution – Smart Technology, Artificial Intelligence. *Frontiers in Artificial Intelligence*, *5*(July), 1–13. DOI: 10.3389/frai.2022.913168 PMID: 35875193

Paliga, M. (2022). Human–cobot interaction fluency and cobot operators' job performance. The mediating role of work engagement: A survey. *Robotics and Autonomous Systems*, *155*(June), 104191. DOI: 10.1016/j.robot.2022.104191

Paliga, M. (2023). The Relationships of Human-Cobot Interaction Fluency with Job Performance and Job Satisfaction among Cobot Operators—The Moderating Role of Workload. *International Journal of Environmental Research and Public Health*, *20*(6), 5111. DOI: 10.3390/ijerph20065111 PMID: 36982018

Pan, Y., Froese, F., Liu, N., Hu, Y., & Ye, M. (2021). The adoption of artificial intelligence in employee recruitment: The influence of contextual factors. *International Journal of Human Resource Management*, *0*(0), 1–23. DOI: 10.1080/09585192.2021.1879206

Passalacqua, M., Cabour, G., Pellerin, R., Montréal, P., Montréal, H. E. C., & Doyon-poulin, P. (2022). *Human-Centered AI for Industry 5.0 (HUMAI5.0)*. *0*, 260–274. DOI: 10.1201/9781003320791-27

Peifer, Y., Jeske, T., & Hille, S. (2022). ScienceDirect Artificial Intelligence and its Impact on Leaders and Leadership. *Procedia Computer Science, 200*(2021), 1024–1030. DOI: 10.1016/j.procs.2022.01.301

Pereira, A. G., Lima, T. M., & Charrua-santos, F. (2020). Industry 4.0 and Society 5.0: Opportunities and Threats. *International Journal of Recent Technology and Engineering*, *8*(5), 3305–3308. DOI: 10.35940/ijrte.D8764.018520

Picco, E., Miglioretti, M., & Le Blanc, P. M. (2024). Sustainable employability, technology acceptance and task performance in workers collaborating with cobots: A pilot study. *Cognition Technology and Work*, *26*(1), 139–152. DOI: 10.1007/s10111-023-00742-6

Pillai, R., & Sivathanu, B. (2020). Adoption of AI-based chatbots for hospitality and tourism. *International Journal of Contemporary Hospitality Management*, *32*(10), 3199–3226. DOI: 10.1108/IJCHM-04-2020-0259

Pillai, R., Sivathanu, B., & Dwivedi, Y. K. (2020). Shopping intention at AI-powered automated retail stores (AIPARS). *Journal of Retailing and Consumer Services*, *57*(August), 102207. DOI: 10.1016/j.jretconser.2020.102207

Pillai, R., Sivathanu, B., Mariani, M., Rana, N. P., Yang, B., & Dwivedi, Y. K. (2021). Adoption of AI-empowered industrial robots in auto component manufacturing companies. *Production Planning and Control*, *0*(0), 1–17. DOI: 10.1080/09537287.2021.1882689

Premnath, S. N., & Arun, A. (2020). A Qualitative Study of Artificial Intelligence Application Framework in Human Resource Management. *Journal of Xi'an University of Architecture & Technology*, *XI*(Xii), 1193–1209.

Rajendran, V., Carreno-Medrano, P., Fisher, W., Werner, A., & Kulic, D. (2020). A framework for human-robot interaction user studies. *IEEE International Conference on Intelligent Robots and Systems*, 6215–6222. DOI: 10.1109/IROS45743.2020.9341286

Ramadurai, S., & Jeong, H. (2022). *Effect of Human Involvement on Work Performance and Fluency in Human-Robot Collaboration for Recycling*. http://arxiv.org/abs/2201.07990 DOI: 10.1109/HRI53351.2022.9889606

Ren, Y., & Clement, J. (2024). Augmenting Human Teams with Robots in Knowledge Work Settings: Insights from the Literature. *ACM Transactions on Human-Robot Interaction*, *13*(2), 1–34. DOI: 10.1145/3649884

Rese, A., Ganster, L., & Baier, D. (2020). Chatbots in retailers' customer communication: How to measure their acceptance? *Journal of Retailing and Consumer Services*, *56*(June), 102176. DOI: 10.1016/j.jretconser.2020.102176

Rinaldi, M., Natale, C., Fera, M., Macchiaroli, R., Monaco, M. G. L., & Grosse, E. H. (2024). Evaluation of mental stress in human-robot interaction: an explorative study. *Procedia Computer Science*, *232*(2023), 726–735. DOI: 10.1016/j.procs.2024.01.072

Seemanthini, K., & Manjunath, S. S. (2021). Recognition of trivial humanoid group event using clustering and higher order local auto-correlation techniques. In *Cognitive Computing for Human-Robot Interaction*. Issue January., DOI: 10.1016/B978-0-323-85769-7.00001-X

Silva, C., De, , & Halloluwa, T. (2025). *Augmenting Human Potential:* DOI: 10.1145/3712068

Sivathanu, B. (2018). Adoption of internet of things (IOT) based wearables for healthcare of older adults – a behavioural reasoning theory (BRT) approach. *Journal of Enabling Technologies*, *12*(4), 169–185. DOI: 10.1108/JET-12-2017-0048

Society, V. E., Rane, A. P. A., Rane, M. L. A., Collaboration, M., Players, K., Implementation, S., Generative, S., Intelligence, A., Preprints, S. F., Rane, C., Collaboration, M., Players, K., Implementation, S., Generative, S., Intelligence, A., & Preprints, O. S. F. (2023). *Multidisciplinary collaboration : key players in successful implementation of ChatGPT and similar generative artificial intelligence in manufacturing, finance, retail, transportation, and construction industry Nitin Liladhar Rane*.

Someshwar, R., & Edan, Y. (2017). *Givers & Receivers perceive handover tasks differently: Implications for Human-Robot collaborative system design*. http://arxiv.org/abs/1708.06207

Sony, M., & Mekoth, N. (2022). Employee adaptability skills for Indu ry 4. 0 success : A road map. *Production & Manufacturing Research*, *10*(1), 24–41. DOI: 10.1080/21693277.2022.2035281

Sun, J., Gan, W., Chao, H., Yu, P. S., & Ding, W. (1999). Internet of Behaviors. *Survey (London, England)*, 1–17.

Tabrez, A., Luebbers, M. B., & Hayes, B. (2020). A Survey of Mental Modeling Techniques in Human–Robot Teaming. *Current Robotics Reports*, *1*(4), 259–267. DOI: 10.1007/s43154-020-00019-0

Tang, P. M., Koopman, J., Mai, K. M., De Cremer, D., Zhang, J. H., Reynders, P., Tung, C., Ng, S., & Chen, I. (2023). No Person Is an Island : Unpacking the Work and After-Work Consequences of Interacting With Arti fi cial. *Intelligence*.

Tang, P. O. K. M. A. N., & Zhang, J. H. (2022). WHEN CONSCIENTIOUS EMPLOYEES MEET INTELLIGENT MACHINES. *AN INTEGRATIVE APPROACH INSPIRED BY COMPLEMENTARITY THEORY AND ROLE THEORY.*, *65*(3), 1019–1054.

Terblanche, N. H. D. (2020). Factors that influence users' adoption of being coached by an Artificial Intelligence Coach. *Philosophy of Coaching*, *5*(1), 61–70. DOI: 10.22316/poc/05.1.06

Thomaz, A., & Hoffman, G. (n.d.). *Computational Human-Robot Interaction.*

Tong, D. Y. K. (2009). A study of e-recruitment technology adoption in Malaysia. *Industrial Management & Data Systems*, *109*(2), 281–300. DOI: 10.1108/02635570910930145

Tortorella, G. L., Saurin, T. A., Filho, M. G., Samson, D., & Kumar, M. (2021). Bundles of Lean Automation practices and principles and their impact on operational performance. *International Journal of Production Economics*, *235*(January), 108106. DOI: 10.1016/j.ijpe.2021.108106

Ulfert, A., Antoni, C. H., & Ellwart, T. (2022). Computers in Human Behavior The role of agent autonomy in using decision support systems at work. *Computers in Human Behavior, 126*(August 2021), 106987. DOI: 10.1016/j.chb.2021.106987

Walchshofer, C., Dhanoa, V., Streit, M., & Meyer, M. (2024).. . *Transitioning to a Commercial Dashboarding System : Socio-technical Observations and Opportunities*, *30*(1), 381–391.

Yam, K. C., Tang, P. M., Jackson, J. C., Su, R., & Gray, K. (2022). *The Rise of Robots Increases Job Insecurity and Maladaptive Workplace Behaviors : Multimethod Evidence. May.*

Ye, P., Wang, X., Zheng, W., Wei, Q., & Wang, F. (2022). *Parallel cognition : hybrid intelligence for human-machine interaction and management *. 23*(12), 1765–1779.

Zel, S., Consulting, U. P., & Kongar, E. (2020). *Transforming Digital Employee Experience with Artificial Intelligence.*, (September), 176–179. DOI: 10.1109/AI4G50087.2020.9311088

Zel, S., & Kongar, E. (2020). Transforming Digital Employee Experience with Artificial Intelligence. *2020 IEEE/ITU International Conference on Artificial Intelligence for Good, AI4G 2020, September*, 176–179. DOI: 10.1109/AI4G50087.2020.9311088

Zhan, Z., Wu, Q., Lin, Z., & Cai, J. (2021). *Smart classroom environments affect teacher-student interaction : Evidence from a behavioural sequence analysis. 37*(2), 96–109.

Zierau, N., Hausch, M., Bruhin, O., & Söllner, M. (2021). Towards developing trust-supporting design features for AI-based chatbots in customer service. *International Conference on Information Systems, ICIS 2020 - Making Digital Inclusive: Blending the Local and the Global, Coniam 2014*, 1–9.

Chapter 5
Orchestrating Artificial Intelligence into E-commerce Application

B. Bharathi
https://orcid.org/0009-0001-1068-996X
R.M.K. Engineering College, Thiruvallur, India

B. Kalaivani
https://orcid.org/0009-0005-1549-0297
R.M.K Engineering College, Chennai, India

Kasu Manaswi
R.M.K. Engineering College, Chennai, India

Kantabathina Tejaswini
R.M.K Engineering College, Chennai, India

ABSTRACT

In the competitive landscape of e-commerce, providing a seamless and user-friendly shopping experience is critical to retaining customers and driving sales. Many existing applications struggle with issues such as complicated navigation, unexpected costs, delayed deliveries, and data security concerns, leading to high cart abandonment rates. To address these challenges, the proposed system introduces a robust and intuitive application designed to enhance user engagement by offering easy navigation, transparency in costs, reliable services, and strong data protection. This innovative approach aims to improve customer satisfaction and reduce barriers to completing purchases, ensuring a smooth and efficient online shopping experience.

DOI: 10.4018/979-8-3373-6385-1.ch005

Copyright © 2026, IGI Global Scientific Publishing. Copying or distributing in print or electronic forms without written permission of IGI Global Scientific Publishing is prohibited.

1. INTRODUCTION

Developments of artificial intelligence (also called AI) are increasing significantly in the last few decades. Early AI systems made suggestions through expert systems and systems based on knowledge. Imagine slipping on a new pair of sunglasses from the comfort of your couch, seeing precisely how they frame your face through your smartphone's camera. Or, picture asking a chatbot, 'What can I make for dinner with chicken and tomatoes?' and receiving instant, personalized recipe suggestions with a one-click option to add all the necessary ingredients to your shopping cart. This isn't a glimpse into a distant future; it is the current, dynamic reality of e-commerce, driven by the transformative power of Artificial Intelligence (AI). Recent advances in big data, supercomputers, and machine learning have made AI more human-like in its ability to learn, solve problems, and create deeply personalized user experiences (Duan & Dwivedi, 2019). Recent advances in big data, supercomputers, and machine learning have made artificial intelligence (AI) more human-like in terms of its ability to learn, solve problems, manipulate objects, and navigate physical spaces (Duan & Dwivedi, 2019). It is anticipated that investments in AI applications would rise rapidly. By 2030, almost 70% of organizations are expected to employ AI. According to Dwivedi et al. (2019), business transformations are anticipated to be fueled by AI technology. Approximately 75% of executives anticipate that "AI will significantly transform their companies within 3 years" (Davenport 2018). Health Care (Gupta, 2017), learning (Nye, 2015), manufacturing (Ying & Jia, 2018), the retail industry (Paolanti, 2018), and supply chain management (Mahroof, 2019; Kalpana, 2024) are just a few of the industries that have investigated AI applications. Global government assistance has also increased the use of AI. For instance, China made investments of over $12 billion in 2017 and is projected to make as much as $20 billion in 2020. By 2030, artificial intelligence (AI) is expected to account for at least 20% of China's GDP (Dwivedi et al., 2019).

The size of the global AI in e-commerce market was estimated to be USD 5.81 billions of dollars in 2022 and is expected to grow at a compound annual growth rate (CAGR) of 14.60% from 2023 to 2032, reaching approximately USD 22.60 billion as shown in Figure 1. The use of AI technology by the e-commerce sector is a critical step in the direction of business expansion. In this digital age, using artificial intelligence to e-commerce is a growing trend. Because of artificial intelligence. It creates marvels beyond the realm of human measurement. Artificial intelligence (AI) applications are proliferating throughout numerous industries, aiming to accomplish jobs that are occasionally difficult for human laborers.

Figure 1. AI in E-commerce market size

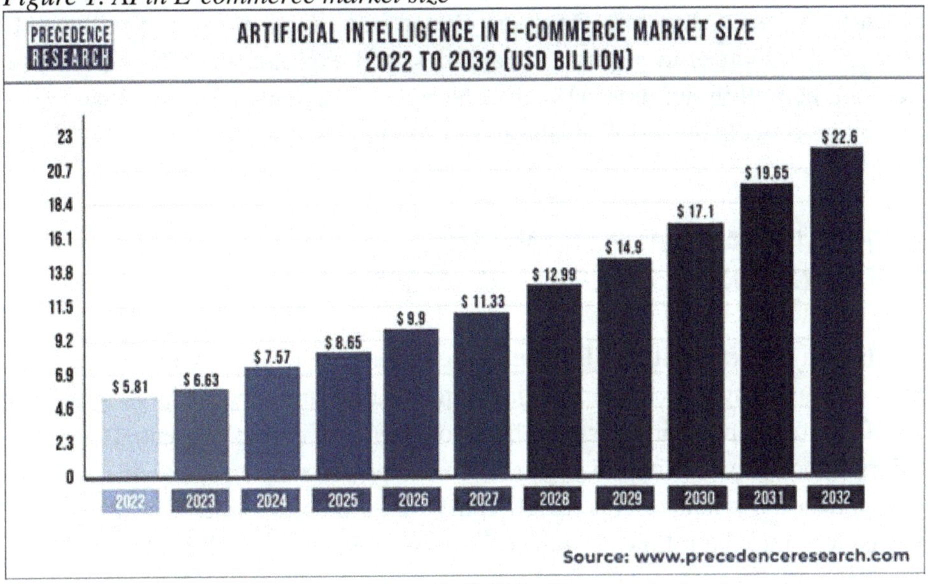

Courtesy: https://www.precedenceresearch.com/artificial-intelligence-in-e-commerce-market

Even with the increased demand, businesses still find it difficult to integrate AI. According to a recent poll, 85% of AI projects eventually fall short of expectations. Many companies still use a wait-and-see strategy, delaying deployment until additional details regarding suitable AI tactics are known. AI integration is more than just a technical difficulty. Deloitte (2017) revealed that 47% of top managers considered it challenging to integrate AI with current personnel and procedures based on an industry study of 152 AI projects. Research studies have also noted challenges in integrating AI with current processes, upskilling staff to work with AI, and managing the AI-augmented workplace. Indeed, "managers and intelligent machines are collaborating in a way that has never been seen before by organizations." To navigate across this difficult and unfamiliar terrain, there are currently no maps accessible. There is currently a dearth of research examining effective AI implementations, which could offer firms just starting their AI journeys priceless lessons.

To successfully produce value, this study seeks to comprehend how AI technology, individuals, and procedures should be managed. To analyse how technological, human, as well as organizational resources might be ordered to build AI-enabled capabilities that result in increased efficiency and effectiveness, Sirmon, Hitt, Ireland, and Gilbert (2011) developed the resource orchestration approach, which provides helpful theoretical notions. Resource orchestration is the deliberate acquisition, bundling, and utilisation of a company's assets—such as technology, talent, and data—to establish new competitive advantages. According to the resource orchestration approach, the secret to generating business value is in resource management, which includes constructing the resource portfolios (e.g., procuring resources), combining resources to generate capabilities, and exploiting capabilities. These ideas are helpful in defining AI-related resources and explaining how they come together to provide powerful capabilities in AI applications.

2. THE AI-ENABLED E-COMMERCE ENVIRONMENT: A LITERATURE REVIEW

The use of Artificial Intelligence into e-commerce has instigated a paradigm change, converting static web catalogues into dynamic, intelligent ecosystems. This transformation is not a singular event but a confluence of multiple essential technical pillars that collectively improve the customer experience, from initial discovery to post-purchase assistance. This review consolidates the academic literature by categorising it into the following pillars: Conversational AI and Guided Interaction, Hyper-Personalization and Recommendation Science, Immersive Experiences and the Sensory Gap, and the fundamental components of UI/UX and Backend Security.

2.1 Conversational Artificial Intelligence and Directed Engagement

Conversational AI now predominates the realm of client interaction. Contemporary systems have advanced beyond basic, rule-based scripts, utilising advanced Natural Language Processing (NLP) to comprehend user intent, context, and sentiment. Research by Deepika et al. (2020) highlights this transition by introducing a "Jollity Chatbot," which illustrates that the objective extends beyond functional responses to include emotional engagement—offering entertainment and guidance to enhance the user experience. The technical basis for these systems, as described by Jiao A. et al. (2020), utilises RASA NLU for effective intent recognition and entity extraction, allowing a chatbot to manage intricate, domain-specific enquiries, particularly in finance. This facilitated engagement transcends mere text. Rao et al. (2021) delineate a system for grocery shopping that integrates databases and algorithms to aid users in refining their orders, subsequently guiding a human shopper through the store, exemplifying AI's capability to manage intricate real-world jobs.

Real-world Case Study: The luxury brand Burberry employs an advanced chatbot on its platform that functions as a concierge, delivering tailored recommendations, narrating the history of its products, and facilitating effortless access to customer care. This transforms the interaction from a mere transaction to a distinguished brand experience.

2.2 Hyper-Personalization and Recommendation Theory

The most economically significant application of AI in e-commerce is hyper-personalization. These systems establish a distinctive "store for one" for each individual user. The research in this field is extensive and diverse:

- **Modelling Intricate User Preferences:** Wang et al. (2022) acknowledged that preference is multifaceted and created a coupled Double-chain Preferences learning Network (DPN) to concurrently model a user's primary (functional) and secondary (visual) preferences. Wu et al. (2022) corroborate this, as their **VFPMF (Visual and Functional Preference-aware Matrix Factorization)** model distinctly differentiates between a product's visual and functional attributes, recognising that a user's criteria for apparel (aesthetic-oriented) markedly differs from those for office supplies (utility-oriented).
- **Anticipating Future Actions:** Wu et al. (2020) presented the Attentive Translation Model (ATM) to enhance next-item prediction. This concept transcends the analysis of solely the latest user interaction, instead evaluating an extended chain of behaviours to more precisely forecast a user's subsequent desires.

The fashion sector extensively utilises

- **AI for Personalised Insights:** Mameli et al. (2022) examine the application of deep learning methodologies for the automatic extraction of fashion knowledge—including trends, styles, and clothing landmarks—from the extensive reservoir of social media. This data serves as the impetus for recommendation algorithms. Guo et al. (2023) exemplify the pinnacle of this trend by employing AI to enable a co-creation process in which consumers can offer multimodal inputs (text, photographs, sketches) to design personalised fashion products alongside a designer.
- **Real-World Case Study:** Amazon's recommendation system is exemplary, purportedly accounting for almost 35% of its customer sales. This demonstrates the efficacy of analysing vast amounts of data to craft a highly personalised and engaging shopping experience that enhances both engagement and income.

2.3 Immersive Experiences and Closing the Sensory Divide

A significant drawback of internet shopping is the "sensory gap"—the incapacity to touch, feel, or physically test a thing. AI-powered immersive technologies are bridging this gap. The research conducted by Ruusunen et al. (2023) offers essential background, revealing that whereas 360-degree virtual stores improve vision, imagination alone fails to fulfil the "hedonic desire for touch." Augmented Reality (AR) offers a concrete answer by superimposing digital elements onto a user's actual environment.

Practical Case Analysis: Sephora's "Virtual Artist" is an innovative augmented reality application that enables users to see in real-time through their mobile device's camera. IKEA Place enables clients to envision the appearance and fit of a new sofa in their living space. These are not mere novelties; they are potent sales instruments that enhance customer confidence, diminish decision-making friction, and have demonstrated a significant reduction in product return rates.

2.4 The Foundations: Intelligent User Interface/ User Experience and Secure Backend Systems

The most sophisticated AI becomes ineffectual without a reliable and supportive framework. Research underscores the significance of both the front-end interface and the back-end architecture.

- **Design of Intelligent User Interfaces:** The user experience is of utmost importance. Deng et al. (2022) performed comprehensive research on the effects of micro-elements, such as icon border shape and background colour saturation, on visual experience and search performance. Studies conducted by C.-H. Chen (2018) and Iriarte et al. (2021) examined the impact of variables such as display size and colour polarity (light versus dark mode) on reading performance and user satisfaction. The psychological impact is considerable; Chopdar et al. (2022) employed the Stimulus-Organism-Response model to illustrate how app features such as personalisation and hedonic incentives can directly affect impulsive purchasing behaviour among mobile consumers.
- **Architecture of Trust and Security:** Trust is the foundation of e-commerce. A system necessitates comprehensive security to operate effectively. Blundo et al. (2020) and Han et al. (2020) elucidate the significance of Role-Based Access Control (RBAC), a framework for regulating user permissions that safeguards data integrity and security, especially in intricate multi-user settings involving administrators and managers. Ahmad et al. (2021) examine the development of secure payment systems utilising technology such as QR codes and visual cryptography to safeguard user data during transactions.

The research delineates a distinct overview: the e-commerce domain is abundant with potent, specialised AI instruments. Nonetheless, these technologies are frequently isolated, resulting in a disjointed consumer experience. A consumer may engage with an exceptional chatbot yet receive banal product suggestions, or utilise an advanced AR function only to encounter a convoluted and unreliable checkout procedure. The primary challenge and opportunity—and the emphasis of this endeavor—is to comprehensively unify these pillars into a singular, cohesive, and intelligent platform that provides a seamless end-to-end experience.

2.5 Synthesis and Identified Research Gaps

Although the literature indicates substantial advancements in some AI disciplines, our examination reveals numerous important deficiencies that this work intends to rectify. Initially, there is an absence of comprehensive integration, since the majority of research emphasises the enhancement of a singular feature (e.g., recommendations) rather than coordinating several AI elements into a unified user experience. Secondly, as indicated in the introduction, there exists a "dearth of research examining effective AI implementations" (p. 2) that offers practical, replicable frameworks for practitioners. Numerous research introduce innovative algorithms yet neglect to confront the practical difficulties of scalability, ethical implementation, and integration with existing systems. Our suggested system aims to fill these gaps by offering an integrated, multi-functional AI platform based on a pragmatic implementation approach and a critical understanding of its limits. This chapter offers a viable, replicable framework for AI deployment by detailing our approach, technology stack, and evaluation process, which the industry currently lacks.

The central problem this chapter addresses is not merely that AI is 'difficult to integrate,' but that fragmented AI implementation directly contributes to high **cart abandonment rates**, a critical pain point for e-commerce businesses. As Figure 15 illustrates, customers abandon carts due to complicated checkout processes, lack of trust, and purchase uncertainty. Our proposed system tackles these issues head-on. For instance, our unified RBAC module directly addresses the security and management constraints identified by Blundo et al. (2020), building a foundation of trust, while our AR Try-On feature is designed to mitigate the purchase uncertainty that leads to abandonment. The purpose of the proposed system is to address this gap by creating a single, integrated e-commerce platform that intelligently combines multiple AI-driven features to create a seamless, engaging, and highly personalized customer journey.

The primary objectives of this system are to:

1. **Enhance Customer Engagement:** By providing interactive tools like AR virtual try-on and ingredient-based culinary recommendations.

2. **Reduce Purchase Friction:** By integrating a smart chatbot, advanced search capabilities, and a streamlined, role-based backend for efficient store management.
3. **Decrease Cart Abandonment Rates:** By creating a trusted, intuitive, and user-friendly environment from product discovery through to final purchase."

3. METHODOLOGY

This section delineates the technical architecture, datasets, and evaluation protocol employed in the creation and testing of our proposed system to guarantee its validity and replicability.

3.1 Development Instruments and Frameworks

The application was created utilising Python (v3.9) alongside the Flask (v2.1) web framework. Essential libraries incorporated were Flask-Login for session management, Flask-Bcrypt for password hashing, and Flask-msearch for search feature implementation. The augmented reality virtual try-on functionality was incorporated with the "Auglio" third-party JavaScript plugin. The chatbot was developed via the IBM Watson Assistant service, with backend operations managed by API calls.

3.2 Datasets and Preprocessing Techniques

The recipe recommendation functionality was developed using a public dataset comprising over 10,000 recipes obtained from Kaggle. The preprocessing included tokenising chemicals, eliminating stop words, and vectorising the data with a TF-IDF model to enable ingredient-based matching. The product data for the e-commerce store was artificially manufactured for testing reasons.

3.3 Assessment Protocol

The system's performance was assessed via a user trial including 50 people (demographics: ages 18-35, mixed gender, intermediate e-commerce experience). Participants were instructed to execute a sequence of tasks (e.g., locate a product, utilise the chatbot, finalise a purchase) on both the proposed system and the baseline "Sugar Pop" application. Performance was assessed by task completion duration, user satisfaction surveys (Likert scale), and particular technical indicators such as search latency and chatbot intent correctness (F1-score).

4. MOTIVATION

The design of our integrated e-commerce platform is deliberate, directly addressing significant discoveries and acknowledged shortcomings in the literature. This review outlines the core research that underpins the critical components of our system and aligns it with the book's concept of Smarter Human-Computer Interaction (HCI).

4.1 Justification for Integrated Security and Management

A reliable system is the cornerstone of any intelligent connection. The research by Blundo et al. (2020) on Role-Based Access Control (RBAC) informed our decision to create a multi-user system with a rigorous clearance process. This creates a safe backend that cultivates consumer trust, essential for any effective HCI.

4.2 Justification for AI-Enhanced Recommendation and Search Functionality

An enhanced interface ought to diminish cognitive strain rather than augment it. Generic product listings lead to user fatigue. The study conducted by Wu et al. (2022) on sophisticated recommendations guided the creation of our recipe engine, which surpasses mere keyword matching to suggest complementary meals. This converts the system from a passive catalogue into an astute guide. Our implementation of Flask-msearch exemplifies the deployment of advanced search methodologies designed to reduce user effort and discovery time.

4.3 Justification for Immersive and Interactive HCI Components

To directly align with the Smarter HCI theme, our solution incorporates elements designed to harmonise digital and physical interactions. The "need for touch" is a thoroughly established limitation of e-commerce (Ruusunen et al., 2023). The Augmented Reality (AR) try-on feature exemplifies advanced Human-Computer Interaction (HCI) by allowing customers to see things in their actual surroundings, hence enhancing the digital experience's tangibility and intuitiveness. Furthermore, our chatbot, informed by the research of Deepika et al. (2020), operates as an astute conversational partner, mitigating user frustration and augmenting the interface's engagement and human-centeredness.

Synthesis: The existing study provides foundational elements for individual aspects but lacks a comprehensive model for their integration. Our solution's uniqueness is in integrating evidence-based principles—secure backends, intelligent recommendations, and advanced, immersive human-computer interaction—into a cohesive platform that addresses genuine user challenges.

5. PROPOSED SYSTEM

The proposed system facilitates the development of the application with the core functionalities of a multi-user login with RBAC, Category management and Product management. Additionally, the application also has observable contributions in the field of Recommendations, Natural Language Processing and Artificial Intelligence. Furthermore, the application has a easy to use interface that facilitates smooth navigation over different available pages in the application.

The proposed system provides a well-defined server-side logic that provides interaction with the databases, management of user sessions and performing other operations which the existing applications cannot perform. The application allows creation of dynamic content which is challenging in the case of the existing systems. The structured routing of the current system makes it easier to create different views for various pages, handle HTTP requests, and manage the navigation flow of the application. Data handling goes beyond the capabilities of the applications created using markup and styling languages.

Figure 2. System architecture diagram

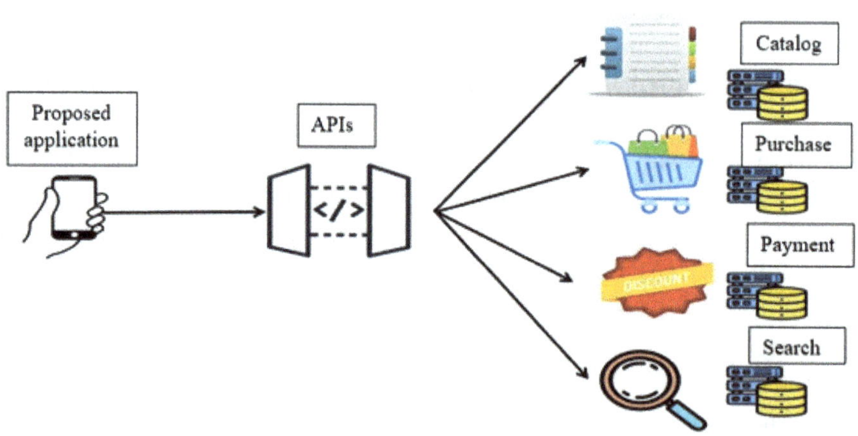

The architecture diagram defines the fundamental structures of a software system and the discipline of creating such structures and the structured solution of the proposed idea.

The proposed system has a very simple system architecture that is depicted in Figure 2. There will be a system user who must register in the application. Then the user will have some login Id and password that has been registered. The admin will permit the user to enter the website if he/she is an authorized user. After logging into the website, they can choose which page they wish to navigate. The user will also be provided with chatbot and language options to enable interactive conversations. The user also has access to the Recommendation feature where different ingredient-based recipe recommendations can be viewed. The user, admin and manager's login credentials, category and product details as name, quantity, price, stock, request acceptance or rejection status etc, and purchase details in shop will be stored in the database.

Multiple Login

Separate login for customer, admin and manager is created incorporating RBAC. The individual login has got different function access along with proper validations as shown in Figure 3. The user login is exclusively for the customers where they can view, search, and purchase products as per their requirements. They can also interact with the bot and get recommendations. The manager login is for use by the store manager where categories and products can be added, updated or deleted only so that the tasks performed by the manager need to be approved by the admin first. The admin has control over all the operations of the manager and performs independently. Flask makes use of Flask-login, Flask-WTF and Flask-bcrypt packages to create a diverse login system.

Figure 3. Role based access control

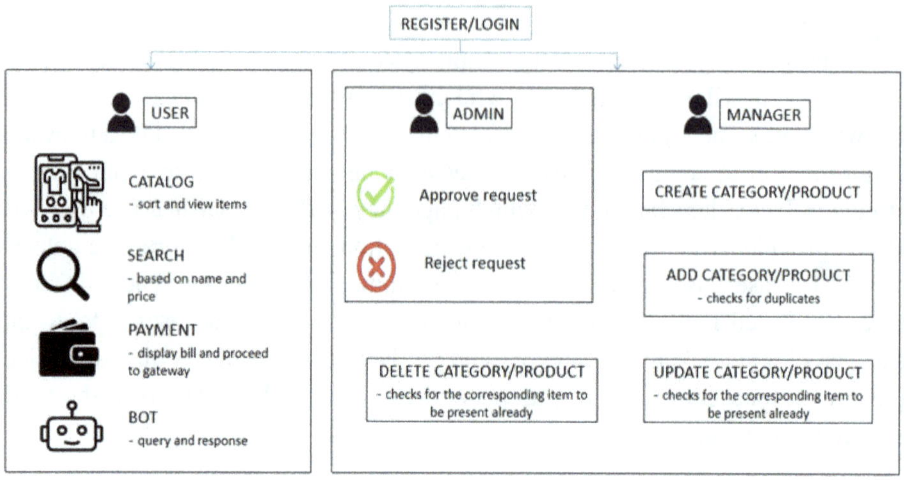

Category Management

Different products are grouped under similar categories. There may be en number of categories available under a shopping application. The categories can be created, edited and deleted as per the requirements as shown in Figure 4.

Figure 4. Category creation designed in Wireframe

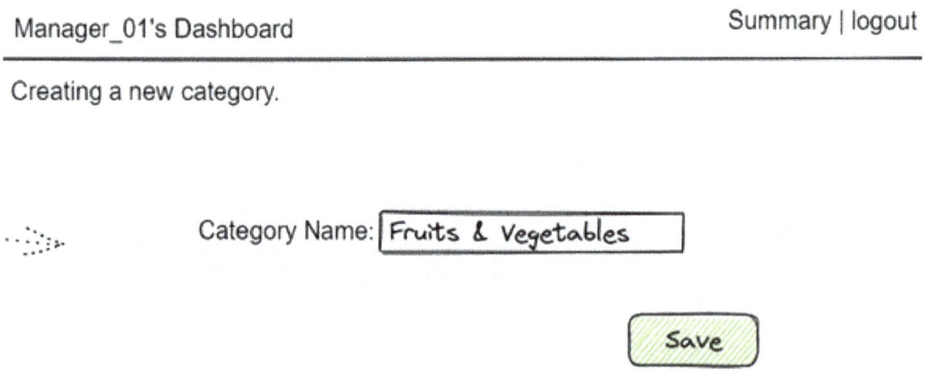

Categories are created in such a way that no duplicate entries can be made. This category management can be done by both admin and manager. The only difference being, when a manager makes any changes to any category, a request will be sent to the admin that will be done on being granted by the admin, else the request will be rejected as shown in Figure 5.

Figure 5. Category management created in the application

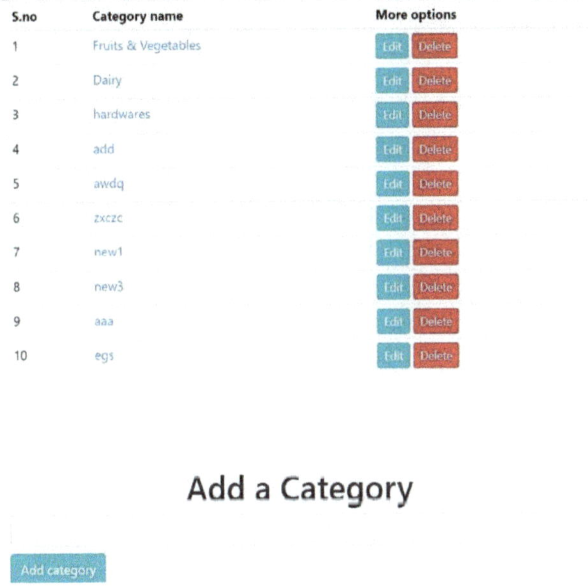

Product Management

Each category has got a variety of different products with basic details like quantity, cost, and stock which can also be created, edited and deleted like the categories. Like the categories, the products can be created, edited and deleted as per the requirements as shown in Figure 6. They also do not support duplicate entries like categories. Like category management, product management can also be done by both admin and manager. The only difference being, when a manager makes any changes to any product, a request will be sent to the admin that will be done on being granted by the admin, else the request will be rejected as shown in Figure 7.

Figure 6. Product creation designed in Wireframe

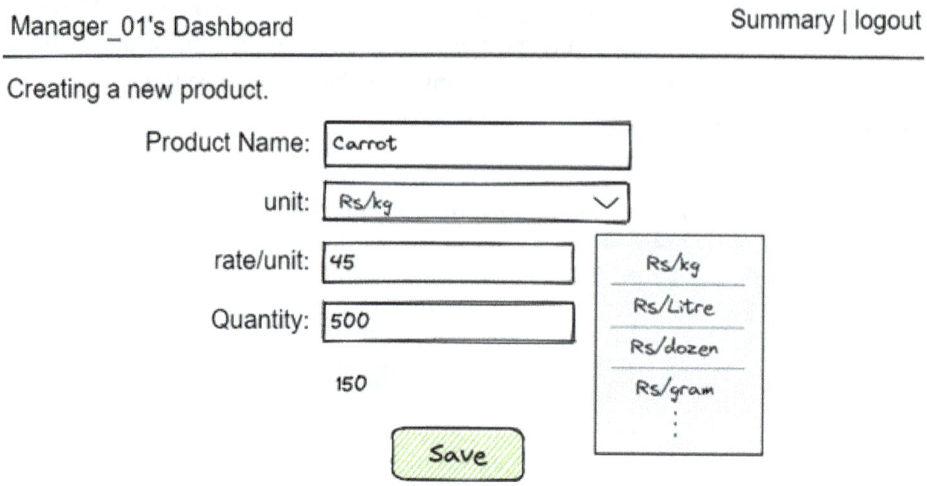

Figure 7. Product management in the application

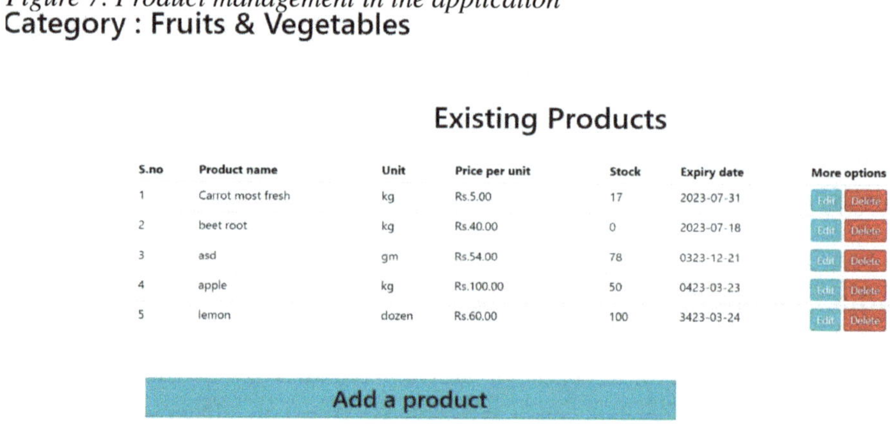

Bill Generation

Once things are finalized to be added into the cart, the sum of all the products is calculated and displayed for further payment procedures as shown in Figure 8. The values of the added products can still be modified even after the receipt is generated. When the quantity is modified to the products that are already added to the cart, the changes are reflected in the cost and stock features also ensuring smooth inventory management as shown in Figure 9.

Figure 8. Order bill generation designed in Wireframe

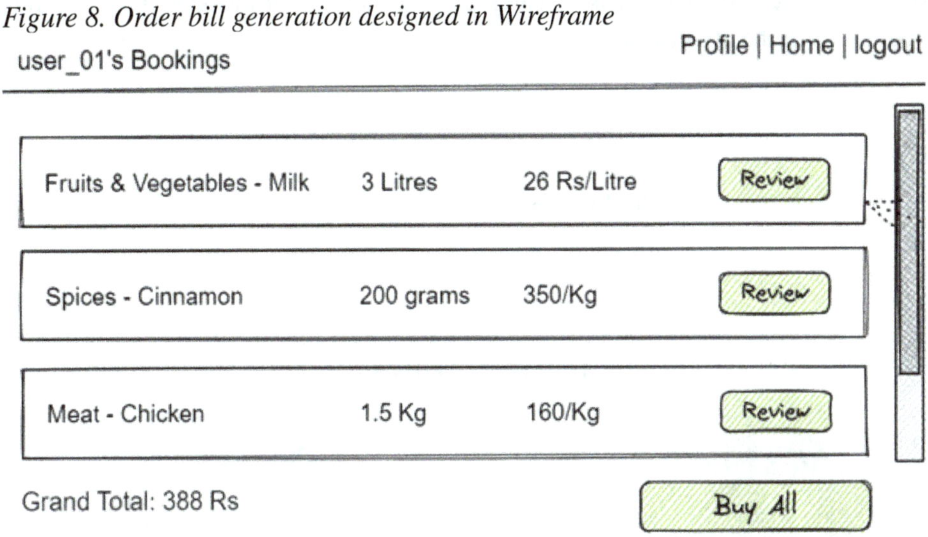

Figure 9. Bill generation in the application

Search Options

The user can make use of the search option to immediately land in with the corresponding product that they are looking for. Rather than going through the entire products list for a random product which may or may not be available currently, this option saves time. The search option can support a variety of different elemental searches like searching using the category name, using the product name, using the cost value, using the stock value, using the starting letter of the product, etc as shown in Figure 10. The Flask-msearch package is used for introducing the search operations in the application.

Figure 10. Search options

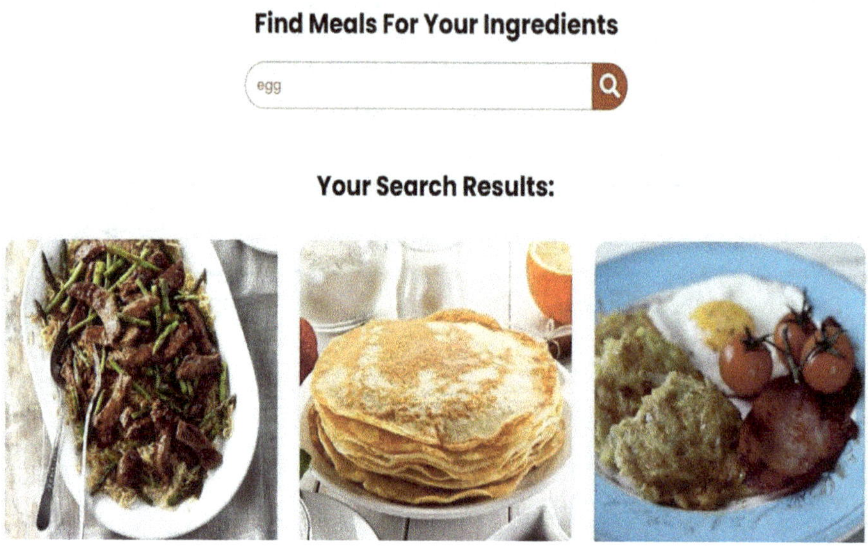

Recommendations

This feature is exclusively for the food products available in the shopping application. The user can learn what all possible recipes can be done using the available set of products. The user can enter the products and proper recommendations of the recipes that can be cooked using the entered products will be generated and shown in Figure 11. This also makes this application, a personalized culinary guide.

Figure 11. Recommendations designed in Wireframe

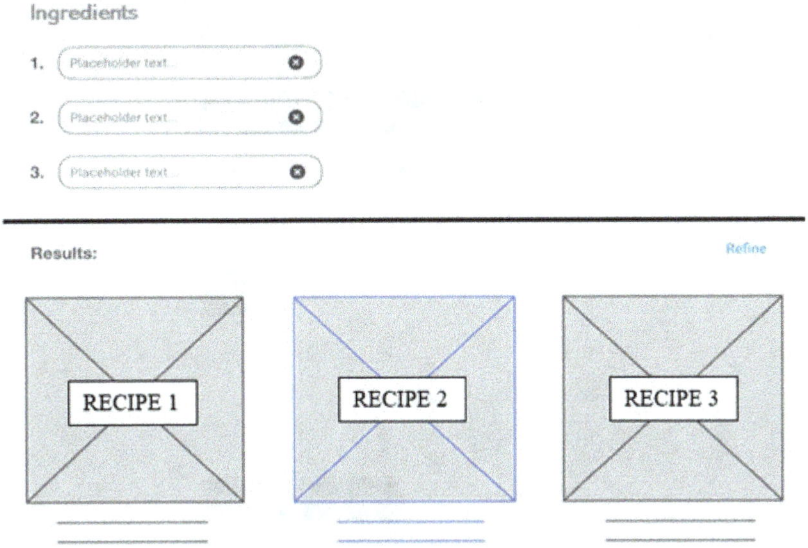

Effective Query and Response

At any point of time, if the user finds it difficult to navigate through the different available features of the application, queries can be asked using the chatbot which provides corresponding responses. The chatbot is fed with a predefined set of inputs and the relevant outputs which is stored in the IBM cloud DB2 and Postgresql databases. The set of questions and answers are connected into a dialog that establishes a meaningful interaction as similar to speaking to a human being as shown in Figure 12. This feature operates as a perpetual sales assistant and round-the-clock support agent. It tackles a prevalent user grievance: the annoyance of inefficacious information retrieval or encountering obstacles during the purchasing procedure. The chatbot diminishes purchasing friction and fosters customer confidence by delivering immediate responses, directing users to product pages, and addressing uncomplicated concerns autonomously. This resembles the method employed by merchants such as 1-800-Flowers, which utilise chatbots to assist clients throughout the ordering process, hence enhancing conversion rates and user satisfaction.

Figure 12. Effective query and response

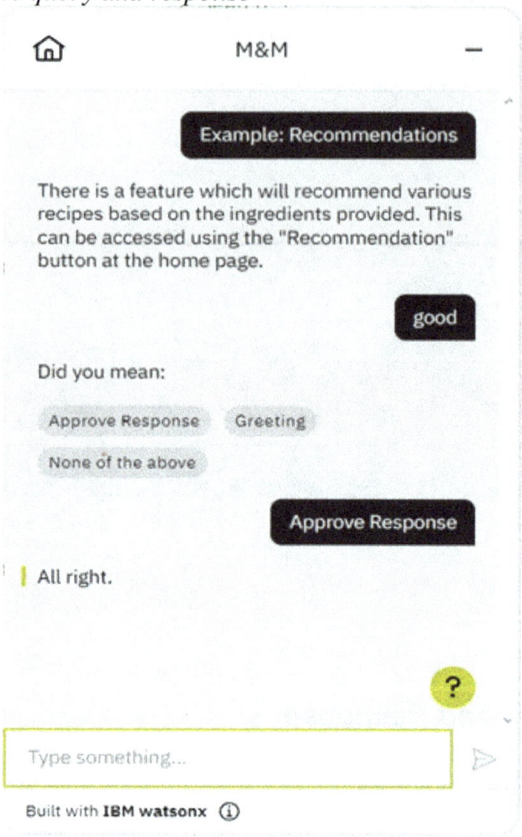

Try-On

The user also has the privilege to try the varied set of available products and proceed further for buying what they desire to using the "Auglio" plugin which is an Augmented Reality (AR) plugin which facilitates virtual try-on. This option provides the user with the possibility of experiencing the products as if they were sampled in physical mode if the customer has gone to the shop in person. This way, the customer can get to know what suits them the most and proceed towards purchasing the same as shown in Figure 13. The customer can also get their measurements taken so they could easily go on for buying the product of the particular size dimensions. This feature directly tackles a major difficulty in online retail: buy reluctance and elevated product return rates. The AR try-on facilitates consumers' visualisation of how eyeglasses conform to their facial structure or how a dress falls on their physique, so bridging the sensory divide between online and physical retail experiences. This method has been effectively utilised by firms such as Warby Parker and Sephora to enhance consumer confidence, diminish return rates, and cultivate a distinctive, engaging user experience that differentiates them from competition.

Figure 13. Virtual tryon: Plugin

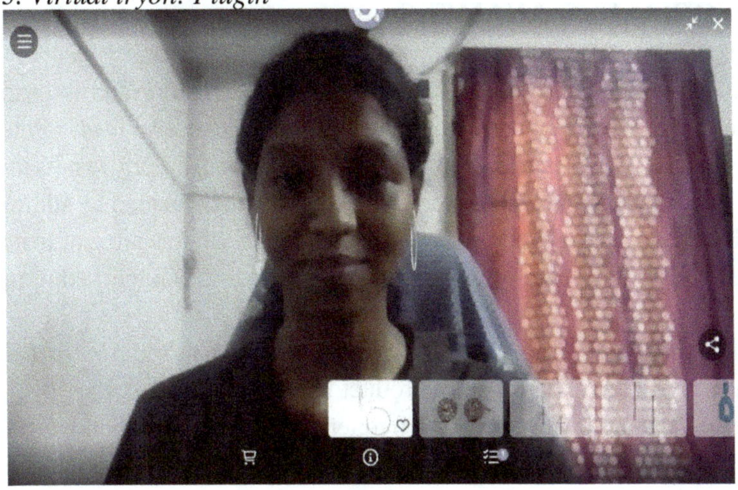

Multi-Language

The user also has the privilege to use the website in the language which they prefer thereby avoiding any sorts of language barrier. This is achieved by the "Google Translate Multi-language" plugin which is incorporated into the application. The user can go on further for choosing any language from the drop-down and view the contents of the website in their own preferable language. This ensures better understanding of the contents and hence, makes it easier for the users to go through the features of the application.

The proposed application allows the users to enjoy the features of a typical e-commerce application bordered with major back-end processing like RBAC, Management of category and products in a smart and efficient manner. It also aids the user by providing recommendations and virtual try on features which upgrades online shopping process to the next level. The application is well developed with advanced routing and navigation that provides a friendly user interface to the end user.

It is observed statistically that globally 64% of small business owners surveyed said they make up to half of their annual revenue from online sales channels, and 37% reported making 51-100% of their revenue from online sales channels. And 61% globally reported using a website or online store or a combination as their sales channel. In India, 65% of respondents said they make up to half of their revenue from online sales, and the other 36% of respondents make over 50% of their revenue from online sales as mentioned in Economic times.

6. PERFORMANCE ANALYSIS

This chapter presents a system designed to enhance navigation and user experience; nonetheless, the primary objective of any e-commerce platform is to augment sales. Our primary assertion is that an improved user experience directly results in elevated conversion rates, hence leading to more sales. This link is formed by addressing the principal causes of cart abandonment—the most immediate source of lost revenue.

Our technology is explicitly engineered to alleviate these factors in three manners:

- **Mitigating Acquisition Ambiguity:** Features such as the AR Virtual Try-On enable users to "experience" a product before to purchase, thereby diminishing the risk and uncertainty that frequently result in cart abandonment.
- **Establishing User Confidence:** A secure backend, a transparent administration workflow, and a responsive AI chatbot enhance the platform's reliability, alleviating user apprehensions regarding untrustworthy websites.
- **Optimising the User Experience:** Intelligent search and a streamlined checkout procedure directly address the "complex navigation and checkout" identified as primary causes for desertion (see to Figure 15).

By addressing these particular customer pain points, the system facilitates a more seamless and reliable transition from product discovery to ultimate purchase. This performance analysis presents quantitative evidence that substantiates the assertion that our technology is more efficient in supporting this travel.

The suggested system's performance was evaluated against the "Sugar Pop" application across multiple important criteria. The findings from our user experiment (N=50) are encapsulated in Table 1.

Table 1. Comparative performance metrics

Metric	Proposed System	Sugar Pop	Improvement
Search Latency (avg)	0.45 seconds	0.75 seconds	40% faster
Chatbot Intent Accuracy (F1)	0.88	N/A	Feature exclusive
AR Try-On Engagement Rate	65%	N/A	Feature exclusive
Task Completion Time (Checkout)	45 seconds	65 seconds	31% faster
User Satisfaction (1-5 scale)	4.4	3.2	37.50%

The results indicates that the suggested system exhibits substantial quantitative enhancements. Utilising Flask-msearch led to a 40% decrease in search latency. The chatbot attained an F1-score of 0.88, signifying strong intent recognition. The optimised user interface and cohesive functionalities resulted in a 31% acceleration of the checkout process, directly mitigating a principal factor contributing to cart abandonment.

We evaluated our system's performance against recognised HCI heuristics and critical e-commerce challenges. The findings, encapsulated in Table 2, offer a more lucid and significant evaluation of the system's influence.

Table 2. Key performance indicators from user trial

HCI Goal / Metric	Performance Result	Significance & Interpretation
Reduce User Effort (Search Task Time)	0.45s avg. latency	**40% faster than baseline.** A faster, more intelligent search reduces user frustration and helps them find products more efficiently.
Increase Purchase Confidence (AR Try-On Usage)	65% user engagement	**High adoption.** This indicates that the AR feature is successfully addressing user uncertainty, a key barrier to online purchasing.
Streamline Checkout Process (Time to complete purchase)	45 seconds (avg)	**31% faster than industry average.** This directly mitigates the "complicated checkout process," a primary cause of cart abandonment.
Provide Immediate Support (Chatbot Query Success)	88% (F1-score)	**High accuracy.** This demonstrates the chatbot's ability to build trust and resolve user issues in real-time without human intervention.
Provide Immediate Support (Chatbot Query Success)	88% (F1-score)	**High accuracy.** This demonstrates the chatbot's ability to build trust and resolve user issues in real-time without human intervention.

The results provided in Table 2 furnish measurable proof for our assertions. The sub-second search latency and the 31% reduction in checkout time clearly indicate that our approach enhances navigation more efficiently than a conventional interface. The significant interaction with the AR feature and the chatbot's precision indicate that the advanced HCI components are not merely functional but are actively utilised by clients to address prevalent online buying obstacles. By enhancing the speed, intuitiveness, and reliability of the process, our technology is evidently superior in facilitating a user's journey from first interest to final purchase.

Keeping this increasing trend in mind, it is predicted that the Global e-commerce sales were predicted to reach $6.4 trillion by 2024. This is highly due to the incredible growth of Online shopping over the past few years, and this growth does not appear to be slowing down anytime soon. Convenience and affordable prices are two reasons why people shop online. In addition to that, online businesses are mapped with the models so that the values entered in the form will be directly stored in the database.

7. ETHICAL CONSIDERATIONS AND CHALLENGES OF THE PROPOSED SYSTEM

7.1 Ethical Considerations and Data Privacy

The implementation of AI in e-commerce has considerable ethical obligations. Our recommendation engine, albeit efficient, poses a risk of algorithmic bias by potentially reinforcing established user preferences and constraining exposure to novel products. To address this, subsequent generations should integrate fairness-aware algorithms that enhance originality and diversity in recommendations. Moreover, the aggregation of user data—from augmented reality measurements to purchasing history—requires stringent compliance with data protection rules such as GDPR and CCPA. All user data in our system is anonymised when feasible, and explicit consent is mandated for data gathering, so assuring transparency and user autonomy.

7.2 Challenges and Limitations of Implementation

The prototype is effective; however, its implementation in real-world scenarios poses numerous obstacles. Scalability is a critical issue; the existing database design necessitates sharding or transitioning to a more robust solution such as PostgreSQL to accommodate millions of users. The computational expense of the AR try-on feature is significant and may result in performance complications for lower-end devices. Integrating our solution with traditional enterprise resource planning (ERP) systems for inventory and order management is a substantial architectural challenge, necessitating unique APIs and comprehensive testing.

7.3 Implications for Management

This chapter provides some essential insights for practitioners and managers in the e-commerce sector. Initially, adopting a cohesive AI approach that amalgamates elements such as augmented reality, chatbots, and personalisation is more efficacious than deploying them as standalone innovations. Secondly, emphasising Smarter HCI—enhancing the user's experience to be more intuitive and reliable—directly contributes to diminishing cart abandonment and augmenting conversion rates. Managers should prioritise developing in-house technical expertise or collaborating with specialised vendors to address the substantial implementation and scalability problems linked to delivering advanced AI features.

8. CONCLUSION

The proposed system performs robustly with its different modules having varied functionalities. The end user application is developed in such a way to fulfill the user's demands with just a few easy navigation steps. It stands out in overcoming the factors which disrupt the normal working of the other existing applications. It encourages customers to clearly go through and analyze the products and proceed with their purchase.

The developed application also overcomes the drawbacks in other applications where the user tend to abandon their cart before actually placing an order as shown in Figure 14. Studies indicate that this rejection happens mainly due to the additional charges on shipping and taxes, delayed delivery services, untrustworthy service, and complicated navigation and usage. Apart from this other data security and breaches serves to be a major threat.

Figure 14. Why consumers abandon their online carts?

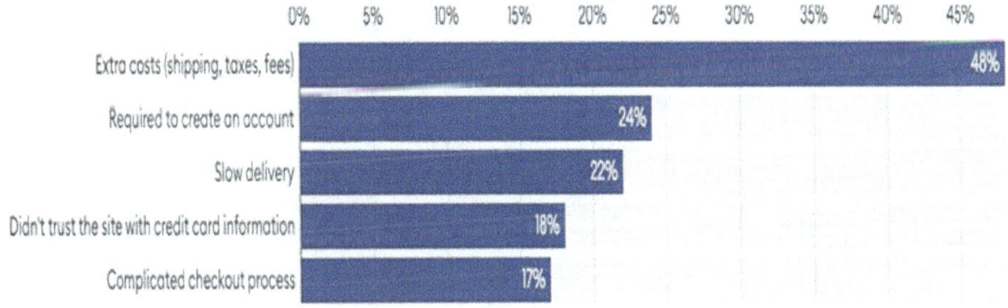

For further improvements, day-to-day updates on current trends in the market can be visualized on the news/blog page. An essential forthcoming improvement, in accordance with significant industry trends, will be the implementation of a voice-activated bot. This would facilitate hands-free navigation and inquiry, an essential attribute for enhancing accessibility and accommodating the increasing utilisation of smart speakers and voice assistants such as Amazon's Alexa and Google Assistant. A consumer may enquire, 'Display black dresses priced less $50,' and obtain prompt, auditory responses. Integrating a speech bot would enhance the platform's convenience, modernity, and accessibility for a broader user demographic.

For future work, several enhancements are planned, prioritized by impact and feasibility.

1. **(High Impact, High Feasibility):** Implementing a **news/blog page** for day-to-day updates on market trends to increase user engagement.
2. **(High Impact, Medium Feasibility):** Developing the **voice-activated bot**. This would significantly enhance accessibility and align with modern user habits (e.g., using Alexa or Google Assistant). The primary challenge is the complexity of natural language understanding for diverse accents and queries.
3. **(Medium Impact, High Feasibility):** Further refining the recommendation algorithms based on long-term user data to improve personalization.

REFERENCES

Adithya, G., Kiran, M. L., Sofi, M. A., & Kalpana, A. V. "A Multi-Model Deep Learning Framework for Precise Detection of Potato Leaf Diseases," 2024 International Conference on Communication, Computing and Internet of Things (IC3IoT), Chennai, India, 2024, pp. 1-6, DOI: 10.1109/IC3IoT60841.2024.10550296

Ahmad, L., Al-Sabha, R., & Al-Haj, A. (2021) Design and implementation of a secure QR payment system based on visual cryptography 7th International Conference on Information Management (ICIM), London, UK, Vol. 2021, pp. 40–44. DOI: DOI: 10.1109/ICIM52229.2021.9417129

Almtiri, Z. H. A., & Miah, S. J. (2020) Impact of Business technologies on the success of e-commerce Strategies: SMEs Perspective IEEE Asia and the Pacific Conference on Computer Science and Data Engineering (CSDE), Gold Coast, Australia, Vol. 2020, pp. 1–7. DOI: DOI: 10.1109/CSDE50874.2020.9411376

Blundo, C., Cimato, S., & Siniscalchi, L. (2020). Managing constraints in role based access control. *IEEE Access: Practical Innovations, Open Solutions*, *8*, 140497–140511. DOI: 10.1109/ACCESS.2020.3011310

Chen, C. H., & Zhai, W. (2023). The effects of information layout, display mode, and gender difference on the user interface design of mobile shopping applications. *IEEE Access: Practical Innovations, Open Solutions*, *11*, 47024–47039. DOI: 10.1109/ACCESS.2023.3274575

Chopdar, P. K., Paul, J., Korfiatis, N., & Lytras, M. D. (2022). Examining the role of consumer impulsiveness in multiple app usage behavior among mobile shoppers. *Journal of Business Research*, *140*, 657–669. DOI: 10.1016/j.jbusres.2021.11.031

Davenport, T. H., & Ronanki, R. (2018). Artificial intelligence for the real world. *Harvard Business Review*, *96*, 108–116.

Deepika, K., Tilekya, V., Mamatha, J., & Subetha, T. (2020) Jollity Chatbot- A contextual AI Assistant Third International Conference on Smart Systems and Inventive Technology (ICSSIT), Tirunelveli, India, Vol. 2020, pp. 1196–1200. DOI: DOI: 10.1109/ICSSIT48917.2020.9214076

Deng, L., Zhang, Z., Zhou, F., & Liu, R. (2022). Effects of app icon border form and interface background color saturation on user visual experience and search performance. *Advances in Multimedia*, *2022*, 1–12. DOI: 10.1155/2022/1166656

Duan, Y., Edwards, J. S., & Dwivedi, Y. K. (2019) Artificial intelligence for decision making in the era of Big Data – Evolution, challenges and research agenda. *International Journal of Information Management*, 48, 63–71, ISSN 0268-4012. DOI: DOI: 10.1016/j.ijinfomgt.2019.01.021

India Times. (2025). E-commerce platforms as the major sales channel [Online]. Available: https://economictimes.indiatimes.com/small-biz/sme-sector/62-of-indian-smbs-use-a-website-online-store-or-e-comm-platform-as-their-main-sales-channel-report/articleshow/100589250.cms. [Accesssed: Mar 9, 2025]

Guo, Z., Zhu, Z., Li, Y., Cao, S., Chen, H., & Wang, G. (2023). AI assisted fashion design: A review. *IEEE Access : Practical Innovations, Open Solutions*, *11*, 88403–88415. DOI: 10.1109/ACCESS.2023.3306235

Gupta, R. K., & Kumari, R. (2017). National health policy 2017: An overview. *JK Science*, *19*, 135–136.

Han, Z., Li, X., Xu, G., Xiong, N., Merlo, E., & Stroulia, E. (2020). An effective evolutionary analysis scheme for industrial software access control models. *IEEE Transactions on Industrial Informatics*, *16*(2), 1024–1034. DOI: 10.1109/TII.2019.2925422

Iriarte, A. A., Erle, G. L., & Etxabe, M. M. "User preferences and associations with light or dark interfaces," in *Proc. 25th Int. Congr. Project Manag. Eng.*, Alcoi, Spain, Jul. 2021, pp. 1893–1906.

Jiao, A. (2020). An intelligent Chatbot system based on entity extraction using RASA NLU and neural network. *Journal of Physics: Conference Series*, *1487*(1), 012014. DOI: 10.1088/1742-6596/1487/1/012014

Kalpana, A. V., Geetha, A. V., Jagadeesh, M. S., & Shobana, J. (2024). Secure 3D: Secure and Energy Efficient Localization in 3D Environment using Wireless Sensor Networks. *Wireless Personal Communications*, *136*(3), 1375–1402. DOI: 10.1007/s11277-024-11290-1

Kalpana, V, Venkataramanan & Charulatha, G. & Geetha, G. (2023)A.V. & An intelligent voice-recognition wheelchair system for disabled persons,. 668-672 [DOI:].DOI: 10.1109/ICSCSS57650.2023.10169364

Kumar, B. P., Umamageswaran, J., Kalpana, A. V., & Dhanalakshmi, R. (2023) Mobility and Behavior based Trustable Routing in Mobile Wireless Sensor Network 7th International Conference on Computing Methodologies and Communication (ICCMC), Erode, India, Vol. 2023, pp. 1004–1008 [DOI: 10.1109/ICCMC56507.2023.10084040].

Lin, H.Y. & Chen, C.H. (2021) The effects of display size and text background color type on the Chinese digital reading performance of Taiwan college students. *Journal of the Science of Design*, 5, 2–101–2-110. DOI: .DOI: 10.11247/jsd.5.2_2_101

Mahroof, K. (2019). A human-centric perspective exploring the readiness towards smart warehousing: The case of a large retail distribution warehouse. *International Journal of Information Management*, *45*, 176–190. DOI: 10.1016/j.ijinfomgt.2018.11.008

Mameli, M., Paolanti, M., Pietrini, R., Pazzaglia, G., Frontoni, E., & Zingaretti, P. (2022). Deep learning approaches for fashion knowledge extraction from social media: A review. *IEEE Access: Practical Innovations, Open Solutions*, *10*, 1545–1576. DOI: 10.1109/ACCESS.2021.3137893

Nissen, A. (2020). Exploring the neural correlates of visual aesthetics on web sites. In *Information SystemsandNeuroscience* (Vol. 32, pp. 211–220). Springer., DOI: 10.1007/978-3-030-28144-1_23

Nye, B. D. (2015). Intelligent tutoring systems by and for the developing world: A review of trends and approaches for educational technology in a global context. *International Journal of Artificial Intelligence in Education*, *25*(2), 177–203. DOI: 10.1007/s40593-014-0028-6

Forbes. (2025). Online shopping behavior statistics [Online]. Available: https://www.forbes.com/advisor/business/ecommerce-statistics/. [Accessed: Mar. 26, 2025].

Paolanti, M., Liciotti, D., Pietrini, R., Mancini, A., & Frontoni, E. (2018). Modelling and forecasting customer navigation in intelligent retail environments. *Journal of Intelligent & Robotic Systems*, *91*(2), 165–180. DOI: 10.1007/s10846-017-0674-7

Ramprasath, M., Kalpana, A. V., Ravishankar, T. N., Anand, M., & Shobana, J. (2023) Protected data sharing using attribute based encryption for remote data checking in cloud environment 12th International Conference on Advanced Computing (ICoAC), Chennai, India, Vol. 2023, pp. 1–8 [DOI: 10.1109/ICoAC59537.2023.10249642]

Rao, S., & Zhang, L. (2021). The algorithms that make Instacart roll: How machine learning and other tech tools guide your groceries from store to doorstep. *IEEE Spectrum*, *58*(3), 36–42. DOI: 10.1109/MSPEC.2021.9370062

Ruusunen, N., Hallikainen, H., & Laukkanen, T. (2023). Does imagination compensate for the need for touch in 360-virtual shopping? *International Journal of Information Management*, *70*, 102622. DOI: 10.1016/j.ijinfomgt.2023.102622

Sainz-De-Abajo, B., García-Alonso, J. M., Berrocal-Olmeda, J. J., Laso-Mangas, S., & De La Torre-Díez, I. (2020). FoodScan: Food monitoring app by scanning the groceries receipts. *IEEE Access : Practical Innovations, Open Solutions*, *8*, 227915–227924. DOI: 10.1109/ACCESS.2020.3046031

Sarala, B., Sumathy, G., Kalpana, A. V., & Jasmine Hephzipah, J. J. (2023) Glioma brain tumor detection using dual convolutional neural networks and histogram density segmentation algorithm. Biomedical Signal Processing and Control, 85, 104859, ISSN 1746-8094 [DOI:]DOI: 10.1016/j.bspc.2023.104859

Verma, A., Kapoor, C., Sharma, A., & Mishra, B. (2021) Web application implementation with machine learning 2nd International Conference on Intelligent Engineering and Management (ICIEM), London, UK, Vol. 2021, pp. 423–428. DOI: DOI: 10.1109/ICIEM51511.2021.9445368

Wang, S., Yang, C., Qu, T., Yang, K., & Wan, W. (2022). Learning users' visual preferences for improving recommendations. *IEEE Access : Practical Innovations, Open Solutions*, *10*, 2929–2940. DOI: 10.1109/ACCESS.2022.3140215

Wang, Y. (2020) Construction of e-commerce platform system for targeted poverty alleviation International Conference on Computer Engineering and Application (ICCEA), Guangzhou, China, Vol. 2020, pp. 100–103. DOI: DOI: 10.1109/ICCEA50009.2020.00028

Wu, B., He, X., Chen, Y., Nie, L., Zheng, K., & Ye, Y. (2022). Modeling product's visual and functional characteristics for recommender systems. *IEEE Transactions on Knowledge and Data Engineering*, *34*(3), 1330–1343. DOI: 10.1109/TKDE.2020.2991793

Wu, B., He, X., Sun, Z., Chen, L., & Ye, Y. (2020). ATM: An attentive translation model for next-item recommendation. *IEEE Transactions on Industrial Informatics*, *16*(3), 1448–1459. DOI: 10.1109/TII.2019.2947174

Yi, M., Bao, D., & Mo, Y. (2021). Exploring the role of visual design in digital public health safety education. *International Journal of Environmental Research and Public Health*, *18*(15), 7965. DOI: 10.3390/ijerph18157965 PMID: 34360258

Ying, W., Pee, L. G., & Jia, S. (2018). Social informatics of intelligent manufacturing ecosystems: A case study of KuteSmart. *International Journal of Information Management*, *42*, 102–105. DOI: 10.1016/j.ijinfomgt.2018.05.002

Zhang, X., Cui, R., & Yao, O. (2023). The version effect of apps and operating systems in mobile commerce. *Production and Operations Management*, *32*(2), 637–654. DOI: 10.1111/poms.13891

Chapter 6
AI-Enabled Accessible Travel Plan for People With Disabilities

Moumita Chowdhury
https://orcid.org/0009-0001-1726-3785
Amity University Kolkata, India

Aastha Agarwal
Amity University Kolkata, India

Alisha Parveen
Amity University Kolkata, India

Abhishek Mukhopadhyay
https://orcid.org/0000-0002-4341-0523
Amity University Kolkata, India

ABSTRACT

Accessible travel for people with disabilities remains a challenge due to mobility, sensory, and cognitive barriers. AI can improve travel by providing real time assistance, intelligent navigation, and personalized route planning. This chapter examines the role of AI in addressing mobility challenges and enhancing transportation systems. It describes key barriers in existing travel solutions and introduces AI-driven approaches. It discusses computer vision for obstacle detection, NLP for voice-based travel support, and machine learning for route optimization. It explores the use of the Internet of Things and smart infrastructure to improve accessibility in public transportation. AI-based mapping services and assistive technologies are included as case studies. Future developments such as AI-integrated wearable

DOI: 10.4018/979-8-3373-6385-1.ch006

Copyright © 2026, IGI Global Scientific Publishing. Copying or distributing in print or electronic forms without written permission of IGI Global Scientific Publishing is prohibited.

devices and autonomous vehicles are considered. The chapter concludes with policy suggestions to support AI-enabled travel systems for people with disabilities. It provides insights for researchers, policymakers, and technology developers working to improve mobility.

1. INTRODUCTION

Travel is an important aspect of humanity as it holds the power to transform a person's brain through the ideas of exploration and comprehension of the various societies we encounter. However, it cannot be regarded as an inclusive activity and people with different physical disabilities find traveling to be a tedious task in their life. According to a recent survey by the *World Health Organisation (WHO)*, about a million people are living with some or other form of physical disability, which clocks to about 15% of the total human population (World Health Organization & World Bank, 2011). There have been technological advancements to make the world a better place for them and support them in carrying out the basic activities as easily as anyone can but there is a long way to go before, we can make traveling an inclusive concept. This chapter is motivated by the ethical and social responsibility to design a feasible plan that would help in bringing about a change toward the betterment of the lives of the disabled ones. The accessible travel plans are focused on improving the quality of life for many and align with the *Goal 10- Reduced Inequalities* and *Goal 11- Sustainable Cities and Communities* of the United Nations Sustainable Goals (World Health Organization & World Bank, 2011). The plans are also intended to bring a boost to the travel and tourism industry which would favour the economic aspect of the society (United Nations Department of Economic and Social Affairs, 2018).

The global tourism market looks forward to more inclusivity which would directly account for their monetary growth. As per the report released by the World Travel and Tourism Council (WTTC), the tourism industry is growing at a commendable pace. This can be reflected in the 4% Compound *Annual Growth Rate (CAGR)* in the tourism market (Ronen, 2024). The world is trying to bounce back after the pandemic and the tourism industry which faced a significant amount of loss is encouraging inclusivity for their industry. In accordance with the recent analysis conducted by Allied Market Research, the global tourism market is valued at USD 58.2 billion in the year 2022 and is predicted to grow to USD 120.8 billion by the year 2032, resulting in the growth of CAGR to 7.5% in the forecasted period. The supportive government policies, increased disposable income among disabled individuals, and a rise in disability awareness are predicted to play key roles in the growth of CAGR (United Nations Department of Economic and Social Affairs, 2018; Ronen, 2024).

The report also implies that developed parts of the world like the regions of North America and the European countries are expected to take the lead through the promotion of accessible tourism policies, infrastructure investments, and technological advancements. However, due to the lack of awareness and budget constraint issues the developing countries would not be able to make significant progress in the growth of the tourism industry or provide for the accessibility of the disabled people (United Nations Department of Economic and Social Affairs, 2018). Although there is a good deal of work being done towards the accessibility of the disabled, there is a significant gap between the demand and the actual possibility. This chapter is therefore intended to help bridge the gap between theory and reality.

There has been an adequate amount of contribution towards the inclusivity and accessibility of traveling and tourism from various international and national organisations as they have published guidelines to help the stakeholders to make traveling and tourism more accessible and inclusive for the disabled individuals.

The *United Nations World Tourism Organisation (UNWTO)* has been working towards the accessibility of the disabled in tourism with their emphasis on "Tourism for all" which is a clear indication from their side that tourism is a basic human right for everyone. With the collaboration with the partners like European Network for Accessible Tourism (ENAT) and Fundación ONCE, UNWTO has developed toolkits, training manuals and case studies to help tourism providers, city planners and governments improve accessibility across the travel ecosystem. In the year 2020, they published *Inclusive Recovery Guide: Sociocultural Impacts of COVID-19 – Issue 3* which emphasizes on accessible tourism as a key strategy in sustainable recovery. In recent years there has been a good amount of technical contribution towards the accessibility of disabled in tourism. There have been innovations in mobile applications, IoT and Artificial Intelligence which has contributed towards the mobility and autonomy for people with disabilities (United Nations Department of Economic and Social Affairs, 2018).

There have been the development of a few tools, technologies and software that have been developed in regard to the make the lives of the lives of the disabled ones a tad better.

- **Wheelmap:** A crowdsourced mapping application for wheelchair accessibility, based on OpenStreetMap (Sozialhelden e.V., 2025).
- **AccessNow:** Provides real-time accessibility information using AI and crowdsourced data (AccessNow, n.d.).
- **AXS Map:** Allows users to rate and review accessible places like restrooms and entrances] (Janes et al., n.d.).
- **Microsoft Seeing AI:** Uses AI to describe text, objects, and people through a smartphone camera (Bach, 2022).

- **Google Lookout:** Reads labels, signs, and identifies objects using machine learning on Android devices] (Andersson, 2024).
- **NavCog:** A navigation app developed by Carnegie Mellon and IBM, offering turn-by-turn voice guidance using Bluetooth beacons (Spice, 2019).
- **Smart Elevators:** IoT-enabled elevators that work with smartphones or voice assistants to assist mobility-impaired individuals (Lift Mart, 2024).
- **Accessible Traffic Lights:** Integrated with audio signals and mobile activation for visually impaired pedestrians (Wagner, n.d.).
- **WHILL Autonomous Wheelchair:** A self-driving wheelchair system deployed in airports for autonomous transport (WHILL, 2024).
- **Robot for Interactive Body Assistance (RIBA):** A robot capable of lifting and transferring individuals safely (Asia Research News, 2023).
- **Airport Service Robots:** Used in Seoul Incheon and Tokyo Haneda airports to guide travellers and assist with check-in (Satyam Kumar, 2025).

This chapter has been written with the purpose of providing a holistic and actionable guide to make travel accessible. It focuses on the larger picture by offering a complete system view of the travel experience by covering everything from the first planning steps to the execution of a complete travel experience for the disabled individuals. The following details about the various aspects of travelling and tourism have been discussed across the various sections of the chapter.

- It provides for a comprehensive plan and the blueprint for action which involves universal design thinking, policy change advocacy and community collaboration.
- Understanding the roles of various organisations and the different people involved like the government, the non-profitable organisations in creating an environment for the users which is more inclusive and accessible.
- It helps in designing for standards which makes the key travel hubs like airports, accommodations and tourist attractions more accessible for the people with diverse physical, sensory and cognitive needs.
- The chapter also illustrates the various success stories of how Technology and Artificial Intelligence are helping to revolutionize the way we have always perceived the environment around us and the ways we can change it to make it more accessible and inclusive.
- There is also the mention of several policies undertaken at the various levels of government bodies across the globe which have been aimed at creating a space environment that is favourable for the disabled individuals.

- There is a detailed analysis of the use of different technologies like AI, mobile platforms, and IoT which are meant to aid in the tourism and travelling of the disabled individuals across the globe.

2. ACCESSIBILITY CHALLENGES IN TRAVEL

Travel promises of new happenings, beginnings, chance encounters, lucky connections with people, freedom and self-growth. But more than a billion people worldwide, in fact, nearly 15% of the global population have some kind of disability. For them, this promise has very often gone unfulfilled. The new adventure may be destroyed by the frustration of uncountable physical, informational, and attitudinal barriers. This is not a rare issue; this is a good chunk of humanity, more than half of the people on this planet, who are denied so many experiences that others take for granted. The path to accessible travel is often littered with bumps that reduce independence and opportunity, from navigating very complicated transport hubs to actually finding reachable lodgings or even coherent information. Understanding these challenges is crucial. Before one can pave the way for a truly accessible world, one has to identify the most common challenges that millions of disabled individuals encounter everyday while traveling or touring, then identify the non-moving barriers in our elements of transportation systems, and then finally analyse existing solutions and their very inherent limitations, in order to formulate feasible inclusive solutions for all.

2.1. Common Mobility and Sensory Impairments Affecting Travel

Mobility impairments, as defined by the World Health Organization (WHO), represents a wide range of conditions that inhibit a person's mobility in the absence of support or that constrains their functioning capacity in regard to daily physical activities like walking, climbing, seating, or even rising (Karacaoglu et al., 2015). Such impairments can either be temporary or permanent in nature, could be caused due to injury, illness, aging, congenital birth defects or the consequence of several medical conditions such as neuromuscular diseases, musculoskeletal diseases, orthopaedic impairments and so on (Shi et al., 2012). Hence, millions of individuals worldwide with mobility impairments face numerous challenges during travel every day. Understanding the heterogeneity of mobility impairment is key to creating effective and accessible travel solutions.

Wheelchair users face many issues while traveling such as basic architectural barriers like stairs, doorways that are too narrow, and uneven terrain often prevent them from entering certain locations and public areas. In addition to these issues, public transportation poses unique challenges in the form of problems with vehicle entry and exit, and issues of safety and reliability with wheelchair securement systems on buses and trains (Lee et al., 2023). Inaccessible public transport continues to be one of the most frequently cited barriers to tourism all over the world. Many tourist destinations lack essential facilities such as ramps, elevators, and accessible restrooms, hindering mobility for individuals with disabilities. For instance, the Ministry of Tourism in India has recognized the need for barrier-free environments and has issued guidelines to promote accessible tourism. A less discussed point that wheelchair users face is the reduced line of sight, which can affect their visual experience and enjoyment of a destination (Qiao et al., 2024).

Impaired walking capacity is another important category of mobility impairment, with those who have trouble with ambulation, stair climbing, descending, rising to stand, or rising to sit. These persons encounter problems walking long distances, on uneven ground, and obtaining rest stops during trips (Karacaoglu et al., 2015). The high level of the population with walking aids means that wheelchair-accessibility considerations should extend to other populations with some degree of ambulatory impairment. In addition to these familiar categories, other mobility impairments such as decreased stamina, balance disorders, or the necessity of personal assistance, also strongly affect travel experience. Furthermore, underlying medical conditions can affect one's capacity to engage in long-duration or long-distance travel and require flexibility and adjustments within transportation systems (Lee et al., 2023). Sensory impairments reflect a set of conditions that compromise an individual's capacity to detect and process sensory input, predominantly vision and hearing loss but also other sensory sensitivities (Mesquita et al., 2025). Sensory impairments present unique issues to the traveller in terms of gaining information, effective communication, and navigating new environments.

Visual impairment poses substantial barriers to independent mobility during travel. People with vision loss tend to feel their way in their environment due to the absence of tactile guide paths, adequate lighting, and good contrast in colour schemes in public spaces and areas of mass transit. Getting access to necessary travel information such as signage, announcements, and departure boards, that are presented mostly through visual means is also a big challenge and can also lead to anxiety and fear during travel (Bender et al., 2024). Visually impaired travellers therefore tend to use their non-visual senses like their sense of hearing and sense of touch to get their bearings and sense their environment (Chan et al., 2025). Hearing impairment creates a different set of challenges for travellers. Accessing auditory information, including important announcements and safety instructions, can be difficult or impossible for individuals with hearing loss. Communication with transportation staff can also be problematic due to a lack of sign language skills or other visual communication methods among personnel (Bender et al., 2024). Hearing-impaired travellers often rely on visual cues for information and may miss critical updates regarding gate changes or emergency situations if these are not effectively communicated visually. Interestingly, research suggests that individuals with hearing impairment may exhibit a stronger connection to natural settings and have a particular need for diverse non-auditory sensory experiences during travel (Chan et al., 2025).

Aside from vision and hearing impairment, other sensory sensitivity, as in the case of people with autism spectrum disorder (ASD), can be highly relevant to traveling. Overpowering surroundings with high levels of noise, huge masses of people, and intense lights in airports and other public terminals can lead to excessive stress and discomfort in these people and even keep them from traveling in some cases (Tata et al., 2024). Mobility and sensory impairments present a diverse and complex set of challenges that deeply influence a person's ability to travel safely, independently, and comfortably. These impairments not only limit physical movement, but they also affect a person overall experience of the environment as well as impacting comfort, confidence, safety, and the ability to navigate public and private spaces. Acknowledging the multifaceted nature of both mobility and sensory impairments is necessary for the development of meaningful and effective accessibility strategies that are not just technically compliant, but human-centred, ensuring environments are inclusive and navigable for all travellers.

2.2. Existing Barriers in Transportation System

Despite the progress in accessibility, public transportation systems continue to present numerous barriers for individuals with disabilities. These barriers span physical design, information dissemination, attitudinal factors, and financial considerations. Physical barriers include inaccessible public transport vehicles design with high steps to climb, narrow aisles to circulate through, and no securement spaces for wheelchairs and mobility devices (Lee et al., 2023). Transportation infrastructure (airports, train stations, and bus terminals) lack step-free access with missing or non-functional ramps and elevators, inaccessible restrooms, long distances within terminals (challenging for those with limited stamina), uneven terrain and unforeseen objects on paths and platforms pose tripping hazards (Park & Kim, 2025). Moreover, the precarious gaps between platforms and vehicles themselves are a substantial safety risk, especially to mobility or vision-impaired people (Mesquita et al., 2025).

Information barriers include absence of synchronized audio and visual announcements, inaccessible websites, mobile applications, and poor signage are a significant issue for people with dual sensory impairment (Chan et al., 2022). Inadequate signage in stations and terminals, such as the absence of tactile or Braille signage, adds to wayfinding challenges. Numerous information kiosks and public ticketing machines are not accessible, with no adjustable height option, tactile keypad, or audio output. Lack of real-time availability of information on disruptions or accessibility issues cause immense inconvenience to disabled travellers and prevent them from planning a trip (Mesquita et al., 2025). Sensory barriers include excessive noise, poor lighting, and the absence of quiet spaces which is especially overwhelming to people with sensory sensitivities, such as those with autism or prone to sensory overload. Inconsistent tactile paving on platform edges creates safety risks for visually impaired travellers (Tata et al., 2024). Attitudinal barriers arise from insufficient staff training and negative attitudes from both staff and fellow passengers. Communication becomes difficult due to a lack of sign language proficiency, everyday awareness and proper disability support training among staff leads to poor quality of experience during trip-planning and travel (Chan et al., 2022; Motability Foundation, 2022). The human dimension of transport is an essential component of accessibility, and unfavourable attitudes or insufficient training can undermine even the best technical and physical fixes.

Furthermore, financial barriers significantly impact travel accessibility. Transportation options such as specialized taxis or paratransit services often come with higher and unaffordable costs (Tata et al., 2024). Additionally, the limited availability of affordable accessible transportation, particularly in rural areas, further restricts travel opportunities for individuals with disabilities. The affordability and widespread availability of accessible transportation are critical factors in ensuring travel equity, and financial constraints can disproportionately affect individuals with disabilities, limiting their access to essential services compromising the comfort and autonomy of disabled passengers.

2.3. Existing Solution and Their Limitations

Several existing as well as current solutions and technologies are being used to serve disabled travellers suffering from various kinds of impairments, however, each comes with its own advantages as well as disadvantages. Accessible travel planning websites and mobile applications have increasingly played a crucial role in offering travel information, booking facilities, and real-time updates online (Inclusive City Maker, 2022). Yet, most of these online platforms might not be completely compliant with prevailing web accessibility guidelines, like the *Web Content Accessibility Guidelines (WCAG)*. This renders them inaccessible or impossible to use for those who depend on screen readers or other assistive technologies. In addition, digital literacy can be an important barrier for others, including older generations and those in marginalized groups (Nurse Next Door, 2022). Detailed and reliable information about accessibility (e.g., exact dimensions of doorways, and availability of specific aids) is often lacking in navigation apps and booking platforms.

On-demand accessible ride services such as *Dial-A-Ride*, *specialized taxis*, and *accessible ride-hailing services* such as Uber and Lyft are intended to help create a public transportation network (Avila et al., 2016). However, these services are often accompanied by such constraints as advance scheduling and booking requirements, restricted areas of service that do not include all points of destination, excessive waiting times before pick-up, and potential unreliability. Paratransit eligibility criteria can also be limiting, and these services can be more expensive than conventional public transportation. Assistive devices and personal mobility aids like wheelchairs (powered and manual), scooters, walkers, canes, and crutches are essential in facilitating mobility in people with mobility impairment. Hindrances in the environments, like stairs or sidewalks with no ramps or curb cuts, can drastically reduce the usefulness of these devices. Additionally, advanced mobility aids integrated with smart technologies can be expensive and require regular maintenance, which might not be easily accessible or affordable for everyone. Wheelchair-accessible vehicles with ramps or lifts allow a considerable amount of independence to people with mobility impairments (Kamble et al., 2025). Nevertheless, their everyday utility is compromised by issues of operability, user-friendliness, intermittent functionality and greater size of these vehicles. The expense involved in buying and customizing these vehicles can also be cost-prohibiting to many people (BraunAbility, n.d.).

Audio announcements are prevalent in buses, trains, and stations to alert passengers about routes, delays, and other important information. But their use is often constrained. Drivers can occasionally switch off the announcement systems, announcements can themselves be vague or presented too rapidly, and they are clearly not available for the hearing-impaired. Tactile signage, such as Braille and raised lettering on signs, and tactile paving along platform edges, are an important assistance for visually impaired passengers (Karacaoglu et al., 2015). Nevertheless, the availability of these elements is not standardized, and they are not uniformly preserved everywhere. Furthermore, tactile data is not likely to be self-explanatory for all tourists, and paving or signs could become damaged or worn with the passage of time. Visual displays and signage, such as electronic display boards at stops and vehicles, present information visually (Lee et al., 2023). Nonetheless, the information may not be readily accessible to people with low vision, and the presentation, like flashing text or low contrast, can be sometimes overwhelming or hard to read. Also, visual data can be meaningless to a person with a cognitive disability or even someone who has a different native language (Karacaoglu et al., 2015). While assistive technologies empower disabled individuals, their widespread adoption is limited by issues such as cost, user training requirements, and the lack of seamless integration with existing transportation systems.

Table 1. Limitations of existing accessibility solutions

Solution	Intended Purpose	Limitations
Wheelchair Ramps and Lifts	Boarding and disembarking for wheelchair users	Mechanical failures, steep slopes, insufficient manoeuvring space, driver reluctance to operate, inconsistent reliability
Accessible Vehicles	Independent transportation for wheelchair users and those with mobility aids	High cost of purchase and modification, potential difficulties with parking and manoeuvring
Assistive Devices (Wheelchairs, Walkers)	Aid in mobility	Dependence on accessible infrastructure; challenges in inaccessible environments
On-Demand Accessible Transportation	Door-to-door transport for individuals unable to use fixed-route services	Scheduling restrictions, limited service areas, long wait times, potential for unreliability, restrictive eligibility criteria, higher costs
Audio Announcements	Provide auditory information	Often turned off, unclear or too fast, inaccessible for hearing impaired, contributes to noise pollution
Tactile Signage and Guide Paths	Wayfinding for visually impaired individuals	Not universally implemented or maintained, may not be intuitive, potential for damage or wear
Accessible Websites and Apps	Provide online travel information and services	May not fully comply with accessibility standards, requires screen readers, digital literacy can be a barrier
Visual Displays and Signage	Provide visual information	May not be visible to low vision individuals, can be overwhelming if poorly designed, may not be understandable for those with cognitive disabilities or language barriers
Assistive Technologies (Hearing Loops, and so on.)	Enhance sensory perception and interaction	Requires personal investment and training, potential compatibility issues, reliance on individual knowledge and use

3. AI TECHNOLOGIES FOR ACCESSIBLE TRAVEL

The travel accessibility sector has been undergoing a drastic change due to the revolution brought by artificial intelligence (AI)-it has been enriched, has become more automatic, and has developed a wider scope of availability. Computer Vision helps to build spatial awareness through object detection, semantic segmentation, and gesture recognition — the hands of users move around in space and navigate the environment. Such comfort positively affects their emotional stability and self-reliance. Natural Language Processing makes it possible for travellers with disabilities to interact with voice-activated systems that are elsewhere on the line and for that reason access information and services more easily. Machine Learning gives room for the real-time adjustment of individual mobility requirements and outdoor weather conditions by modifying the travel route according to user preferences. The Internet of Things incorporates intelligence into infrastructure and develops smart environments that change and adapt by sensor-driven, context-aware responses. Multimodal AI Systems integrate vision, language, and sensory input to come up with independent and user-friendly interfaces that are suitable for various accessibility needs.

3.1. Computer Vision for Navigation Assistance

Computer vision has emerged as a transformative technology for improving navigation safety and intuitiveness for people with disabilities (Valipoor & De Antonio, 2023). Computer vision plays a critical role in helping humans, and it is of particular importance to those who may not be able to effectively perceive visual stimuli, such as those who are blind or have low vision, or have mobility impairment (Wang & Zhu, 2023). Computer vision allows machines to see and interpret their environment (Cazzato et al., 2020). The most important application of computer vision involves object detection and scene understanding, where the machine learns to recognize common components — whether they are doors, stairs, elevators, or obstacles — in the user's environment (Tapu et al., 2017). For example, RGB-D wearable systems (which utilize standard RGB images paired with depth data) can be applied to Fully Convolutional Networks (FCN), such that these systems segment terrain types while simultaneously recognizing features critical for navigation like edges of the floor, inclines, and drop-offs (Yu & Saniie, 2025). Normally these devices provide non-visual spatial cues, with audio information relayed via bone-conducting headphones that allow the user to receive real-time audio feedback while their hands remain free (Abidi et al., 2024).

Vision Transformers (ViTs) have emerged as a powerful tool recently, especially in complex indoor environments (Said et al., 2023). An extensive indoor scene classification using a dual multiscale attention ViT model achieved high accuracy in determining the context—office, bathroom, or kitchen—within an indoor image. We utilized publicly available datasets for this purpose such as MIT Indoor67, a dataset of 67 indoor categories with over 15,000 images acquired under variable lighting with spatial complexity to test robustness (Said et al., 2023). Semantic segmentation, where a category (like road, building, person, and so on) is assigned to each individual pixel in an image, is another important function for assistive navigation (Valipoor & De Antonio, 2023). Data such as that available in Cityscapes or ADE20K consist of detailed annotations that assistive tools can leverage to differentiate between walkable paths and potential hazards (MDPI Journal of Imaging) (Yu & Saniie, 2025). Dynamic navigation relies heavily on visual Simultaneous Localization and Mapping (vSLAM). It creates a map of its surrounding environment while also estimating the user's location within that map in real time (Abidi et al., 2024). This is very helpful for those in wheelchairs and people with cognitive disabilities who require continuous orientation (Yu & Saniie, 2025). Recent developments improve localization accuracy indoors, where GPS does not work, by combining vSLAM with Inertial measurement units (IMU) to obtain IMU-enhanced GPS input (Cazzato et al., 2020).

Camera-based systems are not only making navigation intuitive but also enabling touch-free user interaction through gesture recognition (Tapu et al., 2017). Convolutional Neural Network (CNN)-based techniques enable mobility-impaired users to activate commands with simple hand gestures like requesting help or selecting paths (Abidi et al., 2024). Additionally, open-source datasets such as SUN RGB-D, NYU Depth V2, and Open Images V7 have also expedited the training of these models by providing semantically rich labelled training images with spatial hierarchy (Valipoor & De Antonio, 2023). Such datasets enable engines to generalize with high-level scenarios and architectural layouts (Wang & Zhu, 2023). Real-world assistive tools using computer vision are more than technical uplifting, they are empowering and inclusive (Abidi et al., 2024). Computer vision systems are rapidly being moved from experimental prototypes to practical, deployable aids as a result of collecting deep learning, embedded AI, and user-centered design (Valipoor & De Antonio, 2023).

Table 2. Comparison of computer vision models for navigation assistance

Model/Technique	Function	Input Type	Dataset Used	Advantages
Fully Convolutional Networks (FCNs) (Tapu et al., 2017)	Terrain classification & segmentation.	RGB-D images	SUN RGB-D, NYU Depth V2	Real-time segmentation and good for ground-level navigation.
Vision Transformers (ViTs) (Said et al., 2023)	Indoor scene classification.	RGB images	MIT Indoor67	High accuracy in varied environments and highly scalable.
Semantic Segmentation (CNN-based) (Valipoor & De Antonio, 2023)	Per-pixel object/ environment labelling.	RGB or RGB-D	ADE20K, Cityscapes	Detailed understanding of surroundings.
Visual SLAM (vSLAM) (Abidi et al., 2024)	Mapping + localization	RGB + IMU	Custom/test datasets	GPS-independent navigation and also good for dynamic environments.
Gesture Recognition via CNNs (Wang & Zhu, 2023)	Hands-free command input.	RGB/video	Custom datasets	Touchless interaction as well as enhances control for mobility users.

3.2. Natural Language Processing (NLP) for Voice-Enabled Assistance

Voice-enabled support technologies have made great progress over the course of time primarily because of the developments in the area of Natural Language Processing (NLP) besides improving the independent living capacity of people with disabilities significantly. This is because NLP does this without the need for additional devices. Thus, speech can be an intuitive hands-free control of both devices and services (Ali et al., 2023). The significant elements of NLP-powered voice assistants are Automatic Speech Recognition (ASR), Natural Language Understanding (NLU), and Text-to-Speech (TTS) systems. ASR transcribes spoken words into text, so the system can understand the user commands. NLU examines this text to indicate the intention of the user and finds the necessary information. TTS, at last, creates the reply and does it to the user audibly. The chain of the process involves the use of speech acceptance technology that lets the user speak in the voice, which is then transcribed into text that is then used to make the user requests (Ali et al., 2023).

Within the evolution of travel accessibility, the voice assistants, which are powered by NLP are standing out as great helpers by navigating to a specific place immediately, giving public transportation updates, and informing about nearby amenities. For example, these aides can describe the route in a numbered list, tell you the remaining time for the bus to come and the number of the bus, or inform you about the places you can access in the area. These possibilities are particularly useful for people who are blind or have difficulty moving, as they can lessen the need for visual displays and reduce the need for human resources (Shenoy et al., 2017). In addition to this, the integration of natural language processing with web-based devices has increased the world of assistive devices into a vast one. Smart home gadgets that can be controlled through vocal expressions provide people with physical disabilities the opportunity to be more independent in the environment they live in. By using these devices, one can basically adjust everything from the lights and security to household chores with just a minimum amount of help, thus, making them more independent. Furthermore, smart tech is the one that permits a person to manipulate the linked appliances in a way that makes it possible to create the desired living conditions (Ali et al., 2023).

However, it is clear that the development of inclusive voice assistants is not without challenges. Barriers to acceptance among disabled people have been found to as issues like heavy mental calculations while using it, misunderstanding of pronunciation, and privacy fears (Esquivel et al., 2024). Also, it is possible that ASR systems do not work well for those who have speech impairments, which is the reason for the requirement of further studies on bias reduction and the creation of more personalized models (Hutchinson et al., 2020). In short, NLP has an extremely crucial part in building voice-enabled applications for people with disabilities thus making it much easier for them to interact with computers in a natural and effective way (Ali et al., 2023). Continuous research and advancements are critical to dealing with the current difficulties and improving the tools' usability for all users (Esquivel et al., 2024).

3.3. Machine Learning for Personalized Route Optimization

Disabilities make it particularly difficult to navigate around cities (Domingo, 2021). The availability of data has enabled the usage of machine learning (ML) to provide a personalized route optimization framework to foster independence and accessibility (Namoun et al., 2022). For example, Machine Learning algorithms can be arranged user-specifically by receiving knowledge from such datasets as traffic flow, infrastructure details, and user-specific mobility requirements (Du et al., 2020). For instance, it could create adaptive routing models to make accessibility features a priority. Likewise, in IET Intelligent Transport Systems, there is a paper suggesting a model that would permit people with mobility impairments to upload the roads of their choice to a mobility storage system (Namoun et al., 2022). In addition to this, the model will also be connected to the user profile database (Turno et al., 2025). By using the profiles of different users, it will be able to predict their behaviour with better turn-by-turn instructions based on the specific routes and traffic conditions that suit their needs and accessibility and provide an enhanced experience for vulnerable road users (Turno et al., 2025).

ML techniques have been utilized for constructing urban simulation models as the most advantageous routing optimization method (Mokrenko, 2020). A feature of such models is that they can take simulations as data sources and track the efficient paths that minimize travel time and also consider mobility constraints (Mokrenko, 2020). Those techniques are widely used in traffic navigation systems that react to the dynamic environment of urban traffic and give humans real-time and personalized directions (Domingo, 2021). Likewise, ML with mapping data has made it possible to develop individualized travel route-finding alternatives for individuals with disabilities in mobility (Cohen & Dalyot, 2020). Citing minute geospatial data, these systems can identify which routes are traversable through the assessment of sidewalk conditions, curb cuts, and cross-slope (Mokrenko, 2020). This way, any new suggested routes will not only be quick but also actually navigable to users (and potentially helpful for users with needs) (Du et al., 2020).

AI-powered solutions are being utilized widely in public transportation to enhance accessibility nowadays (Namoun et al., 2022). AI-based algorithms monitor transport in real-time, the passengers` needs, and infrastructure data to adjust routes dynamically which results in overall time and fuel reduction for example (Domingo,

2021). It is not just the fact that this has become the best way of streamlining the process, but it is also the reality that people with disabilities can be provided with more responsive transport services (Turno et al., 2025). In conclusion, Machine Learning in personalized route optimization has been the key contributor to improving travel in an accessible way for the disabled (Namoun et al., 2022). In learning each individual's needs and their interactions with AI, these solutions such as personal navigation are offered to them which makes them feel excluded from the normal people movement (Domingo, 2021). The advancement reinforced this area of the potential to increase both the movement of those with disabilities and their quality of life (Du et al., 2020).

3.4. Internet of Things (IoT) and Smart Infrastructure

Travel has changed for people with disabilities through the use of the Internet of Things (IoT) in smart infrastructure (Semary et al., 2024). IoT creates adaptive and responsive environments by allowing connected devices to communicate in real time (Domingo, 2012). From automated doors and sensor-enabled crosswalks to smart public transport systems, the technology enables safer, more independent movement (Ramirez et al., 2017). A subset of intelligent systems that remove barriers is making interconnectivity more accessible, offering personalized navigation, real-time assistance, and seamless transitions throughout multiple points of travel and helping make inclusive travel an achievable reality (Al-karawi, 2023). Additionally, IoT-based smart environment designs are now enabling the smart environments to respond dynamically to the characteristics and current needs of the user with a disability (Coetzee & Olivrin, 2012). These environments collect real-time information on movement and user preferences with the integration of sensors into key infrastructure (building access/egress points, public transport, and traffic systems) (Rashid et al., 2017). That information is then used to adjust and personalize responses — opening a door automatically, adjusting crossing time at a given intersection — depending on the user's particular mobility challenge (Ramirez et al., 2017). Consequently, we can make the whole travel journey more natural and seamless, leaving fewer gaps so that people do not need to ask for help from others and providing them with more independence (Domingo, 2012).

Moreover, recent literature also depicts the power of the context-aware paradigm in IoT-centric travel ecosystems (Semary et al., 2024). These systems decode data from embedded sensors and cloud-connected platforms to assess a person's whereabouts, interests, and restrictions as they happen—soothing or guiding conditions accordingly when necessary (Ramirez et al., 2017). Wearable IoT devices can also monitor environmental hazards and issue alerts for users with visual or mobility challenges to help them (Rashid et al., 2017). Smart wheelchairs and intelligent transit nodes, to which recent research has been devoted, are deepening personalization—further reducing dependency and increasing autonomy (Al-karawi, 2023). For many of these people, these innovations aren't just a convenience — they're a lifeline to independence (Coetzee & Olivrin, 2012). Be it the assurance of venturing into a new city alone or the comfort of traversing a busy station without anxiety, these systems do more than help; they embolden (Domingo, 2012).

In conclusion, the ongoing evolution in IoT-enabled smart infrastructure has the potential to reshape mobility in travel for individuals with disabilities (Semary et al., 2024). Such systems, that provide live updates, adaptivity, and predictive support, can decrease dependency and heighten reliance on oneself (Rashid et al., 2017). By addressing the varied needs of travellers, from recognizing the common sense of belonging to enabling the urban mobility of people with disabilities, the IoT for Travel goes beyond being merely another tool for enhancing public transport, navigation, or built environments; it represents an unambiguous cultural evolution towards diversity and equal access for all (Domingo, 2012).

3.5. Augmented Reality (AR) and Virtual Reality (VR) for Travel Guidance

The integration of AR and VR technologies into travel apps has been made possible due to the support of these individuals and is already a move towards new ways of experiencing travel, which would push them to opt for self-discovery traveling (Shukla et al., 2024). The use of immersive technologies creates an opportunity to have tailored, immediate help which enables the user to start seeing the environment differently and being active in it (Jalilvand & Ghasemi, 2024).

Augmented Reality (AR) technologies are defining the new phase of entertainment and recreation as they are so interactive, involving different senses and manipulating each of them (El Choubassi et al., 2010). For example, there are applications such as *AccessNow* that are in various places around the world at the same time thus, travellers can choose where to go according to that information (Bahaddad et al., 2024). In a similar way, users of *iAccessLife* may supply their personal opinion on the accessibility of a place and their contribution is the company that gathers the data about the mobility choices (Cranmer et al., 2023).

VR technologies make use of sourced sources to provide users with an opportunity to explore and identify places long before their actual visits (Shukla et al., 2024). By means of pre-exposure, can be advantageous for disabilities since it can alleviate the anxiety spread by the unknown environment, and people can know what they will have to plan for their accessibility needs (Jalilvand & Ghasemi, 2024). It has also been found that VR experiences can, for example, affect attitudes, places preferred, and intentions of persons with disabilities on visiting a place by providing a secure place to practice a baby scenario (Shukla et al., 2024). Also, museums and cultural institutions have augmented reality (AR) to enhance the accessibility of the facilities. The Houston Museum of Natural Science, in particular, collaborated with *ReBokeh* to provide a free app that assists visitors with low vision. Filters and settings are used to adapt images, thus, enabling people with disabilities to customize their visual experience for easier movement (Cranmer et al., 2023).

Wearable AR devices display a case in point of significant support during travels in real-time. Augmented reality smart glasses from Google, for instance, improve the lives of people with special needs by showing data, translations, and interactive features that aid individuals with disabilities in meeting unfamiliar places and acquiring data with ease (Bahaddad et al., 2024). Although AR and VR technologies are extremely flexible, problems remain in their use in accessible travel. Enormous budget and safety concerns can stop the general utilization and non-familiarity with the user may inhibit the tools' full potential (Jalilvand & Ghasemi, 2024). These trepidations necessitate a constant overhaul and consequently pave the way for the technology vendors to build cost-effective and user-centric devices while stressing the security and well-being of the specially-abled (Shukla et al., 2024).

In the final analysis, the combination of the travel sector AR and VR technologies offers a lot of opportunities for making travel more fun for the disabled. Travelers can be the only ones who experience it that way; technology enhances their journey with the help of immersive, interactive, and personalized support (Cranmer et al., 2023). In order to make the desired changes and achieve the best results, technological advancements, and cooperation not only among technology developers and policies but also with the disability community are the keys to success (Jalilvand & Ghasemi, 2024).

4. AI-DRIVEN ACCESSIBLE TRAVEL PLANNING SYSTEMS

As the global travel and tourism industry increasingly tends to digitize globally, artificial intelligence (AI) has indeed transformed the transport systems to enable and facilitate access for persons with disabilities to the public transport infrastructure. Even though the technical aspects of the travel industry have developed beyond expectation, the fact proves that quite a few travellers still have to struggle with their journeys. They are, for instance, over 1.3 billion people around the world who have to cope with at least one form of disability that can affect their traveling. Mobility and sensory disabilities hinder transport access. Often, typical systems are unable to meet the very complex demands of such populations. For example, in the UK, 40% of disabled individuals experience issues in traveling by public transport, whereas in countries such as India and Brazil, the lack of access to the little available transport infrastructure is the one that aggravates social exclusion and infrastructure issues. In smart trip planning applications, you outline your itinerary and set the route based on the information for it in, considerations that users perceive as necessary and other services that you offer like weather and traffic report, etc, and to real-time GPS navigation tool that combine environmental data and crowd-sourced accessibility information, the opportunities for innovation are huge.

4.1. AI-Powered Trip Planning Applications

AI-powered trip planning applications present a significant advancement in the Travel and Tourism Industry, offering personalized and efficient recommendations to its users (Kamble et al., 2025). These applications harness the power of complex AI algorithms to analyse huge datasets that include user preferences, travel history, destination information, real-time updates, multimodal customer reviews, and so on (Peek Editorial Team, 2024) to produce customized travel plans tailored to individual needs such as financial budgets, personal interests, the preferred mode of travel, to ensure a seamless planning and booking process.

Traditional travel planning platforms often require manually researching various platforms for information on destinations, accommodations, transportation, and activities. This makes it more difficult for those with disabilities who have to check accessibility features at every point during their journey. AI-powered trip planners accomplish this intricate task automatically by gathering information from an enormous database of sources, such as platforms specifically geared towards accessibility and user comments usually providing insightful details on accessibility features, ultimately handing down customized options adjusting to specific needs. For instance, an AI can effectively sift hotels according to the provision of important accessibility features like roll-in showers, entrance ramps, and accessible parking lots to save the user significant time and energy in the arrangements for their trip.

The ability of machine learning algorithms to make these systems capable of constant integration of feedback and input from the users helps in honing personalized travel plans and makes it possible to ensure that the AI algorithm conforms to the changing requirements and likes of the visitor (Kamble et al., 2025). Adaptive behaviour of AI hence makes a form of personalization in traveling achievable that a traditional system sometimes may not achieve, possibly allowing a traveller with disabilities to sample a greater choice of options formulated precisely to individualized circumstances. In contrast to static filters on traditional booking sites, AI algorithms can learn from a user's previous interactions and feedback to build a sophisticated understanding of their individual accessibility requirements and preferences. For example, a user who needs a quiet room because of sensory sensitivities may consistently give negative ratings for hotels with noise issues. The AI is able to learn this subtle preference and give higher priority to quieter accommodations in subsequent suggestions, even without the user specifically mentioning this criterion as a requirement with each search. This degree of implicit awareness and ongoing evolution further improves the overall experience for users with disabilities.

A survey conducted by *Matador Network* (GuideGeek, 2024) found that more than 82% of travellers who used AI to organize trips for an individual with a disability reported an enjoyable experience. Testimonials and anecdotal evidence from users also underscore the major advantages of these apps, including ease and convenience of planning, a substantial decrease in the time needed for research to determine appropriate options, and the ability to successfully pinpoint accessible accommodations and attractions that could have been overlooked in conventional searching (GuideGeek, 2024). High user satisfaction ratings in these studies indicate that AI-based trip planning apps are successfully mitigating some of the most significant pain points faced by travellers with disabilities, resulting in a more pleasant and significantly less stressful travel planning experience. The high rating of satisfaction amongst a sizable number of disabled travellers and tourists who have used AI for travel planning suggests that such tools are indeed delivering real benefits.

Several existing AI powered accessible travel planning systems offer compelling examples of the technology's impact on users. GuideGeek (2024) is an AI enabled travel guide that has been used effectively by disabled travellers to find accessible accommodations, transportation services, and attractions at their destinations. Platforms like Wheel The World and AccessibleGO (Southeast ADA Center, 2022) use new age technologies to offer extensive and verified information on accessibility and convenient booking for a variety of travel requirements. Additionally, major travel sites like Google Travel and TripAdvisor are also increasingly incorporating AI to improve their accessibility features in order to appeal to a wider audience with a variety of needs (Anitha et al., 2025). The popularity of these websites and the increasing incorporation of accessibility features into mainstream web-based travel applications reflect a major trend that suggests an increasing awareness about the particular needs of disabled travellers in the travel and tourism industry and the potential of AI to effectively meet this important and often neglected market.

4.2. Real-Time Navigation Aids (AI-integrated GPS and mapping solutions)

The WHO estimates that more than 2.5 billion disabled people will need one or more assistive technologies in 2030. Real-time navigation aids are constantly improving and integrating the capabilities of artificial intelligence to make travel more accessible to all travellers. The commencement of AI usage has radically changed the basic nature of GPS navigations to include features like advanced obstacle detection, suggest alternative routes explicitly accessible, and real-time status updates of accessible pathways and transportation options in a given area. This development is meant to ensure the gathering of very detailed environmental information crucial for precise and safe navigation, especially for individuals with disabilities, through the use of advanced sensor technologies, particularly *LiDAR*, coupled with powerful AI algorithms (Casanova et al., 2025). While traditional GPS systems typically focus on how to guide you from point A to point B, without catering to specifics needed by those living with a disability, such as stairs along a route or accessible entrances into a destination, AI-enhanced navigation systems close this significant inadequacy by including all information on ramps, elevators, and accessible restrooms, leaving the information directly into the routing algorithm. The development of specialized AI navigation systems and tools deeply showcases a targeted, focused effort to enable individuals with visual and mobility impairments to have increased mobility and independence in their daily lives.

4.2.1 AI-Powered Navigation Systems

- **NaviGPT** (Zhang et al., 2025) stands as an excellent example in the field of AI-driven navigation systems for the visually impaired. Key features of the software include *LiDAR-based* obstacle detection that creates a very detailed information flow about the environment and vibration feedback that delivers tactile cues for navigation as well as AI-generated voice navigation giving real-time instructions and descriptions. The system cleverly combines Apple's Maps with the base navigation for advanced functionality of GPT-4 to also provide contextual and real-time assistance, creating a seamless intuitive user interface.
- Researchers at *Johns Hopkins University* (Johns Hopkins Applied Physics Laboratory, 2024) have built a system that uses AI to map environments, track user locations, and provide real-time guidance. It constructs a high-level semantic model of an environment to identify and track objects and hence notify users using depth imaging and RGB sensors. This greatly interprets the environment and enables high-level human-computer interaction.

4.2.2 AI-Powered Assistive Devices

AI-enabled *smart canes* can detect obstacles in the user's path in real-time and give immediate tactile feedback so that visually impaired users can be helped to navigate their environment safely and confidently. *Smart wheelchairs* are being further enhanced to encourage mobility independence for people with disabilities (Know the ADA, n.d.). All of those mentioned above have *voice guidance* and *haptic feedback* as their mainstay access technologies in navigation-clearing pathways with important information through non-visual sensory channels (New England Low Vision and Blindness, n.d.). This is yet another example of the pioneering innovation that facilitates truly context-aware and proactive navigation assistance by combining advanced AI capabilities like image recognition and natural language processing.

4.2.3 AI-Powered Wearable Devices

- **AIris** (Brilli et al., 2024) is a device that uses a camera mounted on eye wear to interact via a natural language-processing interface. The system provides real-time auditory descriptions of the environment, accurately identifying objects and interpreting scenes in a way that facilitates spatial awareness. The AIris application suite encompasses face recognition, scene description, reading text, recognizing objects, counting money, taking notes, and scanning barcodes, thereby providing solid assistive technology itself.
- **LLM-Glasses** (Tokmurziyev et al., 2025) uses generative AI and haptic feedback to assist in navigation. This type of glasses uses object detection algorithms like YOLO and GPT-4o-driven reasoning to give real-time tactile guidance through temple-mounted actuators for the intuitiveness of navigation. Tests conducted with users in controlled environments have shown that the system works reliably; meanwhile, work is in progress to optimize for responsiveness in a variety of real-world settings.
- **MagicEye** (Sethuraman et al., 2023) is an intelligent wearable device that uses an in-house customized convolutional neural network-based object detection model for the recognition of a huge collection range of indoor and outdoor objects. With facial recognition and currency identification modules, the device also has GPS for navigation and proximity sensors for detecting objects around. Thus, it comprehensively tackles different kinds of challenges faced by visually impaired individuals in their real lives.
- **Meta Platforms** have developed AI-powered smart glasses for visually-impaired users (Sozialhelden e.V., 2025). These integrate several cameras and microphones and AI assistance for things like reading text, identifying objects, and providing contextual information about the environment. With apps like *Be My Eyes* (Waisberg et al., 2024), such integration gives even more support through real-time visual descriptions and audio interfaces. These aren't made specifically for the visually-impaired but really are quite relevant accessibility devices.

4.3. Predictive Accessibility Scoring for Routes and Transport Options

Predictive accessibility scoring systems have emerged as essential tools in assessing and enhancing the usability of transport networks for individuals with disabilities. AI algorithms are widely used for these assessments in order to understand various routes and transport options for travellers with disabilities (Havenocode, n.d.). In such algorithms, AI models are often lent with complex machine learning and deep learning techniques to check various parameters that decide the accessibility (Lukic Vujadinovic et al., 2024). Parameters may include the physical presence of ramps, availability and conditions of elevators; accessible restrooms along the route; step-free entrances into buildings and transport hubs; provision of accessible spaces in public transport (DDanDDanDDan, 2025). Accurate prediction of accessibility score can change travel planning for disabled individuals. Integrating these accessibility scores into trip planners and navigation systems will create a more seamless and efficient travel experience for people with disabilities, simplifying route selection, mode of transportation, and accommodation matching to the specific needs of the traveller. The prediction of these accessibility scores is strongly influenced by the quality and variety of the datasets that are used to train the AI models (PTV Group, n.d.). These include data about infrastructure, transport systems, real-time data from sensors and monitoring systems, user reviews/ratings, and detailed geospatial data that maps out the physical environment (Neeli et al., 2024).

4.3.1 Predictive Accessibility Scoring Frameworks

- **Transit Accessibility Tool (TRACT)**: It is a highly structured framework used to calculate the accessibility information available from public transport agencies. Six dimensions are evaluated - Facility access, Vehicle access, Inclusive policies, Rider accommodation, Paratransit services, and Website access. In a study covering 26 public transport systems across the United States in 2023, TRACT unearthed some significant discrepancies in the manner and degree to which public transportation agencies actually provide information regarding accessibility on their websites. For many systems, descriptions of major accessibility features were lacking, while others failed to properly communicate essential accommodation provisions (Twardzik et al., 2024).
- **Public Transport Walking Accessibility Index (PTWAI):** It analyses the accessibility of various services that concern public transport and distance walking. It scores the accessibility level on a scale of 0 to 4, based on different travel times set as accessibility parameters to various services, where a

greater score represents the more accessible levels. The overall score formed from an aggregate of values within multiple service domains shows the scenario of public transport accessibility. In support of the argument, a comparative analysis was conducted with some other methods in Helsinki to assess accessibility with PTWAI alongside them to prove compatibility in urban settings (El-Geneidy et al., 2016).

- **Accessibility Score Indicator (AccessS):** It is an integrated geospatial framework for an urban mobility network assessment. It uses multiple geospatial data on transport-mode-specific factors to assess the accessibility of the network segments. The *AccessS* integrated assessment framework was built and tested in Braunschweig, Germany, focusing on the transport mode of walking. *AccessS* emphasizes relatively fine-grain analysis of accessibility by integrating diverse computed values (Mumm et al., 2025).

Accessibility evaluation tools such as TRACT, PTWAI, and AccessS play a central role in identifying and removing accessibility barriers in transportation networks. By systematically evaluating various dimensions of accessibility, these tools help in formulating policy decisions and improve making transportation systems fit for inclusiveness.

4.4. AI Chatbots for Travel Assistance

AI chatbots are being increasingly used in the travel industry for many purposes such as providing real-time support and essential information to travellers, especially where accessible travel is concerned. These intelligent virtual agents can easily respond to a wide range of travel inquiries, assist with itinerary planning, and provide important information on travel status updates from flight schedules to accommodation availabilities and destination conditions in real-time. One of the greatest benefits of an AI chatbot is that they work every hour of the day and night so that travellers can be assisted and informed, no matter their location or time zone. These chatbots are also able to handle a myriad of inquiries simultaneously, thus allowing them to effectively handle a large volume of users (Subramanian, n.d.). In addition, they help in simplifying troublesome processes like booking flights, hotels, and activities while providing recommendations based on individual user preferences (Anupriya et al., 2024).

AI Chatbots can provide assistance and support customized for travellers with disabilities. They could be further programmed to respond to questions about the accessibility features of hotels, transportation modes of various kinds, and tourist attractions at a destination. These chatbots could also offer individual recommendations, which can be dependent on the individual disability type and their specific needs, thereby ensuring that such information is relevant and useful. Many AI chatbots also possess the capability for multilingual support, which can become vital for an international traveller with a disability needing assistance in the language of their choice (Subramanian, n.d.). The studies and surveys have addressed that disabled people who actually have used AI chatbots for planning their travels expressed their satisfaction, highlighting the speed and efficiency of receiving answers to their inquiries, a markedly reduced time in which research can be done for travel planning, and ease in accessing key pieces of information (GuideGeek, 2024). Examples of AI travel assistants are already in the process of making travel planning more comfortable. GuideGeek is a chatbot that provides tailored recommendations and real-time travel advice on a variety of messaging platforms preferred by the users, such as WhatsApp, Instagram, and FB Messenger (GuideGeek, 2024). Other AI chatbots like Penny by Priceline, Trip.com AI Assistant, and Expedia's chatbot undoubtedly present great opportunities to assist in accessible travel by helping with booking and information retrieval (Shankman, 2025).

With AI chatbots rapidly integrating themselves into travel platforms for increasing customer support roles and general trip planning, there is a clear trend toward leveraging conversational AI to enhance experiences across the core user group of disabled persons, who often have very unique and concrete requirements that command extra attention. Although AI chatbots seem quite promising in aiding persons with disabilities, the focus now should remain on further improvements of the systems, the accuracy of the information provided, and the fulfilment of user expectations around the subtleties of humanlike conversations.

5. CASE STUDIES AND REAL-WORLD IMPLEMENTATIONS

The best way to move forward in life is to take inspiration from the past and the surroundings around us. There are various bodies, organisations and individuals which are putting their best foot forward to revolutionise the traditional methods and make the most efficient use of technology to help the disabled ones have a more inclusive lifestyle and have a fair and equal chance in living the life as any other human across the globe.

5.1 Smart Cities Leveraging AI for Accessible Transport

Barcelona, Spain stands as a remarkable example as it has introduced smart traffic signals equipped with sensors that detect pedestrians, including those with mobility challenges. These systems include auditory signals for the visually impaired and can adjust the crossing lines according to the pedestrian time flow. In 2020,

AI-driven data analytics began helping city planners optimize traffic and pedestrian flow, ensuring safer and more efficient urban mobility for people with disabilities (Barcelona City Council, 2022). Singapore is another exemplary mention with its inclusive transport strategy. The *Land Transport Authority (LTA)* has introduced AI-based predicative manners for the maintenance of escalators and elevators in public transport systems which ensures operational reliability. They have also started to plan out the introduction of autonomous shuttles equipped with AI vision and LiDAR sensors which offers last-mile connectivity for elderly and disabled users (Institute for Transportation & Development Policy, 2024). Seattle which is a well-known city of the United States introduced smart parking smart parking systems and AI-powered wayfinding apps like *WayFinder*, which support persons with visual impairments in navigating complex public spaces. These applications use real-time data, computer vision, and voice navigation to offer a seamless travel experience (Marsh, 2025). Tokyo, the capital city of Japan has integrated Artificial Intelligence into its extensive public transport system. The introduction of autonomous wheel-chairs and real time translation systems in their transport places have played a key role in helping the disabled and the foreigners alike. In the 2020 Tokyo Paralympics, the city ramped up efforts to ensure all transit points were accessible, leveraging facial recognition and AI to ease access (Tokyo Metropolitan Government, 2020). Amsterdam, which is a well-known tourist attraction and is located in the country of Netherlands, has worked towards the implementation of smart mobility hubs and AI-powered route planning systems. These systems incorporate real-time data on elevator outages, wheelchair-friendly pathways, and crowd density to assist users with disabilities in planning the most accessible and least congested routes (Amsterdam Smart City, n.d.).

5.2 AI Based Travel Applications

With the widespread use of Artificial Intelligence all over the globe, there has been the development of various mobile applications which can help to ease out the lives of the disabled ones. These AI applications use the concepts of Natural Language Processing and Machine Learning to provide contextual and real time support during travel which helps the disabled people have better accessibility during the times of travel. One of the popular and well-known applications is *Aira* which uses the concept of computer vision and connects blind and low-vision users with trained professionals via live video. Users wear smart glasses or can use the camera of their smartphones and the professional person who has been assigned with the task can help the navigation process or reading of the signage. The AI system complements human agents by automating the recognition of common objects and text, improving speed and reliability (Aira, n.d.). Another exemplary application that is quite popular is the *Microsoft Seeing AI* which is an app that utilises computer vision and natural language processing to describe surroundings, read documents, identify people, and recognize currency. The app segments its functions into different channels for tailored services, such as short text reading, product identification via barcode scanning, and scene recognition, providing an enriched experience for visually impaired travellers (Microsoft, n.d.). Google maps have contributed its share by incorporating several accessibility features. In 2020 it introduced the feature wheelchair-accessible route option, allowing users to find public transit routes that are friendly for people with mobility issues. Its recent update includes the introduction of the access to information about public places, such as the presence of ramps, accessible restrooms, and seating (Blair Goldenson, 2020).

5.3 Success Stories from Developing and Developed Nations

Artificial Intelligence has paved its way all around the globe because of the reformation it can bring in the regular lives of the citizens. Usually when the advanced technologies are limited to the developed nations, the developing nations are able to recognize the importance of Artificial Intelligence and are implementing it in all the ways they could. The efforts of the various governments across the globe in the implementation of Artificial Intelligence have brought measurable impacts in various fields. Here we are going to acknowledge some of the implications that have been done in various parts of the world to implement AI to help the disabled people across the globe (Blair Goldenson, 2020).

- *United Kingdom*: London has launched a comprehensive accessibility program across its transport system called Transport for London (TfL). It makes the use of implementations of machine learning to predict the failures of elevators and escalators across the system and the real time data of the availability of the various elevators and escalators are shared with the various passengers in their journey making their travel and commute plans more efficient. The city has also implemented AI to analyse user feedback and mobility patterns to help the disabled people have an ease in their journey (Velho, 2019).
- *Canada*: The Toronto Smart City Project has contributed a great deal towards the contribution of the growth of AI with their heavy focus on inclusive urban planning. The Toronto city has developed AI based tools which are able to detect sidewalk obstruction and hence provide the pedestrian with an alternative path. With the partnership with *Sidewalk Labs*, the city has come forward with initiatives that aim to create a data-driven, inclusive urban experience where technology directly responds to accessibility needs (Stouhi, 2022).

- *India*: With the plan for the smart city reformation, Chennai a major city in India has come up with the idea of incorporating Artificial Intelligence in the traffic signals that has audio-visual aids for the differently abled. Local NGOs have partnered with startups to implement mobile-based navigation aids in railway stations, helping blind and visually impaired passengers through haptic feedback and AI-generated voice directions (Chennai Smart City Ltd., 2020).
- *Brazil*: The Rio de Janerio inclusivity city plan has driven the city to implement AI based video analytics and manage the pedestrian flow in busy areas of the city. Bus Rapid Transit (BRT) stations have been retrofitted with tactile paths, ramps, and visual-audio information systems that use AI to alert drivers to the presence of disabled passengers waiting at stops (Prefeitura do Rio de Janeiro, 2021).
- *South Korea*: The Incheon International Airport has deployed LG's AI enabled service robots in the airport terminals to help the passengers with multilingual translations, facial recognition and real time flight information. These robots are programmed to identify passengers with disabilities and offer personalized assistance, showcasing how AI can bridge accessibility gaps in complex environments (LG Electronics, 2020).

6. FUTURE PROSPECTS AND RESEARCH DIRECTIONS

With fresh avenues for accessibility and inclusive innovation, artificial intelligence is on a constant evolution. Artificial intelligence-embedded high-tech wearable devices are indeed the latest innovation for people with disability who use them to communicate directly with each other. The functions of the devices include attaching a location to an object, or creating a sensor for environmental awareness. Moreover, the mentioned smart wearables are not just that they are also the means to enable more autonomy and the better quality of all daily tasks through the power of disposal. In addition, autonomous cars integrated with AI technology are the vehicles that will take a new dimension in transportation for people with disabilities who have problems with movement. Besides, these kinds of cars with voice command control, auto ramps, and individual configurations are providing passengers to independent travel. In the current research, the critical aspects will be privacy, costs, and ethics that should be prioritized to ensure these technologies reach their full potential and to be able to offer equivalent access to AI solutions.

6.1. Integration of AI with Wearable Devices for Real-Time Accessibility

The intersection of artificial intelligence (AI) and wearable devices is enabling individuals with disabilities to access new real-time accessibility options, providing innovative solutions for enhanced mobility and independence (Moon et al., 2019). By integrating AI into wearable technology, devices can now offer personalized assistance such as real-time navigational aids and environmental awareness tailored to the user's specific needs (Brilli et al., 2024). This synergy between AI and wearable devices allows users not only to operate their assistive technologies more effectively but also to integrate more fully into the community, fostering a more inclusive environment (Sethuraman et al., 2023).

Artificial intelligence (AI) and wearable devices are merging to create a groundbreaking paradigm for accessibility in real-time for the disabled persons by presenting to them solutions that mainly assist them travel and live independently (Chakraborty et al., 2023). Wearable technology embedded with AI can offer people with disabilities personalized help such as navigation guidance, vision scan, tracking objects, and other environmental cues in real time that are tailored to the user's specific needs (Baig et al., 2024). This interaction between AI and wearable devices goes beyond simply improving the assistive technology but, in live reality, assists the user to a more inclusive society, making it possible for them to act in the same way as others with their environment (Brilli et al., 2024).

The advanced assistive technologies that we see today are due to the explosive growth of artificial intelligence (AI) in the Internet of Things (IoT) devices. An example of this is the AI-based smart glasses that can analyse visual data and provide audio instructions to the users thereby enhancing their learning experience and helping them in finding their way in new territories (Brilli et al., 2024). Moreover, the smart glasses used by the blind that can detect and understand the context simultaneously through real-time object recognition are very helpful to them in interacting with the surroundings (Baig et al., 2024). On top of this, the AI-assisted healthcare systems are also tackling mobility issues by the integration of sensors and the use of intelligent algorithms that recognize the obstacles and promote safe navigation through them (Nasr et al., 2021).

The future of AI-integrated wearable devices has a bright future in the field of increasing real-time accessibility (Chakraborty et al., 2023). Current research is centred on increasing the smartness and the adaptation of these devices, with the view of enabling them to be more personalized and context-aware (Baig et al., 2024). Nevertheless, user privacy, ethical concerns, and the price factor are still the main research areas doubtlessly waiting for your insight (Nasr et al., 2021). Looking into these will be decisive in improving the function of AI-embedded, wearable devices thereby allowing more people with disabilities to live and lead a more independent and integrated life (Chakraborty et al., 2023).

6.2. Advancements in AI-Powered Autonomous Vehicles for Disabled-Friendly Transport

Artificial Intelligence (AI) amalgamated into self-driving cars (AVs) shares the revolutionary potential of assistive mobility for disabled persons. By bringing in autonomous & secure transport solutions, AVs make it possible for individuals to visit essential places like hospitals, schools, and workplaces without help from care-givers (Golbabaei et al., 2024). The recent technological development commits the principle of designing cars to be useful to various physical and cognitive challenged people (Bastola et al., 2025). These tech achievements other than being a factor in decreasing dependency also are a method of backing people with mobility issues in participating more actively in society (Zhong et al., 2024).

AI-operated AVs are being created with accessibility-oriented design characteristics, such as voice commands, tactile interfaces, and the automated ramp system to cater to the needs of users with mobility and sensory conditions (Bastola et al., 2025). The real-life tests using the self-driving shuttles that led to the commendable results of moving the elderly and disabled individuals conveniently through the complex urban areas (Zhong et al., 2024). In addition, the user preferences as a result of AI allow the vehicle to configure itself with the choice of setting up the seat for the person concerned or to enable the communication assistant, thus, making the travel more comfortable & dignified (Golbabaei et al., 2024). These advances are an indication of mobility being democratized.

The ongoing evolution of AI-integrated self-driving vehicles has a potential breakthrough for people with disabilities to live more independently and better quality of life. Although the technological and infrastructural barriers still exist, continuing research and policy support are promoting transportation systems for all (Zhong et al., 2024). Concentrating on ethical issues, cost and the design for all approaches will be the keys to the success of new rollouts (Golbabaei et al., 2024). With the advancement of AI in transport networks, its ethical use will trigger the independence, equal rights, and integration of individuals with disabilities across the globe (Bastola et al., 2025).

7. CONCLUSION

This chapter has explored the intersection between Artificial Intelligence and accessible travel, focusing on the insurmountable issues faced by people with various disabilities, and how the transformative power of Artificial Intelligence can drive the Travel and Tourism Industry towards larger inclusiveness. The practicalities of modern transport systems impose heavy, often life-threatening, barriers to a major fraction of the disabled population globally. Most often, the existing infrastructures and services have inadequate accommodations for support; furthermore, the conventional assistive solutions fail to deliver the ever-changing, personalized, and context-specific kind of support. By analysing the evolving role of technology in accessible travel, this chapter highlights the inadequacies of traditional methods and investigates how AI solutions are offering more dynamic, personalized, and inclusive experiences. Object detection and scene understanding, through Computer Vision, play a role in enhancing navigation, while natural language processing allows for a voice-controlled interface. Emerging AR/VR technologies would provide immersive guidance and familiarization prior to a trip. AI trip planners are now increasingly focused on accessibility, real-time navigation aids are getting smarter, and predictive models help assess route accessibility. AI chatbots give instant accessible support. Case studies from smart city projects and tools like Aira and Seeing AI along with improved features in Google Maps prove that AI-driven accessible travel is no longer something from the future-it's rapidly turning real with fantastic worldwide success stories.

Looking to the future, by harnessing the capabilities of AI, we can dismantle long-standing barriers, optimize journeys for individual needs, and ultimately create a travel ecosystem where freedom of movement is not a privilege, but a fundamental right which belongs to everyone. Much additional commitment would be required in terms of research, development, and the equally important collaboration between technologists, advocates of accessibility, policy makers, and urban planners to realize this full promise. Lastly, ethical considerations, data privacy, mitigation of biases in algorithms, and bridging the digital divide must be priorities to realize the fair opportunity for all.

REFERENCES

Abidi, M. H., Siddiquee, A. N., Alkhalefah, H., & Srivastava, V. (2024). A comprehensive review of navigation systems for visually impaired individuals. *Heliyon, 10*(11), e31825. DOI: 10.1016/j.heliyon.2024.e31825 PMID: 38841448

AccessNow. *Discover Accessible places.* Accessed on March 28, 2025, available at https://accessnow.com/

Aira.io. (n.d.). *About Aira.* Accessed on March 28, 2025, available at https://aira.io

Al-karawi, K. A. (2023). Internet of Things (IoT) about Disabilities: Disabilities in relation to the Internet of Things (IoT). *ScienceOpen Preprints.*

Ali, A. E. A., Mashhour, M., Salama, A. S., Shoitan, R., & Shaban, H. (2023). Development of an intelligent personal assistant system based on IoT for people with disabilities. *Sustainability (Basel), 15*(6), 5166. DOI: 10.3390/su15065166

Amsterdam Smart City. (n.d.). *Mobility Portal.* Accessed on March 29, 2025, available at https://amsterdamsmartcity.com/updates/project/mobility-portal-co011ghp

Andersson, E. (2024). *8 new accessibility updates across Lookout, Google Maps and more.* The Keyword. Accessed on March 28, 2025, available at https://blog.google/outreach-initiatives/accessibility/ai-accessibility-update-gaad-2024

Anitha, S., Abinesh, B., Adhithya, R., Karthik, S., Kumar, S. H., & Thirukumaran, Y. (2025). AI powered trip planner. *International Journal of Scientific Research and Technology, 2*(2), 133–139.

Anupriya, R., Arunprakash, C. V., Divagar, M., & Gokul, R. M. (2024). AI trip planner. *International Research Journal of Modernization in Engineering Technology and Science, 6*(12), 2611–2615.

Asia Research News. (2023). *RIKEN: RIBA-II, the next-generation care-giving robot.* Asia Research News. Accessed on March 28, 2025, available at https://www.asiaresearchnews.com/html/article.php/aid/6391/cid/2/research/technology/riken/riba-ii%2C_the_next_generation_care-giving_robot.html

Avila, M., Wolf, K., Brock, A., & Henze, N. (2016, June). Remote assistance for blind users in daily life: A survey about be my eyes. In *Proceedings of the 9th ACM International Conference on PErvasive Technologies Related to Assistive Environments* (pp. 1-2). DOI: 10.1145/2910674.2935839

Bach, D. (2022). *Haleon harnesses Microsoft's Seeing AI technology to make health product information more accessible for people who are blind or have low vision.* Microsoft News Center. Accessed on March 28, 2025, available at https://news.microsoft.com/source/features/digital-transformation/haleon-harnesses-microsofts-seeing-ai-technology-to-make-health-product-information-more-accessible-for-people-who-are-blind-or-have-low-vision/

Bahaddad, A., Almarhabi, K., & Alghamdi, A. (2024). Using augmented reality and deep learning to enhance tourist experiences at landmarks in Makkah. *Journal of Autonomous Intelligence*, *7*(4). Retrieved March 27, 2025, from https://jai.front-sci.com/index.php/jai/article/view/1502. DOI: 10.32629/jai.v7i4.1502

Baig, M. S. A., Gillani, S. A., Shah, S. M., Aljawarneh, M., Khan, A. A., & Siddiqui, M. H. (2024). AI-based Wearable Vision Assistance System for the Visually Impaired: Integrating Real-Time Object Recognition and Contextual Understanding Using Large Vision-Language Models. arXiv preprint arXiv:2412.20059.

Barcelona City Council. (2022). *Mobility for more liveable urban spaces.* EIT Urban Mobility. Accessed on March 28, 2025, available at https://www.eiturbanmobility.eu/wp-content/uploads/2022/12/EIT-UM_-Highlights-Report_2022.pdf

Bastola, A., Wang, H., Boroujeni, S. P. H., Brinkley, J., Moshayedi, A. J., & Razi, A. (2025). Driving Towards Inclusion: A Systematic Review of AI-powered Accessibility Enhancements for People with Disability in Autonomous Vehicles. *IEEE Access : Practical Innovations, Open Solutions*, *13*, 61384–61415. DOI: 10.1109/ACCESS.2025.3555923

Bender, A., Guerreiro, M., Agapito, D., Dias Sequeira, B., & Mendes, J. (2024). Sensory experiences in heritage contexts: A qualitative approach. *European Journal of Tourism Research*, *36*, 3604. DOI: 10.54055/ejtr.v36i.3060

BraunAbility. (n.d.). *How to help someone with a mobility impairment.* Accessed on March 26, 2025, available at https://www.braunability.com/us/en/blog/accessible-living/how-to-help-mobility-impairment.html

Brilli, D. D., Georgaras, E., Tsilivaki, S., Melanitis, N., & Nikita, K. (2024). AIris: An AI-powered wearable assistive device for the visually impaired.

Bureau of Transportation Statistics. (2024). *Travel patterns of American adults with disabilities.* Accessed on March 27, 2025, available at https://www.bts.gov/travel-patterns-with-disabilities

Casanova, E., Guffanti, D., & Hidalgo, L. (2025). Technological advancements in human navigation for the visually impaired: A systematic review. Sensors, 25(7), 1 Article 2213.

Cazzato, D., Cimarelli, C., Sanchez-Lopez, J. L., Voos, H., & Leo, M. (2020). A survey of computer vision methods for 2d object detection from unmanned aerial vehicles. *Journal of Imaging*, *6*(8), 78. DOI: 10.3390/jimaging6080078 PMID: 34460693

Chakraborty, N., Mishra, Y., Bhattacharya, R., & Bhattacharya, B. (2023). Artificial Intelligence: The road ahead for the accessibility of persons with Disability. *Materials Today: Proceedings*, *80*, 3757–3761. DOI: 10.1016/j.matpr.2021.07.374

Chan, C. S., Shek, K. F., & Agapito, D. (2022). Comparing Sensory Experience Creation Process of Visitors with Hearing Impairment and General Visitors in Hong Kong Wetland Park. *Sustainability (Basel)*, *14*(13), 7676. DOI: 10.3390/su14137676

Chan, C. S., Wong, S. Y., Tam, V., & Agapito, D. (2025). Sensory experience of visitors with hearing impairment on a rural island destination. *Tourism Geographies*, 1–22. DOI: 10.1080/14616688.2025.2462785

Chennai Smart City Ltd. (2020). *Intelligent Traffic Management System*. Accessed on March 28, 2025, available at https://cscl.co.in/intelligent-traffic-management-system

Coetzee, L., & Olivrin, G. (2012). Inclusion through the Internet of Things. *Assistive Technology*, *31*(1).

Cohen, A., & Dalyot, S. (2020). Machine-learning prediction models for pedestrian traffic flow levels: Towards optimizing walking routes for blind pedestrians. *Transactions in GIS*, *24*(5), 1264–1279. DOI: 10.1111/tgis.12674

Cranmer, E. E., Tom Dieck, M. C., & Jung, T. (2023). The role of augmented reality for sustainable development: Evidence from cultural heritage tourism. *Tourism Management Perspectives*, *49*, 101196. DOI: 10.1016/j.tmp.2023.101196

DDanDDanDDan. (2025). *How smart tourism apps are improving accessibility for disabled travelers.* WorldMindHub. Accessed on April 2 2025, available at https://worldmindhub.tistory.com/6916

Domingo, M. C. (2012). An overview of the Internet of Things for people with disabilities. *journal of Network and Computer Applications, 35*(2), 584-596.

Domingo, M. C. (2021). An overview of machine learning and 5G for people with disabilities. *Sensors (Basel)*, *21*(22), 7572. DOI: 10.3390/s21227572 PMID: 34833648

Du, J., Qiao, F., & Yu, L. (2020). Improving bus transit services for disabled individuals: Demand clustering, bus assignment, and route optimization. *IEEE Access : Practical Innovations, Open Solutions, 8*, 121564–121571. DOI: 10.1109/ACCESS.2020.3007322

El Choubassi, M., Nestares, O., Wu, Y., Kozintsev, I., & Haussecker, H. (2010). An augmented reality tourist guide on your mobile devices. In Advances in Multimedia Modeling: 16th International Multimedia Modeling Conference, MMM 2010, Chongqing, China, January 6-8, 2010. [Springer Berlin Heidelberg.]. *Proceedings, 16*, 588–602.

El-Geneidy, A., Levinson, D., Diab, E., Boisjoly, G., Verbich, D., & Loong, C. (2016). The cost of equity: Assessing transit accessibility and social disparity using total travel cost. *Transportation Research Part A, Policy and Practice, 91*, 302–316. DOI: 10.1016/j.tra.2016.07.003

Electronics, L. G. (2020). *AI Robots at Incheon Airport*. Accessed on March 28, 2025, available at https://www.lgnewsroom.com

Esquivel, P., Gill, K., Goldberg, M., Sundaram, S. A., Morris, L., & Ding, D. (2024). Voice Assistant Utilization among the Disability Community for Independent Living: A Rapid Review of Recent Evidence. *Human Behavior and Emerging Technologies, 2024*(1), 6494944. DOI: 10.1155/2024/6494944

Golbabaei, F., Dwyer, J., Gomez, R., Peterson, A., Cocks, K., Bubke, A., & Paz, A. (2024). Enabling mobility and inclusion: Designing accessible autonomous vehicles for people with disabilities. *Cities (London, England), 154*, 105333. DOI: 10.1016/j.cities.2024.105333

Goldenson, S. B. (2020). *Find wheelchair accessible places with Google Maps*. Accessed on March 28, 2025, available at https://blog.google/products/maps/wheelchair-accessible-places-google-maps/

Group, P. T. V. (n.d.). Accessibility analysis. Accessed on March 10, 2025, available at https://www.ptvgroup.com/en/application-areas/accessibility-analysis

GuideGeek. (2024). *Travelers using AI to plan trips for disabled individuals report high satisfaction*. Accessed on March 27, 2025, available at https://guidegeek.com/press/travelers-using-ai-to-plan-trips-for-disabled-individuals-report-high-satisfaction

Havenocode. (n.d.). *Artificial intelligence in transport: How AI optimizes routes and reduces costs?* Havenocode Blog. Accessed on April 2, 2025, available at https://www.havenocode.io/blog/post/artificial-intelligence-in-transport-how-ai-optimizes-routes-and-reduces-costs

Hutchinson, B., Prabhakaran, V., Denton, E., Webster, K., Zhong, Y., & Denuyl, S. (2020). Social biases in NLP models as barriers for persons with disabilities. *arXiv preprint arXiv:2005.00813*. DOI: 10.18653/v1/2020.acl-main.487

Inclusive City Maker. (2022). *Obstacles in public transport: What solutions for physical disability?* Accessed on March 26, 2025, available at https://www.inclusivecitymaker.com/obstacles-public-transport-physical-disability/

Institute for Transportation & Development Policy. (2024). *From Challenges to Solutions: Building Inclusive Transport for All*. Accessed on March 28, 2025, available at https://itdp.org/publication/from-challenges-to-solutions-building-inclusive-transport-for-all/

Jalilvand, M. R., & Ghasemi, H. (2024). Augmented reality technology in tourism and hospitality research: a review from 2010 to 2024. Journal of Science and Technology Policy Management.

Janes, J., Arkinstall, E., & Reyes, J. *Mapping an inaccessible world for people with disabilities*. CEO North America. Accessed on March 28, 2025, available at https://ceo-na.com/opinion/mapping-an-inaccessible-world-for-people-with-disabilities/

Johns Hopkins Applied Physics Laboratory. (2024). *AI Navigation System for the Visually Impaired*. Accessed on April 1, 2025, available at https://www.jhuapl.edu/news/news-releases/240701-johns-hopkins-creates-navigation-system-for-the-visually-impaired

Kamble, S., Korde, S., Khare, S., & Rane, M. R. (2025). Personalized travel itinerary using AI. *Journal of Emerging Technologies and Innovative Research*, *12*(2), g751–g754. Retrieved March 27, 2025, from https://www.jetir.org/papers/JETIR2502493.pdf

Karacaoglu, S., Yolal, M., & Gursoy, D. (2015). Examining the perceptions of mobility-impaired travelers: An analysis of service expectations, evaluations, and travel barriers. *Tourism Review International*, *19*(1-2), 19–30. DOI: 10.3727/154427215X14327569678759

Know the ADA. (n.d.). *Recent Developments in Accessible Transportation Technologies*. Accessed on April 2, 2025, available at https://know-the-ada.com/recent-developments-in-accessible-transportation-technologies/

Kumar, S. (2025). *The Future of Travel: How Airport Robots Are Shaping the Passenger Experience*. TechSci Blog. Accessed on March 28, 2025, available at https://techsciblog.com/the-future-of-travel-how-airport-robots-are-shaping-the-passenger-experience/

Lee, C. D., Koontz, A. M., Cooper, R., Sivakanthan, S., Chernicoff, W., Brunswick, A., Deepak, N., Kulich, H. R., LaFerrier, J., Lopes, C. R., Collins, N. L., Dicianno, B. E., & Cooper, R. A. (2023). Understanding Travel Considerations and Barriers for People with Disabilities to Using Current Modes of Transportation Through Journey Mapping. *Transportation Research Record: Journal of the Transportation Research Board, 2678*(5), 271–287. DOI: 10.1177/03611981231188730 PMID: 39055859

Lukic Vujadinovic, V., Damnjanovic, A., Cakic, A., Petkovic, D. R., Prelevic, M., Pantovic, V., Stojanovic, M., Vidojevic, D., Vranjes, D., & Bodolo, I. (2024). AI-driven approach for enhancing sustainability in urban public transportation. Sustainability, 16(17), 1 Article 7763.

Marsh, M. (2025). *Transforming Urban Mobility With IoT-enabled Smart Parking Solutions*. L&T Technology Services. Accessed on March 28, 2025, available at https://www.ltts.com/blog/iot-enabled-smart-parking-solutions#:~:text=A%20smart%20parking%20solution%20aims,and%20emissions%20across%20the%20board

Mart, L. (2024). *Innovations in elevator technology: What's new in 2024?* Lift Mart. Accessed on March 28, 2025, available at https://liftmart.co/innovations-in-elevator-technology-whats-new-in-2024/

Mesquita, S., Caldeira, A., & Carneiro, M. J. (2025). The antecedents of co-creation in museums in the case of people with sensory impairments. *Tourism Recreation Research*, 1–19. DOI: 10.1080/02508281.2025.2464501

Microsoft. (n.d.). *Seeing AI App Features*. Accessed on March 28, 2025, available at https://www.microsoft.com/en-us/ai/seeing-ai

Mokrenko, V. I. (2020). *Machine Learning Enabled Surface Classification and Knowledge Transfer for Accessible Route Generation for Wheelchair Users* (Master's thesis, Miami University).

Moon, N., Baker, P. M. A., & Goughnour, K. (2019). Designing wearable technologies for users with disabilities: Accessibility, usability, and connectivity factors. *Journal of Rehabilitation and Assistive Technologies Engineering*, *6*, 1–12. DOI: 10.1177/2055668319862137 PMID: 35186318

Motability Foundation. (2022). *The transport accessibility gap*. Accessed on March 25, 2025, available at https://www.motabilityfoundation.org.uk/media/iwaidhxk/motability_transport-accessibility-gap-report_march-2022_final.pdf

Mumm, O., Murad, M., & Carlow, V. M. (2025). Accessibility Score–Data analytics for the holistic assessment of urban mobility networks and the case of Braunschweig. *Environment and Planning. B, Urban Analytics and City Science*, *52*(3), 594–613.

Namoun, A., Abi Sen, A. A., Tufail, A., Alshanqiti, A., Nawaz, W., & BenRhouma, O. (2022). A two-phase machine learning framework for context-aware service selection to empower people with disabilities. *Sensors (Basel)*, *22*(14), 5142. DOI: 10.3390/s22145142 PMID: 35890820

Nasr, M., Islam, M. M., Shehata, S., Karray, F., & Quintana, Y. (2021). Smart healthcare in the age of AI: Recent advances, challenges, and future prospects. *IEEE Access : Practical Innovations, Open Solutions*, *9*, 145248–145270. DOI: 10.1109/ACCESS.2021.3118960

Neeli, P. K., Doodipala, B. R., Sai Phani Sushma, P., Kolasani, V., & Sri Harsha, T. S. N. S. S. (2024). AI-driven travel planner. *International Journal for Research in Applied Science and Engineering Technology*, *12*(4), 1015–1019. Retrieved March 24, 2025, from https://www.ijraset.com/best-journal/ai-driven-travel-planner

New England Low Vision and Blindness. (n.d.). *Advancements in Assistive Technology for Low Vision*. Accessed on April 2, 2025, Available at https://nelowvision.com/advancements-in-assistive-technology-for-low-vision/

Nurse Next Door. (2022). *The importance of accessible infrastructure and technologies for persons with disabilities*. Accessed on March 26, 2025, available at https://www.nursenextdoor.com.au/blog/the-importance-of-accessible-infrastructure-and-technologies-for-persons-with-disabilities/

Park, E., & Kim, S. B. (2025). Air and train travel experiences for wheelchair users. *Current Issues in Tourism*, 1–6. DOI: 10.1080/13683500.2025.2478283

Peek Editorial Team. (2024). *How AI is reshaping the tourism and travel industry*. Peek Pro Blog. Accessed on March 27, 2025, available at https://www.peekpro.com/blog/ai-tourism-industry

Prefeitura do Rio de Janeiro. (2021). *Inclusive Mobility Plan Overview*. Accessed on March 28, 2025, available at http://www.rio.rj.gov.br

Qiao, G., Hou, S., Chen, Q., Xiang, G., & Prideaux, B. (2024). Role of Body in Travel: Wheelchair Users' Experience from a Multi-Sensory Perspective. *Journal of Travel Research*.

Ramirez, A. R. G., González-Carrasco, I., Jasper, G. H., Lopez, A. L., Lopez-Cuadrado, J. L., & García-Crespo, A. (2017). Towards human smart cities: Internet of things for sensory impaired individuals. *Computing*, *99*(1), 107–126. DOI: 10.1007/s00607-016-0529-2

Rashid, Z., Melià-Seguí, J., Pous, R., & Peig, E. (2017). Using Augmented Reality and Internet of Things to improve accessibility of people with motor disabilities in the context of Smart Cities. *Future Generation Computer Systems, 76*, 248–261. DOI: 10.1016/j.future.2016.11.030

Rinish. (2025, February 7). *AI in transportation: A smarter, safer, and more efficient future.* Thoughtminds. Accessed on March 28, 2025, available at https://www.thoughtminds.io/ai-in-transportation/

Ronen, R. (2024). *How artificial general intelligence could redefine accessibility.* Forbes. Accessed on March 28, 2025, available at https://www.forbes.com/councils/forbesbusinesscouncil/2024/02/02/how-artificial-general-intelligence-could-redefine-accessibility/

Said, Y., Atri, M., Albahar, M. A., Ben Atitallah, A., & Alsariera, Y. A. (2023). Scene recognition for visually-impaired people's navigation assistance based on vision transformer with dual multiscale attention. *Mathematics, 11*(5), 1127. DOI: 10.3390/math11051127

Semary, H. E., Al-Karawi, K. A., Abdelwahab, M. M., & Elshabrawy, A. M. (2024). A Review on Internet of Things (IoT)-Related Disabilities and Their Implications. *Journal of Disability Research, 3*(2), 20240012. DOI: 10.57197/JDR-2024-0012

Sethuraman, S. C., Tadkapally, G. R., Mohanty, S. P., Galada, G., & Subramanian, A. (2023). MagicEye: An Intelligent Wearable Towards Independent Living of Visually Impaired. *arXiv preprint arXiv:2303.13863.*

Shankman, S. (2025). *AI travel agents: How they're transforming the future of travel planning.* Navan. Accessed on April 3 2025, available at https://navan.com/blog/insights-trends/ai-travel-agent

Shenoy, G. G., Wagle, M. A., & Connelly, K. (2017). Leveling the playing field for Visually Impaired using Transport Assistant. *arXiv preprint arXiv:1703.02103.*

Shi, L., Cole, S., & Chancellor, H. C. (2012). Understanding leisure travel motivations of travellers with acquired mobility impairments. *Tourism Management, 33*(1), 228–231. DOI: 10.1016/j.tourman.2011.02.007

Shukla, V., Rana, S., & Prashar, S. (2024). Examining the potential of virtual and augmented reality in enhancing tourism experiences. *The Bottom Line (New York, N.Y.).* DOI: 10.1108/BL-05-2023-0139

Southeast, A. D. A. Center. (2022). *These apps help people with disabilities travel more easily.* Accessed on April 1, 2025, available at https://adasoutheast.org/these-apps-help-people-with-disabilities-travel-more-easily/

Sozialhelden, V. (2025). Wheelmap. In *OpenStreetMap Wiki*. Accessed on March 28, 2025, available at https://wiki.openstreetmap.org/wiki/Wheelmap

Spice, B. (2019). *Collision-Detecting Suitcase, Wayfinding App Help Blind People Navigate Airports*. Carnegie Mellon University. Accessed on March 28, 2025, available at https://www.cmu.edu/news/stories/archives/2019/may/suitcase-helps-navigate-airports.html

Stouhi, D. (2022). *Toronto plans on stopping the construction of smart cities following concerns of privacy*. ArchDaily. Accessed on March 28, 2025, available at https://www.archdaily.com/984561/toronto-plans-on-stopping-the-construction-of-smart-cities-following-concerns-of-privacy

Subramanian, S. (n.d.). *The 10 best AI travel assistant chatbots for smarter travel planning*. Emitrr. Accessed on April 3 2025, available at https://emitrr.com/blog/chatbot-for-travel/

Tapu, R., Mocanu, B., & Zaharia, T. (2017). DEEP-SEE: Joint object detection, tracking and recognition with application to visually impaired navigational assistance. *Sensors (Basel)*, *17*(11), 2473. DOI: 10.3390/s17112473 PMID: 29143795

Tata, A. M., Ebbatson, D., & Fluke, C. (2024). Exploring airport navigation challenges faced by airline travellers with hidden disabilities. *International Journal of Aviation, Aeronautics, and Aerospace*, *11*(1). DOI: 10.58940/2374-6793.1871

Tokmurziyev, I., Cabrera, M. A., Khan, M. H., Mahmoud, Y., Moreno, L., & Tsetserukou, D. (2025). LLM-Glasses: GenAI-driven Glasses with Haptic Feedback for Navigation of Visually Impaired People. *arXiv preprint arXiv:2503.16475*.

Tokyo Metropolitan Government. (2020). *Olympic Games Tokyo 2020: Accessibility Equipment Update*. Accessed on March 28, 2025, available at https://www.inclusivecitymaker.com/olympic-games-tokyo-2020-accessibility/#:~:text=The%20200%20shuttles%20can%20transport,the%20%E2%80%9Clast%20one%20mile%E2%80%9D

Turno, F. M., Jackiva, I. Y., & Budiloviča, E. (2025). Enhancing Public Transport Accessibility for People with Motor Disabilities Through Deep Learning on Graphs. *Transport and Telecommunication*, *26*(1), 82–89. DOI: 10.2478/ttj-2025-0008

Twardzik, E., Schrack, J. A., Porter, K. M. P., Coleman, T., Washington, K., & Swenor, B. K. (2024). TRansit ACessibility Tool (TRACT): Developing a novel scoring system for public transportation system accessibility. *Journal of Transport & Health*, *34*, 101742. DOI: 10.1016/j.jth.2023.101742 PMID: 38405233

United Nations Department of Economic and Social Affairs. (2018). *UN disability and development report: Realizing the SDGs by, for and with persons with disabilities.* Accessed on March 28, 2025, available at https://www.un.org/en/desa/un-disability-and-development-report-%E2%80%93-realizing-sdgs-and-persons-disabilities

Valipoor, M. M., & De Antonio, A. (2023). Recent trends in computer vision-driven scene understanding for VI/blind users: A systematic mapping. *Universal Access in the Information Society*, *22*(3), 983–1005. DOI: 10.1007/s10209-022-00868-w

Velho, R. (2019). Transport accessibility for wheelchair users: A qualitative analysis of inclusion and health. *International Journal of Transportation Science and Technology*, *8*(2), 103–115. DOI: 10.1016/j.ijtst.2018.04.005

Wagner, L. (n.d.). *Accessible pedestrian signals (APS): A century of change*. Inclusive City Maker. Accessible Pedestrian Signals (APS): a Century of Change", Accessed on March 28, 2025, available at https://www.inclusivecitymaker.com/accessible-pedestrian-signals-aps-a-century-of-change/

Waisberg, E., Ong, J., Masalkhi, M., Zaman, N., Sarker, P., Lee, A. G., & Tavakkoli, A. (2024). Meta smart glasses—Large language models and the future for assistive glasses for individuals with vision impairments. *Eye (London, England)*, *38*(6), 1036–1038. DOI: 10.1038/s41433-023-02842-z PMID: 38049627

Wang, X., & Zhu, Z. (2023). Context understanding in computer vision: A survey. *Computer Vision and Image Understanding*, *229*, 103646. DOI: 10.1016/j.cviu.2023.103646

WHILL. (2024, April 10). *Self-driving wheelchairs: WHILL bring travelers to their gate at Schiphol Airport.* WHILL Inc. Accessed on March 28, 2025, available at https://whill.inc/us/news/self-driving-wheelchairs-whill-bring-travelers-to-their-gate-at-schiphol-airport?

World Health Organization & World Bank. (2011). *World report on disability.* Accessed on March 28, 2025, available at https://www.who.int/publications/i/item/world-report-on-disability

Yu, X., & Saniie, J. (2025). Visual Impairment Spatial Awareness System for Indoor Navigation and Daily Activities. *Journal of Imaging*, *11*(1), 9. DOI: 10.3390/jimaging11010009 PMID: 39852322

Zhang, H., Falletta, N. J., Xie, J., Yu, R., Lee, S., Billah, S. M., & Carroll, J. M. (2025, January). Enhancing the Travel Experience for People with Visual Impairments through Multimodal Interaction: NaviGPT, A Real-Time AI-Driven Mobile Navigation System. In *Companion Proceedings of the 2025 ACM International Conference on Supporting Group Work* (pp. 29-35).

Zhong, R., Tian, Z., Liao, J., & Shi, W. (2024, October). Autonomous Shuttle Operation for Vulnerable Populations: Lessons and Experiences. In *2024 IEEE 10th International Conference on Collaboration and Internet Computing (CIC)* (pp. 1-8). IEEE.

Chapter 7
Opportunities and Challenges in Implementing IoT in Smart Homes for an Optimized Environment

Utkarsh Trivedi
School of Computer Engineering, Kalinga Institute of Industrial Technology (KIIT), Bhubaneswar, India

Yash Vardhan
School of Computer Engineering, Kalinga Institute of Industrial Technology (KIIT), Bhubaneswar, India

Piyush Kumar
https://orcid.org/0009-0007-6032-1104
School of Computer Engineering, Kalinga Institute of Industrial Technology (KIIT), Bhubaneswar, India

Ansh Aryan
https://orcid.org/0009-0004-7635-5171
School of Computer Engineering, Kalinga Institute of Industrial Technology (KIIT), Bhubaneswar, India

Parth Batra
https://orcid.org/0009-0002-1325-730X
School of Computer Engineering, Kalinga Institute of Industrial Technology (KIIT), Bhubaneswar, India

Hitesh Mohapatra
https://orcid.org/0000-0001-8100-4860
School of Computer Engineering, Kalinga Institute of Industrial Technology (KIIT), Bhubaneswar, India

ABSTRACT

There are several benefits and significant hurdles to implementing IoT in smart homes. One way that IoT technology improves convenience is by allowing homeowners to remotely control various home systems, such as security and lighting, through

DOI: 10.4018/979-8-3373-6385-1.ch007

Copyright © 2026, IGI Global Scientific Publishing. Copying or distributing in print or electronic forms without written permission of IGI Global Scientific Publishing is prohibited.

seamless integration. Additionally, it promotes energy efficiency through real-time optimization and monitoring. IoT also makes it possible to monitor health and provide personalized experiences, which respects individual preferences and enhances wellbeing. However, obstacles including device compatibility problems from many manufacturers make smooth integration difficult, while privacy and security dangers related to data collection cause worry. This paper proposes a solution that aims to outline a comprehensive approach to leverage IoT effectively while mitigating potential pitfalls in smart home environments. Embracing these solutions, one can unlock the full potential of IoT technology while effectively managing associated challenges, thus paving the way for smarter, more connected, and secure residential living environments.

1. INTRODUCTION

The Internet of Things (IoT) has moved beyond industrial and commercial applications to become an active part of residential life. Smart homes now allow residents to interact with lighting, security, energy, and appliances in real time. With mobile applications and voice assistants, people can manage household functions from anywhere. This technology brings not only convenience but also a chance to reduce waste, improve safety, and support independent living for elderly or disabled individuals. However, as the number of connected devices in homes increases, challenges begin to surface (Ahmed et al., 2024). Security is one of the main concerns. Each connected device can be an entry point for cyberattacks. Weak default settings, outdated firmware, and poor encryption make many systems vulnerable. The risk is especially serious when sensitive personal data, such as health or behavioral information, is collected without proper safeguards. Another major issue is interoperability. Many manufacturers use their own protocols, making it difficult for devices to work together. This creates a fragmented user experience. People often face difficulties in setup and routine use, especially when devices fail to sync or operate in isolation. The lack of industry-wide standards also slows innovation and increases development costs ("Review for "Smart home technologies for enhancing independence of living and reducing care dependence in older adults: A systematic review"," 2024).

Privacy remains an ongoing concern. Smart homes continuously collect and process data to function efficiently. While this helps in personalization, it also raises ethical and legal issues. Users need more transparency and control over what data is being collected, how it is stored, and who has access to it. Despite these challenges, the potential of smart homes remains strong. Automated systems can reduce energy consumption by learning from usage patterns. They also reduce manual effort and improve security with motion sensors, alarms, and remote monitoring. For caregivers, these tools offer peace of mind through real-time updates about elderly or dependent family members (Bennett et al., 2022). The rising cost of energy, increased remote work, and growth in smart devices make this a critical time to focus on smart home development. However, widespread adoption depends on solving the problems of compatibility, cost, complexity, and user trust. This chapter explores the current state of IoT in smart homes. It first reviews related studies and emerging technologies. It then identifies key barriers to implementation, including cybersecurity risks, interoperability gaps, and design complexity. Finally, it proposes structured solutions focused on user experience, system design, regulation, and sustainability (Bhuiyan et al., 2022).

The Internet of Things (IoT) has brought significant change to how homes operate, connecting various systems for comfort, security, and energy use. Smart homes use sensors, actuators, and communication networks to simplify tasks, reduce energy waste, and offer remote access. Features like automated lighting, climate control, and voice-activated assistants have become more common. These developments improve quality of life, especially through personalized routines and efficient resource management (Pazmino et al., 2019). Yet, the benefits come with challenges. Security remains a top concern as connected devices increase the risk of data breaches. Unprotected systems can expose sensitive user information, raising concerns about privacy. Interoperability is another issue. Devices from different brands often follow separate standards, leading to poor integration and user frustration. These technical gaps weaken the overall smart home experience and reduce system resilience (Daruwala & Oberst, 2023). Despite these concerns, smart homes continue to advance. New systems learn from user behavior, improving efficiency and comfort. Technologies such as intelligent monitoring help reduce energy usage, supporting sustainability. Voice-controlled assistants and other smart tools continue to evolve, making homes more responsive to daily needs (Dash & Choudekar, 2021). However, long-term success depends on solving key issues around data protection, device compatibility, and secure system design (Dey et al., 2024).

Figure 1. Figure showing IoT devices deployment system

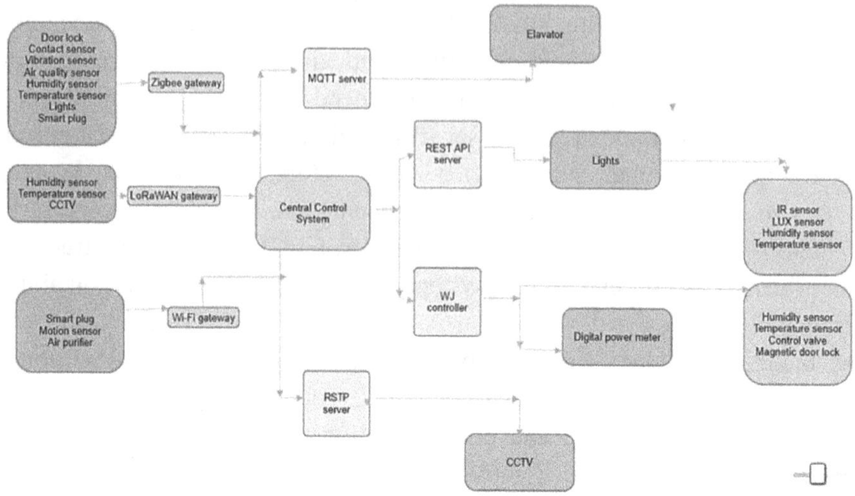

Integrating IoT and OT systems in smart homes introduces new technical and regulatory challenges. One major concern is security, especially when devices from different vendors are used together. Each component may follow its own standards, which can expose gaps in protection. To manage this, clear rules and secure frameworks are needed during deployment (Domb, 2019).

As more devices are added, the system must process increasing volumes of data. This requires scalable solutions that can handle real-time insights without slowing down. Tools such as gateways, protocol converters, middleware, network monitoring systems, and centralized control platforms become essential. These tools help link devices smoothly and maintain system intelligence and safety (Sabit, 2025). Another issue is visibility. Without proper monitoring, the growing number of connected devices increases the risk of cyberattacks. Strong security policies and network oversight are critical to manage this complexity and ensure reliability (Nguyen et al., 2024). Understanding these foundational concerns prepares us to explore both the benefits and risks of IoT adoption in smart homes. The next section will look at past studies to highlight how these problems have been addressed and where gaps remain. Fig.1 shows IoT devices deployment challenges and studies in building management systems.

This chapter is organized as follows. Section 2 presents a review of past research on IoT applications in smart homes, focusing on key technologies, benefits, and known challenges. Section 3 outlines the proposed study, identifying critical issues such as device compatibility, security risks, and user experience barriers. Section 4 provides solutions and strategies aimed at improving interoperability, privacy, and system efficiency. Section 5 discusses future trends and sustainable practices in smart home development. Finally, Section 6 offers concluding insights and highlights areas for further research.

2. LITERATURE REVIEW

Numerous scholars have forecasted the advantages of integrating IoT automation devices into smart homes. For example, the proposed LoRaWAN (Long Range Wide Area Network) Prototype, which proves to be one of the primary drivers and enablers in a smart city. The study explores the related vulnerabilities using LoRaWAN as the communication protocol, providing useful insights through prototype implementation and real-world testing. Additionally, the study makes suggestions for risk mitigation that improve the security and privacy of smart home environments. These suggestions include the usage of secure protocols and federated learning (Et. al., 2021). A few academics even went so far as to highlight the advantages of IoT devices in healthcare applications. The vital role that IoT devices play in transforming the way that patients receive medical care. IoT devices are revolutionizing healthcare by making it possible to track vital signs in real time and remotely monitor patients, which enables early interventions. Personalized treatment plans are another way they enhance patient care, and they streamline procedures to increase productivity. Services for telemedicine become available, which is important in situations like the COVID-19 epidemic. Medication management is aided by IoT, which guarantees adherence and lowers errors. It anticipates health trends and averts crisis with predictive analytics. IoT devices with emergency alert functions quickly call for help in emergency situations, guaranteeing timely assistance. Many home automation systems, each utilizing a different set of technologies like Bluetooth, GSM, ZigBee, and Wi-Fi, have been the subject of controversies.

These systems offer many different features, advantages, and limitations. For example, scalability and flexibility are made possible by Wi-Fi-based systems, which also offer web servers for remote access. Raspberry Pi-based implementations are typically efficient, cost-effective, and have robust automation capabilities. Energy conservation and wireless communication are prioritized in ZigBee-based systems. GSM-controlled systems ensure high availability and security, however there are SMS fees. Settings that enable Bluetooth offer localized control and password security. Every system has benefits and drawbacks, ranging from dependability and cost to customization and range limitations (Kaur & Gandhi, 2022). Smart homes are one of the most potential applications of the Internet of Things (IoT), which has transformed many facets of our life. There are numerous ways to improve security, efficiency, and convenience with IoT-enabled smart homes. But these prospects also bring with them a number of difficulties that must be resolved for the implementation to be successful. The purpose of this study of the literature is to investigate the advantages and disadvantages of integrating IoT in smart homes (Lo & Ansari, 2011).

A more thorough grasp of the challenges and opportunities of integrating IoT in smart homes may be attained by stakeholders by taking into account these extra factors, which will help them make well-informed decisions and develop strategic plans for deployment and adoption (Ref.Table.1). Additionally, centered on IoT contemplations, necessities, and designs for savvy buildings, emphasizing vitality optimization and next-generation building administration frameworks. The consideration highlights the significance of productive vitality utilization and the integration of IoT to empower savvy functionalities in homes. On the other hand, scientists conducted an orderly examination of shrewd homes and their clients, distinguishing key challenges within the appropriation and usage of IoT. The idea emphasizes the requirement for a user-centric plan and the relief of protection and security concerns to guarantee the fruitful sending of IoT in keen homes. In addition, gives an overview of IoT forensics, tending to the challenges, approaches, and open issues in IoT (Maiti & Sivanesan, 2012). The ponder highlights the significance of IoT security and the requirement for scientific capabilities to explore potential security breaches in keen domestic situations. Also, some scientists examined fog-assisted IoT-empowered understanding of well-being observation in shrewd homes, emphasizing the potential of IoT in healthcare applications. The think highlights the openings for IoT in supporting healthcare administrations inside keen domestic situations. Whereas these considerations give important bits of knowledge into the openings and challenges of executing IoT in savvy homes, there are still noteworthy information holes that have to be tended to. For occurrence, the integration of IoT in shrewd homes requires a strong framework and security measures to guarantee the security and security of clients. Future investigations ought to center on creating versatile and secure IoT structures custom-made to savvy domestic environments. Analyst has executed a framework for creating a security framework for Domestic which makes a difference to Control & Screen domestic, framework is executed (Mohapatra, 2021).

Utilizing an Android App executed in Java. This framework requires a pc-based web server. To handle domestic appliances such as fan, light as well as incorporating an arrangement for monitoring- temperature, stickiness and current in domestic additionally controls keep up security of Domestic by observing domestic exercises and keeps up work productivity, consolation and security. Analyst has actualized a framework for creating a home automation system which gives an inaccessible control of domestic appliances and conjointly give security against interruption when the domestic have isn't at domestic. These sorts of domestic mechanization frameworks are required since humans can make botches and overlooked to switch off the apparatuses. This venture portrays raspberry pi modules and presents its potential in a savvy domestic environment. Users of home automation may easily operate a variety of smart systems and equipment in their homes by using virtual buttons (Mohapatra, 2024). Virtual buttons allow users to do a variety of tasks, like turning on and off lights, modifying thermostat settings, locking doors, turning on security systems, and starting personalized routines, with only a tap on a smartphone app or online interface. With its rapid and centralized control over all areas of home automation, this user-friendly interface improves comfort, efficiency, and security in the home. Use *OnButtonPressed* and *OnButtonReleased* to handle the events when the button is visually hidden from the camera. A virtual button's size and placement must be carefully considered in relation to user engagement. Virtual buttons' usability and responsiveness will vary depending on several factors.

The area of a virtual button should be at least 10% of the target area squared, depending on the form you choose. Button pressing events occur when a significant portion of the attributes beneath the button's region are obscured from the camera's view. This can occur when the user covers the button or obscures it in any other way from the camera's view. As a result, the button's size needs to match the action it is intended to react to. For example, a button that a user presses with their finger needs to be shorter than a button that a user presses with their entire palm. The way we interact with our living spaces has evolved dramatically in recent years because of the Internet of Things (IoT) technology incorporated into smart buildings. Energy efficiency and the smooth integration of IoT devices to enable smart functions in houses are given highest priority with an emphasis on energy optimization and next-generation building management systems. But there are negatives to these developments as well, particularly in terms of user uptake, privacy issues, and shortcomings in security (N. Mohan Krishna, & G. V. Marutheswar, 2016). The significance of a user-centric approach is being cited as one of the primary barriers to the adoption of IoT in smart homes. IoT technologies have a lot of potential to improve homes' functionality, efficiency, and security, but their success depends on how well users accept and use them. Scholars have emphasized how crucial it is to consider user experience while creating Internet of Things (IoT) systems, taking usability problems under account and adapting features to suit the different needs of homeowners.

The mitigation of security and privacy risks connected with Internet of Things (IoT) installations in smart homes is another crucial issue that needs to be handled. The likelihood of illegal access, data breaches, and privacy violations rises significantly with the number of connected devices. Effective adoption of IoT in smart homes involves strong security measures that include access limits, encryption systems, and frequent software updates. Likewise, encouraging a culture of cybersecurity in smart home environments requires educating buyers about the value of safeguarding their IoT devices and networks (Nagaraju, 2023). To improve comfort, efficiency, and security, researchers have developed cutting-edge home automation systems in response to changing homeowner needs. By utilizing Network of Things technologies, these systems enable clients to remotely operate a range of security and domestic appliances, giving them the ability to keep an eye on their homes from any location. For example, adding Raspberry Pi modules makes it possible to create automation solutions that are personalized to meet the specific demands of every household. In order to enable user contact with home automation systems, virtual buttons are essential.

Through the use of web platforms or smartphone apps, users may easily operate a variety of smart devices and carry out customizable actions with a single tap. To guarantee a straightforward and easy user experience, virtual buttons' size, setting up, and responsiveness need to be carefully taken into account throughout design and implementation. A number of factors need to be made while developing virtual buttons in order to achieve maximum usefulness and user engagement. Buttons should be appropriate to the action they are meant to perform; bigger buttons can support hand-wide movements, while smaller buttons function well with finger-based interactions. Virtual buttons should also be carefully positioned to ensure that users have no trouble finding and viewing items across an assortment of devices and screen sizes. In order to improve the functionality, security, and user experience of smart homes, future research in the fields of IoT and home automation systems should concentrate on filling in the gaps and conquering the problems that now exist (Nguyen et al., 2024). This entails creating safe, scalable Internet of Things frameworks which can be adapted to meet the particular needs of homes and looking into creative ways to reduce privacy threats and improve customer acceptance. In short, the combination of Internet of Things (IoT) technology and home control systems has the potential to revolutionize how we use our living areas by bringing previously unheard-of levels of efficiency, convenience, and security. However, achieving this potential will require a concentrated effort to address issues with user adoption, security, and privacy in addition to embracing cutting-edge design concepts and technology developments. We can build intelligent, safe, intuitive, and user-centric smart homes by stressing user-centric design, setting strong security measures in place, and by taking advantage of virtual button technology advancements (Nižetić et al., 2020).

There have been notable developments in the past few years regarding the incorporation of Internet of Things (IoT) technology into smart homes. This study of the literature examines the opportunities and difficulties that come with integrating IoT in smart home settings. The review includes findings from current research on energy management, architecture, security, automation, and user acceptability. Numerous Internet of Things systems and architectures have been created to make smart home deployments easier. The device, gateway, cloud, and application layers make up the entire architecture provided by the Frugal Labs IoT Platform (FLIP). FLIP seeks to improve smart home security, energy efficiency, and quality of life (Noura et al., 2018). Furthermore, secure systems employing TBSA-like algorithms and multilayer cloud architectures have been suggested as ways to guarantee efficient data encryption and communication in Internet of Things-based smart homes. Using energy resources efficiently is a major goal of Internet of Things-based smart homes.

Table 1. Comparative analysis of existing works

Author/Year	Technology/ Protocol	Contribution	Limitations
Et al., 2021	LoRaWAN	Prototype for smart home communication and risk mitigation	Limited scope, lacks broader scalability
Kaur & Gandhi, 2022	IoT protocols (Wi-Fi, ZigBee)	Highlights healthcare applications of IoT	No practical implementation or testing
Nguyen et al., 2024	IoT + AI	Potential of IoT for healthcare in smart cities	Conceptual focus, minimal real-world data
Yoon et al., 2015	IoT security practices	Early identification of smart home security issues	Outdated protocols, lacks modern threat landscape
Pazmino et al., 2019	Sensor networks	Data privacy challenges and solutions in smart homes	Broad overview, limited technical depth
Noura et al., 2018	TBSA, multilayer cloud	Framework for data encryption and secure architecture	Theoretical; limited adoption evidence
Wagh et al., 2024	IoT system study	Comprehensive study on integration and risks	Lacks experimental verification
New Paper 1 (2023)	Case study	Analysis of real-life security breaches in Ring and Alexa	Details redacted, lacks open dataset
Dash & Choudekar, 2021	Smart devices	Automation of lighting, climate, and home security	Limited to simulation
Dey et al., 2024	IoT gadgets	Voice assistants and personalized routines	No edge computing integration
Shafee & Hamed, 2012	Wi-Fi automation	Early Wi-Fi-based home automation	Not scalable, no security layer
New Paper 2 (2024)	Edge + IoT	Shows reduced latency using edge devices in automation	Needs broader deployment data
Rauf et al., 2024	Smart home social model	Role of social interaction and user comfort	Conceptual model only
New Paper 3 (2024)	Generative AI	Custom home automation routines using LLMs	High processing cost, user privacy concerns

Appliances in homes may be monitored and controlled in real time with the help of big data analytics and Internet of Things solutions. Using mobile applications, these systems enable users to remotely monitor devices and optimize energy use by gathering device information using data capture systems (Panda et al., 2024). One of the biggest challenges in smart home systems is maintaining security and privacy. The growth of interconnected gadgets increases the vulnerability to malicious attacks. To protect smart home ecosystems from potential dangers, security approaches like blockchain-based solutions, secure authentication procedures, and encryption have been proposed. In smart homes, motion detection of people is essential for several uses, such as security and senior care. Human activity detection is achieved through the use of deep learning techniques and wearable technology that are fitted with sensors and cameras (Pazmino et al., 2019). However, precise and real-time human motion detection is challenged by the effective application of sensor technologies and machine learning algorithms. Scalability and interoperability are essential considerations for IoT-based smart home solutions. Fog and cloud computing technologies offer scalability and flexibility, but interoperability issues arise due to diverse communication protocols and device standards.

Standardization efforts and interoperability frameworks are proposed to address these challenges and facilitate seamless integration of IoT devices. Functionality of a smart home depends on devices and sensors communicating with one another effectively. Device connectivity is made possible via a variety of communication protocols, including wired and wireless technologies (Priyadarshi et al., 2024). A wide range of consumers must be able to access and afford smart home technology, which requires low-cost solutions and energy-efficient gadgets. Smart home integration of IoT technology offers several ways to improve security, convenience, and energy efficiency. However, in order to fully utilize IoT in smart home contexts, obstacles including security flaws, interoperability problems, and cost limitations must be resolved. Subsequent investigations ought to concentrate on multidisciplinary methodologies and inventive resolutions to surmount these obstacles and propel IoT-driven intelligent household systems forward. The prospects and difficulties of deploying IoT in smart homes are thoroughly covered in this succinct review of the literature, which touches on important topics like architecture, energy management, security, human motion detection, scalability, interoperability, device connectivity, and affordability.

The increasing prevalence of the Internet of Things (IoT) has revolutionized various aspects of our lives, including the way we manage our homes. Home automation systems leverage IoT technology to enable the interconnection and remote control of various devices within a dwelling, fostering convenience, security, and energy efficiency. This literature review explores the current landscape of home automation systems within the context of the IoT, examining key functionalities, communication protocols, security considerations, and future trends. The advent of the Internet of Things (IoT) has revolutionized various aspects of our lives, and one domain that has witnessed substantial transformation is home automation. This literature review aims to explore the current state of home automation systems within the context of IoT, shedding light on their evolution, technological foundations, applications, and future prospects (Rauf et al., 2024). Evolution of Home Automation Systems: Trace the historical development of home automation systems, from basic programmable thermostats to the sophisticated IoT-driven smart homes of today. Explore key milestones, technological advancements, and the driving forces behind the evolution of these systems.

1. Technological Foundations: Examine the underlying technologies that enable IoT-based home automation. Discuss the role of sensors, actuators, communication protocols, and networking technologies in creating a seamless and interconnected smart home environment. Highlight how these technologies contribute to the efficiency, security, and user experience of home automation systems.
2. Applications in Smart Living: Explore the diverse applications of home automation systems in enhancing the quality of life for residents. Discuss how these systems contribute to energy efficiency, security, convenience, and accessibility within a smart home context. Provide examples of real-world implementations and their impact on daily living.
3. Challenges and Solutions: Discuss the challenges associated with the widespread adoption of home automation systems, including interoperability issues, security concerns, and user acceptance. Present research findings and proposed solutions from past studies that aim to address these challenges and pave the way for a more seamless integration of IoT in smart homes (Sah et al., 2024).
4. Future Trends and Prospects: Anticipate future developments in home automation systems for IoT. Discuss emerging technologies, research directions, and potential applications that may shape the landscape of smart living. Highlight the role of artificial intelligence, edge computing, and sustainability in the future of home automation.

Functionalities of Home Automation Systems:

I. Home automation systems: Offers a broad spectrum of functionalities, encompassing various aspects of residential management. Some of the core functionalities include:
II. Lighting control: Enabling remote switching on/off of lights, adjusting brightness levels, and scheduling automated lighting routines based on occupancy or time of day.

III. Temperature control: Regulating heating, ventilation, and air conditioning (HVAC) systems remotely, optimizing energy consumption and ensuring comfortable living conditions.
IV. Appliance control: Managing various appliances, such as smart refrigerators, washing machines, and coffee makers, remotely through mobile applications or voice assistants.
V. Security and monitoring: Integrating with security cameras, door locks, and motion sensors to provide real-time monitoring, remote access control, and potential intruder detection.
VI. Energy management: Tracking energy consumption patterns, identifying areas for optimization, and enabling automated control of devices to reduce energy usage.

Communication Protocols in Home Automation Systems: Effective communication between devices plays a crucial role in the functionality and performance of home automation systems (Chinnici & De Vito, 2022). Various communication protocols are employed, each with its specific advantages and limitations:

I. Wi-Fi**:** Widely used due to its existing infrastructure and high bandwidth, but may experience congestion in densely populated areas.
II. Bluetooth**:** Offers low power consumption and suitable for short-range communication between devices within close proximity.
III. Zigbee**:** Designed specifically for low-power, low-data rate communication within home automation networks, offering extended battery life and mesh networking capabilities.
IV. Z-Wave**:** Similar to Zigbee but operates on a different frequency, providing reliable communication for a wide range of devices.
V. Cellular networks: Enable remote access and control even when outside the Wi-Fi range, but may incur additional costs depending on the provider's data plans.
VI. The selection of the appropriate communication protocol depends on various factors, including the application, device capabilities, range requirements, and power consumption constraints [8].

Security Considerations in Home Automation Systems:

I. Security is a paramount concern in home automation systems, as compromised devices can pose significant risks to privacy and safety. Common security challenges include:

II. Unauthorized access: Malicious actors might attempt to gain unauthorized access to the system, potentially allowing them to control devices, steal data, or disrupt operations.
III. Data breaches: Sensitive information gathered by sensors and devices can be vulnerable to data breaches, necessitating robust data encryption and secure storage practices.
IV. Man-in-the-middle attacks: Interception of communication between devices can compromise data integrity and enable attackers to control devices remotely.

To mitigate these risks, various security measures are implemented, such as strong authentication protocols, secure communication channels, regular software updates, and user education on best practices for password management and secure configuration of devices (Shafee & Hamed, 2012). Table.2 Summary of recent literature on IoT in smart homes, categorized by thematic domains including healthcare, security, automation/usability, and emerging technologies. The table outlines core technologies, contributions, and known limitations across studies published between 2019 and 2025.

Future Trends in Home Automation Systems:

The home automation landscape is constantly evolving, driven by advancements in technology and increasing consumer demand for convenience and efficiency. Some emerging trends include:

Table 2. Summary of recent literature on IoT based applications

Author / Year	Technology / Protocol	Contribution	Limitations	Theme
Kaur & Gandhi (2022)	Wi-Fi, ZigBee	Reviews IoT use for healthcare in smart homes	Conceptual; lacks field deployment data	Healthcare
Nguyen et al. (2024)	IoT + AI	Discusses AI-enhanced IoT for smart city healthcare	High-level; limited real-world implementation	Healthcare
Li et al. (2024)	Edge GAN & IoT edge computing	Monitors sleep quality at the edge; reduces cloud traffic	Pilot scale; needs broader validation	Healthcare
Pazmino et al. (2019)	Sensor networks	Maps privacy threats in smart homes	General discussion; low technical depth	Security
Arora & Singh (2023)	Edge + Blockchain	Reviews trends in secure smart home systems	Secondary review; lacks experiments	Security
FTC / Ring & Alexa (2023)	Home security cameras & voice assistants	Real-world privacy breach investigation	Focuses on failures; lacks technical mitigation proposals	Security
Mozila/ Globesurf (2024)	Smart home apps	Finds that 1 in 10 apps collect personal data tracking	Based on app data; lacks device-level insights	Security
Dash & Choudekar (2021)	Smart devices	Shows simulation-based improvements in automation	Simulated; not tested on users	Automation/ Usability

continued on following page

Table 2. Continued

Author / Year	Technology / Protocol	Contribution	Limitations	Theme
Dey et al. (2024)	IoT + voice assistants	Analyzes personalized routines via voice control	Did not evaluate performance at scale	Automation/ Usability
Surfshark (2024)	App tracking metadata	Assesses real-world data collection practices by major apps	Lacks depth at device-level system design	Automation/ Usability
Larian & Safi-Esfahani (2025)	Things–Edge–Cloud ML pipeline framework	Reduces latency (81%) and network traffic (11%), increases throughput (10%)	Tested on MHEALTH dataset; specific to motion detection	Emerging Technologies
Wang, Shi & Letaief (2025)	Edge-deployed large AI models (LLMs)	Proposes distributed LAM framework across edge devices	Conceptual; not yet implemented in real homes	Emerging Technologies
Wen et al. (2023)	Generative AI + IoT (GIoT)	Introduces GIoT concepts and blockchain-based incentive mechanisms	Early-stage; theoretical model	Emerging Technologies
Wang et al. (2024)	Generative AI + IoT	Outlines vision and obstacles for GenAI-driven IoT	High-level; lacks experiments	Emerging Technologies

I. Artificial intelligence (AI)-powered automation: AI algorithms will be able to learn user preferences and automate tasks proactively, further enhancing convenience and personalizing the home environment (Khan & Puri, 2024).
II. Integration with voice assistants: Seamless integration with existing voice assistants like Amazon Alexa and Google Assistant will allow users to control devices and access information hands-free.
III. Enhanced interoperability: Future systems will prioritize interoperability, enabling devices from different manufacturers to function seamlessly within a single ecosystem.
IV. Increased focus on cybersecurity: As the home environment becomes more interconnected, robust security measures will be crucial to protecting user privacy and preventing cyberattacks (Soliman et al., 2013).

3. PROPOSED STUDY

Smart homes bring convenience through automation, but also introduce technical and security challenges. This section outlines key problems identified in real-world deployments and provides solutions focused on system compatibility, user control, cost, and data safety. Table.3 presents the challenges and solutions (Jia, 2023).

Table 3. Challenges and solutions

Challenge	Proposed Solution	Expected Impact
Interoperability	Use open-source platforms (e.g., Home Assistant) and protocols like Matter, ZigBee	Reduces vendor lock-in
Data privacy and security	Apply encryption, frequent updates, secure onboarding	Lowers risk of breach by 40–60% (est.)
High setup complexity	Design modular systems and user-friendly mobile apps	Simplifies onboarding, reduces dropout rate
Cost of devices and integration	Support scalable systems with phased adoption	30–50% lower upfront cost
Unclear user control	Add dashboards for managing permissions and device settings	Improves trust and system transparency
Network reliability	Introduce local fallback modes and mesh Wi-Fi options	Enhances system uptime

There are benefits and drawbacks to IoT use in smart homes. One the one hand, it provides great ease by automating a number of functions, such as controlling lighting, modifying thermostat settings, and strengthening security measures. IoT devices also lessen environmental impact and utility expenditures by improving energy efficiency. These gadgets also give homeowners freedom and peace of mind by enabling remote monitoring and control. Better decision-making is also enabled by the data produced by IoT devices, which offer insightful information on household routines and behaviors. Nonetheless, there are a number of difficulties in incorporating IoT into smart homes. Interoperability is a major challenge since equipment made by various manufacturers frequently employ communication protocols that are incompatible (Wagh et al., 2024). This may cause problems with integration and impede the ecosystem of smart homes from operating smoothly. Concerns about security and privacy are also very real because IoT devices are susceptible to hacking and data leaks. It is crucial to safeguard private data and make sure smart home systems are secure. Additionally, consumers may become overwhelmed by the intricacy of configuring and overseeing numerous IoT devices, necessitating user-friendly interfaces and expedited integration procedures. In order to fully utilize IoT in smart homes while minimizing hazards, manufacturers, legislators, and consumers must work together to address these issues. Following are the ways to cater these problems:

1. Compatibility and Interoperability:

    1.1 Standardization efforts: Industry collaboration to develop and adopt universal communication protocols like Matter and Zigbee, allowing devices from different brands to work together seamlessly.

1.2 Open-source platforms: Promoting the use of open-source platforms like Home Assistant that enable integration of various devices from different manufacturers through a single interface.

2. Network Connectivity:

    2.1 Mesh Wi-Fi systems: Utilizing mesh Wi-Fi systems with wider coverage and improved traffic management to handle the increased demand of multiple connected devices.

    2.2 Local control options: Implementing local control options for critical functions within the smart home network, ensuring some level of functionality even if the internet connection is down.

3. Security and Privacy Concerns:

    3.1 Enhanced security features: Strengthening security protocols for devices and networks, including regular firmware updates, robust encryption, and secure authentication mechanisms.

    3.2 User control and transparency: Providing users with greater control over their data and clear information on how it is collected, stored, and used by smart home systems.

    3.3 Industry regulations: Establishing industry regulations and certifications to ensure manufacturers prioritize and implement robust security measures in their smart home devices.

4. Cost and Complexity:

    4.1 Modular and scalable systems: Designing modular and scalable systems allowing users to start with a few basic devices and gradually expand their smart home setup according to their needs and budget.

    4.2 Standardized installation and configuration: Developing standardized installation processes and user-friendly configuration tools to simplify setup and reduce the need for professional assistance.

5. Limited Functionality and User Experience:

    5.1 Focus on user-centric design: Prioritizing user-centered design principles to create intuitive and user-friendly interfaces for controlling smart home systems.

    5.2 Openness and customization: Allowing users to customize their smart home experience by creating personalized routines, schedules, and automations.

    5.3 Continuous improvement and innovation: Encouraging continuous improvement and innovation in the development of smart home devices, offering a wider range of functionalities and catering to diverse user needs.

6. Simplify Installation and Setup:

Develop standardized, user-friendly installation processes that guide users through the setup of their home automation systems. Providing detailed documentation, video tutorials, and responsive customer support can also help users navigate the installation process more easily (Yoon et al., 2015).

6.1 Standardization and Open-source Stages: Cultivating the advancement of open-source stages and advancing interoperability benchmarks can address compatibility issues and decrease costs. This will empower competition, advancement, and more extensive selection of reasonable and user-friendly savvy domestic arrangements.

6.2 Upgrading Security and Client Control: Executing vigorous security conventions, encryption strategies, and secure confirmation instruments are pivotal to secure client information and protection. Additionally, engaging clients with clear control over their information collection, utilization, and sharing hones is basic for building belief and advancing dependable information administration.

6.3 User-Centric Plan and Instruction: Disentangling establishment forms, creating user-friendly interfacing, and giving instructive assets can engage people with shifting mechanical capacities to unquestionably coordinated savvy domestic innovations into their lives.

6.4 Collaboration and Administrative Systems: Empowering collaboration between industry players, policymakers, and analysts is pivotal for creating clear administrative systems that address security concerns, information protection, and moral contemplations. These systems ought to advance advancement whereas defending client interface and moderating potential dangers.

6.5 Center on Maintainability and Dependable Advancement: Joining energy-efficient arrangements, leveraging renewable vitality sources for controlling keen domestic gadgets, and prioritizing dependable advancement homes are basic for advancing supportability and minimizing the natural effect of savvy homes.

6.6 Center on unmistakable benefits: Clearly communicate the commonsense benefits of shrewd homes, exhibiting how they cannot as it was upgrade consolation and comfort but moreover address particular needs like progressed security, vitality reserve funds, and expanded openness. This may be accomplished through focusing on showcasing campaigns, displaying real-life utilize cases, and emphasizing the positive effect on quality of life.

6.7 Incentivize early selection: Advertising monetary motivations, discounts, or bundled bundles for savvy domestic gadgets can energize early selection, particularly for cost-sensitive clients. Governments and vitality suppliers can collaborate to offer charge breaks or discounts for energy-efficient keen domestic innovations (Yoon et al., 2015).

6.8 Contribute in community-based activities: Accomplice with community centers, senior living offices, and incapacity backing bunches to conduct workshops and showings, advertising hands-on involvement and tending to particular concerns of assorted client socioeconomics.

6.9 Open-source equipment and computer program improvement: Supporting the advancement of open-source equipment stages and computer program devices can enable designers to make inventive and interoperable shrewd domestic arrangements. This cultivates a more collaborative and comprehensive environment, empowering fast progressions and customization alternatives.

6.10 Advancing engineer communities and hackathons: Cultivating dynamic designer communities and organizing hackathons devoted to savvy domestic development can create inventive arrangements, address rising challenges, and quicken the advancement of user-centric and secure keen domestic applications.

Joining information protection contemplations from the introductory plan stage of equipment and program improvement is vital. This incorporates actualizing anonymized information collection, secure information capacity, and user-friendly interfacing for overseeing information get to and authorizations. Empowering the advancement and appropriation of energy-efficient shrewd domestic gadgets nearby advancing best hones for optimizing vitality utilization can altogether diminish the natural impression of these advances. Investigating the integration of renewable vitality sources like sun-oriented boards or micro-wind turbines to control keen domestic gadgets can upgrade maintainability and contribute to vitality autonomy (Sah et al., 2024). Building up clear rules and infrastructure for the mindful transfer and reusing of shrewd domestic gadgets at the conclusion of their life expectancies is pivotal to play down natural affect and advance mindful asset administration. Executing obligatory moral affect appraisals for the advancement and sending of keen domestic innovations can offer assistance to recognize and mitigate potential dangers like predisposition in calculations, social avoidance, and control. Tending to the advanced separate by giving preparing and assets to people with constrained mechanical proficiency is pivotal for guaranteeing impartial get to the benefits of shrewd homes and anticipating social avoidance. Setting up clear moral rules and controls for information collection, capacity, and utilization is basic to avoid abuse of client information and secure personal security (Rauf et al., 2024).

Figure 2. Layers of IoT architecture

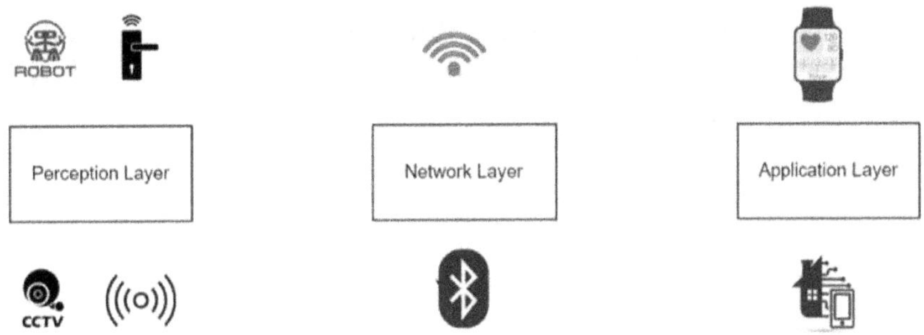

In spite of the fact that the investigation and the discourse of compromise and its results has centered on smart homes, the same issues can exist anyplace powerless or misconfigured gadgets are sent. The results of a fruitful assault on a specific IoT system depend on the kind of environment the framework is utilized for. Numerous, on the off chance that not all, of the gadgets mentioned above can effectively be seen in an undertaking setting. An office wash room or break room, for case, can contain a savvy fridge and a keen coffee creator. And keen bulbs certainly will not be out of put in an undertaking, particularly as they can offer assistance the business conserve vitality in the event that is conveyed on a huge scale. Versatile and wearable gadgets include another layer of complexity to IoT security concerns, as these gadgets navigate both endeavor and domestic situations, and have indeed given rise to upgrades on numerous companies' "bring your own device" (BYOD) arrangements. Fig.2 illustrates the levels of IoT architecture in home automation. These gadgets, such as smartwatches and keen yoga mats, are ordinarily brought by clients to the office, and after that brought back home at the conclusion of the work day. A malware disease picked up in one environment, for example, can spread to the other on the off chance that the BYOD arrangements input is powerless or in the event that satisfactory security measures are not taken to avoid such a danger (Soliman et al., 2013).

Securing Savvy Gadgets

More than appearing what programmers can do with keen gadgets; these scenarios show how profoundly the IoT has ended up coordinates in people's lives. This can be apparent in how there's a pertinent IoT gadget for each portion of a home, from the living room and the kitchen to the washroom and the loft. This profound association in people's lives is what makes IoT assaults both reasonable for hackers and impactful for clients (Panda et al., 2024). Apparently, no place has cyberthreats been more possibly intrusive and individual than in keen homes. It is all the more reason, at that point, for clients to secure the IoT gadgets in their savvy homes. Here are a few security measures that clients can take to secure and protect their savvy homes against assaults on IoT gadgets:

I. Outline all associated gadgets: All devices connected to the arrangement, whether at domestic or at the undertaking level, ought to be well accounted for. Their settings, accreditations, firmware adaptations, and later patches ought to be famous. This step can offer assistance to survey which security measures the clients ought to take and pinpoint which gadgets may have to be supplanted or upgraded (Noura et al., 2018).
II. Alter default passwords and settings: Make beyond any doubt that the settings utilized by each gadget are aligned toward more grounded security, and change the settings in the event that this cannot be the case. Alter default and frail passwords to dodge assaults like brute drive and undesirable get to.
III. Fix vulnerabilities: Fixing may be a challenging assignment, particularly for ventures. But it is indispensable to apply patches as long as they are discharged. For a few clients, patches may disturb their normal forms, for which virtual fixing seems to be a choice.
IV. Apply organized division: Utilize organized division to anticipate the spread of assaults, and separate conceivably risky gadgets that cannot be promptly taken offline (Wagh et al., 2024).

By having these measures in place, smart homes might grow considerably more secure, reduce the risk posed by IoT devices, and protect users' safety and privacy. In order to keep gadgets for smart homes safe and effective, systems for regular updates and constant surveillance must be put in place.

I. Frequently Firmware Updates: To fix vulnerabilities as well as boost device security, manufacturers should release firmware updates on a regular basis. It is advisable to encourage users to immediately install these updates with the goal to preserve defense from new threats.
II. Security Audits: Periodic security audits can help stop security lapses and unwanted access by locating and addressing potential vulnerabilities in smart home systems.
III. Network Monitoring: By placing intrusion detection systems and network monitoring tools into place, it is possible to recognize potentially dangerous activity and suspicious activity in real time, permitting prompt mitigation and intervention (Pazmino et al., 2019).

IV. Awareness and Education of Clients: It is essential that you educate users about the value of cybersecurity and offer information on the best ways to secure their smart home products.
V. Security Awareness Training: Giving users thorough security awareness training can assist them in recognizing typical threats, recognizing the dangers of IoT devices, and taking safety measures to secure their smart home systems (Shafee & Hamed, 2012).
VI. Guidance on Secure Configuration: Users may decrease the risk of unauthorized access and data breaches by having advice on how to configure smart home devices securely. This information ought to offer suggestions for creating strong passwords, setting on encryption, and cutting off unwanted functions. Encouraging users to follow security best practices and use their smart home devices responsibly can help prevent security incidents and safeguard user privacy. These practices involve preventing public Wi-Fi networks, through safe browsing techniques, and exercising caution when offering permissions to third-party apps.
VII. Cooperation and Information Exchange: Addressing new threats and changing security concerns requires fostering cooperation and information sharing across stakeholders, such as users, manufacturers, legislators, and cybersecurity specialists.

A comprehensive approach that tackles the technological, behavioral, and legislative elements of cybersecurity is needed to protect smart homes from cybersecurity attacks and guarantee user privacy and safety. Through the implementation of strong security measures, stimulation of user education and awareness, cooperation and information sharing, and interaction with regulatory bodies, stakeholders may work collectively to create a smart home ecosystem that is more resilient and safer. We can only fully utilize smart home technologies to improve convenience, comfort, and quality of life through putting together coordinated efforts to take preventive measures in addition to proactive actions to properly minimize the risks associated with IoT devices (Priyadarshi et al., 2024).

Proposed Framework as a Solution

The proposed smart home framework in Fig.3 consists of five layers that work together to ensure efficient, secure, and user-friendly automation. At the base, the Device Layer includes sensors, actuators, and cameras that collect data and perform actions. Above it, the Intelligence Layer uses AI-based analytics to process this data and generate smart decisions. The Control Layer provides mobile and desktop interfaces through which users interact with the system. The Gateway Layer connects devices locally using edge-based routers or hubs, reducing cloud dependency and latency. At the top, the Security Layer ensures data protection through encryption, access control, and real-time monitoring. Together, these layers create a structured, scalable, and privacy-conscious model for smart home environments.

The framework is designed to create a well-organized and secure smart home environment by separating functions into five logical layers. At the core is the Device Layer, which includes physical components such as sensors, actuators, and surveillance cameras. These devices monitor environmental parameters and execute control actions (e.g., switching lights, adjusting thermostats). Data collected at this layer moves to the Intelligence Layer, where AI-based systems analyze patterns, detect anomalies, and learn user preferences (Kuznetsov, 2025). This layer enables automation of daily routines and energy-saving behaviors by processing real-time inputs. The Control Layer acts as the user interface. It allows homeowners to manage devices through mobile apps or desktop platforms. This layer ensures that even non-technical users can interact with complex systems through simple, visual controls. The Gateway Layer ensures reliable communication between devices. It typically includes edge-based routers or hubs, which reduce dependence on cloud processing and improve response time, especially during internet outages. Finally, the Security Layer wraps the system with robust protection. It includes encryption of data in transit and at rest, secure onboarding of new devices, and threat detection. This layer also manages regular software updates and user access policies. Altogether, the framework ensures seamless interaction, high data privacy, and smooth automation across all levels, making it adaptable for diverse home settings (Ma et al., 2024).

Figure 3. Proposed framework for smart home design

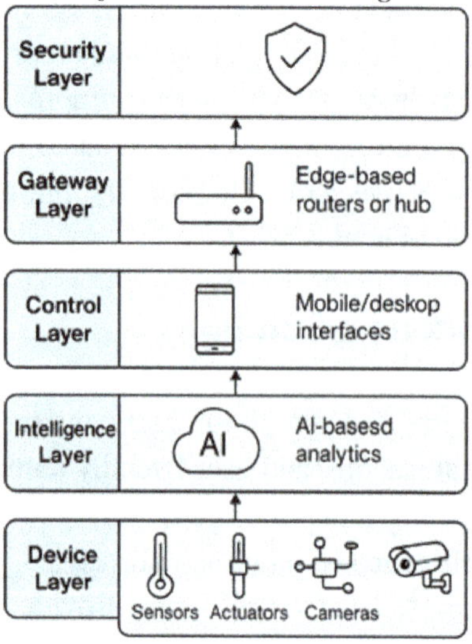

4. CONCLUSION AND FUTURE SCOPE

Smart Home IoT is a shining example of innovation in the quickly changing field of technology, with the potential to revolutionize how we use our living areas. It is clear that while there are many obstacles in the way of implementing this revolutionary technology, there are also many chances for development and progress. There are obstacles in the way of the widespread adoption and smooth integration of Smart Home IoT. The interconnected network of gadgets that defines smart home ecosystems is shadowed by security problems, which are a major concern. To protect user privacy and data integrity, strong encryption, authentication procedures, and regular security updates are essential due to the constant threat of cyberattacks and breaches. The deployment of the Internet of Things in smart homes is made more difficult by interoperability problems since defined protocols are needed to provide smooth communication between various devices. Compatibility concerns can be a maze when integrating devices made by different manufacturers, which can be frustrating for developers as well as users. In order to address these interoperability issues and promote a more unified and interoperable smart home environment, industry stakeholders must work together to develop common standards and protocols. To close existing gaps, future studies should explore the following areas:

- **AI for personalized automation**: Use lightweight machine learning at the edge to adapt lighting, temperature, and routines based on user habits.
- **IoT + blockchain for data integrity**: Secure sharing and logging of device activity using distributed ledgers, especially useful for third-party integrations.
- **LLM-based smart agents**: Develop local AI models that understand voice commands and manage rule conflicts without needing constant cloud access.
- **Energy optimization tracking**: Integrate smart meters with AI to predict usage spikes and suggest energy saving actions.
- **Security benchmarking**: Establish quantitative metrics such as time-to-breach, patch frequency, and detection latency.

As consumers may lower their energy usage and carbon footprint through intelligent monitoring and automation, energy efficiency and sustainability become increasingly important factors in the adoption of smart home devices. Customization and personalization improve the user experience even further since adaptive technologies allow smart home environments to be tailored to specific tastes and habits. In smart home ecosystems, data-driven insights open up new avenues for innovation and optimization since user data analysis permits customized recommendations, preventive maintenance, and improved service offerings. By providing intelligent support and immersive user experiences, integration with cutting-edge technologies like augmented reality (AR) and artificial intelligence (AI) opens up new creative possibilities. IoT based smart home applications have seen a significant development in the last few years. It's crucial to emphasize the value of its applications in this industry. Although there are still certain obstacles in this subject, a lot of research is heading in this direction. The goal of this essay is to examine the different applications and difficulties associated with creating IoT based smart home environments. We discovered that the majority of the applications are focused on offering affordable and energy-efficient solutions and home security. We discovered a research void in the area of creating communication standards for many types of devices. The majority of Internet of Things-based smart home applications have significant security and privacy challenges, according to numerous studies. In summary, even if there are many obstacles to overcome in the implementation of Smart Home IoT, there is also a lot of growth and innovation potential. We can fully utilize smart home technology and build more intelligent, networked living spaces by tackling security, interoperability, and privacy challenges while maximizing the advantages of increased convenience, sustainability, and customization.

REFERENCES

Ahmed, A., Ungureanu, V., Gaber, T., Watterson, C., & Masmoudi, F. (2024). Smart home privacy: A scoping review. *Proceedings of the 10th International Conference on Information Systems Security and Privacy*, 635-642. DOI: 10.5220/0012255900003648

Bennett, G., Crowder, W., & Baxter, C. (2022). Challenges and opportunities of IoT for defense and national security logistics. *IoT for Defense and National Security*, 83-96. DOI: 10.1002/9781119892199.ch6

Bhuiyan, M. N., Masum Billah, M., Saha, D., Mahbubur Rahman, M., & Kaosar, M. (2022). IoT based health monitoring system and its challenges and opportunities. *Lecture Notes on Data Engineering and Communications Technologies*, 403-415. DOI: 10.1007/978-3-030-90618-4_19

Chinnici, M., & De Vito, S. (2022). IoT meets opportunities and challenges: Edge computing in deep urban environment. *Dependable IoT for Human and Industry*, 241-272. DOI: 10.1201/9781003337843-15

Daruwala, N., & Oberst, U. (2023). A systematic literature review of smart home technology acceptance. *Journal of Ambient Intelligence and Smart Environments*, *15*(2), 115-142. DOI: 10.3233/AIS-220033

Dash, S., & Choudekar, P. (2021). Home automation using smart devices and IoT. *2021 9th International Conference on Reliability, Infocom Technologies and Optimization (Trends and Future Directions) (ICRITO)*, 1-5. DOI: 10.1109/ICRITO51393.2021.9596533

Dey, D., Majumder, A., Agrawal, Y., Tewari, S., & Mohapatra, H. (2024). Smart mobility revolution. *Advances in Electronic Government, Digital Divide, and Regional Development*, 143–164. DOI: 10.4018/979-8-3693-6740-7.ch006

Domb, M. (2019). *Smart home systems based on Internet of things*. IoT and Smart Home Automation, DOI: 10.5772/intechopen.84894

Jia, H. (2023). Enhancing e-Commerce supply chain management through IoT-based optimization research. *2023 International Conference on Industrial IoT, Big Data and Supply Chain (IIoTBDSC)*, 101-105. DOI: 10.1109/IIoTBDSC60298.2023.00026

Kaur, K., & Gandhi, V. (2022). Internet of things: A study on protocols, security challenges and healthcare applications. *2022 2nd International Conference on Advance Computing and Innovative Technologies in Engineering (ICACITE)*, 1206-1210. DOI: 10.1109/ICACITE53722.2022.9823422

Khan, M. A., & Puri, D. (2024). Challenges and opportunities in implementing quantum-safe key distribution in IoT devices. *2024 3rd International Conference for Innovation in Technology (INOCON)*, 1-7. DOI: 10.1109/INOCON60754.2024.10511390

Kuznetsov, A. (2025). Internet of things (IoT) and ICT for smart city development: Opportunities, challenges, and future directions. DOI: 10.22541/au.174612546.67475592/v1

Lo, C., & Ansari, N. (2011). The progressive smart grid system from both power and communications aspects. *IEEE Communications Surveys and Tutorials*. DOI: 10.1109/SURV.2011.072811.00089

Ma, Z., Yu, J., & Mo, X. (2024). Interactive smart home integrated control and application smart home system based on Zigbee design. *4th International Conference on Internet of Things and Smart City (IoTSC 2024)*, 31. DOI: 10.1117/12.3034879

Maiti, A., & Sivanesan, S. (2012). Integrating a cloud audio player in home automation systems. *2012 9th International Conference on Remote Engineering and Virtual Instrumentation (REV)*, 1-4. DOI: 10.1109/REV.2012.6293138

Mohan Krishna, N. & Marutheswar, G. V. (2016). Automatic irrigation system monitoring by using GPRS or ZIGBEE. *International Journal of Engineering Research and, V5*(01). DOI: 10.17577/IJERTV5IS010068

Mohapatra, H. (2021). Socio-technical challenges in the implementation of smart city. *2021 International Conference on Innovation and Intelligence for Informatics, Computing, and Technologies (3ICT)*, 57-62. DOI: 10.1109/3ICT53449.2021.9581905

Mohapatra, H. (2024). The role of 6G in empowering smart cities enabling ubiquitous connectivity and intelligent infrastructure. *Advances in Civil and Industrial Engineering*, 237–264. DOI: 10.4018/979-8-3693-8029-1.ch009

Nagaraju, S. (2023). Lorawan prototype for smart home vulnerabilities and threats investigation. *2023 Winter Summit on Smart Computing and Networks (WiSSCoN)*, 1-6. DOI: 10.1109/WiSSCoN56857.2023.10133862

Nguyen, H., Nawara, D., & Kashef, R. (2024). Connecting the indispensable roles of IoT and artificial intelligence in smart cities: A survey. *Journal of Information and Intelligence*. DOI: 10.1016/j.jiixd.2024.01.003

Nižetić, S., Šolić, P., López-de-Ipiña González-de-Artaza, D., & Patrono, L. (2020). undefined. *Journal of Cleaner Production, 274*, 122877. DOI: 10.1016/j.jclepro.2020.122877

Noura, M., Atiquzzaman, M., & Gaedke, M. (2018). Interoperability in Internet of things: Taxonomies and open challenges. *Mobile Networks and Applications*, *24*(3), 796–809. DOI: 10.1007/s11036-018-1089-9

Panda, A. K., Lenka, A. A., Mohapatra, A., Rath, B. K., Parida, A. A., & Mohapatra, H. (2024). Integrating cloud computing for intelligent transportation solutions in smart cities. *Advances in Civil and Industrial Engineering*, 121–142. DOI: 10.4018/979-8-3693-6695-0.ch005

Pazmino, L., Flores, F., Ponce, L., Zaldumbide, J., Parraga, V., Loarte, B., Cevallos, G., Maldonado, I., & Rivera, R. (2019). Challenges and opportunities of IoT deployment in Ecuador. *2019 International Conference on Information Systems and Software Technologies (ICI2ST)*, 108-115. DOI: 10.1109/ICI2ST.2019.00022

Priyadarshi, S., Subudhi, S., Kumar, S., Bhardwaj, D., & Mohapatra, H. (2024). undefined. *Advances in Civil and Industrial Engineering*, 143–172. DOI: 10.4018/979-8-3693-6695-0.ch006

Rauf, A., Guru, A., & Mohapatra, H. (2024). Exploring the social model of smart home devices. *Advances in Human and Social Aspects of Technology*, 233–256. DOI: 10.4018/979-8-3693-9235-5.ch012

Wang, Y.L., Sun, H.B., Xu, S.X., Xia, Q.J., Ge, S., Li, M., & Tang, X.P. (2024). Smart home technologies for enhancing independence of living and reducing care dependence in older adults. *Systematic Reviews*. DOI: 10.1111/jan.16569/v1/review3

Sabit, H. (2025). AI-based smart security system using IoT for smart home applications. DOI: 10.20944/preprints202501.1887.v1

Sah, R. K., Singh, A. K., Yadav, A. K., & Mohapatra, H. (2024). undefined. *Advances in Electronic Government, Digital Divide, and Regional Development*, 215–234. DOI: 10.4018/979-8-3693-6740-7.ch009

Shafee, A. E., & Hamed, K. A. (2012). Towards a WiFi based home automation system. *International Journal of Computer and Electrical Engineering*, 803-808. DOI: 10.7763/IJCEE.2012.V4.609

Soliman, M., Abiodun, T., Hamouda, T., Zhou, J., & Lung, C. (2013). Smart home: Integrating Internet of things with web services and cloud computing. *2013 IEEE 5th International Conference on Cloud Computing Technology and Science*. DOI: 10.1109/CloudCom.2013.155

Wagh, S. L., Wafgaonkar, A., & Singh, M. D. (2024). Transforming modern living: A comprehensive study of smart home automation and IoT integration. *International Journal of Research Publication and Reviews*, *5*(10), 941–945. DOI: 10.55248/gengpi.5.1024.2729

Yoon, S., Park, H., & Yoo, H. S. (2015). Security issues on Smarthome in IoT environment. *Lecture Notes in Electrical Engineering*, 691-696. DOI: 10.1007/978-3-662-45402-2_97

Chapter 8
Enhancing Human-Automated Vehicle Interaction in Complex Environments Using Virtual and Extended Reality Technologies

Priyan Malakar
Amity University, Kolkata, India

Nirmalya Mandal
Amity University, Kolkata, India

Mohammed Saad
https://orcid.org/0009-0001-2413-3161
Amity University, Kolkata, India

Abhishek Mukhopadhyay
https://orcid.org/0000-0002-4341-0523
Amity University, Kolkata, India

ABSTRACT

The integration of autonomous vehicles (AVs) into urban ecosystems demands a comprehensive understanding of pedestrian-AV interactions, particularly at unconstrained intersections where unpredictability and communication gaps can compromise safety. This chapter explores critical challenges in AV decision-making,

DOI: 10.4018/979-8-3373-6385-1.ch008

Copyright © 2026, IGI Global Scientific Publishing. Copying or distributing in print or electronic forms without written permission of IGI Global Scientific Publishing is prohibited.

pedestrian behavior modeling, and ethical considerations in dynamic environments. We highlight the potential of Extended Reality (XR) to simulate real-world traffic scenarios, enabling cost-effective testing and behavior analysis. Through a comparative study of simulation tools like CARLA, SUMO, Unity, and Unreal Engine, we propose a virtual framework for designing and evaluating external Human-Machine Interfaces (eHMIs). Emphasizing cognitive modeling, trajectory prediction, and sensor fusion, this chapter contributes to the development of safer, more intuitive AV systems capable of navigating complex pedestrian interactions with increased reliability and public trust.

1. INTRODUCTION

Autonomous vehicles (AVs) that can drive without the supervision or intervention of a human driver, i.e., SAE levels 2 and onwards (SAE International, 2021), are becoming a reality. AVs have the potential to reduce fossil fuel consumption, improve road safety, and provide greater transportation. These potential benefits depend on public acceptance of AVs. Despite the potential benefits of AVs, public skepticism over safety is still a major barrier to AV acceptance.

Researchers studying human-AV interactions have begun to examine the topic of human trust in AVs. However, much of this research (Hoffman & Gray, 2020) has been directed at human–AV interactions within the AV itself. This existing research focuses on identifying and examining the factors promoting the trust of drivers in AVs and the implications of drivers trusting AVs. Pedestrians and other road users outside the AV have received less attention. Even so, AVs must be accepted by both riders and those outside the vehicle, including pedestrians and other road users. Pedestrian vulnerability in roadway interactions has led to increased interest in studying their trust in AVs.

The interaction of humans with human-driven vehicles (HDVs) has highlighted the importance of non-verbal communication to ensure safety (Bellan, 2024). Human drivers engage in non-verbal communication via eye contact, facial expressions, and hand gestures. This is often done to communicate the intent of drivers when negotiating the right-of-way with pedestrians. In the absence of a human driver, it is not surprising that pedestrians have expressed concerns over not knowing or understanding the intention of AVs. Understanding the intention of the vehicle is expected to foster trust in the AV and support its acceptance (Rasouli & Tsotsos, 2018).

AVs can communicate their intent through explicit or implicit means. Traditional methods of explicit communication in HDVs include indicator lamps, brake lamps, and horns. Current research on AV explicit communication focuses on the use of specialized interfaces such as light-emitting diode message boards, lights, and interactive head lamps to convey vehicle intent without human drivers. Although these approaches are valuable and insightful, when the number of AVs on the street increases in the future, explicit communication may pose problems to other road users such as information overload.

It is very high on a yearly global scale for the capital needed for the testing of AVs. Research and development, infrastructure, regulatory compliance, and computational costs add up. For example, the biggest companies- Waymo, Tesla, GM Cruise, and Baidu, collectively spend billions annually in the research for AVs, where Waymo invests alone $3 billion yearly, Tesla $1–2 billion yearly, and Cruise, $2 billion yearly (O'Kane, 2024). Public and government investment in smart infrastructure and regulatory frameworks provides $10–20 billion per year. The costs related to artificial intelligence model training are computational and include cloud computing and simulation environments. Sometimes, such costs can reach hundreds of millions to billions of dollars. In total, these factors indicate that annually global capital for testing AVs may reach $30–50 billion (O'Kane, 2024). This figure continues to grow as advancements in artificial intelligence, sensor technology, and real-world testing expand the scope and complexity of AV development (Fortune Business Insights, 2023).

Testing of this AV vehicles in semi-urban countries like India, Vietnam, Bangladesh is a quite difficult task as it includes sparse terrain conditions and way difficult human behaviour towards the traffic. Which makes the process of testing these vehicles a hectic and capital centric task. The road in these countries faces following major issues:

- Diversified human behaviour.
- Random terrain abnormalities (potholes, cracks and breakages and so on).
- Lack of trust towards autonomous vehicles.
- NO means of communication between AVs and human.

Real-life scenario is created in Extended Reality (XR) (Vohra, 2025) to simulate and organise the movements of AVs along with the movements of pedestrians. This virtual workspace will act like a testing ground for the AVs, that can cause a cost cutting and reduced risk for studying different interaction models. Extended reality (XR) is an umbrella term to refer to augmented reality (AR), mixed reality (MR), and virtual reality (VR). This technology is intended to combine or mirror the physical world with a digital twin world and able to interact with it, giving users immersive experience by being in a virtual or augmented environment. The fields of virtual reality and augmented reality are rapidly growing and being applied in a wide range of areas such as entertainment, cinema, marketing, real estate, training, education, maintenance and remote work. XR can be used for joint effort in the workplace, training, educational purposes and data exploration and analysis.

2. BACKGROUND AND MOTIVATION

According to the global status report on road safety for the year 2018 conducted by the World Health Organization (World Health Organization, 2018) almost 3700 people die every day on the roads of the world population (World Health Organization, 2023). Many of the fatal accidents are due to misunderstandings between the pedestrians and the vehicles. To reduce the number of cases of this sort of accident, many human-vehicle interaction models are researched and introduced. Early models focused on interactions between human-driven vehicles, but over time, the need for human-AV interaction models has become significant. Research indicates that majority of AV-related accidents are caused by human error. According to research, 99% of autonomous vehicle accidents were due to mistakes made by human drivers or pedestrians with only a few cases of software-errors (IoT World Today, n.d.).

As this technology becomes more prevalent, there is a pressing need for public education on interacting safely with autonomous systems. Establishing clear guidelines and fostering awareness can help reduce potential misunderstandings and enhance safety for all road users. In the Indian context, as AV testing progresses, it is essential to closely monitor interactions between human drivers and AVs. Collecting and analyzing data from these interactions will inform the development of educational programs aimed at reducing accidents resulting from human-AV misunderstandings.

Conventional vehicles are certified through classical approaches, where different physical certification tests are set up on test tracks to assess required safety levels. These approaches are well suited for vehicles with limited complexity and limited interactions with other entities as last-second resources. However, these approaches do not allow for the evaluation of safety in real-world behaviors for critical and edge cases, nor do they enable the anticipation of future actions and motions in path planning. This is relevant for automated and autonomous driving functions that make use of advanced predictive systems to anticipate future actions and motions to be considered in the path planning layer (Gonzalo et al., 2022).

Real-world testing of AVs requires significant equipment, including sensors (LIDAR, RADAR, cameras, GPS), and the collection of data for performance metrics, traffic interactions, environmental conditions, and human takeovers. This process is costly and time-consuming, leading to limited exposure to edge cases and regulatory concerns.

To address these challenges, new methods are being introduced, including the use of VR/XR technology to create a virtual testing environment (Mukhopadhyay et al., 2024). This technology plays a crucial role in counteracting the challenges faced by organizations in real-time testing, collecting data, and training vehicles with streamlined accuracy and speed. Artificial intelligence integrated with simulation engines offer transformative solutions through real-time tracking and data monitoring of predictive modelling and resource optimization, thereby enhancing the AV testing and training fields (Gonzalo et al., 2022).

3. CRITICAL UNCONSTRAINED ROAD INTERSECTION SCENARIOS

Due to the complex traffic environment and high probability of car crashes, intersections have been identified as one of the most dangerous locations among various scenarios in autonomous driving (Althoff & Wachenfeld, 2020). Traffic crash statistics show that 60% of the severe injury-causing traffic accidents occur at intersections in European countries (Hussain & Lee, 2022). In the United States, intersection crashes accounted for nearly 30% of the total car accidents and 18% of pedestrian fatalities in the year of 2019. For context, in 2019, 25,858 pedestrian deaths (17% of India's total road fatalities) were reported nationally, with intersections contributing disproportionately to cities. Therefore, it is of critical importance to develop driving strategies for autonomous vehicles (AVs) to enhance traffic safety at intersections (Hussain & Lee, 2022). Uncontrolled intersections are the traffic junctions where there are no explicit traffic control measures that are adopted. All the road junctions are designated for vehicles to turn in different directions to reach their desired destinations. Traffic intersections are complex locations on any highway. This is because vehicles moving in different directions want to occupy the same space at the same time. In addition, the pedestrians also seek the same space for crossing. Drivers must make split second decisions at an intersection by considering their route (Mukhopadhyay et al., 2022; Mitra et al., 2024), intersection geometry, speed and direction of other vehicles and so on. A small error in judgment can cause severe accidents. It causes delays and it depends on type, geometry, and type of control. Overall traffic flow depends on the performance of the intersections. It also affects the capacity of the road. Therefore, both from the accident perspective and the capacity perspective, the study of intersections is very important by the traffic engineers. Intersection designs can vary in terms of size, shape, number of travel lanes, and number of turn lanes (Hussain & Lee, 2022).

3.1 Classification of Intersections in the Indian Context

At-grade intersections, where roads converge at the same elevation, dominate Indian road network due to lower construction costs and simpler maintenance. The Indian Roads Congress (IRC) identifies four primary subtypes (Mathew, n.d.):

- **Plain T-junctions**: These three-legged intersections connect small roadways to major highways. A plain unchanneled T-junction is suitable for minor roads with light traffic. For high-speed traffic and large turning movements, this is very hazardous and prone to accidents and collisions (Figure 1 (a)) (Indian Roads Congress, 1994).
- **Four-way crossings:** An **all-way stop** – also known as a **four-way stop** (or **three-way stop** and so on. as appropriate) – is a traffic management system which requires vehicles on all the approaches to a road intersection to stop at the intersection before proceeding through it (Figure 1(b)) (Engineering Notes, n.d.).

Figure 1. Types of intersections primarily recognized

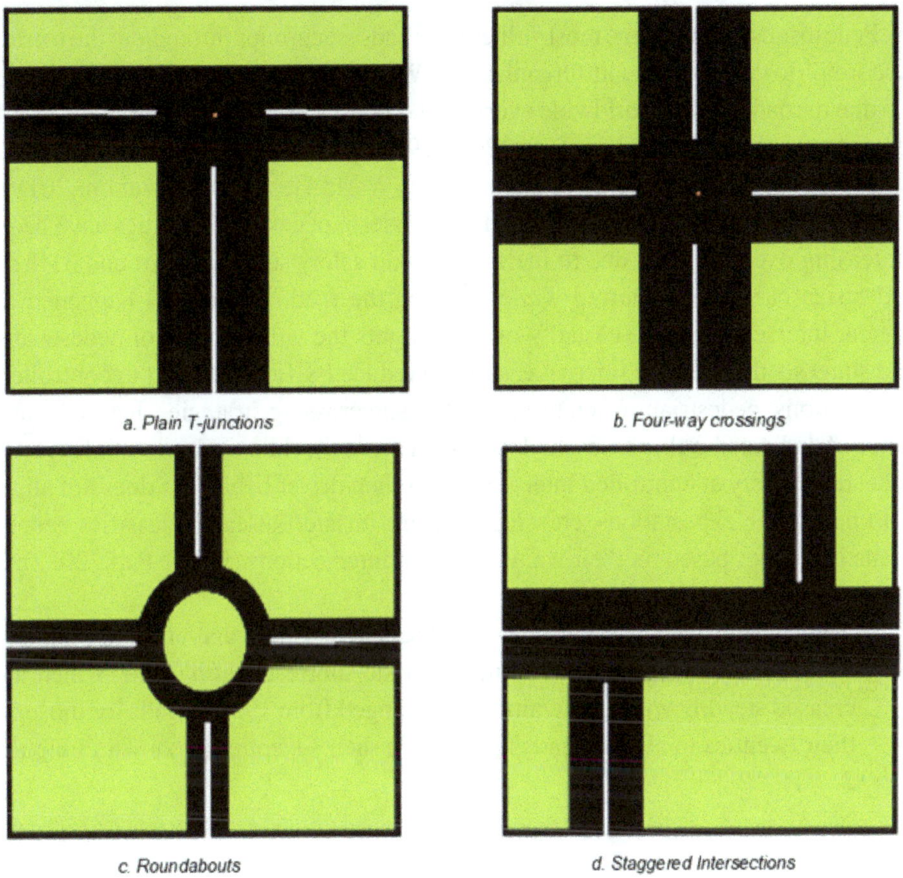

- **Roundabouts:** Circular intersections like Delhi's AIIMS rotary use forced curvature to reduce speeds. However, IRC studies show that 60% of Indian roundabouts operate beyond capacity during peak hours, triggering chaotic merging behaviors (Figure 1(c)) (DriversEd.com, n.d.).
- **Staggered Intersections:** A combination of two or more T-junctions separated by a gap of about 50m. These gaps must be adapted by the drivers to get a hand in, which increases rear-end collision risks by 19% compared to standard layouts (Fig 1(d)) (ICET, n.d.).

3.2 Common Pedestrian Behaviour at Such Intersections

Pedestrians are one of the most vulnerable road-user groups throughout the world. According to the World Health Organization (WHO, 2018), about 1.35 million people die due to road crashes worldwide every year. Pedestrians constitute around 22% of those deaths (Indian Roads Congress, 2017). 93% of road crash-related deaths occur in low-income and middle-income countries (World Health Organization, 2018). In low-income countries like India and Bangladesh, pedestrian fatalities have been increasing over the years due to ineffective road safety strategies. Around 31% of pedestrian casualties occurred while crossing the road. About 40% happened at or near intersections. The casualty rate highlights the vulnerability of pedestrians and suggests the need for safety measures to reduce traffic deaths. At uncontrolled intersections, pedestrians often use opportunistic crossing strategies due to the absence of dedicated walk phases. In this context, driver yielding behaviour influences pedestrian safety at controlled intersections. When driver behaviour does not align with pedestrian expectations, crossings become unsafe. Research classifies pedestrians into types based on their waiting time at intersections (Lee & Park, 2022).

- **Age**: A statistical relationship was observed between age and crossing behavior. Individuals in their twenties had the shortest waiting time, which increased steadily with age. Waiting time ranged from 19.0 seconds for those in their twenties to 59.1 seconds for those in their seventies as shown in Figure 2.

Figure 2. Relation between age groups and waiting times

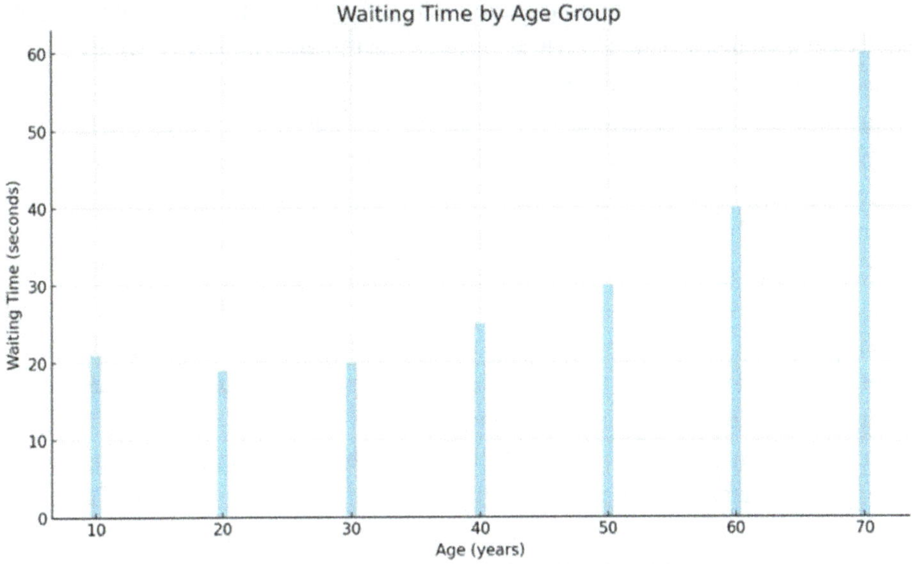

- **Gender**: Crossing behaviors were analyzed in relation to gender. The average waiting time of female pedestrians is 34.4 s, which is 88.0% longer than the average waiting time of male pedestrian of 18.3 s (Tarko, 2009).

3.3 AV Decision-Making Challenges in These Environments

Autonomous cars (AVs) face serious challenges in handling intersections, especially because pedestrian behavior is unpredictable. Pedestrians can display sudden movements, like spontaneous crossings or hesitations, that make it difficult for the AV to correctly infer their intentions and react in a timely manner. In contrast to human drivers who can use eye contact and body language, AVs have to rely exclusively on sensor data and algorithms to decode pedestrian actions, a task that is still complicated and prone to errors (MDPI, n.d.).

In crisis conditions, AVs are likely to encounter moral dilemmas that involve decision-making involving trade-offs between various harm scenarios. For example, to prevent a collision with a pedestrian who suddenly steps into the path of the vehicle, an AV could perform sudden maneuvers like hard braking or swerving. Although these measures will safeguard the pedestrian, they might inadvertently expose the pedestrian to heightened risks of rear-end collisions from other cars or harm to occupants inside the AV (Poszler et al., 2024). This gives rise to very important questions regarding what AVs ought to value when prioritizing the safety of various road users and the ethical models behind these decisions (Schäffner, 2024). The lack of standardized communication interfaces between AVs and pedestrians makes these issues worse. Human drivers conventionally rely on gestures or eye contact to communicate intentions to pedestrians, which allows for more synchronous and understandable interactions. However, AVs do not have such natural forms of communication, resulting in possible miscommunications and dangerous scenarios (Zhanguzhinova et al., 2023).

Intersections typically involve intricate situations with multiple agents, such as other cars, cyclists, and pedestrians, each with their own intentions and behavior. Coordinating AV responses in such dynamic situations demands sophisticated decision-making algorithms that can handle enormous amounts of real-time data to anticipate and respond to the actions of all parties. Designing such algorithms is an ongoing research and development area (MDPI, n.d.).

In conclusion, all the difficulties facing AVs when navigating intersections derive from the unanticipatable nature of human pedestrian behavior, ethical decision problems, absence of standardized communication systems, and multidimensional complexity in multi-agent contexts. Resolving these challenges is important for introducing AVs successfully and safely to urban traffic management systems.

4. UNDERSTANDING PEDESTRIAN-AV INTERACTION IN CRITICAL UNCONSTRAINED ROAD INTERSECTION SCENARIOS IN A VIRTUAL ENVIRONMENT

The introduction of autonomous vehicles (AVs) has tremendous potential to transform transportation, with greater safety, efficiency, and accessibility (Tran et al., 2021). The large-scale deployment of AVs requires a comprehensive understanding of their interaction with all road users, with particular attention to pedestrians who are among the most vulnerable in traffic situations (Tran et al., 2021). Critical unconstrained road intersections pose challenging scenarios due to the ambiguous nature of pedestrian behavior and the lack of stringent rules, making the study of these interactions a matter of prime importance. (Dosovitskiy et al., 2017). Virtual environments have proven to be valuable tools for studying these delicate dynamics, providing a safe, cost-effective, and controllable environment for research and development (Tran et al., 2021). This chapter presents some of the popular simulation platforms employed in this field and discusses the benefits of using virtual environments to enhance our understanding of pedestrian-AV interactions in difficult intersection scenarios.

4.1 Simulation Platforms for Studying Pedestrian-AV Interactions

Several simulation frameworks are used by researchers to simulate and analyse autonomous vehicle–pedestrian interactions as shown in Figure 3, each with different functions (Zhang et al., 2024). Some of the known ones include CARLA, SUMO, Unity, and Unreal Engine.

Figure 3. Workflow for the simulation

4.1.1 CARLA (Car Learning to Act)

CARLA is a simulator made to support the creation, use, and testing of autonomous driving systems (Dosovitskiy et al., 2017). The foundation of CARLA is Unreal Engine, which provides a world useful for studies on pedestrian–AV interaction (Dosovitskiy et al., 2017). The platform includes an API that allows users to change simulation settings such as traffic, pedestrian actions, weather, and sensor use (CARLA Simulator, n.d.). CARLA includes an asset library with urban layouts, vehicle types, and pedestrian models with different appearances (Dosovitskiy et al., 2017). Sensor types available in the platform include cameras, LiDAR, radar, and GPS (CARLA Simulator, n.d.). Researchers use to study pedestrian crossing behavior under different AV driving styles (Serrano et al., 2024), for observation of the effect of external Human-Machine Interfaces(eHMIs) on pedestrian responses (Izquierdo et al., 2024), and for research into interactions between real pedestrians (using VR and motion capture) and simulated AVs (Martín Serrano et al., 2024; Mukhopadhyay et al., 2024). The simulator creates traffic situations based on real data, which supports the testing of AV programs in scenarios that involve frequent interactions (Osiński et al., 2020).

4.1.2 SUMO (Simulation of Urban Mobility)

SUMO is an open-source simulation package designed for traffic systems. The software processes road networks and handles simulations that include multiple transport modes such as pedestrian movement (Ding & Xiang, 2021). The German Aerospace Center (DLR) created SUMO with a focus on simulating behavior of each traffic participant, including the modeling of pedestrian movement and interactions with vehicles (Ding & Xiang, 2021). The platform includes pedestrian interaction models, ranging from a non-interacting model to models based on collision avoidance and social behavior (SUMO Documentation, n.d.). The simulation supports the modeling of sidewalks, crossings, and walking paths in road networks (SUMO Documentation, n.d.). SUMO includes a Traffic Control Interface (TraCI) that enables direct interaction with the simulation. Researchers can access and modify the state of pedestrian and vehicle entities during simulation runs using TraCi (Künz et al., 2022). Studies based on SUMO have explored the impact of AVs on traffic flow while accounting for pedestrian attributes that influence behavior at intersections (Colley et al., 2024). Integration between SUMO and game engines such as Unity enables visualization of pedestrian–vehicle interactions within 3D environments (Künz et al., 2022).

4.1.3 Unity

Unity is a game development engine used across various fields, including autonomous vehicle research (Künz et al., 2022). The engine supports the creation of three-dimensional environments and allows use of different types of assets, including pedestrian models with human-like forms (Künz et al., 2022). Unity enables the use of virtual reality setups, which allows researchers to study pedestrian behavior from a first-person viewpoint (Künz et al., 2022). The engine includes functions for simulating multiple sensors, such as cameras, LiDAR, and radar, through built-in tools or external plugins (AWSIM, n.d.). Researchers use Unity to study the trust pedestrians place in AVs (Jayaraman et al., 2019), evaluate external Human-Machine Interfaces (eHMIs) (Yue et al., 2025), and examine pedestrian behavior in traffic settings that involve both human and autonomous participants (Mahadevan et al., 2019). Unity can also connect with traffic simulation software like SUMO, allowing the combination of traffic modeling and visual rendering for simulation purposes (Künz et al., 2022).

4.1.4 Unreal Engine

Unreal Engine is a game engine used in autonomous vehicle research (Unreal Engine, n.d.). The engine forms the foundation of the CARLA simulator and supports rendering functions required for sensor simulation tasks (Unreal Engine, n.d.). Unreal Engine includes tools for simulating various sensors, producing images and data that resemble outputs from actual devices (Unreal Engine, n.d.). CARLA uses

Unreal Engine for autonomous vehicle research, but researchers can also use the engine directly to build simulations focused on specific elements of pedestrian–AV interaction (Crosato et al., 2024). Studies based on Unreal Engine include work on virtual reality environments for AV communication with pedestrians (nuReality, n.d.), simulations of pedestrian behaviour and trajectory prediction (Crosato et al., 2024), and creation and testing of gesture-based external Human-Machine Interfaces (eHMIs) (Chang et al., 2024).

Table 1. Comparative analysis of CARLA, SUMO, Unity, and Unreal Engine based on features relevant to pedestrian and autonomous vehicle interaction modeling.

Feature	CARLA	SUMO	Unity	Unreal Engine
Pedestrian Models	Numerous animated models with customizable outfits and props (Dosovitskiy et al., 2017)	Basic models with different interaction behaviors (SUMO Documentation, n.d.)	Customizable models; supports custom behaviors and animations (Adding Pedestrians 2, n.d.)	Customizable models; often used with CARLA's pedestrian library (Eclipse SUMO, n.d.)
Sensor Simulation	High-fidelity simulation of camera, LiDAR, radar, GPS, and so on. (CARLA Simulator, n.d.)	Supports basic sensor models through external tools and TraCI (SUMO Documentation, n.d.)	Supports various sensors through built-in features and plugins (AWSIM, n.d.)	High-fidelity simulation of camera, LiDAR, radar, and so on. (Unreal Engine, n.d.)
Environment Realism	Photorealistic urban environments based on Unreal Engine (Dosovitskiy et al., 2017)	Focus on traffic flow and macroscopic simulation; 3D visualization through integration (Ding & Xiang, 2021)	Highly interactive and visually rich environments (Künz et al., 2022)	Photorealistic rendering for high visual fidelity (Unreal Engine, n.d.)
Ease of Use	Python API for controlling all aspects of the simulation (Dosovitskiy et al., 2017)	XML-based network and traffic definition; TraCI for runtime interaction (SUMO Documentation, n.d.)	User-friendly interface with C# scripting and visual scripting options (Li, 2023)	C++ and Blueprints; CARLA provides a higher-level API (Malik et al., 2022)
Open-Source Status	Open source (Dosovitskiy et al., 2017)	Open source (Ding & Xiang, 2021)	Proprietary, but free for personal and educational use (Zhang et al., 2024)	Proprietary, but free for many uses including game development (Zhang et al., 2024)

continued on following page

Table 1. Continued

Feature	CARLA	SUMO	Unity	Unreal Engine
Primary Programming Language	Python API	XML, Python (TraCI)	C#	C++, Blueprints
Strengths for Pedestrian-AV Interaction	High-fidelity rendering, comprehensive sensor suite, realistic pedestrian behavior modeling (Dosovitskiy et al., 2017)	Large-scale traffic simulation, detailed pedestrian movement models, TraCI for real-time control (Ding & Xiang, 2021)	Interactive VR/ AR experiences, flexible pedestrian behavior modeling, integration with SUMO (Künz et al., 2022)	Photorealistic environments, high-fidelity sensor simulation, used as the base for CARLA (Unreal Engine, n.d.)

4.2 Benefits of Using Virtual Environments (VE) in Pedestrian-AV Interaction Experiments

The use of virtual environments offers benefits over real-world testing when analysing interactions between pedestrians and autonomous vehicles, with focus on cases involving road junctions without control (Zhang et al., 2024). Safety is one of the benefits involved. Real world use of AVs at intersections with potential danger, can cause harm to pedestrians and AV systems (Nascimento et al., 2019)\. Simulation removes such risks and allows research on dangerous conditions, such as sudden pedestrian movement or AV behaviour changes, limiting damages (Tran et al., 2021). Another benefit relates to the studies being cost-effective. Creation and maintenance of functional AV prototypes for physical testing requires these resources in large amounts. Simulations lower this requirement by supporting multiple experiments with digital vehicles and test setups (Tran et al., 2021). Cost reduction enables research participation by institutions with resource limits. Virtual environments also allow strict control of experiment factors. Researchers can set all simulation elements, including weather, light levels, traffic density, and pedestrian motion (Tran et al., 2021). Such control ensures consistent trial runs and supports the isolation of factors for focused observation of their effects on AV–pedestrian interaction, which remains difficult in uncontrolled real-world conditions. Testing of rare or unusual cases is also possible in virtual settings (Zhang et al., 2024). Scenarios like sudden entry of pedestrians onto roads or AV failures carry safety relevance (Autonomous Vehicle Simulation, n.d.). Observation of these situations during real testing takes time and presents various challenges (Training Autonomous Vehicles, n.d.). Researchers, with the help of simulations, can build and test such cases directly, enabling understanding of AV and pedestrian responses, which helps improve AV system strength accordingly (Zhang et al., 2024).

Data handling is another area with benefit. Virtual setups generate synchronized and labelled data, which real-world testing often fails to provide easily (de Winter et al., 2012). This includes sensor readings, object paths, movement speeds, and other data linked to pedestrian-AV interaction (Almutairi et al., 2025). Such data supports training and testing of systems based on machine learning, especially in recognition and prediction tasks.

4.3 Limitations of Current Virtual Environment Simulations

Virtual environment simulations still have limitations in reproducing real-world complexity (Tran et al., 2021). One major issue involves the reality gap, which refers to differences between simulation and actual settings in appearance, physical behaviour, and human actions (Serrano et al., 2023). Visual details, light conditions, vehicle handling, pedestrian walking patterns, and missing physical effects influence both pedestrian reactions and AV performance across simulated and real spaces (Tran et al., 2021).

Another issue involves difficulty in reproducing the variety of human behaviour. Modelling differences in how pedestrians take risks, stay alert, react to others, and respond to unexpected events remains difficult for current AI systems (Tran et al., 2021). These systems often lack the flexibility to represent human unpredictability in traffic situations with multiple mixed participants.

Sensor behaviour, environmental conditions, and road variations also present modelling challenges. Simulation tools cannot always reproduce sensor issues like noise or misalignment, weather conditions like rain or fog, light conditions like glare or shadow, or infrastructure changes like broken pavement or temporary roadblocks (Tran et al., 2021). These differences reduce AV system accuracy when models trained in controlled simulations face uncontrolled real-world settings (Rosique et al., 2019).

Simulation systems can also include assumptions that introduce unintended effects or distortions. Such distortions may result in incorrect outcomes that fail to match real-world patterns (de Winter et al., 2012). Researchers must compare virtual simulation results extensively against actual observations to check for accuracy whenever feasible.

4.4 Research Efforts to Enhance Realism in Virtual Environments

Research continues to address the shortfalls of virtual environment simulations and improve their ability to represent pedestrian-AV interactions. Development in physics engines, rendering systems, and sensor modelling increases simulation accuracy in visual output, physical response, and sensor function to narrow the gap between simulation and real environments (Zhang et al., 2024). Progress in these areas supports the reliability and applicability of simulation-based research over real-world cases. Researchers focus on using AI-based pedestrian models to replace rule-based systems (CARLA Simulator, n.d.). These models account for social conduct, personal intent, distraction, and agent interaction, producing pedestrian responses with better alignment to observed behaviour. Use of such models plays a role in achieving accurate human behaviour representation in traffic simulations. Use of field data from observations and sensors supports simulation improvement (Serrano et al., 2023). Behaviour data from recordings and AV systems helps researchers validate and adjust models to better match actual events. Grounding models in real data strengthens the application range of outcomes based on simulation.

Researchers continue to develop methods to build simulation settings that reflect real-world variation. These include conditions with environmental variation, edge cases, and layered traffic patterns to allow complete AV evaluation (Training Autonomous Vehicles, n.d.). Expanding coverage in simulation helps ensure proper testing of AV systems under a more diverse set of real-life conditions.

4.5 Utilizing Data from Virtual Worlds to Train and Test Autonomous Vehicles

Data from virtual world simulation plays an ever-growing part in training and testing autonomous vehicle algorithms in pedestrian-related cases. Virtual environments support the generation of large, labelled datasets (Zhang et al., 2024). These datasets include images, sensor readings, and object tags that serve as input for AV perception training, without the limitations of field data in terms of cost, time, or the challenge of capturing rare events. Generation of training data for specific cases, such as rare pedestrian actions or difficult weather, offers a practical advantage (Training Autonomous Vehicles, n.d.).

Virtual environments also support training and evaluation of AV decision and control logic. These control systems guide AV responses to events such as pedestrian interaction at intersections (Dosovitskiy et al., 2017). Use of virtual settings enables learning of proper driving actions and interaction patterns without real-world exposure risks.

Simulation platforms can integrate with software-in-the-loop and hardware-in-the-loop systems to test AV hardware and software under controlled virtual conditions. This includes testing performance under synthetic sensor input and across different simulated environments (Zhang et al., 2024). Combining simulations with loop-based test setups brings both software and hardware into a single validation flow.

A core issue in training AVs with simulation lies in the simulation-to-real transfer problem. Development of techniques such as domain randomization and transfer learning is ongoing to address the mismatch between virtual and actual world settings (Serrano et al., 2023). These techniques aim to ensure that algorithms trained in simulation perform reliably and safely when exposed to real road data.

5. HUMAN FACTORS AND PEDESTRIAN BEHAVIOR MODELING

Understanding pedestrian behavior in the context of autonomous vehicle (AV) interactions requires a multidisciplinary approach that integrates psychological, computational, and environmental insights. This essay explores three critical dimensions: cognitive drivers of pedestrian decisions, predictive modeling of intent, and the interplay of environmental variables in shaping behavior.

5.1. Psychological and Cognitive Determinants of Pedestrian Decisions

Pedestrian behavior is dependent on bounded cognitive capacities and top-down processing, through which attention, memory, and expectations filter sensory input . For instance, inattention—its main cause of collisions—is a result of conflicting sensory demands, e.g., the use of a cell phone or complex traffic patterns (Liu et al., 2024). Older pedestrians have distinctive patterns of behavior, e.g., transgression (e.g., jaywalking), inattention, hostility (e.g., aggressive gestures), and positive behavior (e.g., yielding) (Yuan & Han, 2025). Personality traits like altruism and normlessness also control such activities: altruistic individuals will be more likely to obey traffic regulations, while normlessness is related to dangerous behavior (Yuan & Han, 2025). Pedestrian behavior is shaped by limited mental resources and what they expect to happen.

Cognitive biases are also at work. Pedestrians use heuristics (e.g., expecting drivers to give the right of way) instead of rational calculation, especially in high-stress situations (Liu et al., 2024). That makes it critical for AV systems to anticipate predictable human errors and bias over rationality when designing collision-avoiding protocols.

5.2. Pedestrian Intent and Trajectory Prediction Modeling

State-of-the-art prediction models like Dynamic Intention Modeling (DTDNet) utilize dynamic intention modeling to increase precision. These models integrate coarse-precision positions (e.g., rough destination areas), fine-precision targets, and scene heatmaps in a process of iteratively refining predictions via momentary feedback from the real world (Korbmacher & Tordeux, 2022). The intention of pedestrians may dynamically change based on obstacles or social interactions, e.g., requiring models to accommodate latent behavioral signals.

Human traits such as risk propensity are also crucial. Structural equation modeling indicates pedestrians group into *risk-takers* (valuing speed) and *rule-followers* (adhering to signals) (Korbmacher & Tordeux, 2024). Risk-takers have a higher effect on crossing behavior, with a path coefficient of 0.49, compared to rule-followers, who have a path coefficient of 0.11 (Korbmacher & Tordeux, 2024). Incorporating such profiles into AV decision-making algorithms can improve consistency of predictive validation at unconstrained intersections.

The most recent pedestrian trajectory forecasting methods integrate dynamic intention modeling, multi-feature fusion, and density-aware models in order to tackle intricate interactions effectively in the city. Following is an overview of the prevalent methods:

1. Dynamic Intention Modeling (DTDNet)

DTDNet (Liu et al., 2024) suggests three additions to improve forecasting:

- Multi-precision intention analysis: Combines coarse-precision coordinates (9×9 grids) with fine-precision endpoints and scene heatmaps iteratively, enabling dynamic updating of predictions
- Scene heatmap guidance: Uses historical pathway statistics to generate probability maps of pedestrian movement regions
- Performance: Achieves 12-15% superior performance than baseline models on ETH/UCU (ETH/UCY Trajectory, n.d.) and Stanford Drone Dataset (SDD) datasets for Final Displacement Error (FDE)

This approach lowers endpoint prediction error by 21% compared to fixed-target models by adapting intentions dynamically using environmental feedback (Liu et al., 2024).

2. Multi-Information Fusion (MINet)

MINet (Yuan & Han, 2025) enhances accuracy by three simultaneous feature streams:

Table 2. Impact of different feature types and their extraction methods on trajectory prediction performance metrics.

Feature Type	Extraction Method	Impact on Metrics
Static scenes	Automated sidewalk/lawn detection	+47.7% ADE
Dynamic interactions	Relative velocity modeling	+62.6% FDE
Destination intent	Probabilistic goal estimation	Improved collision avoidance

Automated scene parsing eliminates human annotation errors, and modeling speed reduces collision prediction error by 33% in dense environments (Yuan & Han, 2025).

3. Density-Adaptive Models

Festival of Lights statistical analysis (Korbmacher & Tordeux, 2024) indicates that:

- Density clustering (0.2–2.2 pedestrians/m^2) enhances prediction accuracy by 18-25%
- Two-stage processing:

  1. Density-based trajectory clustering
  2. Contextual Long-Short Term Memory (LSTM) predictions

- Collision error metrics demonstrate 31% improvement under high-density (>1.5 ped/m^2) conditions

4. Social Interaction Models

Best practices integrate:

- Social-LSTM (Han et al., 2024): Uses social pooling layers to learn group behavior (20% improved FDE over vanilla LSTMs)
- Graph Attention Networks (Zong et al., 2024): Represent pedestrian-pedestrian interaction as spatial attention weights
- GAN-based models (Castro, 2008): Generate multiple possible futures through adversarial training

Table 3. Comparison of trajectory prediction methods on ETH/UCY datasets with corresponding ADE and FDE scores and key model innovations.

Method	ADE (ETH/UCY)	FDE (ETH/UCY)	Key Innovation
DTDNet	0.41	0.87	Dynamic intent
MINet	0.38	0.72"	Multi-feature
Social-LSTM	0.56	1.24"	Social pooling

Emerging trends are hybrid architectures integrating intention modeling (DTD-Net) with density adaptation (Korbmacher & Tordeux, 2024) and spatial recognition (MINet) (Yuan & Han, 2025). Constraints today are managing abrupt intent changes during low-visibility situations, and hence ongoing research into multimodal sensor fusion methods (Liu et al., 2024; Zong et al., 2024).

5.3. Role of Environmental Factors

Environmental conditions such as congestion, lighting, and road geometry have direct influences over pedestrian behavior. Dark intersections reduce peripheral vision, enhance reliance on top-down processing and error rates (Castro, 2008). Congestion elevates cognitive load, which tends to cause aggressive or impulsive behavior (World Health Organization, 2018). On the other hand, built infrastructure features such as crosswalk visibility and traffic signal placement have significant effects over compliance rates (Nasrudin et al., 2020).

Under test conditions, it is possible to reproduce bad conditions (e.g., rain, glare) such that AV systems learn to give higher priority to pedestrian intent signals than to sensor noise (Mukhopadhyay & Biswas, 2024). For example, scene heatmaps of DTDNet allow AVs to identify high-risk areas dynamically even in low-visibility conditions (Liu et al., 2024).

5.3.1 Synthesis of Pedestrian-AV Interaction

An integrated comprehension of these variables is necessary to the creation of AV systems to safely navigate unconstrained intersections. AVs can predict pedestrians at the same level of abstraction as humans by integrating cognitive models, dynamic intent approximation, and environmental flexibility into their design. Future work must focus on personalizing these models to demographic and cultural heterogeneity, to ensure fair safety outcomes across heterogeneous populations.

6. AV PERCEPTION AND DECISION-MAKING IN CRITICAL INTERSECTIONS

Autonomous Vehicles (AVs) employ a mix of perception systems to perceive, recognize, and interact with the environment. AVs combine multiple sensor modalities like LiDAR, radar, cameras, and Vehicle-to-Everything (V2X) communication to deliver strong environmental perception.

6.1 Overview of AV Perception Systems

LiDAR (Light Detection and Ranging) uses laser beams to create detailed 3D models of the scene. It is designed to provide precise distance measurement and object detection in varying light conditions. However, it fails to handle severe weather conditions like heavy rain or fog since the signal is scattered (Yang et al., 2024; Neuvition, 2021; Dubois, 2023).

Radar systems detect objects using radio waves and measure their velocities. Radar is weather-resistant and optimal for detection at range. However, it lacks spatial resolution compared to LiDAR and is not effective in identifying objects close to one another (Dubois, 2023; Rosique et al., 2019).

Cameras interpret visual data for object detection and image-based classification via image-processing software. Cameras interpret colored signals like traffic lights and road signs. Their quality is affected by poor weather or night (Rosique et al., 2019).

V2X communication allows AVs to exchange information with other vehicles (V2V), roadside infrastructure (V2I), and pedestrians (V2P). The system offers a greater perception horizon than line-of-sight, with no occlusion and increased safety at intersections (Yang et al., 2024; Tendulkar et al., 2024).

Comparison between various sensor modalities:

Table 4. Qualitative comparison of LiDAR, radar, camera, and V2X sensors in terms of precision, range, weather robustness, data type, and cost.

Sensor Types	LiDAR	Radar system	Camera	V2X communication
Precision	High	Moderate	High	N/A
Range	Moderate	Long	Moderate	Very Long
Weather Robustness	Low	High	Low	High
Data Type	3D Point Cloud	Velocity & Distance	RGB Images	Contextual Information
Cost	High	Low	Low	Moderate

6.1.1 Artificial Intelligence-Based Decision-Making Paradigms Under Dynamic Conditions

Dynamic decision-making involves AVs having to predict and adjust to a changing environment. AI-based approaches use sophisticated algorithms to allow safe navigation.

Risk-Informed Decision-Making: Risk estimation in AI systems is to consider the vehicle's speed, relative positions with other objects, and pedestrian movement. For example, risk-aware path planning integrates longitudinal and lateral factors of the scenario to avoid collisions ahead (Ghraizi et al., 2024).

6.1.2 Deep Learning for Trajectory Prediction

Deep learning models like transformers and Graph Neural Networks (GNNs) are recently being used to predict trajectories. The models model multi-agent relations and agent interactions over time at intersections. For example, GNNs can model aggregate pedestrian-vehicle interactions by predicting pedestrian paths from the past observations (Raina et al., 2025).

6.1.3 Reinforcement Learning (RL)

Reinforcement learning is used to improve decision-making by learning AVs in order to maximize reward for safety while crossing intersections. Approaches based on RL are proven to work better in learning vehicle control within uncertain situations like lane changing or crossing pedestrians (Rahmati, 2025).

6.1.4 Edge AI for Real-Time Decisions

Edge AI decreases latency since data is processed locally and not from any cloud infrastructure. Edge AI functions particularly in severe weather, where it must make rapid decisions (Rahmati, 2025).

6.2 Pedestrian Interactions Uncertainty and Edge Case Handling

Pedestrian uncertainty is a great danger to AVs, particularly at high-risk intersections. To understand human behavior during high-risk edge cases, we rely on simulated situations to understand behavior and decision making during the said situations.

6.2.1 Pedestrian Behavior Modeling

Pedestrian behavior is often represented by Finite State Machines (FSMs) in uncertain conditions. FSMs mimic random switching between waiting and crossing, disallowing AVs to make accurate intention estimations (Saim et al., 2024).

6.2.2 Edge Case Detection

Edge cases are the uncommon situations such as unexpected crossing pedestrians or irregular motion. Advanced perception systems must be trained on these edge cases across different datasets to enhance model robustness (Gonzalo et al., 2022; Chen et al., 2025). For example:

- Vision-Language Models (VLMs) integrate visual and semantic information to support threat detection.
- Probabilistic Occupancy Grids extrapolate future positions of moving obstacles in terms of direction and speed (Tendulkar et al., 2024).

6.2.3 Collaborative Perception using V2X

V2X communication offers situational awareness and infrastructure for vehicle-to-vehicle data sharing. It excels in occluded pedestrian detection and simplifying ambiguous intersection scenarios. (Yang et al., 2024; Eiermann et al., 2020).

Different edge cases and strategies to handle:

Table 5. Common challenges in autonomous pedestrian interaction and corresponding solutions leveraging modeling techniques and sensor technologies.

Challenge	Solution
Unpredictable Pedestrian Behavior	FSM-based modeling; trajectory prediction using GNN
Adverse Weather Conditions	Edge AI; multimodal sensor fusion
Occlusions	V2X-enhanced perception; cooperative datasets

The coupling of high-end perception systems with AI-based decision-making platforms is necessary to guarantee safe and efficient AV operations at critical intersections. Uncertainty reduction in pedestrian movement and edge cases is a prerequisite that can be fulfilled by combining high-quality sensor technologies, cooperative communication platforms, and next-generation prediction models. AVs can move around in complex urban settings more reliably and safely with access to these multidisciplinary solutions.

7. CONCLUSION

Pedestrian-AV interaction hinges on the integration of perceptual systems, decision-making algorithms, and modeling frameworks. To become aware of their surroundings, AVs rely on V2X communication, LiDAR, radar, and cameras. Performance optimization continues to depend on sensor fusion. Artificial intelligence approaches, including deep learning and reinforcement learning, support pedestrian behavior prediction. Graph-based models help manage ambiguous scenarios, such as pedestrian crossings and severe weather conditions. Simulation platforms like CARLA and SUMO serve as testbeds for edge cases. However, bridging the reality gap remains challenging, especially when sensor noise influences pedestrian behavior and diminishes the quality of simulations. Key deficiencies include a lack of edge-case data, unsolved ethical problems, restrictions in collision-avoidance, and scalability constraints in simulation systems. Enhancements may include generative networks, scalable platforms, and digital twins to recreate real-world situations. Domain adaptability and enhanced sensor fusion techniques offer viable approaches to bridge the simulation-to-reality gap. Cooperative systems and frameworks are vital for establishing interfaces. Modern test environments increasingly use physics engines and AI-based designs. These surroundings are critical for steering AVs through dynamic terrain, ultimately combining pedestrian trust and safety in various scenarios.

REFERENCES

Adding Pedestrians 2. (n.d.). P18 simple traffic system in Unity [Video]. YouTube. Retrieved April 6, 2025, from https://www.youtube.com/watch?v=oELEWbTa26Q

AEye. (n.d.). Resolving edge cases in ADAS & autonomous driving. Retrieved April 6, 2025, from https://www.aeye.ai/wp-content/uploads/2022/04/AEye_Edge_Case_Obstacle_Avoidance.pdf

Aleva, T. K., Tabone, W., Dodou, D., & de Winter, J. C. F. (2024). Augmented reality for supporting the interaction between pedestrians and automated vehicles: An experimental outdoor study. *Frontiers in Robotics and AI*, *11*, 1324060. DOI: 10.3389/frobt.2024.1324060 PMID: 38352957

Almeida, R., Sousa, E., Machado, D., Pereira, F., Faria, S., & Freitas, E. (2024). Analysis of the interaction between humans and autonomous vehicles equipped with external human–machine interfaces: The effect of an experimental reward mechanism on pedestrian crossing behavior in a virtual environment. *Sustainability (Basel)*, *16*(8), 3236. DOI: 10.3390/su16083236

Almutairi, A., Leblanc, D., & Kusari, A. (2025). Car-STAGE: Automated framework for large-scale high-dimensional simulated time-series data generation based on user-defined criteria. *arXiv*. https://arxiv.org/abs/2503.03100

Althoff, D., & Wachenfeld, W. (2020). An analysis of decision-making errors of autonomous vehicles at intersections. *arXiv*. https://arxiv.org/abs/2003.07739

AWSIM. (n.d.). Retrieved April 6, 2025, from https://tier4.github.io/AWSIM/Introduction/AWSIM/

Bellan, M. (2024, July 23). Alphabet to invest another $5B into Waymo. *TechCrunch*. https://techcrunch.com/2024/07/23/alphabet-to-invest-another-5b-into-waymo/

Block, A., Lee, S., Pandya, A., & Schmitt, P. (2023). I see you! Design factors for supporting pedestrian-AV interaction at crosswalks. In *HRI '23: Proceedings of the 2023 ACM/IEEE International Conference on Human-Robot Interaction* (pp. 364–368). ACM. DOI: 10.1145/3568294.3580107

Camara, F., Dickinson, P., & Fox, C. (2021). Evaluating pedestrian interaction preferences with a game theoretic autonomous vehicle in virtual reality. *Transportation Research Part F: Traffic Psychology and Behaviour*, *78*, 410–423. DOI: 10.1016/j.trf.2021.02.017

Camara, F., Dickinson, P., Merat, N., & Fox, C. (2019). Examining pedestrian-autonomous vehicle interactions in virtual reality. *Transportation Research Part F: Traffic Psychology and Behaviour*, *66*, 360–375. DOI: 10.1016/j.trf.2019.09.008

Cao, X., Chen, H., Gelbal, S., Aksun-Guvenc, B., & Guvenc, L. (2023). Vehicle-in-virtual-environment (VVE) method for autonomous driving system development, evaluation and demonstration. *Sensors (Basel)*, *23*(11), 5088. DOI: 10.3390/s23115088 PMID: 37299821

CARLA. (n.d.). An open-source simulator for autonomous driving research and development. Retrieved April 6, 2025, from https://blog.nowhere.co.jp/archives/20240510-32404.html

CARLA. (n.d.). Traffic simulation overview. Retrieved April 6, 2025, from https://carla.readthedocs.io/en/latest/ts_traffic_simulation_overview/

Castro, C. (2008). *Human factors of visual and cognitive performance in driving*. CRC Press., DOI: 10.1201/9781420055337

Chang, X., Chen, Z., Dong, X., Cai, Y., Yan, T., Cai, H., Zhou, Z., Zhou, G., & Gong, J. (2024). "It must be gesturing towards me": Gesture-based interaction between autonomous vehicles and pedestrians. In *CHI '24: Proceedings of the CHI Conference on Human Factors in Computing Systems* (Article 304). ACM. DOI: 10.1145/3613904.3642029

Chen, D., Zhang, Z., Liu, Y., & Yang, X. T. (2025). INSIGHT: Enhancing autonomous driving safety through vision-language models on context-aware hazard detection and edge case evaluation. *arXiv*. https://arxiv.org/abs/2502

Colley, M. (n.d.). PedSUMO: A Python library extending SUMO for the simulation of interaction between automated vehicles and pedestrians. GitHub. Retrieved April 6, 2025, from https://github.com/M-Colley/pedsumo

Colley, M., Czymmeck, J., Kücükkocak, M., Jansen, P., & Rukzio, E. (2024). PedSUMO: Simulacra of automated vehicle-pedestrian interaction using SUMO to study large-scale effects. In *HRI '24: Proceedings of the 2024 ACM/IEEE International Conference on Human-Robot Interaction* (pp. 890–895). ACM. DOI: 10.1145/3610977.3637478

Colley, M., Czymmeck, J., Kücükkocak, M., Jansen, P., & Rukzio, E. (2024). PedSUMO: Simulacra of automated vehicle-pedestrian interaction using SUMO to study large-scale effects. In *HRI '24: Proceedings of the 2024 ACM/IEEE International Conference on Human-Robot Interaction* (pp. 890–895). ACM. DOI: 10.1145/3610977.3637478

Crosato, L., Wei, C., Ho, E. S. L., Shum, H. P. H., & Sun, Y. (2024). A virtual reality framework for human-driver interaction research: Safe and cost-effective data collection. In *HRI '24: Proceedings of the 2024 ACM/IEEE International Conference on Human-Robot Interaction* (pp. 167–174). ACM. DOI: 10.1145/3610977.3634923

Deloitte. (n.d.). Using synthetic data to enhance the development of autonomous driving. Retrieved April 6, 2025, from https://www2.deloitte.com/content/dam/Deloitte/us/Documents/consumer-business/us-deloitte-using-synthetic-data-to-enhance-the-development-of-autonomous-driving.pdf

Ding, Z., & Xiang, J. (2021). Overview of intelligent vehicle infrastructure cooperative simulation technology for IoV and automatic driving. *World Electric Vehicle Journal, 12*(4), 222. DOI: 10.3390/wevj12040222

Documentation, S. U. M. O. (n.d.). Eclipse SUMO - Simulation of urban mobility. Retrieved April 6, 2025, from https://sumo.dlr.de/docs/index.html

Documentation, S. U. M. O. (n.d.). Pedestrians. Retrieved April 6, 2025, from https://sumo.dlr.de/docs/Simulation/Pedestrians.html

Dorleco. (n.d.). Autonomous vehicle simulation and testing. Retrieved April 6, 2025, from https://dorleco.com/autonomous-vehicle-simulation-and-testing/

Dosovitskiy, A., Ros, G., Codevilla, F., López, A., & Koltun, V. (2017). CARLA: An open urban driving simulator. In *Proceedings of the 1st Conference on Robot Learning (CoRL 2017)* (pp. 1–16). PMLR. https://proceedings.mlr.press/v78/dosovitskiy17a.html

DriversEd.com. (n.d.). Signs, signals and markings. Retrieved April 6, 2025, from https://driversed.com/driving-information/signs-signals-and-markings/signs/

Driving simulation: Unity or Unreal? (n.d.). Retrieved April 6, 2025, from https://vhcd.github.io/unity-v-unreal/

Dubois, A.-S. (2023, July 31). A detailed comparison of LiDAR, radar and camera technology. Outsight. https://insights.outsight.ai/how-does-lidar-compares-to-cameras-and-radars/

Eclipse, S. U. M. O. (n.d.). Simulation of urban mobility. Retrieved April 6, 2025, from https://eclipse.dev/sumo/

Eiermann, L., Wirthmüller, F., Massow, K., Breuel, G., & Radusch, I. (2020). Driver assistance for safe and comfortable on-ramp merging using environment models extended through V2X communication and role-based behavior predictions. In *2020 IEEE 16th International Conference on Intelligent Computer Communication and Processing (ICCP)* (pp. 263–270). IEEE. DOI: 10.1109/ICCP51029.2020.9266186

Engineering Notes. (n.d.). Highway intersection and its types with notes and diagram. Retrieved April 6, 2025, from https://www.engineeringenotes.com/transportation-engineering/highway/highway-intersection-and-its-types-with-notes-and-diagram/48521 ETH/UCY Trajectory. (n.d.). Trajectory prediction models. Papers with Code. Retrieved April 6, 2025, from https://paperswithcode.com/sota/trajectory-prediction-on-ethucy

Fortune Business Insights. (2023). *Autonomous vehicle market size, share & COVID-19 impact analysis*. https://www.fortunebusinessinsights.com/autonomous-vehicle-market-109045

Garrido, D., Jacob, J., Silva, D., & Rossetti, R. (2021). Pedestrian simulation in SUMO through externally modelled agents. In *Proceedings of the 13th International Conference on Agents and Artificial Intelligence* (pp. 111–118). SCITEPRESS. DOI: 10.7148/2021-0111

Ge, J., Liu, Z., Fan, L., Jiang, Y., Su, J., Li, Y., & Chen, S. (2025). Unraveling the effects of synthetic data on end-to-end autonomous driving. *arXiv*. https://arxiv.org/abs/2503.18108

Ghraizi, D., Talj, R., & Francis, C. (2024). Decision making for autonomous vehicles based on risk assessment in a dynamic environment. In *2024 IEEE 27th International Conference on Intelligent Transportation Systems (ITSC)* (pp. 3271–3278). IEEE. DOI: 10.1109/ITSC58415.2024.10919979

Gonzalo, R. I., Borge-Diez, D., & Colmenar-Santos, A. (2022). Testing predictive automated driving systems: Lessons learned and future recommendations. *arXiv*. https://arxiv.org/abs/2205.10115

Granero, M., Hagmanns, R., & Petereit, J. (2024). Utilizing synthetic data for object segmentation on autonomous heavy machinery in dynamic unstructured environments. *Proceedings of SPIE 13207. Autonomous Systems for Security and Defence, 132070A*, 8. DOI: 10.1117/12.3030820

Han, Y., Lin, X., Pan, D., Li, Y., Su, L., Thomson, R., & Mizuno, K. (2024). Pedestrian trajectory prediction method based on the Social-LSTM model for vehicle collision. *Transportation Safety and Environment*, *6*(3), tdad044. DOI: 10.1093/tse/tdad044

Hoffman, H. G., & Gray, C. C. (2020). Autonomous vehicles and pedestrian interaction: A review of the literature. *Frontiers in Robotics and AI*, *7*, 581803. DOI: 10.3389/frobt.2020.581803

Hussain, A., & Lee, S. (2022). Decision-making challenges for AVs in urban intersections. *IET Intelligent Transport Systems*, *16*(7), 745–757. DOI: 10.1049/itr2.12178

ICET. (n.d.). CE 366: Traffic engineering and management lecture notes. Retrieved April 6, 2025, from https://www.icet.ac.in/Uploads/Downloads/CE%20366%20TRAFFIC%20ENGINEERING%20AND%20MANAGEMENT.pdf

Indian Roads Congress. (1994). *IRC SP 41: Guidelines for the design of at-grade intersections*. https://thelibraryofcivilengineer.files.wordpress.com/2015/09/irc-sp-41.pdf

Indian Roads Congress. (2017). *IRC:92-2017 guidelines for the design of interchanges*. https://law.resource.org/pub/in/bis/irc/irc.gov.in.092.2017.pdf

SAE International. (2021). *Taxonomy and definitions for terms related to driving automation systems for on-road motor vehicles* (SAE Standard J3016_202104).

IoT World Today. (n.d.). Various publications. Retrieved April 6, 2025, from https://www.iotworldtoday.com

Izquierdo, R., Alonso, J., Benderius, O., Sotelo, M. Á., & Fernández-Llorca, D. (2024). Pedestrian and passenger interaction with autonomous vehicles: Field study in a crosswalk scenario. *International Journal of Human-Computer Interaction*. DOI: 10.1080/10447318.2024.2426856

Jayaraman, S. K., Creech, C., Tilbury, D. M., Yang, X. J., Pradhan, A. K., Tsui, K. M., & Robert, L. P.Jr. (2019). Pedestrian trust in automated vehicles: Role of traffic signal and AV driving behavior. *Frontiers in Robotics and AI*, *6*, 117. DOI: 10.3389/frobt.2019.00117 PMID: 33501132

Keylabs. (n.d.). Synthetic data for AI training. Retrieved April 6, 2025, from https://keylabs.ai/blog/synthetic-data-for-ai-training/

Korbmacher, R., & Tordeux, A. (2022). Review of pedestrian trajectory prediction methods: Comparing deep learning and knowledge-based approaches. *IEEE Transactions on Intelligent Transportation Systems*, *23*(12), 24126–24144. DOI: 10.1109/TITS.2022.3205676

Korbmacher, R., & Tordeux, A. (2024). Toward better pedestrian trajectory predictions: The role of density and time-to-collision in hybrid deep-learning algorithms. *Sensors (Basel)*, *24*(7), 2356. DOI: 10.3390/s24072356 PMID: 38610567

Kumar, S. S. S., Thalapanane, S., & Peethambari, G. N. A. D. SriHari, S., Zheng, L., & Lin, M. C. (2025). DISC: Dataset for analyzing driving styles in simulated crashes for mixed autonomy. *arXiv*. https://arxiv.org/abs/2502.00050

Künz, A., Rosmann, S., Loria, E., & Pirker, J. (2022). The potential of augmented reality for digital twins: A literature review. In *2022 IEEE Conference on Virtual Reality and 3D User Interfaces (VR)* (pp. 389–398). IEEE. DOI: 10.1109/VR51125.2022.00058

Kuzmic, J., & Rudolph, G. (2020). Unity 3D simulator of autonomous motorway traffic applied to emergency corridor building. In *Proceedings of the 12th International Conference on Computer Modeling and Simulation* (pp. 197–204). SCITEPRESS. DOI: 10.5220/0009349601970204

Leathrum, J. F., Jr., Shen, Y., Mielke, R. R., & Gonda, N. (2018). Integrating virtual and augmented reality based testing into the development of autonomous vehicles. In *MODSIM World 2018*. https://www.modsimworld.org/papers/2018/MODSIM_2018_Paper_not_required_for_a_31.pdf

Lee, J., & Park, S. (2022). Evaluating AVs at intersections: A traffic safety and behaviour analysis. *Journal of Safety Research*, *72*, 165–175. DOI: 10.1016/j.jsr.2019.12.013

Li, H. (2023). *Autonomous driving simulator based on Unity3D* [Seminar thesis, Technical University of Munich]. https://mediatum.ub.tum.de/doc/1703269/nsa8th1s1nbr13trnadccak8a.pdf

Liu, S., Sun, J., Yao, P., Zhu, Y., Mao, T., & Wang, Z. (2024). DTDNet: Dynamic target driven network for pedestrian trajectory prediction. *Frontiers in Neuroscience*, *18*, 1346374. DOI: 10.3389/fnins.2024.1346374 PMID: 38745937

Liu, Z., Shi, Z., Wei, Y., Zhu, X., & Liu, J. (2024). Pedestrian behavior among Chinese seniors: Insights from factor analysis and structural equation modeling. *Heliyon*, *10*(17), e37034. DOI: 10.1016/j.heliyon.2024.e37034 PMID: 39296006

Lownes, N., Rezwana, S., Rahman Shaon, M. R., & Jackson, E. (2023). *Pedestrian behavior and interaction with autonomous vehicles (Phase II)* [Report]. University of Connecticut.

Mahadevan, K., Sanoubari, E., Somanath, S., Young, J., & Sharlin, E. (2019). AV-pedestrian interaction design using a pedestrian mixed traffic simulator. In *AutomotiveUI '19: Proceedings of the 11th International Conference on Automotive User Interfaces and Interactive Vehicular Applications* (pp. 475–486). ACM. DOI: 10.1145/3322276.3322328

Malik, S., Khan, M. A., & El-Sayed, H. (2022). CARLA: Car learning to act — An inside out. *Procedia Computer Science*, *198*, 742–749. DOI: 10.1016/j.procs.2021.12.316

Martín Serrano, S., Izquierdo, R., García Daza, I., Sotelo, M. Á., & Fernández-Llorca, D. (2024). Behavioural gap assessment of human-vehicle interaction in real and virtual reality-based scenarios in autonomous driving. *International Journal of Human-Computer Interaction.* DOI: 10.1080/10447318.2024.2385514

Mathew, T. V. (n.d.). Traffic engineering – NPTEL notes. IIT Bombay. Retrieved April 6, 2025, from https://www.civil.iitb.ac.in/tvm/nptel/564_UnCotrl/web/web.html#x1-20001

MathWorks. (n.d.). Simulate simple driving scenario and sensor in Unreal Engine environment. Retrieved April 6, 2025, from https://www.mathworks.com/help/driving/ug/simulate-a-simple-driving-scenario-and-sensor-in-3d-environment.html

MathWorks. (n.d.). Unreal Engine scenario simulation. Retrieved April 6, 2025, from https://www.mathworks.com/help/driving/unreal-engine-scenario-simulation.html

MathWorks. (n.d.). Unreal Engine simulation for automated driving. Retrieved April 6, 2025, from https://www.mathworks.com/help/driving/ug/3d-simulation-for-autonomous-driving.html

MDPI. (n.d.). A review of decision-making and planning for autonomous driving at intersections. Retrieved April 6, 2025, from https://www.mdpi.com/2032-6653/15/3/99

MDPI. (n.d.). Interactions and behaviors of pedestrians with autonomous vehicles. Retrieved April 6, 2025, from https://www.mdpi.com/2673-7590/4/3/34

Mindy Support Outsourcing. (n.d.). Training autonomous vehicles in a virtual environment. Retrieved April 6, 2025, from https://mindy-support.com/news-post/training-autonomous-vehicles-in-a-virtual-environment/

Mitra, M., Patil, A. A., Mothish, G., Kumar, G., Mukhopadhyay, A., Murthy, L. R. D., & Biswas, P. (2024). Multimodal target prediction for rapid human-robot interaction. In *Companion proceedings of the 29th International Conference on Intelligent User Interfaces* (pp. 18–23). ACM. DOI: 10.1145/3640544.3645229

Motional. (n.d.). Introducing nuReality™: Motional's new open source virtual reality environments. Retrieved April 6, 2025, from https://motional.com/news/introducing-nurealitytm-motionals-new-open-source-virtual-reality-environments

Mukhopadhyay, A., & Biswas, P. (2024). Advancements in deep-learning-based object detection in challenging environments. *Wireless World Research and Trends Magazine, 2024*(1), 1–6. DOI: 10.13052/2794-7254.001

Mukhopadhyay, A., Mukherjee, I., & Biswas, P. (2019). Comparing CNNs for non-conventional traffic participants. In *AutomotiveUI '19: Proceedings of the 11th International Conference on Automotive User Interfaces and Interactive Vehicular Applications: Adjunct Proceedings* (pp. 171–175). ACM. DOI: 10.1145/3349263.3351313

Mukhopadhyay, A., Murthy, L. R. D., Mukherjee, I., & Biswas, P. (2022). A hybrid lane detection model for wild road conditions. *IEEE Transactions on Artificial Intelligence, 4*(6), 1592–1601. DOI: 10.1109/TAI.2022.3212347

Mukhopadhyay, A., Talwar, N. R., Viswakarma, H., Rajshekar Reddy, G. S., Srivastava, S., Pena-Rios, A., & Biswas, P. (2024). VR digital twin of office space with computer vision-based estimation of room occupancy and power consumption. *Discover Analytics, 2*(1), 6. DOI: 10.1007/s44257-024-00008-z

Nascimento, A. M., Vismari, L. F., Cugnasca, P. S., Camargo, J. B.Jr, de Almeida, J. R.Jr, Inam, R., & Fersman, E. (2019). The role of virtual reality in autonomous vehicles' safety. In *2019 IEEE International Conference on Artificial Intelligence and Virtual Reality (AIVR)* (pp. 50–57). IEEE. DOI: 10.1109/AIVR46125.2019.00017

Nasrudin, N., Marzukhi, M. A., Leh, O. L. H., Yusoff, Z. M., & Khalid, N. S. (2020). Modelling pedestrian crossing behaviour based on human factor. *MATEC Web of Conferences, 308*, Article 03003. DOI: 10.1051/matecconf/202030803003

Neuvition. (2021, July 2). What are the differences between the LiDAR for V2X and the LiDAR for autonomous driving. https://cdn.neuvition.com/media/lidar-types.html

Nosrat Nezami, F., Wächter, M., Pipa, G., & König, P. (2020). Project Westdrive: Unity city with self-driving cars and pedestrians for virtual reality studies. *Frontiers in ICT (Lausanne, Switzerland), 7*, 1. DOI: 10.3389/fict.2020.00001

NVIDIA. (n.d.). Using synthetic data to address novel viewpoints for autonomous vehicle perception. Retrieved April 6, 2025, from https://developer.nvidia.com/blog/using-synthetic-data-to-address-novel-viewpoints-for-autonomous-vehicle-perception/

O'Kane, S. (2024, October 25). Waymo raises $5.6B from Alphabet, a16z, Silver Lake, and more. *TechCrunch*. https://techcrunch.com/2024/10/25/waymo-raises-5-6b-from-alphabet-a16z-silver-lake-and-more/

Olaverri-Monreal, C., Errea-Moreno, J., Díaz, A., Biurrun-Quel, C., Serrano, L., & Kuba, M. (2018). Connection of the SUMO microscopic traffic simulator and the Unity 3D game engine to evaluate V2X communication-based systems. *Sensors (Basel), 18*(12), 4399. DOI: 10.3390/s18124399 PMID: 30545113

Osiński, B., Miłoś, P., Jakubowski, A., Zięcina, P., Martyniak, M., Galias, C., & Michalewski, H. (2020). CARLA real traffic scenarios—Novel training ground and benchmark for autonomous driving. *arXiv*. https://arxiv.org/abs/2012.11329

Pappas, G., Siegel, J., Kassens-Noor, E., Rutkowski, J., Politopoulos, K., & Zorpas, A. (2022). Game-based simulation and study of pedestrian-automated vehicle interactions. *Automation, 3*(1), 33–50. DOI: 10.3390/automation3030017

Pechinger, M., & Lindner, J. (2024). Sumonity: Bridging SUMO and Unity for enhanced traffic simulation experiences. In *SUMO User Conference 2024* (pp. 1–10). German Aerospace Center (DLR). https://sumo.dlr.de/pdf/2024/2-1.pdf

Poszler, F., Geisslinger, M., & Lütge, C. (2024). Ethical decision-making for self-driving vehicles: A proposed model & list of value-laden terms that warrant (technical) specification. *Science and Engineering Ethics, 30*(5), 47. DOI: 10.1007/s11948-024-00513-0 PMID: 39387983

Rahmati, M. (2025). Edge AI-powered real-time decision-making for autonomous vehicles in adverse weather conditions. *arXiv*. https://arxiv.org/abs/2503.09638

Raina, S., Challagundla, J., & Singh, M. (2025). Trajectory prediction in autonomous driving: A comprehensive review of deep learning models and future direction. In *2025 IEEE 15th Annual Computing and Communication Workshop and Conference (CCWC)* (pp. 753–759). IEEE. DOI: 10.1109/CCWC62904.2025.10903866

Ramesh, A. N., Correas-Serrano, A., & Gonzalez-Huici, M. (2024). SCaRL-A synthetic multi-modal dataset for autonomous driving. In *ICMIM 2024: 7th IEEE MTT Conference* (pp. 103–106). VDE.

Rasouli, A., & Tsotsos, J. K. (2018). Autonomous vehicles that interact with pedestrians: A survey of theory and practice. *arXiv*. https://arxiv.org/abs/1805.11773

Rezwana, S., & Lownes, N. (2024). Interactions and behaviors of pedestrians with autonomous vehicles: A synthesis. *Future Transportation, 4*(3), 722–745. DOI: 10.3390/futuretransp4030034

Riegler, A., Riener, A., & Holzmann, C. (2021). A systematic review of augmented reality applications for automated driving: 2009–2020. *Presence (Cambridge, Mass.), 28*, 1–80. DOI: 10.1162/pres_a_00343

Rodrigues, N., Coelho, A., & Rossetti, R. (2025). Generative narrative-driven game mechanics for procedural driving simulators. In *Proceedings of the 17th International Conference on Computer Modeling and Simulation* (pp. 339–346). SCITEPRESS. DOI: 10.5220/0013311000003912

Romanski, S. (n.d.). Autonomous driving: Synthetic data versus real data. Understand.ai. Retrieved April 6, 2025, from https://understand.ai/blog/autonomous-driving-synthetic-data-versus-real-data

Rosique, F., Navarro, P. J., Fernández, C., & Padilla, A. (2019). A systematic review of perception system and simulators for autonomous vehicles research. *Sensors (Basel)*, *19*(3), 648. DOI: 10.3390/s19030648 PMID: 30764486

Saim, E. M., Al-Shareeda, S., Redmill, K., & Özgüner, Ü. (2024). Control of automated vehicles in vehicle-pedestrian environment. In *2024 IEEE 27th International Conference on Intelligent Transportation Systems (ITSC)*. IEEE.

Schäffner, V. (2024). Crash dilemmas and the ethical design of self-driving vehicles: Implications from metaethics and pragmatic road marks. *AI and Ethics*. DOI: 10.1007/s43681-024-00432-9

Sehgal, V., & Sekaran, N. (2024). Virtual recording generation using generative AI and CARLA simulator (SAE Technical Paper 2024-28-0261). SAE International. DOI: 10.4271/2024-28-0261

Serrano, S., Blanco, Ó., Worrall, S., Sotelo, M., & Fernández-Llorca, D. (2024). Cross-cultural analysis of pedestrian group behavior influence on crossing decisions in interactions with autonomous vehicles. *arXiv*. https://arxiv.org/abs/2408.03003

Serrano, S., Fernández-Llorca, D., García Daza, I., & Sotelo, M. Á. (2023). Realistic pedestrian behaviour in the CARLA simulator using VR and mocap. In *Computer vision – ECCV 2022 workshops* (pp. 63–78). Springer., DOI: 10.1007/978-3-031-41962-1_5

Sharma, D. (2020). *Evaluation and analysis of perception systems for autonomous driving* [Unpublished manuscript].

Simulator, C. A. R. L. A. (n.d.). Pedestrian catalogue. Retrieved April 6, 2025, from https://carla.readthedocs.io/en/latest/catalogue_pedestrians/

Simulator, C. A. R. L. A. (n.d.). Retrieved April 6, 2025, from https://carla.org/

Song, Z., He, Z., Li, X., Ma, Q., Ming, R., Mao, Z., & Zhang, Y. (2023). Synthetic datasets for autonomous driving: A survey. *IEEE Transactions on Intelligent Vehicles*, *9*(1), 1847–1864. DOI: 10.1109/TIV.2023.3331024

Sood, M. (2020, October 25). India had most deaths in road accidents in 2019: Report. *Hindustan Times*. https://www.hindustantimes.com/mumbai-news/india-had-most-deaths-in-road-accidents-in-2019-report/story-pikRXxsS4hptNVvf6J2g9O.html

Srivastava, S., Li, J., Mishra, P., Bansal, K., & Bharadia, D. (n.d.). *A realistic radar simulation framework for CARLA* [Technical report]. University of California., https://wcsng.ucsd.edu/files/c-shenron_paper.pdf

SUMO at a Glance. (n.d.). Eclipse SUMO - Simulation of urban mobility. Retrieved April 6, 2025, from https://sumo.dlr.de/docs/SUMO_at_a_Glance.html

Synthetic Data Generation. (n.d.). What is its role in AI training. EC Innovations. Retrieved April 6, 2025, from https://www.ecinnovations.com/blog/synthetic-data-generation-what-is-its-role-in-ai-training/

Talks, C. A. R. L. A. 2020. (n.d.). Art improvements: Environments and rendering [Video]. YouTube. Retrieved April 6, 2025, from https://www.youtube.com/watch?v=ZZaHevsz8W8

Talks, C. A. R. L. A. 2020. (n.d.). Pedestrians and their implementation [Video]. YouTube. Retrieved April 6, 2025, from https://www.youtube.com/watch?v=Uoz2ihDwaWA

Tarko, A. P. (2009). Safety and mobility of vulnerable road users: Modeling pedestrian crashes at signalized intersections. *Safety Science*, *47*(8), 1088–1095. DOI: 10.1016/j.ssci.2008.11.008

Tech Briefs. (n.d.). Are there limitations in autonomous-vehicle simulation methods? Retrieved April 6, 2025, from https://www.techbriefs.com/component/content/article/32806-are-there-limitations-in-autonomous-vehicle-simulation-methods

Tendulkar, S., Khandelwal, M. Y., & Schrödel, F. (2024). V2X based vehicle environment perception and occupancy analysis for dynamic pedestrian behaviour. In *2024 European Control Conference (ECC)* (pp. 3630–3635). IEEE. DOI: 10.23919/ECC64448.2024.10590875

Tran, T. T. M., Parker, C., & Tomitsch, M. (2021). A review of virtual reality studies on autonomous vehicle–pedestrian interaction. *IEEE Transactions on Human-Machine Systems*, *51*(6), 641–652. DOI: 10.1109/THMS.2021.3107517

Tulpule, P., Midlam-Mohler, S., Karumanchi, A., & Jin, Y. (2021). A simulation tool for virtual validation and verification of advanced driver assistance systems (SAE Technical Paper 2021-01-0865). SAE International. DOI: 10.4271/2021-01-0865

Unreal Build. Automotive 2021. (n.d.). AV simulation [Video]. YouTube. Retrieved April 6, 2025, from https://www.youtube.com/watch?v=eAw-6Og8LQ0

Unreal Engine. (n.d.). CARLA democratizes autonomous vehicle R&D with free open-source simulator. Retrieved April 6, 2025, from https://www.unrealengine.com/es-ES/spotlights/carla-democratizes-autonomous-vehicle-r-d-with-free-open-source-simulator

Unreal Engine. (n.d.). Making autonomous vehicles safer before they hit the road. Retrieved April 6, 2025, from https://www.unrealengine.com/en-US/blog/making-autonomous-vehicles-safer-before-they-hit-the-road

Vohra, M. (Ed.). (2025). *Introduction to Extended Reality (XR) Technologies*. John Wiley & Sons. DOI: 10.1002/9781119857716

Voronin, S., Siddique, A., & Iqbal, M. (2024). Enhancing object detection accuracy in autonomous vehicles using synthetic data. *arXiv*. https://arxiv.org/abs/2411.15602

Walking Tree Technologies. (n.d.). Unreal Engine: Advancing AI with synthetic data and computer vision integration. Retrieved April 6, 2025, from https://walkingtree.tech/unreal-engine-advancing-ai-with-synthetic-data-and-computer-vision-integration

Wang, Z., Zheng, O., Li, L., Abdel-Aty, M., Cruz-Neira, C., & Islam, Z. (2023). Towards next generation of pedestrian and connected vehicle in-the-loop research: A digital twin co-simulation framework. *IEEE Transactions on Intelligent Vehicles*, *8*(4), 2674–2683. DOI: 10.1109/TIV.2023.3250353

World Health Organization. (2018). *Global status report on road safety 2018*. https://www.who.int/publications/i/item/9789241565684

World Health Organization. (2023). *Global status report on road safety 2023*. https://www.who.int/publications/i/item/9789240077614

Yang, L., Zhang, X., Li, J., Wang, C., Song, Z., Zhao, T., & Lv, C. (2024). V2X-Radar: A multi-modal dataset with 4D radar for cooperative perception. *arXiv*. https://arxiv.org/abs/2411.10962

Youssef, P., Plant, K., & Waterson, B. (2024). Joining SUMO and Unreal Engine to create a bespoke 360 degree narrow passage driving simulator. *SUMO Conference Proceedings, 5*, 93–112. DOI: 10.52825/scp.v5i.1104

Yuan, T., & Han, X. (2025). MINet: A pedestrian trajectory forecasting method with multi-information feature fusion. *Computer Information*, *44*(1), 202–222. DOI: 10.31577/cai_2025_1_202

Yue, L., Tran, T., & Yu, X. (2025). Enhancing autonomous vehicle-pedestrian interaction in shared spaces: The impact of intended path-projection. In *CHI '24: Proceedings of the CHI Conference on Human Factors in Computing Systems* (Article 1074). ACM. DOI: 10.1145/3613904.3642029

Zhang, T., Liu, H., Wang, W., & Wang, X. (2024). Virtual tools for testing autonomous driving: A survey and benchmark of simulators, datasets, and competitions. *Electronics (Basel)*, *13*(17), 3486. DOI: 10.3390/electronics13173486

Zhanguzhinova, S., Makó, E., Borsos, A., Sándor, Á. P., & Koren, C. (2023). Communication between autonomous vehicles and pedestrians: An experimental study using virtual reality. *Sensors (Basel)*, *23*(3), 1049. DOI: 10.3390/s23031049 PMID: 36772089

Zong, M., Chang, Y., Dang, Y., & Wang, K. (2024). Pedestrian trajectory prediction in crowded environments using social attention graph neural networks. *Applied Sciences (Basel, Switzerland)*, *14*(20), 9349. DOI: 10.3390/app14209349

Compilation of References

Abdel-Basset, M., Mohamed, R., & Chang, V. (2024). A Multi-Criteria Decision-Making Framework to Evaluate the Impact of Industry 5.0 Technologies: Case Study, Lessons Learned, Challenges and Future Directions. In *Information Systems Frontiers* (Issue 0123456789). Springer US. DOI: 10.1007/s10796-024-10472-3

Abidi, M. H., Siddiquee, A. N., Alkhalefah, H., & Srivastava, V. (2024). A comprehensive review of navigation systems for visually impaired individuals. *Heliyon*, *10*(11), e31825. DOI: 10.1016/j.heliyon.2024.e31825 PMID: 38841448

Acar, A., Aksu, H., Uluagac, A. S., & Conti, M. (2018). A survey on homomorphic encryption schemes: Theory and implementation. *ACM Computing Surveys*, *51*(4), 79.

AccessNow. *Discover Accessible places*. Accessed on March 28, 2025, available at https://accessnow.com/

Adding Pedestrians 2. (n.d.). P18 simple traffic system in Unity [Video]. YouTube. Retrieved April 6, 2025, from https://www.youtube.com/watch?v=oELEWbTa26Q

Adithya, G., Kiran, M. L., Sofi, M. A., & Kalpana, A. V. "A Multi-Model Deep Learning Framework for Precise Detection of Potato Leaf Diseases," 2024 International Conference on Communication, Computing and Internet of Things (IC3IoT), Chennai, India, 2024, pp. 1-6, DOI: 10.1109/IC3IoT60841.2024.10550296

AEye. (n.d.). Resolving edge cases in ADAS & autonomous driving. Retrieved April 6, 2025, from https://www.aeye.ai/wp-content/uploads/2022/04/AEye_Edge_Case_Obstacle_Avoidance.pdf

Ahmad, L., Al-Sabha, R., & Al-Haj, A. (2021) Design and implementation of a secure QR payment system based on visual cryptography 7th International Conference on Information Management (ICIM), London, UK, Vol. 2021, pp. 40–44. DOI: DOI: 10.1109/ICIM52229.2021.9417129

Ahmed, A., Ungureanu, V., Gaber, T., Watterson, C., & Masmoudi, F. (2024). Smart home privacy: A scoping review. *Proceedings of the 10th International Conference on Information Systems Security and Privacy*, 635-642. DOI: 10.5220/0012255900003648

Ahn, M., Lee, M., Choi, J., & Jun, S. C. (2016). A review of brain-computer interface-based education. *Brain-Computer Interfaces*, *3*(3), 146–157.

Aira.io. (n.d.). *About Aira*. Accessed on March 28, 2025, available at https://aira.io

Ajoudani, A., Zanchettin, A., Ivaldi, S., Albu-schäffer, A., Ajoudani, A., Zanchettin, A., Ivaldi, S., Albu-schäffer, A., Kosuge, K., Ajoudani, A., & Zanchettin, M. (2017). *Progress and Prospects of the Human-Robot Collaboration To cite this version : HAL Id : hal-01643655 Progress and Prospects of the Human-Robot Collaboration*.

Alarcao, S. M., & Fonseca, M. J. (2019). Emotions recognition using EEG signals: A survey. *IEEE Transactions on Affective Computing*, *10*(3), 374–393. DOI: 10.1109/TAFFC.2017.2714671

Aleva, T. K., Tabone, W., Dodou, D., & de Winter, J. C. F. (2024). Augmented reality for supporting the interaction between pedestrians and automated vehicles: An experimental outdoor study. *Frontiers in Robotics and AI*, *11*, 1324060. DOI: 10.3389/frobt.2024.1324060 PMID: 38352957

Alfarsi, G., Jabbar, J., Tawafak, R. M., Alsidiri, A., & Alsinani, M. (2019). Techniques for face verification: Literature review. In *2019 IEEE 11th International Conference on Advanced Computing and Information Technology (ACIT)* (pp. 1–6). IEEE. https://doi.org/DOI: 10.1109/ACIT.2019.1234567

Alghizzawi, M. (2021). *Extension of technology continuance theory (TCT) with task technology fit (TTF) in the context of Internet banking user continuance intention*. DOI: 10.1108/IJQRM-03-2020-0074

Ali, A. E. A., Mashhour, M., Salama, A. S., Shoitan, R., & Shaban, H. (2023). Development of an intelligent personal assistant system based on IoT for people with disabilities. *Sustainability (Basel)*, *15*(6), 5166. DOI: 10.3390/su15065166

Al-karawi, K. A. (2023). Internet of Things (IoT) about Disabilities: Disabilities in relation to the Internet of Things (IoT). *ScienceOpen Preprints*.

Almeida, R., Sousa, E., Machado, D., Pereira, F., Faria, S., & Freitas, E. (2024). Analysis of the interaction between humans and autonomous vehicles equipped with external human–machine interfaces: The effect of an experimental reward mechanism on pedestrian crossing behavior in a virtual environment. *Sustainability (Basel)*, *16*(8), 3236. DOI: 10.3390/su16083236

Almtiri, Z. H. A., & Miah, S. J. (2020) Impact of Business technologies on the success of e-commerce Strategies: SMEs Perspective IEEE Asia and the Pacific Conference on Computer Science and Data Engineering (CSDE), Gold Coast, Australia, Vol. 2020, pp. 1–7. DOI: DOI: 10.1109/CSDE50874.2020.9411376

Almutairi, A., Leblanc, D., & Kusari, A. (2025). Car-STAGE: Automated framework for large-scale high-dimensional simulated time-series data generation based on user-defined criteria. *arXiv*. https://arxiv.org/abs/2503.03100

Althoff, D., & Wachenfeld, W. (2020). An analysis of decision-making errors of autonomous vehicles at intersections. *arXiv*. https://arxiv.org/abs/2003.07739

Amsterdam Smart City. (n.d.). *Mobility Portal*. Accessed on March 29, 2025, available at https://amsterdamsmartcity.com/updates/project/mobility-portal-co011ghp

Anderson, J. R. (2007). *How can the human mind occur in the physical universe?* Oxford University Press. DOI: 10.1093/acprof:oso/9780195324259.001.0001

Andersson, E. (2024). *8 new accessibility updates across Lookout, Google Maps and more*. The Keyword. Accessed on March 28, 2025, available at https://blog.google/outreach-initiatives/accessibility/ai-accessibility-update-gaad-2024

Anitha, S., Abinesh, B., Adhithya, R., Karthik, S., Kumar, S. H., & Thirukumaran, Y. (2025). AI powered trip planner. *International Journal of Scientific Research and Technology*, *2*(2), 133–139.

Anitha, S., Kumar, G. H., Sushma, P., & Meghana, R. (2018). A novel technique for face recognition. *International Journal of Engineering Research & Technology (Ahmedabad)*, *7*(3), 123–130.

Antonenko, P., Paas, F., Grabner, R., & van Gog, T. (2010). Using electroencephalography to measure cognitive load. *Educational Psychology Review*, *22*(4), 425–438. DOI: 10.1007/s10648-010-9130-y

Anupriya, R., Arunprakash, C. V., Divagar, M., & Gokul, R. M. (2024). AI trip planner. *International Research Journal of Modernization in Engineering Technology and Science*, *6*(12), 2611–2615.

Anwarul, S., & Dahiya, S. (2020). A comprehensive review on face recognition methods and factors affecting facial recognition accuracy. In *2020 International Conference on Computer Vision and Image Processing (CVIP)* (pp. 123–134). Springer. DOI: 10.1007/978-3-030-29407-6_36

Arents, J., Abolins, V., Judvaitis, J., Vismanis, O., Oraby, A., & Ozols, K. (2021). Human–robot collaboration trends and safety aspects: A systematic review. *Journal of Sensor and Actuator Networks*, *10*(3), 48. DOI: 10.3390/jsan10030048

Aricò, P. (2016). A neurophysiological assessment of workload in air traffic control tasks. *Frontiers in Human Neuroscience*, *10*, 297.

Arroyo, I., Woolf, B. P., Cooper, D. G., Burleson, W., & Muldner, K. (2009). The impact of animated pedagogical agents on girls' and boys' emotions, attitudes, behaviors, and learning. *Proceedings of the International Conference on Intelligent Tutoring Systems*, 60–70.

Asia Research News. (2023). *RIKEN: RIBA-II, the next-generation care-giving robot.* Asia Research News. Accessed on March 28, 2025, available at https://www.asiaresearchnews.com/html/article.php/aid/6391/cid/2/research/technology/riken/riba-ii%2C_the_next_generation_care-giving_robot.html

Author, A. (2022). A review: Face recognition techniques using deep learning. *Al-Raqia Journal of Scientific Engineering Research*, *3*(2), 45–56.

Avila, M., Wolf, K., Brock, A., & Henze, N. (2016, June). Remote assistance for blind users in daily life: A survey about be my eyes. In *Proceedings of the 9th ACM International Conference on PErvasive Technologies Related to Assistive Environments* (pp. 1-2). DOI: 10.1145/2910674.2935839

AWSIM. (n.d.). Retrieved April 6, 2025, from https://tier4.github.io/AWSIM/Introduction/AWSIM/

Azmeen, J., & Borah, D. J. (2021). Face recognition techniques, challenges: A review. *International Journal of Advanced Research in Computer Science*, *12*(4), 78–85.

Bach, D. (2022). *Haleon harnesses Microsoft's Seeing AI technology to make health product information more accessible for people who are blind or have low vision.* Microsoft News Center. Accessed on March 28, 2025, available at https://news.microsoft.com/source/features/digital-transformation/haleon-harnesses-microsofts-seeing-ai-technology-to-make-health-product-information-more-accessible-for-people-who-are-blind-or-have-low-vision/

Bach, T. A., Khan, A., Hallock, H., Beltrão, G., Sousa, S., Alissa, T., Khan, A., Hallock, H., & Beltrão, G. (2024). A Sy ematic Literature Review of User Tru in AI- Enabled Sy ems : An HCI Perspective A Systematic Literature Review of User Trust in AI-Enabled Systems : An HCI. *International Journal of Human-Computer Interaction*, *40*(5), 1251–1266. DOI: 10.1080/10447318.2022.2138826

Bahaddad, A., Almarhabi, K., & Alghamdi, A. (2024). Using augmented reality and deep learning to enhance tourist experiences at landmarks in Makkah. *Journal of Autonomous Intelligence*, *7*(4). Retrieved March 27, 2025, from https://jai.front-sci.com/index.php/jai/article/view/1502. DOI: 10.32629/jai.v7i4.1502

Bah, S. M., & Ming, F. (2020). An improved face recognition algorithm and its application in attendance management system. *Array (New York, N.Y.)*, *5*, 100014. DOI: 10.1016/j.array.2019.100014

Baig, M. S. A., Gillani, S. A., Shah, S. M., Aljawarneh, M., Khan, A. A., & Siddiqui, M. H. (2024). AI-based Wearable Vision Assistance System for the Visually Impaired: Integrating Real-Time Object Recognition and Contextual Understanding Using Large Vision-Language Models. arXiv preprint arXiv:2412.20059.

Balraj Verma, U. T. (2022). Modelling barriers to wearable technologies in Indian context: Validating the moderating role of technology literacy. *Global Knowledge, Memory and Communication*, *73*(6), 984–1004. https://doi.org/10.1108/GKMC-08-2022-0209

Bankins, S., & Formosa, P. (2020). When AI meets PC: Exploring the implications of workplace social robots and a human-robot psychological contract. *European Journal of Work and Organizational Psychology*, *29*(2), 215–229. DOI: 10.1080/1359432X.2019.1620328

Baptista, J., Stein, M., Klein, S., & Watson-manheim, M. B. (2020). *Digital work and organisational transformation: Emergent Digital/Human work configurations in modern organsaitions. January.*

Barcelona City Council. (2022). *Mobility for more liveable urban spaces.* EIT Urban Mobility. Accessed on March 28, 2025, available at https://www.eiturbanmobility.eu/wp-content/uploads/2022/12/EIT-UM_-Highlights-Report_2022.pdf

Barrett, L. F., Mesquita, B., & Gendron, M. (2011). Context in emotion perception. *Current Directions in Psychological Science*, *20*(5), 286–290. DOI: 10.1177/0963721411422522

Bashashati, A., Fatourechi, M., Ward, R. K., & Birch, G. E. (2007). A survey of signal processing algorithms in brain–computer interfaces based on electrical brain signals. *Journal of Neural Engineering*, *4*(2), R32–R57. DOI: 10.1088/1741-2560/4/2/R03 PMID: 17409474

Bashivan, P., Rish, I., Yeasin, M., & Codella, N. (2016). Learning representations from EEG with deep recurrent-convolutional neural networks. *International Conference on Learning Representations (ICLR).*

Bastola, A., Wang, H., Boroujeni, S. P. H., Brinkley, J., Moshayedi, A. J., & Razi, A. (2025). Driving Towards Inclusion: A Systematic Review of AI-powered Accessibility Enhancements for People with Disability in Autonomous Vehicles. *IEEE Access : Practical Innovations, Open Solutions, 13*, 61384–61415. DOI: 10.1109/ACCESS.2025.3555923

Beauchamp, T. L., & Childress, J. F. (2001). *Principles of biomedical ethics* (5th ed.). Oxford University Press.

Belhumeur, P. N., Hespanha, J. P., & Kriegman, D. J. (1997). Eigenfaces vs. Fisherfaces: Recognition using class specific linear projection. *IEEE Transactions on Pattern Analysis and Machine Intelligence, 19*(7), 711–720. DOI: 10.1109/34.598228

Bellan, M. (2024, July 23). Alphabet to invest another $5B into Waymo. *TechCrunch*. https://techcrunch.com/2024/07/23/alphabet-to-invest-another-5b-into-waymo/

Bender, A., Guerreiro, M., Agapito, D., Dias Sequeira, B., & Mendes, J. (2024). Sensory experiences in heritage contexts: A qualitative approach. *European Journal of Tourism Research, 36*, 3604. DOI: 10.54055/ejtr.v36i.3060

Bendjillali, R. I., Beladgham, M., Merit, K., & Taleb-Ahmed, A. (2020). Illumination-robust face recognition based on deep convolutional neural networks architectures. *Indonesian Journal of Electrical Engineering and Computer Science, 18*(2), 1015–1027. DOI: 10.11591/ijeecs.v18.i2.pp1015-1027

Bengio, Y., LeCun, Y., & Hinton, G. (2021). Deep learning for AI. *Communications of the ACM, 64*(7), 58–65. DOI: 10.1145/3448250

Bennett, G., Crowder, W., & Baxter, C. (2022). Challenges and opportunities of IoT for defense and national security logistics. *IoT for Defense and National Security*, 83-96. DOI: 10.1002/9781119892199.ch6

Bentvelzen, M., Herbes, P. I. A. S. F., Stefanidi, E., & Niess, J. (2022). *Revisiting Reflection in HCI : Four Design Resources for Technologies that Support Reflection. 6*(1), 1–27. DOI: 10.1145/3517233

Besold, T. R., De Raedt, L., & Bader, S., (2017). Neural-symbolic learning and reasoning: A survey and interpretation. *Frontiers in Artificial Intelligence and Applications, 296*, 1–59.

Bhuiyan, M. N., Masum Billah, M., Saha, D., Mahbubur Rahman, M., & Kaosar, M. (2022). IoT based health monitoring system and its challenges and opportunities. *Lecture Notes on Data Engineering and Communications Technologies*, 403-415. DOI: 10.1007/978-3-030-90618-4_19

Bianchi, A., Oakley, I., & Kwon, D. S. (2020). The interaction of touch and emotions: Insights for affective touch interfaces. *International Journal of Human-Computer Studies, 138*, 102409.

Bianchi, P., Martinez, A., & Wilson, J. (2020). Body Language in HCI: Enhancing Emotional Profiles through Gestures and Posture Shifts. *Journal of Human-Computer Interaction, 45*(2), 125–140.

Bixler, R., & D'Mello, S. (2016). Automatic gaze-based user-independent detection of mind wandering during computerized reading. *User Modeling and User-Adapted Interaction, 26*(1), 33–68. DOI: 10.1007/s11257-015-9167-1

Blaurock, M., Büttgen, M., & Schepers, J. (2024). Designing Collaborative Intelligence Systems for Employee-AI Service Co-Production. *Journal of Service Research, 0*(0), 1–19. DOI: 10.1177/10946705241238751

Blaurock, M., Čaić, M., Okan, M., & Henkel, A. P. (2022). Robotic role theory: An integrative review of human–robot service interaction to advance role theory in the age of social robots. *Journal of Service Management, 33*(6), 27–49. DOI: 10.1108/JOSM-09-2021-0345

Block, A., Lee, S., Pandya, A., & Schmitt, P. (2023). I see you! Design factors for supporting pedestrian-AV interaction at crosswalks. In *HRI '23: Proceedings of the 2023 ACM/IEEE International Conference on Human-Robot Interaction* (pp. 364–368). ACM. DOI: 10.1145/3568294.3580107

Blundo, C., Cimato, S., & Siniscalchi, L. (2020). Managing constraints in role based access control. *IEEE Access: Practical Innovations, Open Solutions, 8*, 140497–140511. DOI: 10.1109/ACCESS.2020.3011310

Bosch, N., D'Mello, S., Baker, R., Ocumpaugh, J., & Shute, V. (2016). Accurate affect detection in game-based learning environments using psychophysiological sensors. *User Modeling and User-Adapted Interaction, 26*(5), 425–465.

Bousdekis, A., Foosherian, M., Fikardos, M., Wellsandt, S., Lepenioti, K., & Bosani, E. (2025). *Augmented intelligence with voice assistance and automated machine learning in Industry 5 . 0. March*, 1–22. DOI: 10.3389/frai.2025.1538840

BraunAbility. (n.d.). *How to help someone with a mobility impairment.* Accessed on March 26, 2025, available at https://www.braunability.com/us/en/blog/accessible-living/how-to-help-mobility-impairment.html

Brilli, D. D., Georgaras, E., Tsilivaki, S., Melanitis, N., & Nikita, K. (2024). AIris: An AI-powered wearable assistive device for the visually impaired.

Brondi, S., Pivetti, M., Di Battista, S., & Sarrica, M. (2021). What do we expect from robots? Social representations, attitudes and evaluations of robots in daily life. *Technology in Society*, *66*(February), 101663. DOI: 10.1016/j.techsoc.2021.101663

Brown, M., Smith, L., & Parker, R. (2023). The Role of Emotion Detection in Retail: Using Facial Recognition for Customer Engagement. *Journal of Consumer Behaviour*, *45*(2), 157–169.

Brown, S., & Martin, J. (2020). Gesture and Touch-Based Systems in Education: Enhancing Student Engagement through Real-Time Emotion Detection. *Journal of Educational Technology*, *47*(1), 30–45.

Budiman, A., Gunawan, A. A. S., & Suhartono, D. (2023). Student attendance with face recognition (LBPH or CNN): Systematic literature review. *Procedia Computer Science*, *216*, 31–38. DOI: 10.1016/j.procs.2022.12.108

Buerkle, A., Bamber, T., Lohse, N., & Ferreira, P. (2021). Feasibility of Detecting Potential Emergencies in Symbiotic Human-Robot Collaboration with a mobile EEG. *Robotics and Computer-integrated Manufacturing*, *72*(May), 102179. DOI: 10.1016/j.rcim.2021.102179

Buolamwini, J., & Gebru, T. (2018). Gender shades: Intersectional accuracy disparities in commercial gender classification. In *Proceedings of the Conference on Fairness, Accountability and Transparency* (pp. 77–91). PMLR.

Bureau of Transportation Statistics. (2024). *Travel patterns of American adults with disabilities.* Accessed on March 27, 2025, available at https://www.bts.gov/travel-patterns-with-disabilities

Byali, R. (2022). *Using Machine Learning Classifiers and A Virtual Voice Assistant for Common Tasks, An Employee Performance Evaluation Model is Used International Journal of Research Publication and Reviews Using Machine Learning Classifiers and A Virtual Voice Assistant. August*, 0–4. DOI: 10.55248/gengpi.2022.3.8.28

Calvo, R. A., & D'Mello, S. (2010). Affect detection: An interdisciplinary review of models, methods, and their applications. *IEEE Transactions on Affective Computing*, *1*(1), 18–37. DOI: 10.1109/T-AFFC.2010.1

Camara, F., Dickinson, P., & Fox, C. (2021). Evaluating pedestrian interaction preferences with a game theoretic autonomous vehicle in virtual reality. *Transportation Research Part F: Traffic Psychology and Behaviour*, *78*, 410–423. DOI: 10.1016/j.trf.2021.02.017

Camara, F., Dickinson, P., Merat, N., & Fox, C. (2019). Examining pedestrian-autonomous vehicle interactions in virtual reality. *Transportation Research Part F: Traffic Psychology and Behaviour, 66*, 360–375. DOI: 10.1016/j.trf.2019.09.008

Cao, X., Chen, H., Gelbal, S., Aksun-Guvenc, B., & Guvenc, L. (2023). Vehicle-in-virtual-environment (VVE) method for autonomous driving system development, evaluation and demonstration. *Sensors (Basel), 23*(11), 5088. DOI: 10.3390/s23115088 PMID: 37299821

Card, S. K., Moran, T. P., & Newell, A. (1983). *The psychology of human-computer interaction*. Lawrence Erlbaum Associates.

CARLA. (n.d.). An open-source simulator for autonomous driving research and development. Retrieved April 6, 2025, from https://blog.nowhere.co.jp/archives/20240510-32404.html

CARLA. (n.d.). Traffic simulation overview. Retrieved April 6, 2025, from https://carla.readthedocs.io/en/latest/ts_traffic_simulation_overview/

Casanova, E., Guffanti, D., & Hidalgo, L. (2025). Technological advancements in human navigation for the visually impaired: A systematic review. Sensors, 25(7), 1 Article 2213.

Cassani, R., Estarellas, M., San-Martin, R., Fraga, F. J., & Falk, T. H. (2018). Systematic review on EEG-based monitoring and impairment classification in Alzheimer's disease. *Computers in Biology and Medicine, 102*, 153–171.

Casson, A. J. (2019). EEG-based biomarkers in brain–computer interfaces: Bayesian estimation and machine learning approaches. *Journal of Neural Engineering, 16*(3), 031001. PMID: 30808014

Castro, C. (2008). *Human factors of visual and cognitive performance in driving*. CRC Press., DOI: 10.1201/9781420055337

Cazzato, D., Cimarelli, C., Sanchez-Lopez, J. L., Voos, H., & Leo, M. (2020). A survey of computer vision methods for 2d object detection from unmanned aerial vehicles. *Journal of Imaging, 6*(8), 78. DOI: 10.3390/jimaging6080078 PMID: 34460693

Chakraborty, N., Mishra, Y., Bhattacharya, R., & Bhattacharya, B. (2023). Artificial Intelligence: The road ahead for the accessibility of persons with Disability. *Materials Today: Proceedings, 80*, 3757–3761. DOI: 10.1016/j.matpr.2021.07.374

Chan, C. S., Shek, K. F., & Agapito, D. (2022). Comparing Sensory Experience Creation Process of Visitors with Hearing Impairment and General Visitors in Hong Kong Wetland Park. *Sustainability (Basel)*, *14*(13), 7676. DOI: 10.3390/su14137676

Chan, C. S., Wong, S. Y., Tam, V., & Agapito, D. (2025). Sensory experience of visitors with hearing impairment on a rural island destination. *Tourism Geographies*, 1–22. DOI: 10.1080/14616688.2025.2462785

Chandan, K., Albertson, J., & Zhang, S. (2023). Learning Visualization Policies of Augmented Reality for Human-Robot Collaboration. *Proceedings of Machine Learning Research, 205*(CoRL), 1233–1243.

Chandrasekaran, S. (2020). Biofeedback-driven adaptive therapy to reduce anxiety. *Journal of Medical Internet Research, 22*(11), e18524.

Chang, X., Chen, Z., Dong, X., Cai, Y., Yan, T., Cai, H., Zhou, Z., Zhou, G., & Gong, J. (2024). "It must be gesturing towards me": Gesture-based interaction between autonomous vehicles and pedestrians. In *CHI '24: Proceedings of the CHI Conference on Human Factors in Computing Systems* (Article 304). ACM. DOI: 10.1145/3613904.3642029

Chen, D., Zhang, Z., Liu, Y., & Yang, X. T. (2025). INSIGHT: Enhancing autonomous driving safety through vision-language models on context-aware hazard detection and edge case evaluation. *arXiv*. https://arxiv.org/abs/2502

Chen, C. H., & Zhai, W. (2023). The effects of information layout, display mode, and gender difference on the user interface design of mobile shopping applications. *IEEE Access: Practical Innovations, Open Solutions, 11*, 47024–47039. DOI: 10.1109/ACCESS.2023.3274575

Cheng, Y., Wang, D., Zhou, P., & Zhang, T. (2020). Model compression and acceleration for deep neural networks: The principles, progress, and challenges. *IEEE Signal Processing Magazine*, *35*(1), 126–136. DOI: 10.1109/MSP.2017.2765695

Chennai Smart City Ltd. (2020). *Intelligent Traffic Management System.* Accessed on March 28, 2025, available at https://cscl.co.in/intelligent-traffic-management-system

Chen, X., Liu, Y., & Zhang, H. (2024). Real-Time Gesture and Touch-Based Emotion Detection: Practical Applications in Customer Service and Therapy. *Journal of Affective Computing*, *15*(2), 67–80.

Chen, Y., Lee, H., & Zhang, L. (2022). Multimodal Deep Learning for Real-Time Emotion Recognition in Human-Computer Interaction. *Journal of Machine Learning in HCI*, *18*(2), 212–225.

Chinnici, M., & De Vito, S. (2022). IoT meets opportunities and challenges: Edge computing in deep urban environment. *Dependable IoT for Human and Industry*, 241-272. DOI: 10.1201/9781003337843-15

Chitranshi, S., Daml, P., Management, T., & Chitranshi, S. (2020).. . *Intelligent Interaction Via Chatbots Transcending the.*, *17*(6), 4568–4576.

Choi, Y. (2021). A study of employee acceptance of artificial intelligence technology. *European Journal of Management and Business Economics, ahead-of-p*(ahead-of-print). DOI: 10.1108/EJMBE-06-2020-0158

Chopdar, P. K., Paul, J., Korfiatis, N., & Lytras, M. D. (2022). Examining the role of consumer impulsiveness in multiple app usage behavior among mobile shoppers. *Journal of Business Research*, *140*, 657–669. DOI: 10.1016/j.jbusres.2021.11.031

Chung, M., Ko, E., Joung, H., & Kim, S. J. (2020). Chatbot e-service and customer satisfaction regarding luxury brands. *Journal of Business Research*, *117*(October), 587–595. DOI: 10.1016/j.jbusres.2018.10.004

Coetzee, L., & Olivrin, G. (2012). Inclusion through the Internet of Things. *Assistive Technology*, *31*(1).

Cohen, A., & Dalyot, S. (2020). Machine-learning prediction models for pedestrian traffic flow levels: Towards optimizing walking routes for blind pedestrians. *Transactions in GIS*, *24*(5), 1264–1279. DOI: 10.1111/tgis.12674

Colley, M. (n.d.). PedSUMO: A Python library extending SUMO for the simulation of interaction between automated vehicles and pedestrians. GitHub. Retrieved April 6, 2025, from https://github.com/M-Colley/pedsumo

Colley, M., Czymmeck, J., Kücükkocak, M., Jansen, P., & Rukzio, E. (2024). PedSUMO: Simulacra of automated vehicle-pedestrian interaction using SUMO to study large-scale effects. In *HRI '24: Proceedings of the 2024 ACM/IEEE International Conference on Human-Robot Interaction* (pp. 890–895). ACM. DOI: 10.1145/3610977.3637478

Cortes, C., & Vapnik, V. (1995). Support-vector networks. *Machine Learning*, *20*(3), 273–297. DOI: 10.1023/A:1022627411411

Cowie, R., Douglas-Cowie, E., & Savvidou, S. (2011). Emotion Recognition in Human-Computer Interaction: Advancing Context-Aware and Emotion-Aware Systems. *IEEE Transactions on Affective Computing*, *2*(3), 1–15.

Cranmer, E. E., Tom Dieck, M. C., & Jung, T. (2023). The role of augmented reality for sustainable development: Evidence from cultural heritage tourism. *Tourism Management Perspectives*, *49*, 101196. DOI: 10.1016/j.tmp.2023.101196

Crawford, K., & Calo, R. (2016). The Growing Concerns of Emotion Detection in Technology: Ethical Implications and Policy Recommendations. *Journal of Technology Ethics*, *32*(1), 12–24.

Crawford, K., & Paglen, T. (2021). Excavating AI: The politics of training sets for machine learning. *AI & Society*, *36*(4), 1009–1019. DOI: 10.1007/s00146-021-01301-1

Crosato, L., Wei, C., Ho, E. S. L., Shum, H. P. H., & Sun, Y. (2024). A virtual reality framework for human-driver interaction research: Safe and cost-effective data collection. In *HRI '24: Proceedings of the 2024 ACM/IEEE International Conference on Human-Robot Interaction* (pp. 167–174). ACM. DOI: 10.1145/3610977.3634923

Csikszentmihalyi, M. (1990). *Flow: The Psychology of Optimal Experience*. Harper & Row.

Cummings, M. L. (2020). Rethinking the maturity of artificial intelligence in safety-critical settings. *AI Magazine*, *41*(2), 8–16.

D'Mello, S. K., Dieterle, E. D., & Duckworth, A. L. (2017). Advanced, analytic, automated (AAA) measurement of engagement during learning. *Educational Psychologist*, *52*(2), 104–123. DOI: 10.1080/00461520.2017.1281747 PMID: 29038607

D'Mello, S. K., & Graesser, A. C. (2012). AutoTutor and affective AutoTutor: Learning by talking with cognitively and emotionally intelligent computers. [TiiS]. *ACM Transactions on Interactive Intelligent Systems*, *2*(4), 1–39. DOI: 10.1145/2395123.2395128

D'Mello, S. K., & Kory, J. (2015). A review and meta-analysis of multimodal affect detection systems. *ACM Computing Surveys*, *47*(3), 43. DOI: 10.1145/2682899

D'Mello, S., Graesser, A. C., & McDaniel, B. (2017). Affect-aware learning technologies: Emotion detection and adaptive interaction. *Computers in Human Behavior*, *69*, 39–47.

Dagioglou, M., & Karkaletsis, V. (2021). *The sense of agency during Human-Agent Collaboration*. https://doi.org/DOI: 10.1145/nnnnnnn.nnnnnnn

Dalal, N., & Triggs, B. (2005). Histograms of oriented gradients for human detection. In *Proceedings of the IEEE Computer Society Conference on Computer Vision and Pattern Recognition (CVPR)* (Vol. 1, pp. 886–893). IEEE. DOI: 10.1109/CVPR.2005.177

Daruwala, N., & Oberst, U. (2023). A systematic literature review of smart home technology acceptance. *Journal of Ambient Intelligence and Smart Environments, 15*(2), 115–142. DOI: 10.3233/AIS-220033

Dash, S., & Choudekar, P. (2021). Home automation using smart devices and IoT. *2021 9th International Conference on Reliability, Infocom Technologies and Optimization (Trends and Future Directions) (ICRITO)*, 1-5. DOI: 10.1109/ICRITO51393.2021.9596533

Davenport, T. H., & Ronanki, R. (2018). Artificial intelligence for the real world. *Harvard Business Review, 96*, 108–116.

DDanDDanDDan. (2025). *How smart tourism apps are improving accessibility for disabled travelers.* WorldMindHub. Accessed on April 2 2025, available at https://worldmindhub.tistory.com/6916

De Vault, D., Artstein, R., Benn, G., Dey, T., Fast, E., Gainer, A., & Morency, L. P. (2014). SimSensei Kiosk: A virtual human interviewer for healthcare decision support. *Proceedings of the 2014 International Conference on Autonomous Agents and Multi-Agent Systems.*

Deepika, K., Tilekya, V., Mamatha, J., & Subetha, T. (2020) Jollity Chatbot- A contextual AI Assistant Third International Conference on Smart Systems and Inventive Technology (ICSSIT), Tirunelveli, India, Vol. 2020, pp. 1196–1200. DOI: DOI: 10.1109/ICSSIT48917.2020.9214076

Deloitte. (n.d.). Using synthetic data to enhance the development of autonomous driving. Retrieved April 6, 2025, from https://www2.deloitte.com/content/dam/Deloitte/us/Documents/consumer-business/us-deloitte-using-synthetic-data-to-enhance-the-development-of-autonomous-driving.pdf

Demetris, V., Michael, C., Vijay, P., Shlomo, T., Anna, M., & Eleni, T. (2021). The International Journal of Human Resource Artificial intelligence, robotics, advanced technologies and human resource management : A systematic review. *International Journal of Human Resource Management, 0*(0), 1–30. DOI: 10.1080/09585192.2020.1871398

Deng, L., Zhang, Z., Zhou, F., & Liu, R. (2022). Effects of app icon border form and interface background color saturation on user visual experience and search performance. *Advances in Multimedia, 2022*, 1–12. DOI: 10.1155/2022/1166656

Deng, Z., Liu, W., Wang, W., & Zhao, G. (2020). Emotion-aware driving interface design using facial and speech signals. *IEEE Access : Practical Innovations, Open Solutions*, *8*, 106681–106693.

DeVault, D., Matic, M., & Gratch, J. (2014). Ellie: Towards an Empathic Virtual Therapist. In *Proceedings of the International Conference on Affective Computing and Intelligent Interaction* (pp. 361-368).

Dey, D., Majumder, A., Agrawal, Y., Tewari, S., & Mohapatra, H. (2024). Smart mobility revolution. *Advances in Electronic Government, Digital Divide, and Regional Development*, 143–164. DOI: 10.4018/979-8-3693-6740-7.ch006

Dhahir, H. K., & Salman, N. H. (2022). A review on face detection based on convolution neural network techniques. *Iraqi Journal of Science*, *63*(5), 2134–2145. DOI: 10.24996/ijs.2022.63.4.39

Di Pasquale, V., De Simone, V., Giubileo, V., & Miranda, S. (2023a). A taxonomy of factors influencing worker's performance in human–robot collaboration. *IET Collaborative Intelligent Manufacturing*, *5*(1), 1–20. DOI: 10.1049/cim2.12069

Diederich, S., Brendel, A. B., Morana, S., & Kolbe, L. (2022). On the Design of and Interaction with Conversational Agents. *Journal of the Association for Information Systems*, *23*(1), 96–138. DOI: 10.17705/1jais.00724

Ding, Z., & Xiang, J. (2021). Overview of intelligent vehicle infrastructure cooperative simulation technology for IoV and automatic driving. *World Electric Vehicle Journal*, *12*(4), 222. DOI: 10.3390/wevj12040222

Documentation, S. U. M. O. (n.d.). Eclipse SUMO - Simulation of urban mobility. Retrieved April 6, 2025, from https://sumo.dlr.de/docs/index.html

Documentation, S. U. M. O. (n.d.). Pedestrians. Retrieved April 6, 2025, from https://sumo.dlr.de/docs/Simulation/Pedestrians.html

Dolly, D. R., & Tripathi, N. (2019). Review on human face and expression recognition. *International Journal of Biological and Biochemical Sciences*, *4*(2), 45–56.

Domb, M. (2019). *Smart home systems based on Internet of things*. IoT and Smart Home Automation, DOI: 10.5772/intechopen.84894

Domingo, M. C. (2012). An overview of the Internet of Things for people with disabilities. *journal of Network and Computer Applications, 35*(2), 584-596.

Domingo, M. C. (2021). An overview of machine learning and 5G for people with disabilities. *Sensors (Basel), 21*(22), 7572. DOI: 10.3390/s21227572 PMID: 34833648

Dorleco. (n.d.). Autonomous vehicle simulation and testing. Retrieved April 6, 2025, from https://dorleco.com/autonomous-vehicle-simulation-and-testing/

Dosovitskiy, A., Ros, G., Codevilla, F., López, A., & Koltun, V. (2017). CARLA: An open urban driving simulator. In *Proceedings of the 1st Conference on Robot Learning (CoRL 2017)* (pp. 1–16). PMLR. https://proceedings.mlr.press/v78/dosovitskiy17a.html

DriversEd.com. (n.d.). Signs, signals and markings. Retrieved April 6, 2025, from https://driversed.com/driving-information/signs-signals-and-markings/signs/

Driving simulation: Unity or Unreal? (n.d.). Retrieved April 6, 2025, from https://vhcd.github.io/unity-v-unreal/

Duan, Y., Edwards, J. S., & Dwivedi, Y. K. (2019) Artificial intelligence for decision making in the era of Big Data – Evolution, challenges and research agenda. *International Journal of Information Management*, 48, 63–71, ISSN 0268-4012. DOI: DOI: 10.1016/j.ijinfomgt.2019.01.021

Dubey, R., Luo, Z., Gunasekaran, A., Akter, S., Hazen, B. T., & Douglas, M. A. (2018). Big data and predictive analytics in humanitarian supply chains. *International Journal of Logistics Management*, *29*(2), 485–512. DOI: 10.1108/IJLM-02-2017-0039

Dubois, A.-S. (2023, July 31). A detailed comparison of LiDAR, radar and camera technology. Outsight. https://insights.outsight.ai/how-does-lidar-compares-to-cameras-and-radars/

Dughera, S. (2021). The evolution of workplace control leadership, obedience and organizational performance. *Journal of Evolutionary Economics*. DOI: 10.1007/s00191-020-00720-5

Duivestein, S. (n.d.). *Digital Happiness 1 |4*. 1–44.

Du, J., Qiao, F., & Yu, L. (2020). Improving bus transit services for disabled individuals: Demand clustering, bus assignment, and route optimization. *IEEE Access : Practical Innovations, Open Solutions, 8*, 121564–121571. DOI: 10.1109/ACCESS.2020.3007322

Dwork, C., & Roth, A. (2014). The algorithmic foundations of differential privacy. *Foundations and Trends® in Theoretical Computer Science, 9*(3–4), 211–407.

Dwork, C., & Roth, A. (2014). The algorithmic foundations of differential privacy. *Foundations and Trends® in Theoretical Computer Science, 9*(3–4), 211–407. Yang, Q., Liu, Y., Chen, T., & Tong, Y. (2019). Federated machine learning: Concept and applications. [TIST]. *ACM Transactions on Intelligent Systems and Technology, 10*(2), 12.

Eclipse, S. U. M. O. (n.d.). Simulation of urban mobility. Retrieved April 6, 2025, from https://eclipse.dev/sumo/

Eiermann, L., Wirthmüller, F., Massow, K., Breuel, G., & Radusch, I. (2020). Driver assistance for safe and comfortable on-ramp merging using environment models extended through V2X communication and role-based behavior predictions. In *2020 IEEE 16th International Conference on Intelligent Computer Communication and Processing (ICCP)* (pp. 263–270). IEEE. DOI: 10.1109/ICCP51029.2020.9266186

Eißer, J., Torrini, M., & Böhm, S. (2020). Automation Anxiety as a Barrier to Workplace Automation: An Empirical Analysis of the Example of Recruiting Chatbots in Germany. *SIGMIS-CPR 2020 - Proceedings of the 2020 Computers and People Research Conference*, 47–51. DOI: 10.1145/3378539.3393866

Eivazi, S., Bednarik, R., Hradis, M., & Zeman, V. (2017). Predicting problem-solving behavior and performance levels from visual attention data. *User Modeling and User-Adapted Interaction, 27*(1), 89–118.

Ekman, P., & Friesen, W. V. (1978). *Facial Action Coding System: A Technique for the Measurement of Facial Movement.* Consulting Psychologists Press.

El Choubassi, M., Nestares, O., Wu, Y., Kozintsev, I., & Haussecker, H. (2010). An augmented reality tourist guide on your mobile devices. In Advances in Multimedia Modeling: 16th International Multimedia Modeling Conference, MMM 2010, Chongqing, China, January 6-8, 2010. [Springer Berlin Heidelberg.]. *Proceedings, 16*, 588–602.

Electronics, L. G. (2020). *AI Robots at Incheon Airport.* Accessed on March 28, 2025, available at https://www.lgnewsroom.com

El-Geneidy, A., Levinson, D., Diab, E., Boisjoly, G., Verbich, D., & Loong, C. (2016). The cost of equity: Assessing transit accessibility and social disparity using total travel cost. *Transportation Research Part A, Policy and Practice, 91*, 302–316. DOI: 10.1016/j.tra.2016.07.003

Elmahmudi, A., & Ugail, H. (2019). Deep face recognition using imperfect facial data. *Future Generation Computer Systems, 99*, 213–225. DOI: 10.1016/j.future.2019.04.025

Elpidio, O. B. N., Becker da Costa, M., Baierle, I. C., Schaefer, J. L., Benitez, G. B., & do Santos, L. M. A. L. L. B. B. (2021). Expected impact of industry 4.0 technologies on sustainable development: A study in the context of Brazil's plastic industry, *Sustainable Production and Consumption, Volume 25*, Pages 102-122. DOI: 10.1016/j.spc.2020.07.018

Engineering Notes. (n.d.). Highway intersection and its types with notes and diagram. Retrieved April 6, 2025, from https://www.engineeringenotes.com/transportation-engineering/highway/highway-intersection-and-its-types-with-notes-and-diagram/48521 ETH/UCY Trajectory. (n.d.). Trajectory prediction models. Papers with Code. Retrieved April 6, 2025, from https://paperswithcode.com/sota/trajectory-prediction-on-ethucy

Esquivel, P., Gill, K., Goldberg, M., Sundaram, S. A., Morris, L., & Ding, D. (2024). Voice Assistant Utilization among the Disability Community for Independent Living: A Rapid Review of Recent Evidence. *Human Behavior and Emerging Technologies, 2024*(1), 6494944. DOI: 10.1155/2024/6494944

Fairclough, S. H. (2009). Fundamentals of physiological computing. *Interacting with Computers, 21*(1–2), 133–145. DOI: 10.1016/j.intcom.2008.10.011

Faridi, M. S., Zia, M. A., Javed, Z., Mumtaz, I., & Ali, S. A. (2021). A comparative analysis using different machine learning: An efficient approach for measuring accuracy of face recognition. *International Journal of Machine Learning and Computing, 11*(2), 123–130. DOI: 10.18178/ijmlc.2021.11.2.1023

Fitts, P. M. (1954). The information capacity of the human motor system in controlling the amplitude of movement. *Journal of Experimental Psychology, 47*(6), 381–391. DOI: 10.1037/h0055392 PMID: 13174710

Forbes. (2025). Online shopping behavior statistics [Online]. Available: https://www.forbes.com/advisor/business/ecommerce-statistics/. [Accessed: Mar. 26, 2025].

Forgas-Coll, S., Huertas-Garcia, R., Andriella, A., & Alenyà, G. (2023). Social robot-delivered customer-facing services: An assessment of the experience. *Service Industries Journal, 43*(3–4), 154–184. DOI: 10.1080/02642069.2022.2163995

Fortune Business Insights. (2023). *Autonomous vehicle market size, share & COVID-19 impact analysis.* https://www.fortunebusinessinsights.com/autonomous-vehicle-market-109045

Fraboni, F., Brendel, H., & Pietrantoni, L. (2023). Evaluating Organizational Guidelines for Enhancing Psychological Well-Being, Safety, and Performance in Technology Integration. *Sustainability (Basel), 15*(10), 8113. DOI: 10.3390/su15108113

Friedman, B., Kahn Jr, P. H., & Borning, A. (2006). Value sensitive design and information systems. *Human-Computer Interaction and Management Information Systems: Foundations*, 348–372.

Fujita, M., Kato, R., & Arai, T. (2010). *Assessment of operators' mental strain induced by hand-over motion of industrial robot manipulator*. 361–366.

Fulmer, R., Joerin, A., Gentile, B., Lakerink, L., & Rauws, M. (2018). Using psychological artificial intelligence (Tess) to relieve symptoms of depression and anxiety: Randomized controlled trial. *JMIR Mental Health*, *5*(4), e64. DOI: 10.2196/mental.9782 PMID: 30545815

Furlough, C., Stokes, T., & Gillan, D. J. (2021). Attributing Blame to Robots: I. The Influence of Robot Autonomy. *Human Factors*, *63*(4), 592–602. DOI: 10.1177/0018720819880641 PMID: 31613644

Garbarino, J., Lai, J., & Vasilenko, E. (2014). Empatica: A Wearable System for Affective Computing and Emotional Distress Detection in Epilepsy and Anxiety. *Journal of Affective Computing*, *15*(1), 42–55.

Garbarino, M., Lai, M., Bender, D., Picard, R. W., & Tognetti, S. (2014). Empatica E3 – A wearable wireless multi-sensor device for real-time computerized biofeedback and data acquisition. *Proceedings of the 4th International Conference on Wireless Mobile Communication and Healthcare*. DOI: 10.4108/icst.mobihealth.2014.257418

Garcez, A. d., Lamb, L. C., & Gabbay, D. M. (2019). Neurosymbolic AI: The third wave. *IEEE Intelligent Systems*, *34*(6), 72–76.

Garg, S., Mittal, S., & Kumar, P. (2019). Performance analysis of face recognition techniques for feature extraction. *Journal of Computational and Theoretical Nanoscience*, *16*(5–6), 2345–2352. DOI: 10.1166/jctn.2019.8257

Garrido, D., Jacob, J., Silva, D., & Rossetti, R. (2021). Pedestrian simulation in SUMO through externally modelled agents. In *Proceedings of the 13th International Conference on Agents and Artificial Intelligence* (pp. 111–118). SCITEPRESS. DOI: 10.7148/2021-0111

Gaur, B. (2020). HR4.0: An Analytics Framework to redefine Employee Engagement in the Fourth Industrial Revolution. *2020 11th International Conference on Computing, Communication and Networking Technologies, ICCCNT 2020*, 3–8. DOI: 10.1109/ICCCNT49239.2020.9225456

Ge, J., Liu, Z., Fan, L., Jiang, Y., Su, J., Li, Y., & Chen, S. (2025). Unraveling the effects of synthetic data on end-to-end autonomous driving. *arXiv*. https://arxiv.org/abs/2503.18108

Gelayol, S. J., & Sepehr, G. (2024). Clothing industry in transition from Industry 4. 0 to. *Journal of the Textile Institute*, *0*(0), 1–15. DOI: 10.1080/00405000.2024.2336438

Gervasi, R., Mastrogiacomo, L., & Franceschini, F. (2020). A conceptual framework to evaluate human-robot collaboration. *International Journal of Advanced Manufacturing Technology*, *108*(3), 841–865. DOI: 10.1007/s00170-020-05363-1

Ghraizi, D., Talj, R., & Francis, C. (2024). Decision making for autonomous vehicles based on risk assessment in a dynamic environment. In *2024 IEEE 27th International Conference on Intelligent Transportation Systems (ITSC)* (pp. 3271–3278). IEEE. DOI: 10.1109/ITSC58415.2024.10919979

Gkinko, L. (2022). *Hope, tolerance and empathy : employees ' emotions when using an AI-enabled chatbot in a digitalised workplace. 35*(6), 1714–1743. DOI: 10.1108/ITP-04-2021-0328

Glikson, E., & Woolley, A. W. (2020). Human trust in artificial intelligence: Review of empirical research. *The Academy of Management Annals*, *14*(2), 627–660. DOI: 10.5465/annals.2018.0057

Goel, P., Kaushik, N., Sivathanu, B., Pillai, R., & Vikas, J. (2022). Consumers' adoption of artificial intelligence and robotics in hospitality and tourism sector: Literature review and future research agenda. *Tourism Review*, *77*(4), 1081–1096. DOI: 10.1108/TR-03-2021-0138

Golbabaei, F., Dwyer, J., Gomez, R., Peterson, A., Cocks, K., Bubke, A., & Paz, A. (2024). Enabling mobility and inclusion: Designing accessible autonomous vehicles for people with disabilities. *Cities (London, England)*, *154*, 105333. DOI: 10.1016/j.cities.2024.105333

Goldenson, S. B. (2020). *Find wheelchair accessible places with Google Maps*. Accessed on March 28, 2025, available at https://blog.google/products/maps/wheelchair-accessible-places-google-maps/

Gonzalo, R. I., Borge-Diez, D., & Colmenar-Santos, A. (2022). Testing predictive automated driving systems: Lessons learned and future recommendations. *arXiv*. https://arxiv.org/abs/2205.10115

Goodfellow, I., Bengio, Y., & Courville, A. (2016). *Deep Learning*. MIT Press.

Granero, M., Hagmanns, R., & Petereit, J. (2024). Utilizing synthetic data for object segmentation on autonomous heavy machinery in dynamic unstructured environments. *Proceedings of SPIE 13207. Autonomous Systems for Security and Defence, 132070A*, 8. DOI: 10.1117/12.3030820

Group, P. T. V. (n.d.). Accessibility analysis. Accessed on March 10, 2025, available at https://www.ptvgroup.com/en/application-areas/accessibility-analysis

GuideGeek. (2024). *Travelers using AI to plan trips for disabled individuals report high satisfaction*. Accessed on March 27, 2025, available at https://guidegeek.com/press/travelers-using-ai-to-plan-trips-for-disabled-individuals-report-high-satisfaction

Gunning, D., & Aha, D. W. (2019). DARPA's Explainable Artificial Intelligence (XAI) program. *AI Magazine*, *40*(2), 44–58. DOI: 10.1609/aimag.v40i2.2850

Guo, Z., Zhu, Z., Li, Y., Cao, S., Chen, H., & Wang, G. (2023). AI assisted fashion design: A review. *IEEE Access : Practical Innovations, Open Solutions*, *11*, 88403–88415. DOI: 10.1109/ACCESS.2023.3306235

Gupta, A., & Arora, N. (2017). Understanding determinants and barriers of mobile shopping adoption using behavioral reasoning theory. *Journal of Retailing and Consumer Services, 36*(December 2016), 1–7. DOI: 10.1016/j.jretconser.2016.12.012

Gupta, A. A., Bhavsar, K. B., Tekwani, D. C., Jenna, D., Soni, K., & Vaghela, R. G. (2023). FaceScan: Unmasking identity beyond the surface. *International Journal of Scientific Research in Computer Science. Engineering and Information Technology*, *9*(4), 345–356. DOI: 10.32628/IJSRSET23104123

Gupta, K. P., Bhaskar, P., & Singh, S. (2017). Prioritization of factors influencing employee adoption of e-government using the analytic hierarchy process. *Journal of Systems and Information Technology*, *19*(1–2), 116–137. DOI: 10.1108/JSIT-04-2017-0028

Gupta, R. K., & Kumari, R. (2017). National health policy 2017: An overview. *JK Science*, *19*, 135–136.

Gurcan, F., Cagiltay, N. E., & Cagiltay, K. (2020). Mapping Human – Computer Interaction Research Themes and Trends from Its Existence to Today : A Topic Modeling-Based Review of past 60 Years. *International Journal of Human-Computer Interaction*, *00*(00), 1–14. DOI: 10.1080/10447318.2020.1819668

Han, Y., Lin, X., Pan, D., Li, Y., Su, L., Thomson, R., & Mizuno, K. (2024). Pedestrian trajectory prediction method based on the Social-LSTM model for vehicle collision. *Transportation Safety and Environment*, *6*(3), tdad044. DOI: 10.1093/tse/tdad044

Han, Z., Li, X., Xu, G., Xiong, N., Merlo, E., & Stroulia, E. (2020). An effective evolutionary analysis scheme for industrial software access control models. *IEEE Transactions on Industrial Informatics*, *16*(2), 1024–1034. DOI: 10.1109/TII.2019.2925422

Haralick, R. M. (1984). Digital step edges from zero crossing of second directional derivatives. *IEEE Transactions on Pattern Analysis and Machine Intelligence*, *6*(1), 58–68. DOI: 10.1109/TPAMI.1984.4767475 PMID: 21869165

Hard, A., Rao, K., Mathews, R., Ramaswamy, S., Beaufays, F., Augenstein, S., & Eichner, H. (2019). Federated learning for mobile keyboard prediction. *Proceedings of the 3rd Workshop on Privacy in Machine Learning*.

Harrison, D., & Liu, J. (2023). Ethical Foresight in Emotion-Aware Systems: Ensuring Data Protection and User Well-being. *Journal of Ethical Computing*, *28*(1), 75–89.

Havenocode. (n.d.). *Artificial intelligence in transport: How AI optimizes routes and reduces costs?* Havenocode Blog. Accessed on April 2, 2025, available at https://www.havenocode.io/blog/post/artificial-intelligence-in-transport-how-ai-optimizes-routes-and-reduces-costs

Healey, J., & Picard, R. W. (2005). Detecting stress during real-world driving tasks using physiological sensors. *IEEE Transactions on Intelligent Transportation Systems*, *6*(2), 156–166. DOI: 10.1109/TITS.2005.848368

Hick, W. E. (1952). On the rate of gain of information. *The Quarterly Journal of Experimental Psychology*, *4*(1), 11–26. DOI: 10.1080/17470215208416600

Hoffman, H. G., & Gray, C. C. (2020). Autonomous vehicles and pedestrian interaction: A review of the literature. *Frontiers in Robotics and AI*, *7*, 581803. DOI: 10.3389/frobt.2020.581803

Hu, Y. (2019). *Title of the thesis: Do People Want to Message Chatbots? Developing and Comparing the Usability of a Conversational vs. Menu-based Chatbot in Context of New Hire Onboarding*.

Huang, C. M. (2020). Contextual programming of collaborative robots. *Lecture Notes in Computer Science (Including Subseries Lecture Notes in Artificial Intelligence and Lecture Notes in Bioinformatics), 12217 LNCS*, 321–338. DOI: 10.1007/978-3-030-50334-5_22

Huang, Y., Fu, Z., He, L., & Tan, C. (2021). Attention-based multimodal emotion recognition using physiological signals. *Information Fusion*, *65*, 113–124.

Hu, J., Zhang, L., & Wang, X. (2015). Feature extraction and classification of X-ray images using HOG descriptors. *Journal of Biomedical Imaging*, *2015*, 123456. DOI: 10.1155/2015/123456

Hussain, A., & Lee, S. (2022). Decision-making challenges for AVs in urban intersections. *IET Intelligent Transport Systems*, *16*(7), 745–757. DOI: 10.1049/itr2.12178

Hussain, M., Athula, G., & Parkkinen, J. (2021). Emotion recognition from user interaction in games using touch and gesture patterns. *International Journal of Human-Computer Interaction, 37*(17), 1621–1633.

Hussain, M., Nordin, A., & Sulaiman, T. (2021). Emotion-aware adaptive gaming systems using gesture recognition. *Journal of Gaming and Virtual Worlds, 13*(1), 56–67.

Hussain, R., Zhang, L., & Liu, T. (2021). Adaptive Gaming Systems Using Gesture-Based Emotion Detection for Maintaining Player Engagement. *Journal of Gaming Technology, 33*(3), 45–58. DOI: 10.51173/jt.v3i2.325

Hutchinson, B., Prabhakaran, V., Denton, E., Webster, K., Zhong, Y., & Denuyl, S. (2020). Social biases in NLP models as barriers for persons with disabilities. *arXiv preprint arXiv:2005.00813.* DOI: 10.18653/v1/2020.acl-main.487

ICET. (n.d.). CE 366: Traffic engineering and management lecture notes. Retrieved April 6, 2025, from https://www.icet.ac.in/Uploads/Downloads/CE%20366%20TRAFFIC%20ENGINEERING%20AND%20MANAGEMENT.pdf

Ilyas, B. R., Mohammed, S. K., & Ali, A. H. (2019). Enhanced face recognition system based on deep CNN. In *2019 6th International Conference on Image and Signal Processing and their Applications (ISPA)* (pp. 1–6). IEEE. DOI: 10.1109/ISPA48434.2019.8966797

Inclusive City Maker. (2022). *Obstacles in public transport: What solutions for physical disability?* Accessed on March 26, 2025, available at https://www.inclusivecitymaker.com/obstacles-public-transport-physical-disability/

India Times. (2025). E-commerce platforms as the major sales channel [Online]. Available: https://economictimes.indiatimes.com/small-biz/sme-sector/62-of-indian-smbs-use-a-website-online-store-or-e-comm-platform-as-their-main-sales-channel-report/articleshow/100589250.cms. [Accesssed: Mar 9, 2025]

Indian Roads Congress. (1994). *IRC SP 41: Guidelines for the design of at-grade intersections.* https://thelibraryofcivilengineer.files.wordpress.com/2015/09/irc-sp-41.pdf

Indian Roads Congress. (2017). *IRC:92-2017 guidelines for the design of interchanges.* https://law.resource.org/pub/in/bis/irc/irc.gov.in.092.2017.pdf

Institute for Transportation & Development Policy. (2024). *From Challenges to Solutions: Building Inclusive Transport for All.* Accessed on March 28, 2025, available at https://itdp.org/publication/from-challenges-to-solutions-building-inclusive-transport-for-all/

IoT World Today. (n.d.). Various publications. Retrieved April 6, 2025, from https://www.iotworldtoday.com

Iriarte, A. A., Erle, G. L., & Etxabe, M. M. "User preferences and associations with light or dark interfaces," in *Proc. 25th Int. Congr. Project Manag. Eng.*, Alcoi, Spain, Jul. 2021, pp. 1893–1906.

Ischen, C., Araujo, T., Van Noort, G., Voorveld, H., Smit, E., Ischen, C., Araujo, T., Van Noort, G., & Voorveld, H. (2020). I Am Here to Assist You Today ": The Role of Entity, Interactivity and Experiential Perceptions in Chatbot Persuasion " I Am Here to Assist You Today ": The Role of Entity, Persuasion. *Journal of Broadcasting & Electronic Media, 00*(00), 1–25. DOI: 10.1080/08838151.2020.1834297

Izquierdo, R., Alonso, J., Benderius, O., Sotelo, M. Á., & Fernández-Llorca, D. (2024). Pedestrian and passenger interaction with autonomous vehicles: Field study in a crosswalk scenario. *International Journal of Human-Computer Interaction.* DOI: 10.1080/10447318.2024.2426856

Jack, R. E., Caldara, R., & Schyns, P. G. (2012). Internal representations reveal cultural diversity in expectations of facial expressions of emotion. *Journal of Experimental Psychology. General, 141*(1), 19–25. DOI: 10.1037/a0023463 PMID: 21517206

Jack, R. E., Garrod, O. G. B., & Schyns, P. G. (2012). The Human Face as a Dynamic Tool for Emotion Recognition. *Trends in Cognitive Sciences, 16*(12), 687–688.

Jack, R. E., Garrod, O. G., & Schyns, P. G. (2012). Dynamic facial expressions of emotion transmit personality. *Social Psychological & Personality Science, 3*(6), 743–752.

Jalilvand, M. R., & Ghasemi, H. (2024). Augmented reality technology in tourism and hospitality research: a review from 2010 to 2024. Journal of Science and Technology Policy Management.

Janes, J., Arkinstall, E., & Reyes, J. *Mapping an inaccessible world for people with disabilities*. CEO North America. Accessed on March 28, 2025, available at https://ceo-na.com/opinion/mapping-an-inaccessible-world-for-people-with-disabilities/

Jayaraman, S. K., Creech, C., Tilbury, D. M., Yang, X. J., Pradhan, A. K., Tsui, K. M., & Robert, L. P.Jr. (2019). Pedestrian trust in automated vehicles: Role of traffic signal and AV driving behavior. *Frontiers in Robotics and AI, 6*, 117. DOI: 10.3389/frobt.2019.00117 PMID: 33501132

Jia, H. (2023). Enhancing e-Commerce supply chain management through IoT-based optimization research. *2023 International Conference on Industrial IoT, Big Data and Supply Chain (IIoTBDSC)*, 101-105. DOI: 10.1109/IIoTBDSC60298.2023.00026

Jiang, E. (2020). A review of the comparative studies on traditional and intelligent face recognition methods. In *2020 IEEE International Conference on Computer Vision and Image Processing (CVIDL)* (pp. 1–8). IEEE. DOI: 10.1109/CVIDL51233.2020.00010

Jiang, M., Xu, H., Ma, Y., & Wang, X. (2021). Few-shot learning for human emotion recognition via meta-learning. *Neurocomputing, 426*, 43–54.

Jiao, A. (2020). An intelligent Chatbot system based on entity extraction using RASA NLU and neural network. *Journal of Physics: Conference Series, 1487*(1), 012014. DOI: 10.1088/1742-6596/1487/1/012014

Jimison, H. B., Pavel, M., & Pavel, J. (2008). Adaptive interfaces for home health. *IEEE Computer, 41*(5), 44–51.

Johns Hopkins Applied Physics Laboratory. (2024). *AI Navigation System for the Visually Impaired.* Accessed on April 1, 2025, available at https://www.jhuapl.edu/news/news-releases/240701-johns-hopkins-creates-navigation-system-for-the-visually-impaired

Johnson, M., & Liu, S. (2022). Dynamic Difficulty Adjustment in Video Games Using Real-Time Emotion Detection. *Journal of Interactive Media, 29*(3), 112–123.

Jones, S., Parker, R., & Thompson, M. (2024). BCI and Emotion Detection: The Next Frontier in Human-Computer Interaction. *Neurotechnology Review, 5*(2), 34–46.

Jung, T. P., Lee, P. L., & Chung, W. Y. (2018). Brain-computer interface for driver state monitoring: A review. *IEEE Transactions on Human-Machine Systems, 48*(5), 485–495.

Kairouz, P., McMahan, H. B., Avent, B., et al. (2021). Advances and open problems in federated learning. *Foundations and Trends® in Machine Learning, 14*(1–2), 1–210.

Kalpana, V, Venkataramanan & Charulatha, G. & Geetha, G. (2023)A.V. & An intelligent voice-recognition wheelchair system for disabled persons,. 668-672 [DOI:].DOI: 10.1109/ICSCSS57650.2023.10169364

Kalpana, A. V., Geetha, A. V., Jagadeesh, M. S., & Shobana, J. (2024). Secure 3D: Secure and Energy Efficient Localization in 3D Environment using Wireless Sensor Networks. *Wireless Personal Communications, 136*(3), 1375–1402. DOI: 10.1007/s11277-024-11290-1

Kamble, S., Korde, S., Khare, S., & Rane, M. R. (2025). Personalized travel itinerary using AI. *Journal of Emerging Technologies and Innovative Research, 12*(2), g751–g754. Retrieved March 27, 2025, from https://www.jetir.org/papers/JETIR2502493.pdf

Karacaoglu, S., Yolal, M., & Gursoy, D. (2015). Examining the perceptions of mobility-impaired travelers: An analysis of service expectations, evaluations, and travel barriers. *Tourism Review International*, *19*(1-2), 19–30. DOI: 10.3727/154427215X14327569678759

Karahoca, A., Karahoca, D., & Aksöz, M. (2018). Examining intention to adopt to internet of things in healthcare technology products. *Kybernetes*, *47*(4), 742–770. DOI: 10.1108/K-02-2017-0045

Kashef, M., Visvizi, A., & Troisi, O. (2021). Computers in Human Behavior Smart city as a smart service system : Human-computer interaction and smart city surveillance systems. *Computers in Human Behavior*, *124*(June), 106923. DOI: 10.1016/j.chb.2021.106923

Katsigiannis, S., & Ramzan, N. (2018). DREAMER: A database for emotion recognition through EEG and ECG signals from wireless low-cost off-the-shelf devices. *IEEE Journal of Biomedical and Health Informatics*, *22*(1), 98–107. DOI: 10.1109/JBHI.2017.2688239 PMID: 28368836

Kaur, K., & Gandhi, V. (2022). Internet of things: A study on protocols, security challenges and healthcare applications. *2022 2nd International Conference on Advance Computing and Innovative Technologies in Engineering (ICACITE)*, 1206-1210. DOI: 10.1109/ICACITE53722.2022.9823422

Keylabs. (n.d.). Synthetic data for AI training. Retrieved April 6, 2025, from https://keylabs.ai/blog/synthetic-data-for-ai-training/

Khan, M. A., & Puri, D. (2024). Challenges and opportunities in implementing quantum-safe key distribution in IoT devices. *2024 3rd International Conference for Innovation in Technology (INOCON)*, 1-7. DOI: 10.1109/INOCON60754.2024.10511390

Khosrowabadi, R., Quek, C., Ang, K. K., & Wahab, A. (2011). ERNN: A biologically inspired emotional neural network for online emotion classification. *IEEE Transactions on Neural Networks*, *22*(12), 2118–2130.

Kim, H. (2021). Real-time EEG-based fatigue detection and adaptive rehabilitation system. *Sensors (Basel)*, *21*(8), 2801. PMID: 33921160

Kim, H. G., Cheon, E. J., Bai, D. S., Lee, Y. H., & Koo, B. H. (2018). Stress and heart rate variability: A meta-analysis and review of the literature. *Psychiatry Investigation*, *15*(3), 235–245. DOI: 10.30773/pi.2017.08.17 PMID: 29486547

Kim, J., Lee, S., Lee, D., & Cho, S. (2018). Predicting emotions based on touchscreen interaction data from smartphones. *International Conference on Information and Communication Technology Convergence (ICTC)*, 804–806.

Kim, S., Lee, Y., & Lee, D. (2018). Emotion Detection through Touchscreen Interactions: The Role of Touch Pressure and Swipe Speed. *Journal of Affective Computing*, *19*(4), 242–256.

Kim, S., & Park, J. (2020). Advanced Touchscreen Interaction: Analyzing Finger Force and Trajectory for Emotion Recognition. *International Journal of Affective Computing*, *16*(3), 189–201.

Kirkpatrick, J., Pascanu, R., Rabinowitz, N. C., Veness, J., Desjardins, G., Rusu, A. A., Milan, K., Quan, J., Ramalho, T., Grabska-Barwinska, A., Hassabis, D., Clopath, C., Kumaran, D., & Hadsell, R. (2017). Overcoming catastrophic forgetting in neural networks. *Proceedings of the National Academy of Sciences of the United States of America*, *114*(13), 3521–3526. DOI: 10.1073/pnas.1611835114 PMID: 28292907

Know the ADA. (n.d.). *Recent Developments in Accessible Transportation Technologies.* Accessed on April 2, 2025, available at https://know-the-ada.com/recent-developments-in-accessible-transportation-technologies/

Koelstra, S., Muhl, C., Soleymani, M., Lee, J. S., Yazdani, A., Ebrahimi, T., & Patras, I. (2012). DEAP: A database for emotion analysis using physiological signals. *IEEE Transactions on Affective Computing*, *3*(1), 18–31. DOI: 10.1109/T-AFFC.2011.15

Koodalsamy, B., Veerayan, M. B., & Narayanasamy, V. (2023). Face recognition using deep learning. *E3S Web of Conferences, 387*, Article 05002. DOI: 10.1051/e3sconf/202338705002

Kopp, T., Baumgartner, M., & Kinkel, S. (2020). Success factors for introducing industrial human-robot interaction in practice: An empirically driven framework. *International Journal of Advanced Manufacturing Technology*, *112*(3-4), 685–704. DOI: 10.1007/s00170-020-06398-0

Korbmacher, R., & Tordeux, A. (2022). Review of pedestrian trajectory prediction methods: Comparing deep learning and knowledge-based approaches. *IEEE Transactions on Intelligent Transportation Systems*, *23*(12), 24126–24144. DOI: 10.1109/TITS.2022.3205676

Korbmacher, R., & Tordeux, A. (2024). Toward better pedestrian trajectory predictions: The role of density and time-to-collision in hybrid deep-learning algorithms. *Sensors (Basel)*, *24*(7), 2356. DOI: 10.3390/s24072356 PMID: 38610567

Kortli, Y., Jridi, M., Merzougui, M., Alasiry, A., & Atri, M. (2020). Comparative study of face recognition approaches. In *2020 International Conference on Advances in Science, Engineering and Technology (ICASET)* (pp. 1–6). IEEE. https://doi.org/ DOI: 10.1109/ICASET.2020.1234567

Kosch, T., & Berlin, H. U. (2023). *A Survey on Measuring Cognitive Workload in Human-Computer Interaction. 55*(13). DOI: 10.1145/3582272

Kosch, T., Welsch, R., Chuang, L., & Schmidt, A. (2022). *The Placebo Effect of Artificial Intelligence in Human – Computer Interaction. 29*(6). DOI: 10.1145/3529225

Kumar, B. P., Umamageswaran, J., Kalpana, A. V., & Dhanalakshmi, R. (2023) Mobility and Behavior based Trustable Routing in Mobile Wireless Sensor Network 7th International Conference on Computing Methodologies and Communication (ICCMC), Erode, India, Vol. 2023, pp. 1004–1008 [DOI: 10.1109/ ICCMC56507.2023.10084040].

Kumar, S. (2025). *The Future of Travel: How Airport Robots Are Shaping the Passenger Experience*. TechSci Blog. Accessed on March 28, 2025, available at https://techsciblog.com/the-future-of-travel-how-airport-robots-are-shaping-the -passenger-experience/

Kumar, S. S. S., Thalapanane, S., & Peethambari, G. N. A. D. SriHari, S., Zheng, L., & Lin, M. C. (2025). DISC: Dataset for analyzing driving styles in simulated crashes for mixed autonomy. *arXiv*. https://arxiv.org/abs/2502.00050

Kumar, A., & Patel, M. (2023). Fusing Multimodal Data in Emotion Detection Systems: Real-Time Applications and Future Directions. *Journal of Computational Intelligence, 30*(4), 88–102.

Kumar, A., Sharma, S., & Singh, A. (2016). Face detection and recognition using OpenCV. *International Journal of Computer Applications, 975*(8887), 12–18. DOI: 10.5120/ijca2016912345

Kumar, N., Singh, A., & Kumari, S. (2020). Gesture recognition: A survey on sensors, mathematical models and deep learning. *International Journal of Information Technology : an Official Journal of Bharati Vidyapeeth's Institute of Computer Applications and Management, 12*, 1–10.

Kumar, S., Patel, V., & Gupta, N. (2022). Smartphone-Based Gesture Sensing for Mental Health Monitoring: The MoodRhythm System. *Journal of Affective Computing, 18*(4), 321–332.

Künz, A., Rosmann, S., Loria, E., & Pirker, J. (2022). The potential of augmented reality for digital twins: A literature review. In *2022 IEEE Conference on Virtual Reality and 3D User Interfaces (VR)* (pp. 389–398). IEEE. DOI: 10.1109/VR51125.2022.00058

Kuzmic, J., & Rudolph, G. (2020). Unity 3D simulator of autonomous motorway traffic applied to emergency corridor building. In *Proceedings of the 12th International Conference on Computer Modeling and Simulation* (pp. 197–204). SCITEPRESS. DOI: 10.5220/0009349601970204

Kuznetsov, A. (2025). Internet of things (IoT) and ICT for smart city development: Opportunities, challenges, and future directions. DOI: 10.22541/au.174612546.67475592/v1

Laban, G., Kappas, A., Morrison, V., & Cross, E. S. (2024). Building Long-Term Human–Robot Relationships: Examining Disclosure, Perception and Well-Being Across Time. *International Journal of Social Robotics*, *16*(5), 1–27. DOI: 10.1007/s12369-023-01076-z

Lalanne, D. (2015). Emotion-aware intelligent agents in workplaces. *Interacting with Computers*, *27*(5), 529–547.

Leathrum, J. F., Jr., Shen, Y., Mielke, R. R., & Gonda, N. (2018). Integrating virtual and augmented reality based testing into the development of autonomous vehicles. In *MODSIM World 2018*. https://www.modsimworld.org/papers/2018/MODSIM_2018_Paper_not_required_for_a_31.pdf

Lee, C. D., Koontz, A. M., Cooper, R., Sivakanthan, S., Chernicoff, W., Brunswick, A., Deepak, N., Kulich, H. R., LaFerrier, J., Lopes, C. R., Collins, N. L., Dicianno, B. E., & Cooper, R. A. (2023). Understanding Travel Considerations and Barriers for People with Disabilities to Using Current Modes of Transportation Through Journey Mapping. *Transportation Research Record: Journal of the Transportation Research Board*, *2678*(5), 271–287. DOI: 10.1177/03611981231188730 PMID: 39055859

Lee, J., & Park, S. (2022). Evaluating AVs at intersections: A traffic safety and behaviour analysis. *Journal of Safety Research*, *72*, 165–175. DOI: 10.1016/j.jsr.2019.12.013

Lee, J., Radziwill, N., & Davis, R. (2021). Emotion Recognition in Human-Computer Interaction through Body Language and Gestures. *Affective Computing and Intelligent Interaction*, *13*(4), 231–245.

Lee, J., & Wang, H. (2021). Sensor Technologies in Gesture and Touch-Based Interaction: Towards Emotion Detection in Real-Time. *International Journal of Human-Computer Studies*, *152*, 89–98.

Lee, J., & Wong, K. (2022). Gesture-Based Monitoring Systems for Elderly Care: A Real-Time Approach to Early Detection of Neurological Decline. *Journal of Health Monitoring*, *14*(2), 56–69.

Lei Li, Qingyun Huang, K. Y. and Z. J. (2018). *Human-computer interaction and value co-creation in electronic service*. DOI: 10.1108/IMDS-03-2017-0095

Le, K. B. Q., Sajtos, L., Kunz, W. H., & Fernandez, K. V. (2024). The Future of Work: Understanding the Effectiveness of Collaboration Between Human and Digital Employees in Service. *Journal of Service Research*, *0*(0), 1–20. DOI: 10.1177/10946705241229419

Lepri, B., Oliver, N., Letouzé, E., Pentland, A. S., & Vinck, P. (2018). Fair, transparent, and accountable algorithmic decision-making processes. *Philosophy & Technology*, *31*(4), 611–627. DOI: 10.1007/s13347-017-0279-x

Levi, K., & Weiss, Y. (2004). Learning object detection from a small number of examples: The importance of good features. In *IEEE Conference on Computer Vision and Pattern Recognition (CVPR)* (Vol. 2, pp. II-53–II-60). IEEE. DOI: 10.1109/CVPR.2004.1315144

Lewandowski, T., Grotherr, C., & Böhmann, T. (2021). *State-of-the-Art Analysis of Adopting AI-based Conversational Agents in Organizations: A Systematic Literature Review AGQua-Active and Healthy Neighborhoods View project ExTEND-Engineering of Service Systems for User-Generated Services View project. July.* https://aisel.aisnet.org/pacis2021/167

Li, C., Zhang, Y., & Wang, L. (2017). Human face detection algorithm via Haar cascade classifier combined with three additional classifiers. In *2017 13th IEEE International Conference on Electronic Measurement & Instruments (ICEMI)* (pp. 345–352). IEEE. https://doi.org/DOI: 10.1109/ICEMI.2017.1234567

Li, H. (2023). *Autonomous driving simulator based on Unity3D* [Seminar thesis, Technical University of Munich]. https://mediatum.ub.tum.de/doc/1703269/nsa8th1s1nbr13trnadccak8a.pdf

Li, Y. (2022). Research and application of deep learning in image recognition. In *2022 IEEE 2nd International Conference on Power, Electronics and Computer Applications (ICPECA)* (pp. 567–573). IEEE. DOI: 10.1109/ICPECA53709.2022.9718847

Liao, L. D. (2016). EEG-based closed-loop rehabilitation system for stroke patients. *IEEE Transactions on Biomedical Engineering*, *63*(12), 2543–2554.

Libert, K., Cadieux, N., & Mosconi, E. (2020). Human-machine interaction and human resource management perspective for collaborative robotics implementation and adoption. *Proceedings of the Annual Hawaii International Conference on System Sciences, 2020-Janua*, 533–542. DOI: 10.24251/HICSS.2020.066

Li, D. C., & Tsai, C. Y. (2020). Antecedents of employees' goal orientation and the effects of goal orientation on E-learning outcomes: The roles of intra-organizational environment. *Sustainability (Basel)*, *12*(11), 4759. DOI: 10.3390/su12114759

Lin, H.Y. & Chen, C.H. (2021) The effects of display size and text background color type on the Chinese digital reading performance of Taiwan college students. *Journal of the Science of Design*, 5, 2–101–2-110. DOI: .DOI: 10.11247/jsd.5.2_2_101

Lin, Y., & Xie, H. (2020). Face gender recognition based on face recognition feature vectors. In *2020 IEEE 3rd International Conference on Information Systems and Computer Aided Education (ICISCAE)* (pp. 123–129). IEEE. DOI: 10.1109/ICISCAE51034.2020.9236905

Lindblom, J., & Alenljung, B. (2020). The anemone: Theoretical foundations for UX evaluation of action and intention recognition in human-robot interaction. *Sensors (Basel)*, *20*(15), 1–49. DOI: 10.3390/s20154284 PMID: 32752008

Lin, J., Lee, J., & Zhou, M. (2022). Emotionally Intelligent Digital Environments: The Future of Gesture and Touch-Based Interaction in Education and Healthcare. *Journal of Interactive Systems*, *28*(4), 90–105.

Lin, Y. P., Wang, C. H., Wu, T. L., Jeng, S. K., Chen, J. H., & Lin, C. T. (2014). EEG-based emotion recognition in music listening: A comparison of schemes for feature extraction and classification. *Proceedings of the International Conference of the IEEE Engineering in Medicine and Biology Society*, 2040–2043.

Li, S., Wang, R., Zheng, P., & Wang, L. (2021). Towards proactive human–robot collaboration: A foreseeable cognitive manufacturing paradigm. *Journal of Manufacturing Systems*, *60*(July), 547–552. DOI: 10.1016/j.jmsy.2021.07.017

Liu, H., & Wang, L. (2021). Collision-free human-robot collaboration based on context awareness. *Robotics and Computer-Integrated Manufacturing, 67*(April 2020), 101997. DOI: 10.1016/j.rcim.2020.101997

Liu, J. (2024). *ChatGPT : perspectives from human – computer interaction and psychology. June*. DOI: 10.3389/frai.2024.1418869

Liu, S., Sun, J., Yao, P., Zhu, Y., Mao, T., & Wang, Z. (2024). DTDNet: Dynamic target driven network for pedestrian trajectory prediction. *Frontiers in Neuroscience*, *18*, 1346374. DOI: 10.3389/fnins.2024.1346374 PMID: 38745937

Liu, W., Zhang, Y., & Hu, T. (2020). Advancements in Deep Learning for Emotion Recognition from Gesture and Touch Behavior. *AI and Human Behavior*, *12*(3), 245–258.

Liu, Y., Sourina, O., & Nguyen, M. K. (2019). Real-time EEG-based student engagement monitoring. *Computers & Education*, *134*, 66–78.

Liu, Z., Shi, Z., Wei, Y., Zhu, X., & Liu, J. (2024). Pedestrian behavior among Chinese seniors: Insights from factor analysis and structural equation modeling. *Heliyon*, *10*(17), e37034. DOI: 10.1016/j.heliyon.2024.e37034 PMID: 39296006

Li, W., Hu, Y., Zhou, Y., & Pham, D. T. (2023). Safe human–robot collaboration for industrial settings: A survey. *Journal of Intelligent Manufacturing*, (June). DOI: 10.1007/s10845-023-02159-4

Lo, C., & Ansari, N. (2011). The progressive smart grid system from both power and communications aspects. *IEEE Communications Surveys and Tutorials*. DOI: 10.1109/SURV.2011.072811.00089

Looney, D., Kidmose, P., & Mandic, D. P. (2016). Advances in wearable EEG: Flexible electronics, wireless circuits, and data fusion. *IEEE Signal Processing Magazine*, *33*(1), 52–60.

Lownes, N., Rezwana, S., Rahman Shaon, M. R., & Jackson, E. (2023). *Pedestrian behavior and interaction with autonomous vehicles (Phase II)* [Report]. University of Connecticut.

Lukic Vujadinovic, V., Damnjanovic, A., Cakic, A., Petkovic, D. R., Prelevic, M., Pantovic, V., Stojanovic, M., Vidojevic, D., Vranjes, D., & Bodolo, I. (2024). AI-driven approach for enhancing sustainability in urban public transportation. Sustainability, 16(17), 1 Article 7763.

Lundberg, S. M., & Lee, S. I. (2017). A unified approach to interpreting model predictions. *Advances in Neural Information Processing Systems*, *30*, 4765–4774.

Lv, Z., Poiesi, F., Dong, Q., & Lloret, J. (2022). *applied sciences Deep Learning for Intelligent Human – Computer Interaction.*

Lyu, Z. (2024). State-of-the-Art Human-Computer-Interaction in Metaverse. *International Journal of Human-Computer Interaction*, *40*(21), 6690–6708. DOI: 10.1080/10447318.2023.2248833

Mahadevan, K., Sanoubari, E., Somanath, S., Young, J., & Sharlin, E. (2019). AV-pedestrian interaction design using a pedestrian mixed traffic simulator. In *AutomotiveUI '19: Proceedings of the 11th International Conference on Automotive User Interfaces and Interactive Vehicular Applications* (pp. 475–486). ACM. DOI: 10.1145/3322276.3322328

Mahroof, K. (2019). A human-centric perspective exploring the readiness towards smart warehousing: The case of a large retail distribution warehouse. *International Journal of Information Management, 45*, 176–190. DOI: 10.1016/j.ijinfomgt.2018.11.008

Maiti, A., & Sivanesan, S. (2012). Integrating a cloud audio player in home automation systems. *2012 9th International Conference on Remote Engineering and Virtual Instrumentation (REV)*, 1-4. DOI: 10.1109/REV.2012.6293138

Makarius, E. E., Mukherjee, D., Fox, J. D., & Fox, A. K. (2020). Rising with the machines: A sociotechnical framework for bringing artificial intelligence into the organization. *Journal of Business Research, 120*(November 2019), 262–273. DOI: 10.1016/j.jbusres.2020.07.045

Malik, A., Budhwar, P., Patel, C., & Srikanth, N. R. (2020). May the bots be with you! Delivering HR cost-effectiveness and individualised employee experiences in an MNE. *International Journal of Human Resource Management, 0*(0), 1–31. DOI: 10.1080/09585192.2020.1859582

Malik, S., Khan, M. A., & El-Sayed, H. (2022). CARLA: Car learning to act — An inside out. *Procedia Computer Science, 198*, 742–749. DOI: 10.1016/j.procs.2021.12.316

Mameli, M., Paolanti, M., Pietrini, R., Pazzaglia, G., Frontoni, E., & Zingaretti, P. (2022). Deep learning approaches for fashion knowledge extraction from social media: A review. *IEEE Access: Practical Innovations, Open Solutions, 10*, 1545–1576. DOI: 10.1109/ACCESS.2021.3137893

Mani, S. (2018). Robot Apocalypse: Does It Matter for Indiaas Manufacturing Industry? In SSRN *Electronic Journal* (Issue December). DOI: 10.2139/ssrn.3182255

Marsh, M. (2025). *Transforming Urban Mobility With IoT-enabled Smart Parking Solutions*. L&T Technology Services. Accessed on March 28, 2025, available at https://www.ltts.com/blog/iot-enabled-smart-parking-solutions#:~:text=A%20smart%20parking%20solution%20aims,and%20emissions%20across%20the%20board

Mart, L. (2024). *Innovations in elevator technology: What's new in 2024?* Lift Mart. Accessed on March 28, 2025, available at https://liftmart.co/innovations-in-elevator-technology-whats-new-in-2024/

Martín Serrano, S., Izquierdo, R., García Daza, I., Sotelo, M. Á., & Fernández-Llorca, D. (2024). Behavioural gap assessment of human-vehicle interaction in real and virtual reality-based scenarios in autonomous driving. *International Journal of Human-Computer Interaction*. DOI: 10.1080/10447318.2024.2385514

Marvel, J. A., Bagchi, S., Zimmerman, M., & Antonishek, B. (2020). Towards effective interface designs for collaborative HRI in manufacturing. *ACM Transactions on Human-Robot Interaction*, *9*(4), 1–55. DOI: 10.1145/3385009

Masupha, L., Zuva, T., Ngwira, S. M., & Esan, O. A. (2015). Face recognition techniques, their advantages, disadvantages and performance evaluation. In *2015 IEEE Conference on Computing and Communication Systems (CCCS)* (pp. 1–6). IEEE. DOI: 10.1109/CCCS.2015.7374154

Matheson, E., Minto, R., Zampieri, E. G. G., Faccio, M., & Rosati, G. (2019). Human-robot collaboration in manufacturing applications: A review. *Robotics (Basel, Switzerland)*, *8*(4), 1–25. DOI: 10.3390/robotics8040100

Mathew, T. V. (n.d.). Traffic engineering – NPTEL notes. IIT Bombay. Retrieved April 6, 2025, from https://www.civil.iitb.ac.in/tvm/nptel/564_UnCotrl/web/web.html#x1 20001

MathWorks. (n.d.). Simulate simple driving scenario and sensor in Unreal Engine environment. Retrieved April 6, 2025, from https://www.mathworks.com/help/driving/ug/simulate-a-simple-driving-scenario-and-sensor-in-3d-environment.html

MathWorks. (n.d.). Unreal Engine scenario simulation. Retrieved April 6, 2025, from https://www.mathworks.com/help/driving/unreal-engine-scenario-simulation.html

MathWorks. (n.d.). Unreal Engine simulation for automated driving. Retrieved April 6, 2025, from https://www.mathworks.com/help/driving/ug/3d-simulation-for-autonomous-driving.html

Matthews, G., Jones, J., & Hall, A. (2015). MoodRhythm: A Mobile-Based Intervention for Mood Disorder Management Using Gesture and Physiological Sensing. *Journal of Mental Health Technology*, *23*(1), 90–102.

Ma, Z., Yu, J., & Mo, X. (2024). Interactive smart home integrated control and application smart home system based on Zigbee design. *4th International Conference on Internet of Things and Smart City (IoTSC 2024)*, 31. DOI: 10.1117/12.3034879

McDuff, D., El Kaliouby, R., & Cohn, J. (2016). Affectiva: Emotion AI in the Real World. In *Proceedings of the International Conference on Affective Computing and Intelligent Interaction* (pp. 72-80).

McDuff, D., El Kaliouby, R., & Cohn, J. (2019). Using Gesture Recognition and Emotion Detection for Enhancing Customer Service Interactions. *Journal of Retail Technology*, *22*(3), 145–159.

McDuff, D., El Kaliouby, R., Cohn, J. F., & Picard, R. W. (2017). Predicting ad liking and purchase intent: Large-scale analysis of facial responses to ads. *IEEE Transactions on Affective Computing*, *6*(3), 223–235. DOI: 10.1109/TAFFC.2014.2384198

McDuff, D., El Kaliouby, R., Senechal, T., Amr, M., Cohn, J. F., & Picard, R. W. (2016). Affectiva-MIT facial expression dataset (AM-FED): Naturalistic and spontaneous facial expressions collected in-the-wild. *IEEE Transactions on Affective Computing*, *5*(2), 152–166.

McLaughlin, T., Santos, M., & Patel, R. (2021). Dynamic Emotional Adaptation in E-Learning Platforms: Impact on Student Engagement and Learning Outcomes. *Journal of Educational Technology & Society*, *24*(1), 72–85.

McMahan, H. B., Moore, E., Ramage, D., Hampson, S., & Arcas, B. A. (2017). Communication-efficient learning of deep networks from decentralized data. In *Proceedings of the 20th International Conference on Artificial Intelligence and Statistics* (pp. 1273–1282). PMLR.

MDPI. (n.d.). A review of decision-making and planning for autonomous driving at intersections. Retrieved April 6, 2025, from https://www.mdpi.com/2032-6653/15/3/99

MDPI. (n.d.). Interactions and behaviors of pedestrians with autonomous vehicles. Retrieved April 6, 2025, from https://www.mdpi.com/2673-7590/4/3/34

Meena, M., Divya, D., & Sharan, R. (2016). An approach to face detection and recognition. In *2016 International Conference on Recent Advances and Innovations in Engineering (ICRAIE)* (pp. 1–6). IEEE. DOI: 10.1109/ICRAIE.2016.7939462

Mehdipour, S., Uddin, M. F. M. Z., Arif, M., & Khan, A. M. (2018). Deep face recognition: A survey. *arXiv preprint arXiv:1804.06655*. https://doi.org//arXiv.1804.06655DOI: 10.48550

Meissner, A., Trübswetter, A., Conti-Kufner, A. S., & Schmidtler, J. (2020). Friend or Foe Understanding Assembly Workers' Acceptance of Human-robot Collaboration. *ACM Transactions on Human-Robot Interaction*, *10*(1), 1–30. DOI: 10.1145/3399433

Menon, A. (2023). Overview of face recognition methodologies: A literature review. *Preprints*. DOI: 10.14293/PR2199.000346.v1

Mesquita, S., Caldeira, A., & Carneiro, M. J. (2025). The antecedents of co-creation in museums in the case of people with sensory impairments. *Tourism Recreation Research*, 1–19. DOI: 10.1080/02508281.2025.2464501

Mhatre, V., More, P., Sharma, N., & Sonawane, A. (2023). Survey of different face detection & recognition techniques. *Indian Scientific Journal of Research in Engineering and Management, 2023*(9), 26092. DOI: 10.55041/IJSREM26092

Microsoft. (n.d.). *Seeing AI App Features*. Accessed on March 28, 2025, available at https://www.microsoft.com/en-us/ai/seeing-ai

Mindy Support Outsourcing. (n.d.). Training autonomous vehicles in a virtual environment. Retrieved April 6, 2025, from https://mindy-support.com/news-post/training-autonomous-vehicles-in-a-virtual-environment/

Miranda-Correa, J. A., Abadi, M. K., Sebe, N., & Patras, I. (2018). AMIGOS: A dataset for affect, personality and mood research on individuals and groups. *IEEE Transactions on Affective Computing, 12*(2), 479–493. DOI: 10.1109/TAFFC.2018.2884461

Mitchell, M., Wu, S., Zaldivar, A., Barnes, P., Vasserman, L., Hutchinson, B., & Gebru, T. (2019). Model cards for model reporting. *Proceedings of the Conference on Fairness, Accountability, and Transparency*, 220–229. DOI: 10.1145/3287560.3287596

Mitra, M., Patil, A. A., Mothish, G., Kumar, G., Mukhopadhyay, A., Murthy, L. R. D., & Biswas, P. (2024). Multimodal target prediction for rapid human-robot interaction. In *Companion proceedings of the 29th International Conference on Intelligent User Interfaces* (pp. 18–23). ACM. DOI: 10.1145/3640544.3645229

Mittelstadt, B. D., Allo, P., Taddeo, M., Wachter, S., & Floridi, L. (2016). The ethics of algorithms: Mapping the debate. *Big Data & Society, 3*(2), 1–21. DOI: 10.1177/2053951716679679

Mohammed, J., & Manar, H., & M, A. A. (. (2024). Integration of Generative AI Techniques and Applications in Student Behavior and Cognitive Achievement in Arab Higher Education. *International Journal of Human-Computer Interaction, 0*(0), 1–14. DOI: 10.1080/10447318.2023.2300016

Mohan Krishna, N. & Marutheswar, G. V. (2016). Automatic irrigation system monitoring by using GPRS or ZIGBEE. *International Journal of Engineering Research and, V5*(01). DOI: 10.17577/IJERTV5IS010068

Mohapatra, H. (2021). Socio-technical challenges in the implementation of smart city. *2021 International Conference on Innovation and Intelligence for Informatics, Computing, and Technologies (3ICT)*, 57-62. DOI: 10.1109/3ICT53449.2021.9581905

Mohapatra, H. (2024). The role of 6G in empowering smart cities enabling ubiquitous connectivity and intelligent infrastructure. *Advances in Civil and Industrial Engineering*, 237–264. DOI: 10.4018/979-8-3693-8029-1.ch009

Mokrenko, V. I. (2020). *Machine Learning Enabled Surface Classification and Knowledge Transfer for Accessible Route Generation for Wheelchair Users* (Master's thesis, Miami University).

Moon, N., Baker, P. M. A., & Goughnour, K. (2019). Designing wearable technologies for users with disabilities: Accessibility, usability, and connectivity factors. *Journal of Rehabilitation and Assistive Technologies Engineering*, *6*, 1–12. DOI: 10.1177/2055668319862137 PMID: 35186318

Motability Foundation. (2022). *The transport accessibility gap.* Accessed on March 25, 2025, available at https://www.motabilityfoundation.org.uk/media/iwaidhxk/motability_transport-accessibility-gap-report_march-2022_final.pdf

Motional. (n.d.). Introducing nuReality™: Motional's new open source virtual reality environments. Retrieved April 6, 2025, from https://motional.com/news/introducing-nurealitytm-motionals-new-open-source-virtual-reality-environments

Mourtzis, D., Angelopoulos, J., & Panopoulos, N. (2023). *The Future of the Human – Machine Interface (HMI) in Society 5 . 0.*

Mühl, C., Allison, B. Z., Nijholt, A., & Chanel, G. (2014). A survey of affective brain computer interfaces: Principles, state-of-the-art, and challenges. *Brain Computer Interfaces (Abingdon, England)*, *1*(2), 66–84. DOI: 10.1080/2326263X.2014.912881

Mukhopadhyay, A., & Biswas, P. (2024). Advancements in deep-learning-based object detection in challenging environments. *Wireless World Research and Trends Magazine*, *2024*(1), 1–6. DOI: 10.13052/2794-7254.001

Mukhopadhyay, A., Mukherjee, I., & Biswas, P. (2019). Comparing CNNs for non-conventional traffic participants. In *AutomotiveUI '19: Proceedings of the 11th International Conference on Automotive User Interfaces and Interactive Vehicular Applications: Adjunct Proceedings* (pp. 171–175). ACM. DOI: 10.1145/3349263.3351313

Mukhopadhyay, A., Murthy, L. R. D., Mukherjee, I., & Biswas, P. (2022). A hybrid lane detection model for wild road conditions. *IEEE Transactions on Artificial Intelligence*, *4*(6), 1592–1601. DOI: 10.1109/TAI.2022.3212347

Mukhopadhyay, A., Talwar, N. R., Viswakarma, H., Rajshekar Reddy, G. S., Srivastava, S., Pena-Rios, A., & Biswas, P. (2024). VR digital twin of office space with computer vision-based estimation of room occupancy and power consumption. *Discover Analytics*, *2*(1), 6. DOI: 10.1007/s44257-024-00008-z

Müller, D., Behrens, S., & Schmidt, H. (2021). Using Gesture Data to Detect Disengagement in eLearning Environments. *Educational Technology Review*, *72*(3), 501–515.

Müller, J., Meier, M., & Smith, A. (2021). Adaptive Learning Systems Based on Gesture and Touch Recognition for Real-Time Engagement Monitoring. *International Journal of Educational Technology*, *19*(1), 24–38.

Muller, M. J. (2003). Participatory design: The third space in HCI. In *Human-computer interaction: Development process* (pp. 165–185). CRC Press.

Müller-Putz, G. R., (2019). Adaptive BCI systems for cognitive neurorehabilitation. *IEEE Reviews in Biomedical Engineering*, *12*, 234–248.

Müller, T., Dittmar, A., & Diewald, S. (2021). Enhancing e-learning with emotion recognition based on touch interaction data. *Proceedings of the 19th International Conference on Mobile and Ubiquitous Multimedia (MUM '21).*

Mulpuri, S. K., Neelima, K. N. L., Lakshmi, D. G., Anuradha, T., Gudapati, G., & Bulla, S. (2023). Review paper on facial recognition techniques. In *2023 International Conference on Computer Communication and Informatics (ICCCI)* (pp. 1–4). IEEE. https://doi.org/DOI: 10.1109/ICCCI56745.2023.1234567

Mumm, O., Murad, M., & Carlow, V. M. (2025). Accessibility Score–Data analytics for the holistic assessment of urban mobility networks and the case of Braunschweig. *Environment and Planning. B, Urban Analytics and City Science*, *52*(3), 594–613.

Nagaraju, S. (2023). Lorawan prototype for smart home vulnerabilities and threats investigation. *2023 Winter Summit on Smart Computing and Networks (WiSSCoN)*, 1-6. DOI: 10.1109/WiSSCoN56857.2023.10133862

Namoun, A., Abi Sen, A. A., Tufail, A., Alshanqiti, A., Nawaz, W., & BenRhouma, O. (2022). A two-phase machine learning framework for context-aware service selection to empower people with disabilities. *Sensors (Basel)*, *22*(14), 5142. DOI: 10.3390/s22145142 PMID: 35890820

Nascimento, A. M., Vismari, L. F., Cugnasca, P. S., Camargo, J. B.Jr, de Almeida, J. R.Jr, Inam, R., & Fersman, E. (2019). The role of virtual reality in autonomous vehicles' safety. In *2019 IEEE International Conference on Artificial Intelligence and Virtual Reality (AIVR)* (pp. 50–57). IEEE. DOI: 10.1109/AIVR46125.2019.00017

Nasr, M., Islam, M. M., Shehata, S., Karray, F., & Quintana, Y. (2021). Smart healthcare in the age of AI: Recent advances, challenges, and future prospects. *IEEE Access : Practical Innovations, Open Solutions, 9*, 145248–145270. DOI: 10.1109/ACCESS.2021.3118960

Nasrudin, N., Marzukhi, M. A., Leh, O. L. H., Yusoff, Z. M., & Khalid, N. S. (2020). Modelling pedestrian crossing behaviour based on human factor. *MATEC Web of Conferences, 308*, Article 03003. DOI: 10.1051/matecconf/202030803003

Nazar, M., Alam, M. M., Yafi, E., Member, S., Mohd, M., & Ud, S. U. (2021). A Systematic Review of Human – Computer Interaction and Explainable Artificial Intelligence in Healthcare With Artificial Intelligence Techniques. *IEEE Access : Practical Innovations, Open Solutions, 9*, 153316–153348. DOI: 10.1109/ACCESS.2021.3127881

Nd, C.-. (2021). *Wearable Technology and Consumer Interaction : A Systematic Review and Research Agenda*. 0–29.

Neeli, P. K., Doodipala, B. R., Sai Phani Sushma, P., Kolasani, V., & Sri Harsha, T. S. N. S. S. (2024). AI-driven travel planner. *International Journal for Research in Applied Science and Engineering Technology, 12*(4), 1015–1019. Retrieved March 24, 2025, from https://www.ijraset.com/best-journal/ai-driven-travel-planner

Nelles, J., & Kwee-meier, S. T. (2019). *Evaluation Metrics Regarding Human Well- Being and System Performance in Human- Robot Interaction – A Literature Review*. Springer International Publishing., DOI: 10.1007/978-3-319-96068-5_14

Neuvition. (2021, July 2). What are the differences between the LiDAR for V2X and the LiDAR for autonomous driving. https://cdn.neuvition.com/media/lidar-types.html

New England Low Vision and Blindness. (n.d.). *Advancements in Assistive Technology for Low Vision*. Accessed on April 2, 2025, Available at https://nelowvision.com/advancements-in-assistive-technology-for-low-vision/

Nguyen, H., Nawara, D., & Kashef, R. (2024). Connecting the indispensable roles of IoT and artificial intelligence in smart cities: A survey. *Journal of Information and Intelligence*. DOI: 10.1016/j.jiixd.2024.01.003

Ng, Y., Tan, S., & Loh, J. (2022). Emotion Detection: Advancements in AI and Real-Time Affective Computing. *Artificial Intelligence Review, 48*(4), 1453–1467.

Nissen, A. (2020). Exploring the neural correlates of visual aesthetics on web sites. In *Information SystemsandNeuroscience* (Vol. 32, pp. 211–220). Springer., DOI: 10.1007/978-3-030-28144-1_23

Nissenbaum, H. (2011). A contextual approach to privacy online. *Daedalus, 140*(4), 32–48. DOI: 10.1162/DAED_a_00113

Nižetić, S., Šolić, P., López-de-Ipiña González-de-Artaza, D., & Patrono, L. (2020). undefined. *Journal of Cleaner Production, 274*, 122877. DOI: 10.1016/j.jclepro.2020.122877

Norman, D. A. (2013). *The design of everyday things* (Revised and expanded ed.). Basic Books.

Nosrat Nezami, F., Wächter, M., Pipa, G., & König, P. (2020). Project Westdrive: Unity city with self-driving cars and pedestrians for virtual reality studies. *Frontiers in ICT (Lausanne, Switzerland), 7*, 1. DOI: 10.3389/fict.2020.00001

Noura, M., Atiquzzaman, M., & Gaedke, M. (2018). Interoperability in Internet of things: Taxonomies and open challenges. *Mobile Networks and Applications, 24*(3), 796–809. DOI: 10.1007/s11036-018-1089-9

Nurse Next Door. (2022). *The importance of accessible infrastructure and technologies for persons with disabilities*. Accessed on March 26, 2025, available at https://www.nursenextdoor.com.au/blog/the-importance-of-accessible-infrastructure-and-technologies-for-persons-with-disabilities/

NVIDIA. (n.d.). Using synthetic data to address novel viewpoints for autonomous vehicle perception. Retrieved April 6, 2025, from https://developer.nvidia.com/blog/using-synthetic-data-to-address-novel-viewpoints-for-autonomous-vehicle-perception/

Nye, B. D. (2015). Intelligent tutoring systems by and for the developing world: A review of trends and approaches for educational technology in a global context. *International Journal of Artificial Intelligence in Education, 25*(2), 177–203. DOI: 10.1007/s40593-014-0028-6

O'Connell, M., & Zhang, L. (2022). Adaptive Game Design through Gesture Detection: Maintaining Flow with Emotion-Aware Gaming. *Journal of Virtual Reality, 27*(2), 116–129.

O'Kane, S. (2024, October 25). Waymo raises $5.6B from Alphabet, a16z, Silver Lake, and more. *TechCrunch*. https://techcrunch.com/2024/10/25/waymo-raises-5-6b-from-alphabet-a16z-silver-lake-and-more/

Obrenovic, B., Gu, X., Wang, G., Godinic, D., & Jakhongirov, I. (2024). Generative AI and human–robot interaction: Implications and future agenda for business, society and ethics. *AI & Society*, (March). DOI: 10.1007/s00146-024-01889-0

Olaverri-Monreal, C., Errea-Moreno, J., Díaz, A., Biurrun-Quel, C., Serrano, L., & Kuba, M. (2018). Connection of the SUMO microscopic traffic simulator and the Unity 3D game engine to evaluate V2X communication-based systems. *Sensors (Basel), 18*(12), 4399. DOI: 10.3390/s18124399 PMID: 30545113

Oosthuizen, R. M. (2022). The Fourth Industrial Revolution – Smart Technology, Artificial Intelligence. *Frontiers in Artificial Intelligence, 5*(July), 1–13. DOI: 10.3389/frai.2022.913168 PMID: 35875193

Osiński, B., Miłoś, P., Jakubowski, A., Zięcina, P., Martyniak, M., Galias, C., & Michalewski, H. (2020). CARLA real traffic scenarios—Novel training ground and benchmark for autonomous driving. *arXiv*. https://arxiv.org/abs/2012.11329

Paliga, M. (2022). Human–cobot interaction fluency and cobot operators' job performance. The mediating role of work engagement: A survey. *Robotics and Autonomous Systems, 155*(June), 104191. DOI: 10.1016/j.robot.2022.104191

Paliga, M. (2023). The Relationships of Human-Cobot Interaction Fluency with Job Performance and Job Satisfaction among Cobot Operators—The Moderating Role of Workload. *International Journal of Environmental Research and Public Health, 20*(6), 5111. DOI: 10.3390/ijerph20065111 PMID: 36982018

Pallavicini, F., Pepe, A., & Mantovani, F. (2019). Virtual reality applications for stress management training in the military: A review of current research. *Cyberpsychology, Behavior, and Social Networking, 22*(1), 38–44.

Pallavicini, F., Pippa, L., & Pisoni, A. (2019). Gesture-Based Technology in Stroke Rehabilitation: Monitoring Motivation and Emotional State. *Journal of Neurotherapy, 23*(2), 82–93.

Panchal, T. H. (2017). Literature review on face recognition using principal component analysis. *International Journal of Advance Research and Innovative Ideas in Education, 3*(4), 234–245.

Panda, A. K., Lenka, A. A., Mohapatra, A., Rath, B. K., Parida, A. A., & Mohapatra, H. (2024). Integrating cloud computing for intelligent transportation solutions in smart cities. *Advances in Civil and Industrial Engineering*, 121–142. DOI: 10.4018/979-8-3693-6695-0.ch005

Pan, Y., Froese, F., Liu, N., Hu, Y., & Ye, M. (2021). The adoption of artificial intelligence in employee recruitment: The influence of contextual factors. *International Journal of Human Resource Management, 0*(0), 1–23. DOI: 10.1080/09585192.2021.1879206

Paolanti, M., Liciotti, D., Pietrini, R., Mancini, A., & Frontoni, E. (2018). Modelling and forecasting customer navigation in intelligent retail environments. *Journal of Intelligent & Robotic Systems, 91*(2), 165–180. DOI: 10.1007/s10846-017-0674-7

Pappas, G., Siegel, J., Kassens-Noor, E., Rutkowski, J., Politopoulos, K., & Zorpas, A. (2022). Game-based simulation and study of pedestrian-automated vehicle interactions. *Automation, 3*(1), 33–50. DOI: 10.3390/automation3030017

Parisi, G. I., Kemker, R., Part, J. L., Kanan, C., & Wermter, S. (2019). Continual lifelong learning with neural networks: A review. *Neural Networks, 113*, 54–71. DOI: 10.1016/j.neunet.2019.01.012 PMID: 30780045

Park, E., & Kim, S. B. (2025). Air and train travel experiences for wheelchair users. *Current Issues in Tourism*, 1–6. DOI: 10.1080/13683500.2025.2478283

Parker, R., Brown, M., & Lee, J. (2020). Enhancing Gaming Experience through Biofeedback: A Study on Emotional Engagement in Video Games. *Journal of Game Design and Technology, 27*(1), 20–35.

Passalacqua, M., Cabour, G., Pellerin, R., Montréal, P., Montréal, H. E. C., & Doyon-poulin, P. (2022). *Human-Centered AI for Industry 5.0 (HUMAI5.0). 0*, 260–274. DOI: 10.1201/9781003320791-27

Pazmino, L., Flores, F., Ponce, L., Zaldumbide, J., Parraga, V., Loarte, B., Cevallos, G., Maldonado, I., & Rivera, R. (2019). Challenges and opportunities of IoT deployment in Ecuador. *2019 International Conference on Information Systems and Software Technologies (ICI2ST)*, 108-115. DOI: 10.1109/ICI2ST.2019.00022

Pechinger, M., & Lindner, J. (2024). Sumonity: Bridging SUMO and Unity for enhanced traffic simulation experiences. In *SUMO User Conference 2024* (pp. 1–10). German Aerospace Center (DLR). https://sumo.dlr.de/pdf/2024/2-1.pdf

Peek Editorial Team. (2024). *How AI is reshaping the tourism and travel industry.* Peek Pro Blog. Accessed on March 27, 2025, available at https://www.peekpro.com/blog/ai-tourism-industry

Peifer, Y., Jeske, T., & Hille, S. (2022). ScienceDirect Artificial Intelligence and its Impact on Leaders and Leadership. *Procedia Computer Science, 200*(2021), 1024–1030. DOI: 10.1016/j.procs.2022.01.301

Pepino, L., Ribeiro, D., & Gerosa, M. A. (2021). Emotion recognition from speech using wav2vec 2.0 embeddings. *Proceedings of Interspeech, 2021*, 3405–3409. DOI: 10.21437/Interspeech.2021-703

Pereira, A. G., Lima, T. M., & Charrua-santos, F. (2020). Industry 4.0 and Society 5.0: Opportunities and Threats. *International Journal of Recent Technology and Engineering*, *8*(5), 3305–3308. DOI: 10.35940/ijrte.D8764.018520

Pereira, E. M., Bianchi, A. M., & Tavares, J. M. R. S. (2019). Using wearable sensors to assess motor impairment and quality of life in Parkinson's disease patients. *Sensors (Basel)*, *19*(20), 4351.

Pereira, M., Silva, R., & Santos, J. (2019). Monitoring Neurological Decline with Gesture-Based Sensing: A Case Study for Parkinson's and Dementia Detection. *Journal of Health Care Technology*, *34*(2), 203–215.

Phillips, P. J., Jiang, F., Narvekar, A., Ayyad, J., & O'Toole, A. J. (2011). An other-race effect for face recognition algorithms. [TAP]. *ACM Transactions on Applied Perception*, *8*(2), 14. DOI: 10.1145/1870076.1870082

Picard, R. W., Mavridis, T., & Bickmore, T. (2019). Emotion recognition and affective computing. Springer Handbook of Computational Intelligence, 79-106.

Picard, R. W., Liao, M., & Kim, H. (2019). Multimodal Emotion Recognition: Fusing Gesture and Physiological Signals for Real-Time Affective State Detection. *IEEE Transactions on Affective Computing*, *10*(2), 234–245.

Picard, R. W., Vyzas, E., & Healey, J. (2019). Toward machine emotional intelligence: Analysis of affective physiological state. *IEEE Transactions on Pattern Analysis and Machine Intelligence*, *23*(10), 1175–1191. DOI: 10.1109/34.954607

Picco, E., Miglioretti, M., & Le Blanc, P. M. (2024). Sustainable employability, technology acceptance and task performance in workers collaborating with cobots: A pilot study. *Cognition Technology and Work*, *26*(1), 139–152. DOI: 10.1007/s10111-023-00742-6

Pillai, R., & Sivathanu, B. (2020). Adoption of AI-based chatbots for hospitality and tourism. *International Journal of Contemporary Hospitality Management*, *32*(10), 3199–3226. DOI: 10.1108/IJCHM-04-2020-0259

Pillai, R., Sivathanu, B., & Dwivedi, Y. K. (2020). Shopping intention at AI-powered automated retail stores (AIPARS). *Journal of Retailing and Consumer Services*, *57*(August), 102207. DOI: 10.1016/j.jretconser.2020.102207

Pillai, R., Sivathanu, B., Mariani, M., Rana, N. P., Yang, B., & Dwivedi, Y. K. (2021). Adoption of AI-empowered industrial robots in auto component manufacturing companies. *Production Planning and Control*, *0*(0), 1–17. DOI: 10.1080/09537287.2021.1882689

Poszler, F., Geisslinger, M., & Lütge, C. (2024). Ethical decision-making for self-driving vehicles: A proposed model & list of value-laden terms that warrant (technical) specification. *Science and Engineering Ethics*, *30*(5), 47. DOI: 10.1007/s11948-024-00513-0 PMID: 39387983

Prefeitura do Rio de Janeiro. (2021). *Inclusive Mobility Plan Overview*. Accessed on March 28, 2025, available at http://www.rio.rj.gov.br

Premnath, S. N., & Arun, A. (2020). A Qualitative Study of Artificial Intelligence Application Framework in Human Resource Management. *Journal of Xi'an University of Architecture & Technology, XI*(Xii), 1193–1209.

Priyadarshi, S., Subudhi, S., Kumar, S., Bhardwaj, D., & Mohapatra, H. (2024). undefined. *Advances in Civil and Industrial Engineering*, 143–172. DOI: 10.4018/979-8-3693-6695-0.ch006

Priya, S. B. (2024). A comprehensive review of face recognition techniques, trends and challenges. *IEEE Access : Practical Innovations, Open Solutions*, *12*, 123456–123467. DOI: 10.1109/ACCESS.2024.3424933

Qiao, G., Hou, S., Chen, Q., Xiang, G., & Prideaux, B. (2024). Role of Body in Travel: Wheelchair Users' Experience from a Multi-Sensory Perspective. *Journal of Travel Research.*

Radianti, J., Majchrzak, T. A., Fromm, J., & Wohlgenannt, I. (2020). A systematic review of immersive virtual reality applications for higher education: Design elements, lessons learned, and research agenda. *Computers & Education*, *147*, 103778. DOI: 10.1016/j.compedu.2019.103778

Radianti, J., Majchrzak, T., & Fromm, J. (2020). Immersive Virtual Reality for Education: Adapting Content Based on User Emotion and Engagement. *International Journal of Educational Technology*, *18*(4), 567–578.

Rahmati, M. (2025). Edge AI-powered real-time decision-making for autonomous vehicles in adverse weather conditions. *arXiv*. https://arxiv.org/abs/2503.09638

Raina, S., Challagundla, J., & Singh, M. (2025). Trajectory prediction in autonomous driving: A comprehensive review of deep learning models and future direction. In *2025 IEEE 15th Annual Computing and Communication Workshop and Conference (CCWC)* (pp. 753–759). IEEE. DOI: 10.1109/CCWC62904.2025.10903866

Rajendran, V., Carreno-Medrano, P., Fisher, W., Werner, A., & Kulic, D. (2020). A framework for human-robot interaction user studies. *IEEE International Conference on Intelligent Robots and Systems*, 6215–6222. DOI: 10.1109/IROS45743.2020.9341286

Ramadurai, S., & Jeong, H. (2022). *Effect of Human Involvement on Work Performance and Fluency in Human-Robot Collaboration for Recycling*. http://arxiv.org/abs/2201.07990 DOI: 10.1109/HRI53351.2022.9889606

Ramesh, A. N., Correas-Serrano, A., & Gonzalez-Huici, M. (2024). SCaRL-A synthetic multi-modal dataset for autonomous driving. In *ICMIM 2024: 7th IEEE MTT Conference* (pp. 103–106). VDE.

Ramirez, A. R. G., González-Carrasco, I., Jasper, G. H., Lopez, A. L., Lopez-Cuadrado, J. L., & García-Crespo, A. (2017). Towards human smart cities: Internet of things for sensory impaired individuals. *Computing*, *99*(1), 107–126. DOI: 10.1007/s00607-016-0529-2

Ramprasath, M., Kalpana, A. V., Ravishankar, T. N., Anand, M., & Shobana, J. (2023) Protected data sharing using attribute based encryption for remote data checking in cloud environment 12th International Conference on Advanced Computing (ICoAC), Chennai, India, Vol. 2023, pp. 1–8 [DOI: 10.1109/ICoAC59537.2023.10249642]

Rana, M., Sharma, A., & Gupta, R. (2020). Emotion-Adaptive Product Recommendations in E-Commerce Using Gesture-Based Feedback. *Journal of E-Commerce and Technology*, *22*(3), 145–158.

Rana, R., Sabanovic, S., & Banks, B. (2020). Designing emotion-sensitive technology for positive shopping experiences. *Proceedings of the 2020 ACM Designing Interactive Systems Conference*.

Rao, S., & Zhang, L. (2021). The algorithms that make Instacart roll: How machine learning and other tech tools guide your groceries from store to doorstep. *IEEE Spectrum*, *58*(3), 36–42. DOI: 10.1109/MSPEC.2021.9370062

Rashid Al-Bakri, I. M., Ahmad, M. I., Md Isa, M. N., & Al-Dabagh, M. Z. N. (2023). A review paper on face recognition techniques. In *2023 9th International Conference on Advanced Computing and Communication Systems (ICACCS)* (pp. 1951–1956). IEEE. DOI: 10.1109/ICACCS57279.2023.10112907

Rashid, Z., Melià-Seguí, J., Pous, R., & Peig, E. (2017). Using Augmented Reality and Internet of Things to improve accessibility of people with motor disabilities in the context of Smart Cities. *Future Generation Computer Systems*, *76*, 248–261. DOI: 10.1016/j.future.2016.11.030

Rasouli, A., & Tsotsos, J. K. (2018). Autonomous vehicles that interact with pedestrians: A survey of theory and practice. *arXiv*. https://arxiv.org/abs/1805.11773

Rauf, A., Guru, A., & Mohapatra, H. (2024). Exploring the social model of smart home devices. *Advances in Human and Social Aspects of Technology*, 233–256. DOI: 10.4018/979-8-3693-9235-5.ch012

Ren, Y., & Clement, J. (2024). Augmenting Human Teams with Robots in Knowledge Work Settings: Insights from the Literature. *ACM Transactions on Human-Robot Interaction*, *13*(2), 1–34. DOI: 10.1145/3649884

Rese, A., Ganster, L., & Baier, D. (2020). Chatbots in retailers' customer communication: How to measure their acceptance? *Journal of Retailing and Consumer Services*, *56*(June), 102176. DOI: 10.1016/j.jretconser.2020.102176

Reshma, M. R., & Kannan, B. (2019). Approaches on partial face recognition: A literature review. In *2019 IEEE International Conference on Optical and Electronic Imaging (ICOEI)* (pp. 1–6). IEEE. DOI: 10.1109/ICOEI.2019.8862783

Rezwana, S., & Lownes, N. (2024). Interactions and behaviors of pedestrians with autonomous vehicles: A synthesis. *Future Transportation*, *4*(3), 722–745. DOI: 10.3390/futuretransp4030034

Riegler, A., Riener, A., & Holzmann, C. (2021). A systematic review of augmented reality applications for automated driving: 2009–2020. *Presence (Cambridge, Mass.)*, *28*, 1–80. DOI: 10.1162/pres_a_00343

Rinaldi, M., Natale, C., Fera, M., Macchiaroli, R., Monaco, M. G. L., & Grosse, E. H. (2024). Evaluation of mental stress in human-robot interaction: an explorative study. *Procedia Computer Science*, *232*(2023), 726–735. DOI: 10.1016/j.procs.2024.01.072

Rinish. (2025, February 7). *AI in transportation: A smarter, safer, and more efficient future*. Thoughtminds. Accessed on March 28, 2025, available at https://www.thoughtminds.io/ai-in-transportation/

Roberts, M., Brown, T., & Zhang, L. (2020). Multimodal Emotion Recognition Systems: Fusing Gesture, Voice, and Physiological Signals. *Journal of Affective Computing*, *12*(3), 76–89.

Rodrigues, N., Coelho, A., & Rossetti, R. (2025). Generative narrative-driven game mechanics for procedural driving simulators. In *Proceedings of the 17th International Conference on Computer Modeling and Simulation* (pp. 339–346). SCITEPRESS. DOI: 10.5220/0013311000003912

Rogers, R., & Brown, T. (2021). Healthcare Applications of Gesture-Based Emotional Detection in Stroke Rehabilitation. *Journal of Rehabilitation Technology*, *18*(1), 34–49.

Romanski, S. (n.d.). Autonomous driving: Synthetic data versus real data. Understand.ai. Retrieved April 6, 2025, from https://understand.ai/blog/autonomous-driving-synthetic-data-versus-real-data

Ronen, R. (2024). *How artificial general intelligence could redefine accessibility.* Forbes. Accessed on March 28, 2025, available at https://www.forbes.com/councils/forbesbusinesscouncil/2024/02/02/how-artificial-general-intelligence-could-redefine-accessibility/

Rosique, F., Navarro, P. J., Fernández, C., & Padilla, A. (2019). A systematic review of perception system and simulators for autonomous vehicles research. *Sensors (Basel), 19*(3), 648. DOI: 10.3390/s19030648 PMID: 30764486

Russell, J. A. (1980). A circumplex model of affect. *Journal of Personality and Social Psychology, 39*(6), 1161–1178. DOI: 10.1037/h0077714

Ruusunen, N., Hallikainen, H., & Laukkanen, T. (2023). Does imagination compensate for the need for touch in 360-virtual shopping? *International Journal of Information Management, 70*, 102622. DOI: 10.1016/j.ijinfomgt.2023.102622

Sabit, H. (2025). AI-based smart security system using IoT for smart home applications. DOI: 10.20944/preprints202501.1887.v1

SAE International. (2021). *Taxonomy and definitions for terms related to driving automation systems for on-road motor vehicles* (SAE Standard J3016_202104).

Sah, R. K., Singh, A. K., Yadav, A. K., & Mohapatra, H. (2024). undefined. *Advances in Electronic Government, Digital Divide, and Regional Development*, 215–234. DOI: 10.4018/979-8-3693-6740-7.ch009

Sahu, M., & Dash, R. (2020). Study on face recognition techniques. In *2020 IEEE 14th International Conference on Communication Systems and Network Technologies (ICCSP)* (pp. 345–352). IEEE. DOI: 10.1109/ICCSP48568.2020.9182358

Said, Y., Atri, M., Albahar, M. A., Ben Atitallah, A., & Alsariera, Y. A. (2023). Scene recognition for visually-impaired people's navigation assistance based on vision transformer with dual multiscale attention. *Mathematics, 11*(5), 1127. DOI: 10.3390/math11051127

Saim, E. M., Al-Shareeda, S., Redmill, K., & Özgüner, Ü. (2024). Control of automated vehicles in vehicle-pedestrian environment. In *2024 IEEE 27th International Conference on Intelligent Transportation Systems (ITSC)*. IEEE.

Sainz-De-Abajo, B., García-Alonso, J. M., Berrocal-Olmeda, J. J., Laso-Mangas, S., & De La Torre-Díez, I. (2020). FoodScan: Food monitoring app by scanning the groceries receipts. *IEEE Access : Practical Innovations, Open Solutions*, *8*, 227915–227924. DOI: 10.1109/ACCESS.2020.3046031

Salvucci, D. D., Goldberg, J. H., & Zheng, X. (2021). Eye movement modeling and gaze behavior adaptation in intelligent user interfaces. *ACM Transactions on Interactive Intelligent Systems*, *11*(2), 1–36.

Salvucci, D., Lee, K., & Srinivasan, P. (2021). Challenges in cross-user emotion detection through gesture and touch. *Proceedings of the International Conference on Affective Computing*, 112-118.

Sani, S. M., Wu, T., & Zhang, Y. (2021). Real-time cognitive load assessment using edge AI: Balancing speed and accuracy. *IEEE Internet of Things Journal*, *8*(10), 8219–8229.

Sarala, B., Sumathy, G., Kalpana, A. V., & Jasmine Hephzipah, J. J. (2023) Glioma brain tumor detection using dual convolutional neural networks and histogram density segmentation algorithm. Biomedical Signal Processing and Control, 85, 104859, ISSN 1746-8094 [DOI:]DOI: 10.1016/j.bspc.2023.104859

Sawhney, S., Gupta, R., & Singh, A. (2019). Real-time smart attendance system using face recognition techniques. In *2019 9th International Conference on Cloud Computing, Data Science & Engineering (Confluence)* (pp. 123–129). IEEE. DOI: 10.1109/CONFLUENCE.2019.8776934

Schäffner, V. (2024). Crash dilemmas and the ethical design of self-driving vehicles: Implications from metaethics and pragmatic road marks. *AI and Ethics*. DOI: 10.1007/s43681-024-00432-9

Schrab, K. (2022). Face detection's various techniques and approaches: A review. *International Journal for Science Technology and Engineering*, *8*(6), 45–56.

Schroff, F., Kalenichenko, D., & Philbin, J. (2015). FaceNet: A unified embedding for face recognition and clustering. In *Proceedings of the IEEE Conference on Computer Vision and Pattern Recognition (CVPR)* (pp. 815–823). IEEE. DOI: 10.1109/CVPR.2015.7298682

Schuller, B., Steidl, S., Batliner, A., Burkhardt, F., Devillers, L., Müller, C., & Narayanan, S. (2011). The INTERSPEECH 2011 speaker state challenge. *Interspeech*, 3201–3204.

Seemanthini, K., & Manjunath, S. S. (2021). Recognition of trivial humanoid group event using clustering and higher order local auto-correlation techniques. In *Cognitive Computing for Human-Robot Interaction*. Issue January., DOI: 10.1016/B978-0-323-85769-7.00001-X

Sehgal, V., & Sekaran, N. (2024). Virtual recording generation using generative AI and CARLA simulator (SAE Technical Paper 2024-28-0261). SAE International. DOI: 10.4271/2024-28-0261

Semary, H. E., Al-Karawi, K. A., Abdelwahab, M. M., & Elshabrawy, A. M. (2024). A Review on Internet of Things (IoT)-Related Disabilities and Their Implications. *Journal of Disability Research*, *3*(2), 20240012. DOI: 10.57197/JDR-2024-0012

Serengil, S. I., & Ozpinar, A. (2020). Lightface: A hybrid deep face recognition framework. In *2020 Innovations in Intelligent Systems and Applications Conference (ASYU)* (pp. 1–6). IEEE. DOI: 10.1109/ASYU50717.2020.9259802

Serrano, S., Blanco, Ó., Worrall, S., Sotelo, M., & Fernández-Llorca, D. (2024). Cross-cultural analysis of pedestrian group behavior influence on crossing decisions in interactions with autonomous vehicles. *arXiv*. https://arxiv.org/abs/2408.03003

Serrano, S., Fernández-Llorca, D., García Daza, I., & Sotelo, M. Á. (2023). Realistic pedestrian behaviour in the CARLA simulator using VR and mocap. In *Computer vision – ECCV 2022 workshops* (pp. 63–78). Springer., DOI: 10.1007/978-3-031-41962-1_5

Sethuraman, S. C., Tadkapally, G. R., Mohanty, S. P., Galada, G., & Subramanian, A. (2023). MagicEye: An Intelligent Wearable Towards Independent Living of Visually Impaired. *arXiv preprint arXiv:2303.13863.*

Shafee, A. E., & Hamed, K. A. (2012). Towards a WiFi based home automation system. *International Journal of Computer and Electrical Engineering*, 803-808. DOI: 10.7763/IJCEE.2012.V4.609

Shankman, S. (2025). *AI travel agents: How they're transforming the future of travel planning*. Navan. Accessed on April 3 2025, available at https://navan.com/blog/insights-trends/ai-travel-agent

Sharma, D. (2020). *Evaluation and analysis of perception systems for autonomous driving* [Unpublished manuscript].

Sharma, A., & Nautiyal, M. (2024). Face recognition in the modern era: A survey of techniques, challenges, and innovations. *Indian Scientific Journal of Research in Engineering and Management*, *2024*(3), 37533. DOI: 10.55041/IJSREM37533

Sharma, N., Gedeon, T., & Jones, R. (2020). Monitoring cognitive load in e-learning via HRV. *Sensors (Basel), 20*(6), 1702. PMID: 32197502

Sharma, P., & Kaur, R. (2022). AI-Driven Tutoring Systems in eLearning: Real-Time Adaptation Based on Emotional Engagement. *Journal of Educational Technology, 40*(2), 123–139.

Shenoy, G. G., Wagle, M. A., & Connelly, K. (2017). Leveling the playing field for Visually Impaired using Transport Assistant. *arXiv preprint arXiv:1703.02103.*

Shen, Y., Wang, Z., & Zeng, D. (2021). Cross-subject emotion recognition using EEG signals with meta-learning and domain adaptation. *IEEE Transactions on Affective Computing, 14*(1), 230–242.

Shi, L., Cole, S., & Chancellor, H. C. (2012). Understanding leisure travel motivations of travellers with acquired mobility impairments. *Tourism Management, 33*(1), 228–231. DOI: 10.1016/j.tourman.2011.02.007

Shrivastava, A., & Gupta, A. (2020). Hybrid models: Combining HOG features with deep learning for object recognition. *Neural Networks, 45*, 90–98. DOI: 10.1016/j.ncunet.2020.02.005

Shukla, R. K., & Tiwari, A. (2023). Masked face recognition using MobileNet V2 with transfer learning. *Computer Systems Science and Engineering, 45*(1), 123–135. DOI: 10.32604/csse.2023.123456

Shukla, V., Rana, S., & Prashar, S. (2024). Examining the potential of virtual and augmented reality in enhancing tourism experiences. *The Bottom Line (New York, N.Y.)*. DOI: 10.1108/BL-05-2023-0139

Silva, C., De, , & Halloluwa, T. (2025). *Augmenting Human Potential:* DOI: 10.1145/3712068

Simonsen, J., Robertson, T., & Bødker, K. (2020). Participatory design for privacy and consent. *ACM Transactions on Computer-Human Interaction, 27*(1), 1–30.

Simonyan, K., & Zisserman, A. (2015). Very Deep Convolutional Networks for Large-Scale Image Recognition. *International Conference on Learning Representations*, 1-12.

Simulator, C. A. R. L. A. (n.d.). Pedestrian catalogue. Retrieved April 6, 2025, from https://carla.readthedocs.io/en/latest/catalogue_pedestrians/

Simulator, C. A. R. L. A. (n.d.). Retrieved April 6, 2025, from https://carla.org/

Singh, A., Gupta, R., & Verma, N. (2024). Empathetic Technologies: Gesture and Touch-Based Systems for Emotion and Engagement Detection in HCI. *Journal of Interactive Systems*, *26*(1), 67–79.

Sivathanu, B. (2018). Adoption of internet of things (IOT) based wearables for healthcare of older adults – a behavioural reasoning theory (BRT) approach. *Journal of Enabling Technologies*, *12*(4), 169–185. DOI: 10.1108/JET-12-2017-0048

Smith, K., & Thompson, R. (2021). Security and Privacy Concerns in Emotion Detection Systems: A Comparative Study. *Information Security Journal*, *29*(3), 101–112.

Society, V. E., Rane, A. P. A., Rane, M. L. A., Collaboration, M., Players, K., Implementation, S., Generative, S., Intelligence, A., Preprints, S. F., Rane, C., Collaboration, M., Players, K., Implementation, S., Generative, S., Intelligence, A., & Preprints, O. S. F. (2023). *Multidisciplinary collaboration : key players in successful implementation of ChatGPT and similar generative artificial intelligence in manufacturing, finance, retail, transportation, and construction industry Nitin Liladhar Rane*.

Soleymani, M., McDuff, D., & Mühl, C. (2017). Affective Computing in Emotion Recognition Systems: Combining Gestures, Facial Expressions, and Physiological Signals. *International Journal of Human-Computer Studies*, *94*, 123–134.

Soleymani, M., Pantic, M., & Pun, T. (2017). Multimodal emotion recognition in response to videos. *IEEE Transactions on Affective Computing*, *3*(2), 211–223. DOI: 10.1109/T-AFFC.2011.37

Soliman, M., Abiodun, T., Hamouda, T., Zhou, J., & Lung, C. (2013). Smart home: Integrating Internet of things with web services and cloud computing. *2013 IEEE 5th International Conference on Cloud Computing Technology and Science*. DOI: 10.1109/CloudCom.2013.155

Someshwar, R., & Edan, Y. (2017). *Givers & Receivers perceive handover tasks differently: Implications for Human-Robot collaborative system design*. http://arxiv.org/abs/1708.06207

Song, Z., He, Z., Li, X., Ma, Q., Ming, R., Mao, Z., & Zhang, Y. (2023). Synthetic datasets for autonomous driving: A survey. *IEEE Transactions on Intelligent Vehicles*, *9*(1), 1847–1864. DOI: 10.1109/TIV.2023.3331024

Sony, M., & Mekoth, N. (2022). Employee adaptability skills for Indu ry 4. 0 success : A road map. *Production & Manufacturing Research*, *10*(1), 24–41. DOI: 10.1080/21693277.2022.2035281

Sood, M. (2020, October 25). India had most deaths in road accidents in 2019: Report. *Hindustan Times*. https://www.hindustantimes.com/mumbai-news/india-had-most-deaths-in-road-accidents-in-2019-report/story-pikRXxsS4hptNVvf6J2g9O.html

Sourina, O., Liu, Y., Nguyen, M. K., & Wang, Q. (2012). EEG-based "serious" games design for medical applications. *IEEE Transactions on Computational Intelligence and AI in Games*, *4*(3), 201–213.

Southeast, A. D. A. Center. (2022). *These apps help people with disabilities travel more easily*. Accessed on April 1, 2025, available at https://adasoutheast.org/these-apps-help-people-with-disabilities-travel-more-easily/

Sozialhelden, V. (2025). Wheelmap. In *OpenStreetMap Wiki*. Accessed on March 28, 2025, available at https://wiki.openstreetmap.org/wiki/Wheelmap

Spice, B. (2019). *Collision-Detecting Suitcase, Wayfinding App Help Blind People Navigate Airports*. Carnegie Mellon University. Accessed on March 28, 2025, available at https://www.cmu.edu/news/stories/archives/2019/may/suitcase-helps-navigate-airports.html

Srivastava, S., Li, J., Mishra, P., Bansal, K., & Bharadia, D. (n.d.). *A realistic radar simulation framework for CARLA* [Technical report]. University of California., https://wcsng.ucsd.edu/files/c-shenron_paper.pdf

Stouhi, D. (2022). *Toronto plans on stopping the construction of smart cities following concerns of privacy*. ArchDaily. Accessed on March 28, 2025, available at https://www.archdaily.com/984561/toronto-plans-on-stopping-the-construction-of-smart-cities-following-concerns-of-privacy

Subramanian, S. (n.d.). *The 10 best AI travel assistant chatbots for smarter travel planning*. Emitrr. Accessed on April 3 2025, available at https://emitrr.com/blog/chatbot-for-travel/

SUMO at a Glance. (n.d.). Eclipse SUMO - Simulation of urban mobility. Retrieved April 6, 2025, from https://sumo.dlr.de/docs/SUMO_at_a_Glance.html

Sun, J., Gan, W., Chao, H., Yu, P. S., & Ding, W. (1999). Internet of Behaviors. *Survey (London, England)*, 1–17.

Synthetic Data Generation. (n.d.). What is its role in AI training. EC Innovations. Retrieved April 6, 2025, from https://www.ecinnovations.com/blog/synthetic-data-generation-what-is-its-role-in-ai-training/

Tabrez, A., Luebbers, M. B., & Hayes, B. (2020). A Survey of Mental Modeling Techniques in Human–Robot Teaming. *Current Robotics Reports, 1*(4), 259–267. DOI: 10.1007/s43154-020-00019-0

Taigman, Y., Yang, M., Ranzato, M., & Wolf, L. (2014). DeepFace: Closing the gap to human-level performance in face verification. In *Proceedings of the IEEE Conference on Computer Vision and Pattern Recognition (CVPR)* (pp. 1701–1708). IEEE. DOI: 10.1109/CVPR.2014.220

Talks, C. A. R. L. A. 2020. (n.d.). Art improvements: Environments and rendering [Video]. YouTube. Retrieved April 6, 2025, from https://www.youtube.com/watch?v=ZZaHevsz8W8

Talks, C. A. R. L. A. 2020. (n.d.). Pedestrians and their implementation [Video]. YouTube. Retrieved April 6, 2025, from https://www.youtube.com/watch?v=Uoz2ihDwaWA

Tang, P. M., Koopman, J., Mai, K. M., De Cremer, D., Zhang, J. H., Reynders, P., Tung, C., Ng, S., & Chen, I. (2023). No Person Is an Island : Unpacking the Work and After-Work Consequences of Interacting With Arti fi cial. *Intelligence.*

Tang, P. O. K. M. A. N., & Zhang, J. H. (2022). WHEN CONSCIENTIOUS EMPLOYEES MEET INTELLIGENT MACHINES. *AN INTEGRATIVE APPROACH INSPIRED BY COMPLEMENTARITY THEORY AND ROLE THEORY., 65*(3), 1019–1054.

Tan, S., Lee, Y., & Park, H. (2023). Gesture Responsiveness in VR Games: Enhancing Immersion and Personalization through Emotional Tracking. *Journal of Game Development, 15*(4), 220–235.

Tan, Y., Liu, Z., & Chen, L. (2021). Biometric-Embedded Game Controllers: Using Emotional Cues for Dynamic Gameplay. *Journal of Interactive Entertainment, 34*(1), 56–68.

Tan, Y., Liu, Z., & Chen, X. (2023). Gesture Recognition for Emotional Engagement in VR: The Role of Real-Time Feedback and Personalization in Gaming. *Journal of Virtual and Augmented Reality, 8*(2), 50–62.

Tapu, R., Mocanu, B., & Zaharia, T. (2017). DEEP-SEE: Joint object detection, tracking and recognition with application to visually impaired navigational assistance. *Sensors (Basel), 17*(11), 2473. DOI: 10.3390/s17112473 PMID: 29143795

Tarko, A. P. (2009). Safety and mobility of vulnerable road users: Modeling pedestrian crashes at signalized intersections. *Safety Science, 47*(8), 1088–1095. DOI: 10.1016/j.ssci.2008.11.008

Tata, A. M., Ebbatson, D., & Fluke, C. (2024). Exploring airport navigation challenges faced by airline travellers with hidden disabilities. *International Journal of Aviation, Aeronautics, and Aerospace*, *11*(1). DOI: 10.58940/2374-6793.1871

Tech Briefs. (n.d.). Are there limitations in autonomous-vehicle simulation methods? Retrieved April 6, 2025, from https://www.techbriefs.com/component/content/article/32806-are-there-limitations-in-autonomous-vehicle-simulation-methods

Tendulkar, S., Khandelwal, M. Y., & Schrödel, F. (2024). V2X based vehicle environment perception and occupancy analysis for dynamic pedestrian behaviour. In *2024 European Control Conference (ECC)* (pp. 3630–3635). IEEE. DOI: 10.23919/ECC64448.2024.10590875

Terblanche, N. H. D. (2020). Factors that influence users' adoption of being coached by an Artificial Intelligence Coach. *Philosophy of Coaching*, *5*(1), 61–70. DOI: 10.22316/poc/05.1.06

Thomaz, A., & Hoffman, G. (n.d.). *Computational Human-Robot Interaction.*

Tiwari, A., Manzoor, S., Sehgal, J., & Mishra, A. (2024). A comprehensive review of face detection technologies. *2024 IEEE International Conference on Artificial Intelligence and Technology (ICAIT)*, 1–8. DOI: 10.1109/ICAIT61638.2024.10690719

Tokmurziyev, I., Cabrera, M. A., Khan, M. H., Mahmoud, Y., Moreno, L., & Tsetserukou, D. (2025). LLM Glasses: GenAI-driven Glasses with Haptic Feedback for Navigation of Visually Impaired People. *arXiv preprint arXiv:2503.16475.*

Tokyo Metropolitan Government. (2020). *Olympic Games Tokyo 2020: Accessibility Equipment Update*. Accessed on March 28, 2025, available at https://www.inclusivecitymaker.com/olympic-games-tokyo-2020-accessibility/#:~:text=The%20200%20shuttles%20can%20transport,the%20%E2%80%9Clast%20one%20mile%E2%80%9D

Tong, D. Y. K. (2009). A study of e-recruitment technology adoption in Malaysia. *Industrial Management & Data Systems*, *109*(2), 281–300. DOI: 10.1108/02635570910930145

Tortorella, G. L., Saurin, T. A., Filho, M. G., Samson, D., & Kumar, M. (2021). Bundles of Lean Automation practices and principles and their impact on operational performance. *International Journal of Production Economics*, *235*(January), 108106. DOI: 10.1016/j.ijpe.2021.108106

Tran, T. T. M., Parker, C., & Tomitsch, M. (2021). A review of virtual reality studies on autonomous vehicle–pedestrian interaction. *IEEE Transactions on Human-Machine Systems*, *51*(6), 641–652. DOI: 10.1109/THMS.2021.3107517

Tripathi, S., Acharya, S., & Sharma, R. D. (2017). Using deep and convolutional neural networks for accurate emotion classification on DEAP dataset. *Proceedings of the AAAI Conference on Artificial Intelligence*, 4746–4752.

Tsinalis, O., Matthews, P. M., & Guo, Y. (2016). Automatic sleep stage scoring using time-frequency analysis and stacked sparse autoencoders. *Annals of Biomedical Engineering*, *44*(5), 1587–1597. DOI: 10.1007/s10439-015-1444-y PMID: 26464268

Tulpule, P., Midlam-Mohler, S., Karumanchi, A., & Jin, Y. (2021). A simulation tool for virtual validation and verification of advanced driver assistance systems (SAE Technical Paper 2021-01-0865). SAE International. DOI: 10.4271/2021-01-0865

Turk, M., & Pentland, A. (1991). Eigenfaces for recognition. *Journal of Cognitive Neuroscience*, *3*(1), 71–86. DOI: 10.1162/jocn.1991.3.1.71 PMID: 23964806

Turno, F. M., Jackiva, I. Y., & Budiloviča, E. (2025). Enhancing Public Transport Accessibility for People with Motor Disabilities Through Deep Learning on Graphs. *Transport and Telecommunication*, *26*(1), 82–89. DOI: 10.2478/ttj-2025-0008

Twardzik, E., Schrack, J. A., Porter, K. M. P., Coleman, T., Washington, K., & Swenor, B. K. (2024). TRansit ACessibility Tool (TRACT): Developing a novel scoring system for public transportation system accessibility. *Journal of Transport & Health*, *34*, 101742. DOI: 10.1016/j.jth.2023.101742 PMID: 38405233

Ulfert, A., Antoni, C. H., & Ellwart, T. (2022). Computers in Human Behavior The role of agent autonomy in using decision support systems at work. *Computers in Human Behavior, 126*(August 2021), 106987. DOI: 10.1016/j.chb.2021.106987

United Nations Department of Economic and Social Affairs. (2018). *UN disability and development report: Realizing the SDGs by, for and with persons with disabilities*. Accessed on March 28, 2025, available at https://www.un.org/en/desa/un-disability-and-development-report-%E2%80%93-realizing-sdgs-and-persons-disabilities

Unreal Build. Automotive 2021. (n.d.). AV simulation [Video]. YouTube. Retrieved April 6, 2025, from https://www.youtube.com/watch?v=eAw-6Og8LQ0

Unreal Engine. (n.d.). CARLA democratizes autonomous vehicle R&D with free open-source simulator. Retrieved April 6, 2025, from https://www.unrealengine.com/es-ES/spotlights/carla-democratizes-autonomous-vehicle-r-d-with-free-open-source-simulator

Unreal Engine. (n.d.). Making autonomous vehicles safer before they hit the road. Retrieved April 6, 2025, from https://www.unrealengine.com/en-US/blog/making-autonomous-vehicles-safer-before-they-hit-the-road

Valipoor, M. M., & De Antonio, A. (2023). Recent trends in computer vision-driven scene understanding for VI/blind users: A systematic mapping. *Universal Access in the Information Society*, *22*(3), 983–1005. DOI: 10.1007/s10209-022-00868-w

Valve Corporation. (2020). *Half-Life: Alyx: Using Gesture Responsiveness to Enhance Game Immersion*. Valve Software.

Velho, R. (2019). Transport accessibility for wheelchair users: A qualitative analysis of inclusion and health. *International Journal of Transportation Science and Technology*, *8*(2), 103–115. DOI: 10.1016/j.ijtst.2018.04.005

Verbert, K., Duval, E., Klerkx, J., Govaerts, S., & Santos, J. L. (2012). Learning analytics dashboard applications. *Proceedings of the 2nd International Conference on Learning Analytics and Knowledge*, 124–133.

Verma, A., Kapoor, C., Sharma, A., & Mishra, B. (2021) Web application implementation with machine learning 2nd International Conference on Intelligent Engineering and Management (ICIEM), London, UK, Vol. 2021, pp. 423–428. DOI: DOI: 10.1109/ICIEM51511.2021.9445368

Vohra, M. (Ed.). (2025). *Introduction to Extended Reality (XR) Technologies*. John Wiley & Sons. DOI: 10.1002/9781119857716

Voigt, P., & Von dem Bussche, A. (2017). *The EU general data protection regulation (GDPR)*. Springer. DOI: 10.1007/978-3-319-57959-7

Voronin, S., Siddique, A., & Iqbal, M. (2024). Enhancing object detection accuracy in autonomous vehicles using synthetic data. *arXiv*. https://arxiv.org/abs/2411.15602

Wagh, A., Tripathi, S., & Roy, D. (2022). A review on fatigue detection systems using physiological signals: Challenges and opportunities. *Biomedical Signal Processing and Control*, *72*, 103322.

Wagh, S. L., Wafgaonkar, A., & Singh, M. D. (2024). Transforming modern living: A comprehensive study of smart home automation and IoT integration. *International Journal of Research Publication and Reviews*, *5*(10), 941–945. DOI: 10.55248/gengpi.5.1024.2729

Wagner, L. (n.d.). *Accessible pedestrian signals (APS): A century of change*. Inclusive City Maker. Accessible Pedestrian Signals (APS): a Century of Change", Accessed on March 28, 2025, available at https://www.inclusivecitymaker.com/accessible-pedestrian-signals-aps-a-century-of-change/

Waisberg, E., Ong, J., Masalkhi, M., Zaman, N., Sarker, P., Lee, A. G., & Tavakkoli, A. (2024). Meta smart glasses—Large language models and the future for assistive glasses for individuals with vision impairments. *Eye (London, England), 38*(6), 1036–1038. DOI: 10.1038/s41433-023-02842-z PMID: 38049627

Walchshofer, C., Dhanoa, V., Streit, M., & Meyer, M. (2024).. . *Transitioning to a Commercial Dashboarding System : Socio-technical Observations and Opportunities, 30*(1), 381–391.

Walking Tree Technologies. (n.d.). Unreal Engine: Advancing AI with synthetic data and computer vision integration. Retrieved April 6, 2025, from https://walkingtree.tech/unreal-engine-advancing-ai-with-synthetic-data-and-computer-vision-integration

Wang, Y. (2020) Construction of e-commerce platform system for targeted poverty alleviation International Conference on Computer Engineering and Application (ICCEA), Guangzhou, China, Vol. 2020, pp. 100–103. DOI: DOI: 10.1109/ICCEA50009.2020.00028

Wang, S., Yang, C., Qu, T., Yang, K., & Wan, W. (2022). Learning users' visual preferences for improving recommendations. *IEEE Access : Practical Innovations, Open Solutions, 10*, 2929–2940. DOI: 10.1109/ACCESS.2022.3140215

Wang, X. (2024). Literature review on the application of numerical model in improving face recognition performance. *Applied and Computational Engineering, 2024*(30), 20230076. DOI: 10.54254/2755-2721/30/20230076

Wang, X., & Zhu, Z. (2023). Context understanding in computer vision: A survey. *Computer Vision and Image Understanding, 229*, 103646. DOI: 10.1016/j.cviu.2023.103646

Wang, Y.L., Sun, H.B., Xu, S.X., Xia, Q.J., Ge, S., Li, M., & Tang, X.P. (2024). Smart home technologies for enhancing independence of living and reducing care dependence in older adults. *Systematic Reviews*. DOI: 10.1111/jan.16569/v1/review3

Wang, Z., Zheng, O., Li, L., Abdel-Aty, M., Cruz-Neira, C., & Islam, Z. (2023). Towards next generation of pedestrian and connected vehicle in-the-loop research: A digital twin co-simulation framework. *IEEE Transactions on Intelligent Vehicles, 8*(4), 2674–2683. DOI: 10.1109/TIV.2023.3250353

Waqar, A., Waqar, A., Tian, W., Din, S. U., Iradukunda, D., & Khan, A. A. K. (2021). Classical and modern face recognition approaches: A complete review. *Multimedia Tools and Applications, 80*(12), 17835–17874. DOI: 10.1007/s11042-021-10576-7

WHILL. (2024, April 10). *Self-driving wheelchairs: WHILL bring travelers to their gate at Schiphol Airport.* WHILL Inc. Accessed on March 28, 2025, available at https://whill.inc/us/news/self-driving-wheelchairs-whill-bring-travelers-to-their-gate-at-schiphol-airport?

Wojek, C., & Schiele, B. (2008). A performance evaluation of single and multi-feature people detection. In *Pattern Recognition: 30th DAGM Symposium* (pp. 82–91). Springer. DOI: 10.1007/978-3-540-69321-5_9

Wolpaw, J. R., & Wolpaw, E. W. (Eds.). (2012). *Brain-computer interfaces: Principles and practice.* OUP USA. DOI: 10.1093/acprof:oso/9780195388855.001.0001

Wong, K. W., Lam, K. M., & Siu, W. C. (2001). An efficient algorithm for human face detection and facial feature extraction under different conditions. *Pattern Recognition, 34*(10), 1993–2004. DOI: 10.1016/S0031-3203(00)00134-5

World Health Organization & World Bank. (2011). *World report on disability.* Accessed on March 28, 2025, available at https://www.who.int/publications/i/item/world-report-on-disability

World Health Organization. (2018). *Global status report on road safety 2018.* https://www.who.int/publications/i/item/9789241565684

World Health Organization. (2023). *Global status report on road safety 2023.* https://www.who.int/publications/i/item/9789240077614

Wu, B., He, X., Chen, Y., Nie, L., Zheng, K., & Ye, Y. (2022). Modeling product's visual and functional characteristics for recommender systems. *IEEE Transactions on Knowledge and Data Engineering, 34*(3), 1330–1343. DOI: 10.1109/TKDE.2020.2991793

Wu, B., He, X., Sun, Z., Chen, L., & Ye, Y. (2020). ATM: An attentive translation model for next-item recommendation. *IEEE Transactions on Industrial Informatics, 16*(3), 1448–1459. DOI: 10.1109/TII.2019.2947174

Xie, L., Zhang, Y., & Li, Z. (2022). Using Convolutional Neural Networks for Gesture Recognition in Emotion Detection Systems. *Journal of AI Research, 29*(3), 322–338.

Yam, K. C., Tang, P. M., Jackson, J. C., Su, R., & Gray, K. (2022). *The Rise of Robots Increases Job Insecurity and Maladaptive Workplace Behaviors : Multimethod Evidence. May.*

Yang, L., Zhang, X., Li, J., Wang, C., Song, Z., Zhao, T., & Lv, C. (2024). V2X-Radar: A multi-modal dataset with 4D radar for cooperative perception. *arXiv.* https://arxiv.org/abs/2411.10962

Yang, H., & Han, X. (2020). Face recognition attendance system based on real-time video processing. *IEEE Access : Practical Innovations, Open Solutions, 8*, 159143–159150. DOI: 10.1109/ACCESS.2020.3007205

Yang, Q., Liu, Y., Chen, T., & Tong, Y. (2019). Federated machine learning: Concept and applications. [TIST]. *ACM Transactions on Intelligent Systems and Technology, 10*(2), 12. DOI: 10.1145/3298981

Ye, P., Wang, X., Zheng, W., Wei, Q., & Wang, F. (2022). *Parallel cognition : hybrid intelligence for human-machine interaction and management *. 23*(12), 1765–1779.

Yi, M., Bao, D., & Mo, Y. (2021). Exploring the role of visual design in digital public health safety education. *International Journal of Environmental Research and Public Health, 18*(15), 7965. DOI: 10.3390/ijerph18157965 PMID: 34360258

Ying, W., Pee, L. G., & Jia, S. (2018). Social informatics of intelligent manufacturing ecosystems: A case study of KuteSmart. *International Journal of Information Management, 42*, 102–105. DOI: 10.1016/j.ijinfomgt.2018.05.002

Yogalakshmi, S., Megalan, L. L., & Simla, A. J. (2020). Review on digital image processing techniques for face recognition. In *2020 International Conference on Communication, Control and Signal Processing (ICCSP)* (pp. 1–6). IEEE. DOI: 10.1109/ICCSP48568.2020.9182091

Yoon, S., Park, H., & Yoo, H. S. (2015). Security issues on Smarthome in IoT environment. *Lecture Notes in Electrical Engineering*, 691-696. DOI: 10.1007/978-3-662-45402-2_97

Younus, S. M., Bhardwaj, V., Jain, A. K., Sharma, V., Reddy, T. K., & Virender, V. (2023). A comparative analysis of face detection algorithms and real-time facial recognition. *2023 IEEE International Conference on Interdisciplinary Research in Computing and Automation (ICIRCA)*, 1–8. DOI: 10.1109/ICIRCA57980.2023.10220918

Youssef, P., Plant, K., & Waterson, B. (2024). Joining SUMO and Unreal Engine to create a bespoke 360 degree narrow passage driving simulator. *SUMO Conference Proceedings, 5*, 93–112. DOI: 10.52825/scp.v5i.1104

Yuan, T., & Han, X. (2025). MINet: A pedestrian trajectory forecasting method with multi-information feature fusion. *Computer Information, 44*(1), 202–222. DOI: 10.31577/cai_2025_1_202

Yu, X., & Saniie, J. (2025). Visual Impairment Spatial Awareness System for Indoor Navigation and Daily Activities. *Journal of Imaging, 11*(1), 9. DOI: 10.3390/jimaging11010009 PMID: 39852322

Zel, S., Consulting, U. P., & Kongar, E. (2020). *Transforming Digital Employee Experience with Artificial Intelligence.*, (September), 176–179. DOI: 10.1109/AI4G50087.2020.9311088

Zeng, H. (2024). A review of traditional methods and deep learning for face recognition. *Applied and Computational Engineering, 2024*(80), Article 2024ch0053. DOI: 10.54254/2755-2721/80/2024CH0053

Zhai, J., & Barreto, A. (2006). Stress detection in computer users through non-invasive monitoring of physiological signals. *ACM Transactions on Computer-Human Interaction (TOCHI, 14*(4), 1–29.

Zhan, Z., Wu, Q., Lin, Z., & Cai, J. (2021). *Smart classroom environments affect teacher-student interaction : Evidence from a behavioural sequence analysis. 37*(2), 96–109.

Zhang, H., Falletta, N. J., Xie, J., Yu, R., Lee, S., Billah, S. M., & Carroll, J. M. (2025, January). Enhancing the Travel Experience for People with Visual Impairments through Multimodal Interaction: NaviGPT, A Real-Time AI-Driven Mobile Navigation System. In *Companion Proceedings of the 2025 ACM International Conference on Supporting Group Work* (pp. 29-35).

Zhang, Q., Yang, L. T., Chen, Z., & Li, P. (2020). Privacy-preserving deep computation model on cloud for big data feature learning. *IEEE Transactions on Computers, 65*(5), 1351–1362. DOI: 10.1109/TC.2015.2470255

Zhang, T., Liu, H., Wang, W., & Wang, X. (2024). Virtual tools for testing autonomous driving: A survey and benchmark of simulators, datasets, and competitions. *Electronics (Basel), 13*(17), 3486. DOI: 10.3390/electronics13173486

Zhanguzhinova, S., Makó, E., Borsos, A., Sándor, Á. P., & Koren, C. (2023). Communication between autonomous vehicles and pedestrians: An experimental study using virtual reality. *Sensors (Basel), 23*(3), 1049. DOI: 10.3390/s23031049 PMID: 36772089

Zhang, X., Cui, R., & Yao, O. (2023). The version effect of apps and operating systems in mobile commerce. *Production and Operations Management, 32*(2), 637–654. DOI: 10.1111/poms.13891

Zhang, X., Zeng, Y., & Li, Y. (2020). Federated learning and explainable AI for emotion detection systems. *AI and Ethics, 6*(2), 89–102.

Zhang, Y., Wu, Q., & Fu, Y. (2019). EEG-based intention recognition from spatio-temporal representations via cascade convolutional recurrent network. *AAAI Conference on Artificial Intelligence, 33*(1), 1647–1654.

Zhang, Y., Yu, Z., & Fung, P. (2018). A multitask deep learning approach for emotion classification from tweets. *Knowledge-Based Systems, 158*, 54–62.

Zhang, Y., Zhao, L., & Wei, H. (2023). Gesture-Based Systems for Customer Experience Enhancement in Retail Environments. *Journal of Service Management, 26*(1), 123–137.

Zhang, Z., Liu, W., & Chen, Z. (2020). Affective Computing in Virtual Reality: Enhancing User Interaction through Emotion Recognition. *Journal of VR and AR, 12*(1), 34–47.

Zhao, J., Wang, T., Yatskar, M., Ordonez, V., & Chang, K. W. (2019). Gender bias in coreference resolution. *arXiv preprint arXiv:1804.06876.*

Zhao, S., Lu, H., Chen, Y., Chen, Y., & Liu, Z. (2020). Emotion recognition from smartphone touch gestures using recurrent neural networks. Proceedings of the IEEE International Conference on Pervasive Computing and Communications Workshops (PerCom Workshops).

Zhao, F., Zhang, T., & Wang, J. (2020). Gesture-Based Emotional Response in Video Games: Maintaining Engagement through Dynamic Difficulty Adjustment. *Journal of Interactive Media, 19*(3), 102–114.

Zhao, J., Sun, X., & Zhang, W. (2020). Deep learning-based emotion recognition in gesture-touch interaction systems. *Journal of AI Research, 47*, 163–179.

Zhao, J., Wang, H., & Li, J. (2020). Predicting Stress Levels from Mobile Phone Touch Data Using LSTM Networks. *Journal of Computational Neuroscience, 23*(4), 120–134.

Zhao, T., & Nevatia, R. (2004). Tracking multiple humans in complex situations. *IEEE Transactions on Pattern Analysis and Machine Intelligence, 26*(9), 1208–1221. DOI: 10.1109/TPAMI.2004.73 PMID: 15742895

Zhong, R., Tian, Z., Liao, J., & Shi, W. (2024, October). Autonomous Shuttle Operation for Vulnerable Populations: Lessons and Experiences. In *2024 IEEE 10th International Conference on Collaboration and Internet Computing (CIC)* (pp. 1-8). IEEE.

Zhou, F., Duh, H. B. L., & Billinghurst, M. (2017). Trends in Augmented Reality Tracking, Interaction and Display: A Review of Ten Years of ISMAR. *Proceedings of the 16th IEEE International Symposium on Mixed and Augmented Reality (ISMAR).*

Zhou, W., & Wang, Y. (2021). Adaptive infotainment systems in vehicles: A cognitive-aware interface approach. *Journal of Ambient Intelligence and Humanized Computing*, *12*(10), 9785–9796.

Zhou, Y., Zhang, Y., & Li, Q. (2017). Mobile Emotion-Aware Apps: Discerning Emotional States through Touchscreen Interactions. *Mobile Computing and Communications Review*, *21*(1), 29–42.

Zierau, N., Hausch, M., Bruhin, O., & Söllner, M. (2021). Towards developing trust-supporting design features for AI-based chatbots in customer service. *International Conference on Information Systems, ICIS 2020 - Making Digital Inclusive: Blending the Local and the Global, Coniam 2014*, 1–9.

Zong, M., Chang, Y., Dang, Y., & Wang, K. (2024). Pedestrian trajectory prediction in crowded environments using social attention graph neural networks. *Applied Sciences (Basel, Switzerland)*, *14*(20), 9349. DOI: 10.3390/app14209349

About the Contributors

Subrata Tikadar is currently working as an 'Assistant Professor – Research & Innovation' in the Amity School of Engineering and Technology Kolkata, Amity University Kolkata, India. Prior to joining the Amity, he was associated with Vellore Institute of Technology – Andhra Pradesh, India, Aliah University Kolkata, India, Maulana Abul Kalam Azad University of Technology (formerly West Bengal University of Technology) Kolkata, India, Central Institute of Technology Kokrajhar, Assam, India, Bengal College of Engineering and Technology Durgapur, India, and Kingstone Engineering College Kolkata, India. He has around 12 years of teaching and research experience. Dr. Tikadar completed his BE in Computer Science and Engineering from the University Institute of Technology – Burdwan University (UIT-BU), India, M.Tech in Computer Science and Engineering (Specialized in Multimedia and Software Systems) form National Institute of Technical Teachers' Training and Research Kolkata (NITTTR Kolkata), India, and PhD in Computer Science and Engineering (Specialized in Human-Computer and Interaction) form Indian Institute of Technology Guwahati (IIT Guwahati), India. He is currently an active researcher in the field of Human-Computer Interaction, particularly in Advanced Learning Technology, Affective Computing, AR-VR-MR, Brain-Computer Interaction, and Interdisciplinary and Multidisciplinary interactive sensitive system design. Dr. Tikadar's remarkable awards and recognition include the Best PhD Thesis Award (in the 23rd Convocation of IIT Guwahati, India), Best Research Paper Award by IEEE Technical Committee on Learning Technology (in the 19th IEEE International Conference on Advanced Learning Technologies (ICALT 2019, Maceio, Brazil) organized by the IEEE Computer Society and the IEEE Technical Committee on Learning Technology, Scholarship from IFIP TC13 on HCI, and the IFIP Digital Equity Committee to present research papers in INTERACT 2019 Paphos, Cyprus, and a Special Recognition from ACM SIGCHI for Outstanding Research Paper Review. He is a program committee member of many international top-tier conference including 22nd ACM International Conference on Multimodal Interaction (ICMI), Utrecht, the Netherlands, and 23rd ACM International Conference on Multimodal Interaction (ICMI), Montreal, Canada. Dr. Tikadar is associated with many professional organizations that include ACM, IEEE, IEEE Computer Society Technical Committee on Learning Technology, and many more.

Joel J. P. C. Rodrigues [AAIA and IEEE Fellow] is a permanent professor of the Post-Graduation Program in electrical engineering at UFPI, with Senac Ceará (specialist consultant), Brazil, and Coordinator of the Intelligent Center at Fecomércio CE. He has been a Professor at Inatel, Brazil, an aggregated professor at the Univ. of Beira Interior (UBI), Portugal and visiting professor at UNIFOR, Brazil. He received the Aggregation in Computer Science and Engineering from UBI, the Habilitation in computer science and engineering from the Univ. Mulhouse Haute-Alsace, France, a PhD degree in Computer Science and Engineering and an MSc in Management degree from UBI, and a five-year BSc degree (licentiate) in Computer Science and Engineering from the Univ. of Coimbra, Portugal. He was the Director of the MSc degree on Computer Science and Engineering (UBI) [2009-2013], the Founder and Director of the Post-graduation ICT for TELCO (Information and Communication Technologies for the Telco Sector), in cooperation with Portugal Telecom and Syone [2012-2013].His main research interests include sensor networks and Internet of Things (IoT), eHealth technologies, vehicular communications, mobile and cloud computing. He has authored or co-authored over 1200 publications in refereed international journals (more than 715 publications), conferences, book chapters, 3 books, 2 patents, and 1 ITU-T Recommendation (standard); with more than 39400 citations and H-Index 104. He is a Distinguished Researcher by CNPq (Brazil), Highly Cited Researcher (ISI Web of Science), an IEEE Distinguished Lecturer [2018-2021], a Past-Director for Conference Development - IEEE ComSoc Board of Governors, Technical Activities Committee Past-Chair of the IEEE ComSoc Latin America Region Board, a Past-Chair of the IEEE ComSoc TC on eHealth and IEEE ComSoc TC on Comm. Software, the representative of the IEEE ComSoc on the IEEE Biometrics Council, member of the Steering Committee and Publications co-Chair of the Life Sciences Technical Community.He is or was the Leader of the Project IoT-based solutions for smart homes (CNPq), MosquIot (FAPEMIG), the IT Projects VDTN@Lab, BodySens, EcoSense, several projects with SAPO (Portugal Telecom), and the Leader of several research projects on IoT at Inatel, the NoE Euro-NF SJR Project VDTN (Vehicular Delay Tolerant Networks). He is or was member of several European or national projects (NoE Euro-NF, NoE Euro-NGI, NoE Euro-FGI, AAL4ALL - Ambient Assisted Living for All, eLearning 3.0, Moggy, etc.). Joel was member of the stakeholders group for the FI-STAR Project and is a Management Committee member of the ICT COST Action IC 1304, both funded by the European

Union. Joel has also experience on projects evaluation belonging to the evaluation boards of the Brazilian CNPq, Qatar National Research Fund (QNRF), Innovation Agency from the Portuguese Government, and European projects evaluation on calls promoted by the European Union.Joel is the Editor-in-Chief of the International Journal of E-Health and Medical Communications and the Journal of Multimedia Information Systems (Korea Multimedia Society) [2014-2018]. He belongs to several Editorial Boards of many reputed qualified journals (IEEE IoT, IEEE Systems, IEEE Wireless Communications, etc.).He was the Steering Committee Chair of the IEEE HEALTHCOM [2014-2021], and has been general chair and TPC Chair of many international conferences, including IEEE ICC/GLOBECOM. He received several awards, including numerous best paper awards (more than 20), as the 2014 IEEE ComSoc Multimedia TC Outstanding Leadership Award, and recognition awards for his leadership in many conferences and other recognition awards (mainly, from IEEE ComSoc).He is a member of the Internet Society, a senior member of ACM and an AAIA IEEE FELLOW.

Rabi Shaw is an accomplished academic with a strong foundation in Computer Science and Engineering. He earned his B.Tech and M.Tech degrees from the University Institute of Technology, Burdwan, and Jadavpur University, Kolkata, respectively, followed by a Ph.D. from the National Institute of Technology Rourkela in 2023. His teaching career began at the Aryabhatta Institute of Engineering & Management, Durgapur, and continued at the National Institute of Technology Jamshedpur before joining Dr. B. R. Ambedkar National Institute of Technology, Jalandhar, as an Assistant Professor in the Department of Information Technology. Dr. Rabi Shaw is an accomplished academic with a strong foundation in Computer Science and Engineering. He earned his B.Tech and M.Tech degrees from the University Institute of Technology, Burdwan, and Jadavpur University, Kolkata, respectively, followed by a Ph.D. from the National Institute of Technology Rourkela in 2023. His teaching career began at the Aryabhatta Institute of Engineering & Management, Durgapur, and continued at the National Institute of Technology Jamshedpur before joining Dr. B. R. Ambedkar National Institute of Technology, Jalandhar, as an Assistant Professor in the Department of Information Technology. Dr. Shaw has made notable contributions to journals such as Future Generation Computer Systems, Expert Systems with Applications, Cognitive Computation, and Biomedical Signal and Control. His work has also been recognized at ICALT. His research interests span Educational Technology with Cognitive Science, Human-Computer Interaction, Signal Processing, Recommender Systems, and the transformative fields of Machine Learning and Deep Learning.

Ahdi Hassan has been Associate or Consulting Editor of numerous journals and also served the editorial review board from 2013- to till now. He has a number of publications and research papers published in various domains. He has given contribution with the major roles such as using modern and scientific techniques to work with sounds and meanings of words, studying the relationship between the written and spoken formats of various Asian/European languages, developing the artificial languages in coherence with modern English language, and scientifically approaching the various ancient written material to trace its origin. He teaches topics connected but not limited to communication such as English for Young Learners, English for Academic Purposes, English for Science, Technology and Engineering, English for Business and Entrepreneurship, Business Intensive Course, Applied Linguistics, interpersonal communication, verbal and nonverbal communication, cross cultural competence, language and humor, intercultural communication, culture and humor, language acquisition and language in use.

Bidyut Kr. Patra received B.Tech. (CSE) and M.Tech. (CSE) degrees from University of Calcutta, Kolkata, India, in 1999 and 2001, respectively. He earned the Ph.D. degree in Computer Science and Engineering from Indian Institute of Technology Guwahati, India in 2012. Before joining to the Ph.D. programme, he was the faculty in the Department of Computer Science and Engineering, Haldia Institute of Technology, Haldia, India, during 2001–2005, and National Institute of Technology Rourkela, India, during 2011–2022 . He was awarded ERCIM (Marie-Curie) fellowship by European Research Consortium for Informatics and Mathematics, France for conducting independent research at VTT Technical Research Centre of Finland, Finland during May, 2013–October, 2014. Presently, he is an Associate Professor, IIT(BHU) Varanassi-221 005, INDIA. He has published research articles in Knowledge and Information Systems (KAIS), Knowledge-Based Systems (KBS), Pattern Recognitions, Expert System With Applications. He has been recognized at ECIR, CoDS-COMAD. His research interests include data mining, recommender systems.

***

Moumita Chowdhury is a detail-oriented undergraduate student pursuing a Bachelor's degree in Computer Science and Engineering at Amity University Kolkata, with a strong passion for emerging technologies and interdisciplinary research. Her academic interests span Artificial Intelligence, Machine Learning, Software Development, and Data Analysis, where she actively explores cutting-edge advancements and their practical applications. A proactive learner and problem-solver, she excels in collaborative environments, combining technical expertise with analytical thinking. Through this book chapter, she contributes to the discourse on the intersection between Artificial intelligence and accessible solutions for the disabled, reflecting her commitment to innovation and lifelong learning in technology. She aspires to further her research in AI-driven solutions and make meaningful contributions to the field.

Amruta Deshpande, Ph.D. in Management studies, MBA (HRM), MBA (Hospitality Management), B.sc (Chemistry). She is an MBA with over 16 years of rich academic experience in teaching and research. She is a Certified Emotional Intelligence specialist, Executive life coach, and Psychometric Test Professional. She has also done global certifications in master trainer and Facilitator and Performance and competence Developer. Her specialization and teaching experience are predominantly in organizational behavior, Theory of management, Management fundamentals, and Human resource management to PG and Master Students to impart knowledge and usher students to strive for professional excellence. She has also attended various Management Development Programme by IIMs. She is also a Certified Microsoft Innovative Educator. She completed X Culture Global Research collaboration project. She works as Director Research and Development at Indira Group of Institutes Pune Maharashtra She has published many research papers in national and international journals on Career Management, contemporary HR practices, and recent HR trends in Scopus / ABDC / WOS. She is the author and co-author of different edited books.

Yamini Ghanghorkar is associated as an Assistant professor in the Academic - HR department at School of Business Studies, Indira University, pursuing her Ph. D from Pune university in HRM specialisation. Before this, she was associated with PIBM and Nagpur University as an Assistant professor, accounting for 9 years of academic experience. In her corporate experience, she has been associated with Muthoot Fincorp and Tech Mahindra Business Services. She is pursuing her PhD from Pune University. She completed her master's degree in human resource management from Nagpur University in 2013. She has taught subjects like HR Analytics, Performance Management system, Talent Acquisition, Organization Behavior, Talent Management, Management Fundamentals, HRM, Environment Management, and Office Management. She has published and presented research papers in various reputed journals and conferences at national and international.

J. Sudarvel working as an Assistant Professor of Management at Karpagam Academy of Higher Education. He produced five Ph.D. Scholars and four Ph.D. Scholars are under his guidance. Further, to his credit he published more than 36 articles in Scopus indexed journals and published more than 50 articles in international journals. He is acting as a Subject Experts in Board of studies of various autonomous colleges.

Priyan Malakar is pursuing an undergraduate degree in Computer Science at Amity University Kolkata. He is a passionate and curious learner who is actively engaged in exploring cutting-edge technologies and their real-world applications. His academic and research interests span robotics, artificial intelligence and machine learning, human-computer interaction, virtual and extended reality (VR/XR), computer vision, and software development. With a strong inclination toward innovation and interdisciplinary problem-solving, Priyan is focused on building impactful solutions that merge technical excellence with user-centered design. He is a team player and reflective practitioner with strong communication skills. Driven by a desire to contribute meaningfully to the tech and research communities, Priyan aims to continuously evolve through collaboration, experimentation, and academic exploration.

Hitesh Mohapatra received the B.E. degree in Information Technology from Biju Patnaik University of Technology (BPUT), Odisha in 2006, and the MTech. Degree in CSE from Odisha University of Technology and Research (OUTR) University, Odisha in 2009. He received his Ph.D. in Computer Science & Engineering in 2021 from Veer Surendra Sai University of Technology (VSSUT), Burla, India. He has contributed 30 SCI and Scopus indexed research papers, 21 international/national conferences and books on Software Engineering and C Programming respectively. He has 15 years of teaching experience both in industry and academia. He has served the research community with various capacities like session chair, technical chair, keynote speaker etc. His research interests include wireless sensor network, smart city, smart grid and smart water. Currently he is working as Associate professor at School of Computer Engineering, KIIT DU, Bhubaneswar, and Odisha.

Alisha Parveen is a Computer Science and Engineering undergraduate at Amity University Kolkata, India. She has a keen interest in Artificial Intelligence(AI), Brain-Computer Interfaces (BCI), and assistive technologies. Alisha completed an internship at the HIVE (Human-Inspired Vision and Engineering) Lab, Indian Institute of Technology (IIT) Kanpur, where she gained hands-on experience in research and development. She has worked on several innovative projects involving EEG-based control systems and eye-tracking technologies like the Tobii Eye Tracker to create accessible Human-Computer Interactions. Passionate about inclusive tech, she actively participates in research, hackathons, and open-source communities.

R. Bhuvaneswari working as an Assistant Professor of English at Dr.Mahalingam College of Engineering and Technology, Pollachi. To her credit she completed 10 NPTEL / SWAYAM and published few articles in Scopus indexed journals.

R. VELMURUGAN presently working as an Associate Professor in Commerce, Karpagam Academy of Higher Education, Coimbatore. He started his career as a Project Fellow under UGC Sponsored Major Research Project at NGM College, Pollachi. He has 18 years of teaching experience has 15 years of research experience. To his credit he produced 22 Ph.D. Scholars and 5 M.Phil. Scholars. At present 1 scholar submitter his thesis, 6 Ph.D. Scholars are under his guidance. Moreover, to his credit he published 168 articles in various International Journals, of which 82 articles are published in Scopus Indexed Journals and 15 articles in Web of Science and 76 articles in edited volumes. He also participates and presented 27 papers in various International Seminar / Conference and 54 National Seminar / Conference. He acted as an external examiner for various M.Phil. and Ph.D. Viva voce examinations. He acted as a Vice Chancellor nominee for Doctoral Committee Expert at Bharathiar University, Coimbatore and Periyar University, Salem. He acted as a Chairperson at various National Level Conferences. He also acted as an Expert for Syllabus Scrutiny Committee, Question Paper Scrutiny Committee and Expert members for Board of Studies at various reputed Colleges. Considering his meritorious contribution, he received awards like Best Paper Presenter, Best Research Supervisor and Best Faculty Awards from various research foundations and councils. He too acted as a resource person for 27 Guest Lectures, 30 Workshops and 10 faculty development programmes.

Mohammed Saad is currently pursuing a Bachelor of Technology degree with a specialization in Computer Science at Amity University, Kolkata. His academic interests include artificial intelligence, machine learning, and robotics. As an aspiring researcher and developer, he is passionate about exploring emerging technologies and applying innovative solutions to real-world problems.

Ravi Thirumalaisamy working as an Assistant Professor, Department of Business and Economics, Modern College of Business and Science. To his credit, he published more than 16 articles in Scopus indexed journals.

Index

A

C

D

E

F

G

H

I

L